THE
PEGASUS
AND
ORNE BRIDGES

THE
PEGASUS
AND
ORNE BRIDGES

Their Capture, Defence and Relief on D-Day

Neil Barber

Pen & Sword
MILITARY

In memory of my friend, Gary Cooper

First published in Great Britain in 2009
and reprinted in this format in 2014 by
Pen & Sword Military
An imprint of
Pen & Sword Books Ltd
47 Church Street
Barnsley
South Yorkshire
S70 2AS

Copyright © Neil Barber 2009, 2014

ISBN 978 1 47382 274 0

Printed and bound in the UK
by CPI Group (UK) Ltd, Croydon, CR0 4YY

Typeset by Phoenix Typesetting,
Auldgirth, Dumfriesshire

Pen & Sword Books Ltd incorporates the Imprints of Pen & Sword Aviation, Pen & Sword Family History, Pen & Sword Maritime, Pen & Sword Military, Pen & Sword Discovery, Wharncliffe Local History, Wharncliffe True Crime, Wharncliffe Transport, Pen & Sword Select, Pen & Sword Military Classics, Leo Cooper, The Praetorian Press, Remember When, Seaforth P

For a complete l
PEN &
47 Church Street, B
E-mail: e
Websit

Contents

The Publishers have included several historically
important wartime photographs that cannot be
reproduced to our usual high standards. It was
felt that they were of sufficient interest to the
reader to be included.

Foreword

June 6th 1944 saw the successful capture by 'D' Company 2nd Battalion, The Oxfordshire and Buckinghamshire Light Infantry of the bridges over the Caen Canal and the River Orne followed by their defence by the 7th (Light Infantry) Battalion, The Parachute Regiment. As you read this brilliant account of the planning of this assault by the 6th Airborne Division and the action that took place in the Ranville area, you will find it difficult to put this book down. With each chapter you will marvel at the bravery and dedication of the men who tell their story of what happened to them during the battles they encountered on 6 June 1944, including the arrival of the seaborne units into the 6th Airborne Divisional area.

I congratulate the author for his devotion in producing such an outstanding, detailed account of the capture of the Pegasus and Orne Bridges, their defence and their relief on D-Day.

Major Jack Watson MC.
13th (Lancashire) Battalion, The Parachute Regiment

Preface

The capture of the Caen Canal and River Orne bridges on D-Day remains one of the most celebrated episodes of the Second World War. Much has been written about the 'Pegasus Bridge Operation', so why another book? The simple reason is that I wanted to know more. For all of the publications in which the operation features, there are only two books specifically dedicated to the action, these being Stephen Ambrose's *Pegasus Bridge* (1984) and *The Pegasus Diaries* (2006) by Major John Howard's daughter, Penny Bates. They are both superb, and naturally concentrate on Howard and the exploits of his *Coup de Main* force.

Where this book largely differs from those, and most others, is that there is more information on the actions of the various formations involved in the defence of the immediate area surrounding the bridges, from Benouville to Ranville on the 6 June 1944. The text follows the thread of the operation from inception to completion and therefore traces the training and actions of the *Coup de Main* party and the 7th Parachute Battalion, who fought a truly valiant battle in Benouville. In order to address the defence of the Ranville area, the 12th and 13th Parachute Battalions and other Airborne units feature from the main parachute drop onwards. Then there is the arrival of the Commandos and the lesser-known actions of the Seaborne Engineers whose presence in Benouville undoubtedly influenced the enemy actions there during the afternoon of D-Day. There is also a short appreciation of the efforts of the French intelligence gathering organisations, particularly the Century Network, whose contribution in the years before D-Day cannot be underestimated.

With regard to the attention given to the capture of the bridges, this book is no different, although I have attempted to address a wider range of men within the party, be it the Oxf and Bucks, the Glider Pilots or the Airborne Engineers.

With so much conflicting information concerning timings, whether personal or officially recorded, I have deliberately placed the emphasis on the chronology of events. The method of doing this has been to explore in greater detail and over a wider area. This has proved fruitful in most cases, but not all. For example, the movements of Brigadier Nigel Poett provide invaluable clues as to the sequence of events (and therefore timing!), but those of Lord Lovat certainly do not! Consequently, there are matters that have proved to be impossible to resolve, but I am optimistic that with subsequent feedback, some of these may well be clarified.

*　　*　　*

The influence of the 6th Airborne Division in this area of the Orne remains to this day, with museums, memorials and of course cemeteries. Yet it is more than that. There is a tangible bond between the local population and the parachute, glider, commando and other veterans who, although their numbers slowly diminish, travel out each year to meet old friends and pay their respects to comrades who were not so fortunate.

This is their story, the soldier's eye-view of what they had to do to make this operation, and D-Day, a success.

Acknowledgements

After five years, there are quite a lot of people to thank, and if I have omitted anyone, please be sure that I am very grateful for your assistance.

I am privileged that Major Jack Watson MC, formerly of the 13th Parachute Battalion and now President of the Airborne Assault Normandy Trust, has written the Foreword. Jack, it has been a pleasure to meet you.

I shall always be indebted to the late Colonel David Wood and the late Geoff Barkway, two absolute gentlemen, for vetting the drafts with regard to the Oxf and Bucks and glider pilot input, and to Michael Pine-Coffin, grandson of Colonel Geoffrey Pine-Coffin, for sharing his expertise on the 7th Parachute Battalion, especially when he is preparing books of his own on the complete history of the battalion. I hope it hasn't delayed you too much!

I am especially grateful to Hugh Ambrose for allowing me to quote from the interviews carried out in 1984 by his father, Stephen, during research for his classic book, *Pegasus Bridge*.

To Penny Bates (daughter of Major John Howard) for allowing me to quote from her marvellous *Pegasus Diaries*. Of the Oxf and Bucks group for their help and encouragement, Barry and Diane Parr, Barry and Michael Tappenden, Ted Barwick, Mike Holland, Geoff Baulk (curator of the Oxf and Bucks Museum Section at Bletchley Park), Joan Packwood, Danny Greeno and especially the late Dennis Edwards. With regard to the gliders, Jim Wallwork, Peter Boyle, Phoebe Grant and Bob Randall. To Eric Barley (and Yves Fohlen) for allowing me to quote from their book *Para Memories*.

My gratitude also goes to Sir David Willison, John Hoare and Brian Raymond Guy of 17 Field Company Group RE.

Others I am indebted to include Brigadier-General Julian Thompson, Major Joseph Molyson, Steve Bennett, John Goddard, Michael W Bowman, 'Cincinnati' Sean, Ian 'Nobby' Clark, Felix Jackson, Laurie Milner, Steve Clare, Mick Mockford, John Webber, Jim Clark, Stephen Wright, David Brook, Silvia Atkinson, Michael Massy-Beresford, Dick Goodwin, Bill Mawson and Walter Wright. Also to Major Phillip Pritchard, Stan Scott, Jimmy Synnott and the late Eddie Simms.

My thanks to all the veterans involved (see sources at the rear). It was marvellous to meet you.

My gratitude also goes to the people at the following museums: Toby Haggith, Matthew

Lee and George Smith at the IWM Film archive, IWM sound archive, IWM art archive, PRO Image library, Allan Williams and Will Adam at Keele University Air Photo Library, Andrew Whitmarsh at the Portsmouth D-Day Museum, Alan Brown at the Airborne Forces Museum, Sergeant Andy Moore at JARIC, the Liddell Hart Archive, The Museum of Army Flying, Firepower The Royal Artillery Museum, The Royal Engineers Museum, Major J. Turquand and David Baynham at the Royal Warwicks Museum.

Thanks to the following periodicals for placing requests for help: The Sapper Magazine, The Antelope (Regimental Magazine for the Royal Warwicks) and Best of British.

For the superb new index I am indebted to the late Francis Vere Hodge, someone who I admired enormously and shall never forget.

There are three excellent websites, The Pegasus Archive, 6commando.com and www.geocities.com/lightackack whose authors, Mark Hickman, Peter Bowe (who is writing a book about 6 Commando) and Tom McCarthy respectively, have all been very helpful. Also, thanks to Mark of the 89/317 Field Security Section Re-enactment Group.

In France the help and hospitality of the inhabitants of Benouville has been truly humbling. I would like to express my appreciation to a good friend, Jean-Pierre Liot, without whom I would not have had a clue what anyone was talking about, the staff of the Memorial Pegasus Museum who have always been so helpful and encouraging, Marc Jacquinot, Mark Worthington, Beatrice Boissée, Valerie Quesnel, Sandrine Cabrol, Martin Jenssen and Nicholas Dumont. Thanks to Arlette Gondrée at the Pegasus Bridge Café, the Mayor of Benouville, Alain Lepareur, René Niepceron, Raymond Falaise, the late Georges Fontenier, Louise Moulin, Nicole Bracci, Francois Hamard, Suzy Scheppers, Gilles Deschamps, André and Christiane Grand, Monsieur Lechartier, Monsieur and Madame Faulin, Benedicte Diallo, Claude Montaland and Corrine and Roger Fosse. Finally, to an ex-member of the Resistance, André Heintz. It was a privilege to meet you.

Thanks to Hugo Mitchell for the photo of Wagger Thornton.

For help provided on the German side of events, Werner Kortenhaus and Hans Höller.

To Jimmy Linton, Joe Michie, Carl Rymen, Stephane St Martin, all my friends of the 9th Battalion, including Gordon Newton, Tony Lea, Alan Edwards, Mike Woodcock, Major Mike Strong, the late Sid Capon, Ron McCaffrey and the 'D-Day crowd' at the Vauban in Merville.

At Pen and Sword, I am indebted to Brigadier Henry Wilson, George Chamier, Jonathan Wright, Jon Wilkinson, Helen Vodden and Malcolm Bates.

To those who have accompanied and helped me during my many trips to Normandy, Ian Pieri, Chip, Ian Puttee and Dave Wright. I would also like to remember Chris Harris. You were a gentleman.

I also have to mention Bill Nelson, whose music has inspired me in so many ways for over thirty years.

As always, thanks to my parents Joan and Bob and brother Colin, for your help and encouragement.

Finally, to my ever-patient wife, Caroline, and son, Max, the centre of my universe.

Abbreviations

AA & QMG	Assistant Adjutant & Quartermaster General
ADMS -	Assistant Director Medical Services
CRA -	Commander Royal Artillery (Divisional)
CRE -	Commander Royal Engineers (Divisional)
DD -	Duplex Drive (used on amphibious tanks)
GAF -	German Air Force
GSO -	General Staff Officer
LMG -	Light Machine Gun
MDS -	Main Dressing Station
MMG -	Medium Machine Gun
NAAFI -	Navy, Army & Air Force Institutes
PIAT -	Projectile Infantry Anti-Tank
RAMC -	Royal Army Medical Corps
RAP -	Regimental Aid Post
RASC -	Royal Army Service Corps
WAAF -	Women's Auxiliary Air Force

Chapter One

Planning

On 17 February 1944 Lieutenant General Frederick 'Boy' Browning, the Commander of British Airborne Forces, visited the Officer Commanding the 6th Airborne Division, Major General Richard Nelson Gale. It was no ordinary meeting. Browning briefed Gale on Operation Overlord, the plan for the invasion and liberation of Western Europe. Gale learned that the landings were to take place along the Normandy coast, with the Americans in the west and the British and Canadians in the east. Prior to the seaborne landings, his Division plus the American 82nd and 101st Airborne Divisions were to be employed to protect the vulnerable flanks. General Richard 'Windy' Gale:

The left flank of the British seaborne assault was bounded by the double water obstacle consisting of the Canal de Caen and the River Orne. The ground to the east of the River Orne, though not high, was sufficiently dominating to overlook the left flank of the British assault. It was not desirable to extend the seaborne landings to the beaches east of the Orne in order to capture this ground, as the sea approaches to these would have come under the fire of the heavy defences of Le Havre. The river and the canal were obstacles of no mean order, and an attack over these would have been a costly and most undesirable operation. The quickest and surest way of seizing the dominating features east of the Orne was therefore, by means of an airborne assault.

Our first task in order of priority was to seize intact the bridges over the Canal de Caen and the River Orne at Benouville and Ranville; and to secure a bridgehead of sufficient depth to ensure that these could be held. The defence must have depth; the bridgehead must be sufficiently far out to have the necessary resilience to stand up against any local success which any well delivered enemy attack might have.

The 6th Airborne Division comprised the 3 and 5 Parachute and 6 Airlanding Brigades, but Browning explained that the size of the force was limited by the number of available aircraft. Consequently, one parachute brigade and an anti-tank battery were to be placed under the command of the 3rd British Infantry Division, one of the seaborne assault divisions. General Gale:

Quite apart from the fact that I feared that so small a force would be inadequate for the task, not of seizing, but of holding the bridgehead, it is a terrible thing for a commander to feel that his formation is being committed piecemeal to battle and even then not under his command. I knew how sympathetic General 'Boy' was to my feelings, and indeed it was knowledge of this and the effect I knew he would make on our behalf that really formed my only solace.

There was of course no argument and so I detailed James Hill [Officer Commanding, 3 Parachute Brigade] and his, the senior brigade, for the task and sent him off to commence his planning. Meanwhile my mind was working rapidly on plans for reinforcing him as speedily as possible.

Great therefore, was my relief when a few days later, on 23 February, I was told that the whole of 38 and 46 Groups RAF would now be available and that thus a Divisional operation would be possible. That ghastly dream had passed.

The Ground Commander of the Allied Armies, General Sir Bernard Montgomery, had analyzed the whole invasion plan. This proposed a landing on a forty mile front from the River Orne to Grandcamp in the west, but he considered the capture of the Cherbourg Peninsula to be vital to the success of the operation and therefore suggested to General Dwight D. Eisenhower, the Supreme Commander Allied Expeditionary Force, that the front be extended by fifty miles to the west. He also suggested that the Airborne presence east of the Orne must have more immediate depth. Eisenhower had come to the same conclusions. The further transport aircraft, gliders and crews required for the increased airlift were to be provided by 46 Group which had been formed within RAF Transport Command, and which came under the operational control of the existing 38 Group. Aircraft from the IX US Troop Carrier Command were to also provide aircraft and crews for the training period. General Gale:

So it came about that on 24 February, the 6th Airborne Division was definitely placed under command of the 1st British Corps for 'Operation Overlord'. For planning, a small party consisting of myself, Bobby Bray my GSO 1, Lacoste my GSO 2 Intelligence, one GSO 3, Shamus Hickie my AA and QMG, MacEwan my Medical Adviser, Jack Norris my CRA and Frank Lowman my CRE with the chief clerk went up to 1st Corps Headquarters in Ashley Gardens, London.

It was here that I received my orders and here that we worked out our outline plan.

James Hill's plan for the seizure of the vital bridges was included in this. General Gale:

I was convinced that once the Germans realized that airborne landings had taken place they would be prepared everywhere. They would certainly be prepared on the bridges which we knew were manned; and they would be ready, immediately they looked like being attacked, to blow these. We knew that virtually all the enemy would have to do would be to press a button or move a switch and up would go these bridges. There is always or nearly always a slip between the cup and the lip; orders are vague; there is uncertainty; has the moment arrived or should one wait? Who is the individual actu-

ally responsible both for working the switch or for ordering the bridges to be blown? These questions are age-old, and on the doubts that might exist in some German mind or minds at the critical moment I based the plan. But a moment or two was all that I knew we would get. The assault on the bridges must therefore come like a bolt from the blue.

A stick of parachutists covers a considerable area: under operational conditions twenty men could expect to cover over one thousand yards. The concentration of such a stick in the dark and on unknown ground would take time. Immediate surprise was the essence of the bridge problem. If three gliders can be landed slap on the objective, a concentration of seventy-five fully armed men is immediately achieved.

Brigadier James Hill

Brigadier Hill's plan was based on these essential requirements of speed and surprise, and proposed this use of gliders to capture the bridges, followed by rapid reinforcement by parachutists. Richard Gale:

It was thus for very good reasons that I decided on two Coup de Main *assaults each by three gliders on each of the two bridges. On account of the necessity for complete surprise this must coincide with the drops of the Independent Parachute Company* [which was setting up navigational aids on the Dropping Zones (DZs) or Landing Zones (LZs) to guide in the reinforcements] *and not follow them. The* Coup de Main *party must in fact be one of the first incidents of the invasion and so must be prepared to come in without any navigational aids.*

To seize and secure the bridges over the canal and river would take one brigade.

Gale allocated this task to Brigadier Hugh Kindersley's gliderborne 6 Airlanding Brigade. Richard Gale:

Having captured the bridges intact the problem would then be to hold them. Initially, there must be a bridgehead on both the western and eastern banks. When the seaborne assault division reached Benouville we would be relieved of the responsibility for that in the west. That on the east would, however, remain our task.

*

The core of the 6th Airborne Division had been formed using the policy of 'converting' battalions to gliderborne or parachute formations. This meant that a regular battalion was chosen for conversion and the men asked to volunteer for the Airborne Forces, with those not interested being transferred, without disgrace, to another battalion. However, volunteering was not enough. They then had to pass the rigorous medical and physical fitness tests and then initial training. Thus the nucleus of a battalion was maintained, and then brought up to strength with volunteers from within the Services who had specifically requested to join the Airborne Forces. Each of the Division's three brigades consisted of three battalions. 3 Parachute Brigade had the 8th and 9th Parachute Battalions and 1st Canadian Parachute Battalion; 5 Parachute Brigade comprised the 7th, 12th and 13th Parachute Battalions, while 6 Airlanding Brigade had the 2nd Battalion, Oxfordshire and Buckinghamshire Light Infantry (The 52nd Light Infantry), the 2nd Battalion, Royal Ulster Rifles and 12th Battalion, The Devonshire Regiment.[1]

Chapter Two

Bugle Horns and Para Wings

O n 25 March the Division began a three-day exercise codenamed 'BIZZ II', which was a full-scale dress rehearsal for the invasion. On the first day, 'D' Company of the 2nd Oxf and Bucks, after exiting from the back of trucks, captured three bridges at Faringdon, while the rest of the battalion arrived in gliders, surrounded the bridges and dug in. The Officer Commanding 'D' Company was Major John Howard, a man with a reputation for being extremely professional. Lance Corporal Arthur Roberts, 'D' Company:

Scarface we used to call him [he had a long scar down the right side of his face] *what he'd got at Rugby. You always knew when he was in a bad mood . . . ,it seemed to light up at you! He was a bloke you wouldn't mess about with. He'd come up the ranks and he knew all the answers!*

Jack, or 'Bill' Bailey as he was better known, was due to join the Anti-Tank Platoon, but met Howard after finding that he was being temporarily placed with 'D' Company:

He sat behind the desk, well he looked a bit of a sod actually . . . I can't put it any other way! I'd already been told, already been warned on the previous night that it was a 'bugger's Company', and it was. Having been there a short while, I found I didn't want to go to the Anti-Tank Platoon. John Howard had . . . in the true sense of the word, 'a bastard Company' in as much as the 52nd were a pre-War regiment with a very, very long history which extended back beyond the Peninsula, and they had a great many between-War soldiers serving with them. They'd only come back from India in about 1940. John Howard, it would appear, had got the nucleus of this [in] *'D' Company. And I'm pretty certain when I say this that 'D' Company probably consisted of fifty percent men other than 52nd. John Howard had to weld this Company, so it was something new for him.[1]*

On first seeing his men, Howard had not been impressed. Corporal Bill 'Smokey' Howard had joined from a Young Soldiers battalion, the 70th Kings Royal Rifles, which had been performing aerodrome guard duties with a solitary Lewis gun shared between the whole battalion:

He looked at us askance when half of us didn't know how to deal with a Bren gun, didn't know how to strip it down, didn't know how to clean it or anything else. We looked at it and that was about all we did. We'd never seen any grenades, knew nothing about Bren guns because we hadn't seen any. We had the old short Lee Enfield rifles, which were good. We had fired those in the days when we first joined up. We might have fired ten rounds . . . Of course when we got to John Howard he was used to seeing real soldiers, not these young layabouts![2]

Gliderborne battalions had four companies, each comprising four platoons, 'D' Company's being numbered 22, 23, 24 and 25. A platoon consisted of a Scout section, two Rifle sections and a HQ section.

The training required to bring the Company to the standard that Howard required had been intense. Wally Parr joined the battalion from the Gloucestershire Regiment:

He was strict, he was firm, but he was fair. He never asked anybody to do anything that he wasn't prepared to do himself first. The training was rigorous. Absolute discipline and above all, physical fitness was his thing. Everybody had to be able to do it.

Private Doug Allen:

Twenty-five mile forced marches, he'd be up the front, making sure we were all OK, moving back to each platoon, coming back again. He'd be doing more than twenty-five miles by the time we got back.

Lance Corporal Tom Packwood:

We didn't know it was anything more exceptional than anyone else was doing. He was the man in charge and you just done what he said. We knew that he was older than us and if he could do it, we could too. He was a fair enough man. If anything went wrong and you had an excuse and that, he was on your side.

Private Nobby Clark:

We sort of moulded to his, John Howard's mannerisms because we knew it was the easy way of pleasing him, but if we dropped him in it, he would take it out on us for weeks on end. But if we went along with what he wanted, we could get away with murder! He thought we were all in favour of him, but we weren't, we were just looking after ourselves! We knew the easy way. But he was a fair bloke anyway.

One of the 'originals', Lance Corporal Ted Tappenden, had been called up into the 52nd Light Infantry in 1941. He was Howard's radio operator:

Major Howard had a saying, when we were on exercises if I wasn't behind him and he wanted to send a message over the '38' set . . . the only expression he ever gave out was, 'Blast your bloody eyes, where are you?' One day, things got a little bit on top of us, he said, 'Blast your bloody eyes!' and I said, 'Blast your bloody eyes!' He stood behind the jeep and laughed his head off. The whole Company idolised him. His men came first, that was his attitude.[3]

Perhaps a 'break' to Ilfracombe for the whole of the battalion epitomised everything about Major Howard and his Company. The trip had been devised to maintain fitness and toughen up the men. This was certainly achieved, but it was the return journey that everyone remembered. Lieutenant Henry 'Tod' Sweeney commanded 23 Platoon:

Major John Howard

They said, "Now you've had a jolly good month down here and you will now march back to Bulford." Well, Bulford was 126 miles away, and over Exmoor which of course is very rugged hill country. So we all set off and I suppose we'd just about got 'D' Company up to strength, we'd been building it up all through 1942. Drafts had been coming in month by month and we now had a Company to work on.

We marched for six days during which time I think we had half a day's rest. The first two days were really hot weather going up over the moors of Exmoor and a lot of people were dropping out throughout the Regiment, but 'D' Company I think lost two men.

I found it, as a young officer, a big test of my own capabilities because I wasn't a frightfully good chap at marching, I didn't have a pair of boots that had been all that well broken in and like many other people, because of the damp weather when we'd been sleeping out at night, I'd started to get blisters. But we struggled on, and John, who was a very good chap at marching, was up and down the column and I always think that was a great factor in pulling 'D' Company together and making them realize that they were a unit that could do things.

Lance Corporal Ted Tappenden:

I was pushing a pushbike. Major Howard had a walking stick and on the bottom was an inch of brass. He wore that completely away and he had more blisters on his hands than I had on my feet. 'Take a turn on the bike, sir.' 'Not likely, I'm leading my Company', he said, 'Throw that into the ditch.' But it was the Company bike so we couldn't throw it into the ditch.

Lieutenant 'Tod' Sweeney:

The halt before the final march down into Bulford was at a place called Larkhill ... We fell out for ten minutes and sat down and put our feet up, rested, maybe had a drink out of our water bottle and then we were falling back in again. You had to get on parade in your threes, the whole Regiment, way back, seven or eight hundred of us, and I looked round for my platoon and the three leading corporals in the platoon behind me had

7

thought that for a joke, they'd just show how worn out they were. They fell in on their knees . . . the idea being that they'd worn their legs down to their knees!

'D' Company arrived first at the camp and with Major Howard leading, marched into Bulford at 145 steps to the minute, singing *Onward, Christian Soldiers.* Sergeant 'Tich' Rayner:

The officers, the poor sods, after the march they had to look at everybody's feet . . . and they were worse than us, believe me. I remember looking at 'Tod' Sweeney. Blood was coming out of his boots, and his fingers, hands were all blistered where he'd been on his walking stick. It was a hell of a march.

Private Dennis Edwards:

While 'D' Company invariably appeared to be the best at everything, we were probably no better or worse than the lads in the other Companies. However, our extraordinarily zealous Company Commander insisted that his Company had to win at everything. This virtually ensured that when a Company from the gliderborne Airlanding Brigade, with a choice from twelve infantry companies from the Oxf and Bucks, Devons and Royal Ulster Rifles, was required for a special mission, 'D' Company had an advantage over the other companies in the Brigade, it was simply because it was led by the most determined and dedicated Company Commander.

*

One of Howard's great friends was the Officer Commanding 25 Platoon, Lieutenant Herbert Denham 'Danny' Brotheridge. He was another man who had come up through the ranks. Corporal Bill Bailey:

He was an unusual man because he was about seven, eight, nine years older than the average of the platoon, he could do everything we could do and he could play a good game

of football, which was unusual with officers. He'd saunter into a barrack room, not to see what we were doing. You can have an officer who comes down and really he's picking holes . . . Old Dan would come down, sit down on one man's or the other's bed, and eventually there'd be a chat going on about football or whatever was the topic of the day.

And to get a bollocking off him, to get a rocket off of Dan Brotheridge, you really felt it. He had that ability, and it was a very quiet, unassuming quality with old Dan, it wasn't the bluster that one so often meets up against, it was cool, calculated, exact. You'd have sooner had a punch in the ear.

Lieutenant Denham
Brotheridge

Brotheridge had a renowned sense of humour. Lieutenant Dennis Fox, Officer Commanding 17 Platoon, 'B' Company:

When there was a lull in an exercise he would say, 'Come on, let's go into the nearest big hotel'... what we used to call safe hotels, where these people who were getting away from the bombs, that sort of thing, had ensconced themselves for the war. After dinner we would be sitting in the lounge of the hotel with these dears playing cards or knitting or something like that. We would be sitting right at one end of the room and he would suddenly decide to attack the grandfather clock! He would give out orders, 'Number 1 Section, you'll take up a firing position there, Number 2 Section...', and the idea was to get to the clock without touching the ground. The poor old dears didn't know what was happening at all!

Lieutenant David Wood, Officer Commanding 24 Platoon:

I'm sorry to say we also played tricks with imaginary clockwork mice, which we wound up and set going on the floor. We hadn't got anything there, but we watched it going round the room and chased it! I think we behaved abominably in a large number of pubs and hotels, both when we went street fighting down in Southampton... or when we went up to London to the Battersea street fighting area and it was normal to go out in the evening and have a few beers. I don't think we ever actually got thrown out of a pub...[4]

*

The glider employed to transport the bulk of the Airlanding Brigade was the Horsa, a huge aircraft with a wing span of eighty-eight feet which had space to carry thirty-one men or such things as a jeep towing a 6-pounder anti-tank gun.[5] The Horsa was manufactured almost entirely from wood, and had a jettisonable (if required) tricycle undercarriage, but was also provided with the 'insurance' of a skid, a wooden, metal-faced shock absorber beneath the fuselage and a small one at the tail. To familiarise the Oxf and Bucks with being transported in gliders, they flew in Horsas as 'live loads' for the training of glider pilots at Brize Norton. Lance Corporal Tom Packwood:

You'd probably go out to do three glider trips and you were finished for the day. It wasn't hard work, you just went there, sat in the glider and off they went. Two circuits round the airfield and back down again. Then you'd probably have a cup of tea and a sandwich and then you're off again. You had to do four glider flights to qualify for your glider badge and your shilling a day.

However, on some occasions things did not always go to plan. Private Fred Weaver, 24 Platoon:

They were getting us used to the long distance in a glider. We were cruising around up there when all of a sudden something went wrong, we went below the tail slipstream or something, so the pilot said, 'I'll have to cast off.' We got shook to pieces. We came down in a country place and the next minute the police were there round us. We had to stop in the glider. Then the Air Force came and said, 'Right, you can get out.' The squire of the village, he took us up to his place and we had tea and cakes up there. After that he said, 'Well, they've sent for the transport to come and pick you up, but I don't know when it'll

Fred Weaver

be. It's Market Day today, so if you go down into the village the pubs are open.' So we were down there having a good time!

After earning their badge, if the troops still volunteered for such a job, they were given the remainder of the day off. Ted Tappenden:

I used to work in the office at Brize Norton in the morning, I used to go flying in the afternoon. I did over 200 flights in the afternoon, and some of our lads, Clive, Bill Bailey . . . I think they got in the gliders in the morning and stayed in there all day!

Although vital, for the glider pilots such 'live loads' did have their drawbacks. Staff Sergeant Jim Wallwork, 'B' Squadron, Glider Pilot Regiment:

The worst thing is that occasionally they're sick. This is the worst thing of all, that's why a 'live load' is never very popular on training exercises, because once one becomes sick in the back, the whole bloody lot go sick. The glider, somehow the air goes through it and brings it all forward into the cockpit!

*

Leading Aircraftsman Bob Randall of the RAF's 15th Glider Echelon, was a Group One qualified carpenter, the highest standard in the Service. He had also been fully trained on the pre-flight preparations for the setting up of gliders. At the beginning of 1944 he was posted to RAF Tarrant Rushton, fifteen miles north-west of Bournemouth:

Up until this time the glider stations had a team from Airspeed. Hamilcars had a team from General Aircraft Limited. They were responsible for working out the weight and balance of the gliders and also doing air tests. This was going to be our job because these people had got to be returned to their works.

Moving between the airfields of Tarrant Rushton and Netheravon, north of Salisbury, he performed these tasks on both the Horsa and the Hamilcar. In early March he was ordered to go to Netheravon to team up with two other 'handlers':

There were six Horsa gliders and six Albermarle tugs, the glider pilots, all 'Top Brass' there. Air Vice-Marshal Leigh-Mallory, Group Captain Cooper from Tarrant Rushton, the CO from Netheravon and all their entourage were all round there with these gliders.

10

Staff Sergeant Wallwork was one of the glider pilots:

No word as to why, in the usual glider pilot style, but we foregathered at mid-field and were addressed by our Colonel, George Chatterton, behind whom appeared a covey of Army and Air Force Brass. Heavy Brass. He pointed out a couple of triangles marked with broad white tape, one here, one there, on the airfield. Not very big but apparently, in his judgement, big enough. Briefing was very succinct: 'You will be towed at one minute intervals to 4,000 feet, which will take about one hour. You will then release three miles away at a point decided by your tug, from where you will be able to see these triangles. Numbers 1, 2 and 3 will land in this one, making a right-hand circuit, and 4, 5 and 6 in t'other from a left-hand circuit. Now, hop off for lunch. All gliders are ready and assembled on the towpath. Take-off 1300 hours.'

No word as to how we were chosen. Perhaps drawn from a hat? Perhaps crews our Squadron Commanders were glad to part with?

Bob Randall:

During this time, Leigh-Mallory was saying that you could never expect Army NCOs to be able to land powerless aircraft the size of a bomber into patches like that, because you need the skill of a bomber pilot to bring the aircraft in, even with engines, and to do it without engines, you couldn't expect it.

Jim Wallwork:

A glider is exactly the same as an aircraft, it's got the same controls, it's got a turn and bank, an altimeter, a speedometer and so on. The only difference between it and an aircraft is that the engine is a hundred yards ahead on the end of a tow rope and someone else opening and closing the throttles. When you cast off, you fly it exactly the same. We all flew powered aircraft, so we knew how to fly pretty well anything.

Each glider had two pilots because the only assistance in flying the Horsa was a compressed air bottle to operate the flaps, helping to descend more rapidly, and another to help actuate the brakes. Everything else was manually controlled:

So we took off and flew a short course, saw the triangles, cast off and landed all six in our correct areas, to our utter astonishment. A mutter of disbelief emanated from the Brass, and a few low-key bragging words about 'his boys' from George. The Royal Air Force cast the doubt ...

Bob Randall

11

Bob Randall:

One of the RAF blokes said, 'Well, it was lucky, obviously it was just luck that they did it.' So Chatterton said, 'We'll do it again,' but there wasn't time to do it again that day, so they had to go back the next day. He said, 'Just to make life difficult this time, I want 1, 2 and 3 in the other patch,' and changed their patches over. They went off . . . , came round, cast off and they did it. 1, 2 and 3, 4, 5 and 6 in their respective patches with hardly a piece of any of the aircraft overhanging the tape, that was the amazing thing.

Eight glider crews, which included two as back-up, *had* in fact been handpicked from various squadrons of the Glider Pilot Regiment. Glider pilots were not just highly skilled fliers, they had also been through the intense training required to be an Airborne soldier. On top of that they were trained to take over all kinds of tasks such as Bren gunner, jeep driver, despatch rider, anti-tank gunner, whatever role was required on the ground at the time. Colonel Chatterton, the Commander Glider Pilots, called his men 'Total soldiers,' and Army Air Corps wings were very proudly worn. Staff Sergeant Oliver Boland:

You become a fairly unusual person, very rare indeed. I used to occasionally get bloody wet by not having an overcoat on in order to make sure everybody [could] see these blue wings! Such is youth!

*

In early April the 2nd Oxf and Bucks moved to Lincolnshire to prepare for an inter-Divisional exercise. The bulk of the battalion were accommodated in Woodhall Spa, but 'D' Company went to Bardney, nine miles to the north-west. Everyone knew that the invasion would happen in the summer and confirmation of the Oxf and Bucks involvement was subsequently given on 15 April, after the de-brief for Exercise 'BIZZ II'. Major Howard:

I was called over by the Colonel, Mike Roberts and told to report to him that afternoon. I was welcomed cordially by my CO and asked to take a seat.
Colonel Roberts faced me across the desk and, holding my eye, told me that 'D' Company, plus two platoons of 'B' Company and thirty Sappers under command, were to have a very important task to carry out when the invasion started. The Colonel went on to tell me that our task would be to capture two bridges intact. My force of 180 men was to land by night in six gliders in the areas indicated and he produced a plan of the area around two bridges which showed a canal running parallel to a river, about a quarter of a mile apart.[6]

Howard had been informed in order to allow him time to think about a plan prior to the exercise later in the month, codenamed 'MUSH'. This pitted the two Airborne Divisions against each other, with the whole of 6 Airlanding Brigade again practising the capture, defence and relief of two bridges. Prior to it, John Howard gave a briefing in the school at Woodhall Spa. Lieutenant 'Tod' Sweeney:

He said that we'd been selected for a particular operation and that we would be joined by two platoons of 'B' Company, that's the Dennis Fox platoon and the Sandy Smith platoon. We didn't know very much about it but he knew it was to do with the capture of two bridges and it was to do with a special operation that was going to take place before anybody else. He thought that the bridges were guarded by a platoon of special German troops, but again we didn't know very much about it, but he just gave that first warning and then swore us all to secrecy.[7]

Stan Evans

As in most battalions, competition between the Companies was strong, although due to Major Howard's stringent requirements for his Company, many of the battalion had always seen them as somewhat mad. Lance-Corporal Stan Evans belonged to Lieutenant Richard 'Sandy' Smith's 14 Platoon, 'B' Company:

We always classed ourselves the best, better than 'D' Company. It was a shock to the lads in 'B' Company to think 'D' Company thought this! 'B' Company was a very, very good Company. I think Lieutenant Smith was a bugger really. He was a Don from Oxford, he wanted everything perfect, which we all did. When you've got a load of lads like Airborne chaps, all volunteers . . . you get some real rough buggers. In my platoon, everlasting, the lads were always fighting amongst themselves . . . but that would be because of drink, a few beers every night time. There'd be an argument, what I'd call playful argument, but it caused a few fracases. Having said that, as much as the fellas used to argue or fight, whatever you'd like to call it, when it came to the crunch, they were all behind Lieutenant Smith. They admired him although he was a bit, as most of the officers were, toffee-nosed type of thing.

Lieutenant Dennis Fox's 17 Platoon contained a high proportion of the pre-War regular soldiers and hence they were all older than him:

I had a magnificent sergeant . . . 'Wagger' Thornton. He was a remarkable man. In barracks, a quiet, unobtrusive man who would as soon sweep the barrack room himself as order a soldier to do it, but in action he was first class, absolutely first class. He virtually commanded the platoon, I was the figurehead.

Exercise 'MUSH' was taking place near Cirencester in Gloucestershire. The six platoons were to capture and hold two bridges at Cerney Wick. To make the assaults as close to reality as possible, Howard had requested that soldiers in German uniform defend the bridges. These turned out to be very enthusiastic members of 1 Polish Parachute Brigade. Lance Sergeant 'Tich' Rayner, 22 Platoon:

13

I stalked this Pole, pulled him over, got him on the ground, as he fell down, his rifle [with fixed bayonet] fell away from him and stuck me up the cheeks of my arse! It stuck in about an inch!

Frank Bourlet, 25 Platoon:

This developed into what can only be described as a 'Battle Royale'. Somebody got hurt, I don't know who it was, and this sort of triggered this sort of vendetta off. In the end they had to calm it down otherwise somebody was going to get seriously hurt.

Lance Corporal Tom Packwood, 25 Platoon:

They didn't speak our language and we didn't speak theirs, so it was more like a bit of a blood and thunder affair. It got a bit hectic I think, but it turned out alright, no-one was court-martialled as far as I know!

Private Doug Allen:

It was alright, it was all clean fun wasn't it? I mean, they enjoyed it as much as we did. There were a few fights, we couldn't shoot them with real bullets so we'd bang 'em one instead!

Following the exercise, the Division returned to Bulford.

*

While the 6th Airborne continued its training, the RAF had maintained an almost constant vigil over the Division's landing area in Normandy. Thousands of photographs were taken and analyzed to assess any changes to the German defences. On 17 April Major Gerry Lacoste of the Division's Intelligence Branch, reported that a multitude of 'dots' had appeared on the proposed Landing Zone for 6 Airlanding Brigade. Lieutenant Colonel Frank Lowman, Divisional Commander Royal Engineers (CRE):

Detailed examination of the air photographs indicated that the obstructions consisted either of wooden poles twelve to eighteen inches in diameter, or of metal girders, in both cases about fifteen feet high and sunk in holes about four feet deep. It was also possible that the tops of the poles were laced together with stout plain or barbed wire. In some areas the holes had been dug but no poles erected at that stage. The spacing of the poles was thirty to sixty yards.

Having also seen the photos, General Gale paid him a visit and asked what he proposed to do about them. The poles meant possible carnage for a massed glider landing in darkness. The only answer was that they had to be removed. And so, to the dismay of Brigadier Kindersley's 6 Airlanding Brigade, General Gale was forced to switch the rôle of the Brigade with that of 5 Parachute Brigade, allowing the Paras time to clear some of the obstacles from the LZ prior to the subsequent glider landings.[8]

Brigadier Nigel Poett was the Officer Commanding 5 Parachute Brigade. He had taken command during its formation in June 1943. Before this he had been the CO of a Durham Light Infantry battalion and had never contemplated becoming a parachutist or having any involvement with the Airborne Forces:

I had a telegram from the Military Secretary, who was the man who looks after all the appointments in the British Army, saying that I had, 'been selected to command a parachute brigade. Was I prepared to parachute?' That was a problem for me. Like John Howard I have a bad knee . . . I'm not a particularly bold man, however I hadn't the courage to say no! So I said, 'Yes, thrilled, thank you very much indeed, delighted.' And then I had my medical and fortunately I had a tame doctor with my Brigade in which I was serving, and knew him very well, and his eyes didn't travel below the waist! I was damned fit . . . except for my knee.

Brigadier Nigel Poett

General Gale's subsequent written orders to him about the tasks for 5 Parachute Brigade stated that for the Ranville task:

It is imperative that you should hold this area. The framework of your defensive plan must rest on the anti-tank and MMG layout. This layout must cover the open ground to the south and the open ground which forms the Landing Zone to the north. The more enclosed country nearer the banks of the river and the orchards to the east must be covered by infantry in depth and PIATs. You will wire and mine the belt of orchards between Herouvillette and Le Mariquet to a depth of 100 yards. This minefield will be well signposted and covered by fire from infantry posts.[9]

The orders also explained the *Coup de Main* method for capturing the bridges and the need to expand the subsequent bridge positions to the west as quickly as possible, before any counter-attack could drive the small Oxf and Bucks force away. This expansion and defence was a battalion-size task.

During Exercise 'BIZZ II' the 7th Parachute Battalion had performed extremely well, gaining special notice from Gale and the comment that 'It was in a good position for getting an important job.' The Commanding Officer, Lieutenant Colonel Pine-Coffin, who had previously commanded the 3rd Parachute Battalion in North Africa, wanted an 'important job' for his new battalion:

During the next few weeks it was important not to undermine this good position by any thoughtless lapse on the part of any individual member of the battalion. Special attention was paid to all matters of discipline, and in order to avoid a large number of minor charges appearing on the conduct sheets, a special period known as 'Ginger Week' was

Lieutenant Colonel Geoffrey
Pine-Coffin

instituted. A 'Ginger Week' is a conscious effort by the whole battalion to ginger itself up for a period of seven days. No single infringement of the smallest regulation was allowed to pass unnoticed and offenders were assembled daily on the square to be drilled till they sweated. The whole week was a period of considerable amusement and was appreciated even by those unlucky enough to find themselves 'gingered'.

Brigadier Poett duly gave the battalion the vital task of defending the western side of the bridgehead.

Defence of the Ranville area against attacks emerging from the south-east was given to the 12th and 13th Battalions. Lieutenant Colonel Alexander Johnson's 12th (Yorkshire) Battalion had been formed in 1943 from the 10th Green Howards, while Lieutenant Colonel Peter Luard's 13th (Lancashire) Battalion had evolved from the 2/4th South Lancashire Battalion. Both battalions had been through the Division's intense training programme for the invasion, and were thoroughly prepared for their assigned tasks.

The 7th Battalion (Light Infantry) the Parachute Regiment had been converted from the 10th Battalion, Somerset Light Infantry. Perpetuating its Light Infantry origin, the battalion wore a green diamond backing behind their beret badge. As with the Oxf and Bucks, 'young soldiers' and general volunteers had brought them up to strength, and the previous CO, Lieutenant Colonel Hilaro Barlow, had been a very influential figure in the moulding of the battalion. Lieutenant Nick Archdale, HQ Company:

In training, he was a frightening man, his standards were absolute. The 7th Battalion was a very special collection of people, I don't know why, but it was immensely friendly and happy in all ranks. We weren't easy going in any way, but Barlow instilled this unforgiving discipline. I mean as a young officer you did not make a mistake or you probably disappeared back to your unit, quietly, without any fuss. He expected the highest standards without being in any way abrupt or noisy or anything like that. You knew that you had to give it everything. He was a very imposing character, quiet but immensely respected.

When Lieutenant David Hunter, formerly of the Royal Scots, had arrived, he immediately noticed this friendliness:

In December 1943 I had a rush of blood to the head and volunteered for the Parachute Regiment. I suspect my main motive was to impress the girls. After two weeks hard physical training and two weeks parachute training, including eight jumps, I found myself at the end of January 1944 with the 7th Parachute Battalion at Bulford Camp in Salisbury Plain. I had transferred from the oldest Regiment in the British Army to the newest. After the Royal Scots it was like a breath of fresh air. The Royal Scots method of dealing with a new officer was to ignore him (with a few honourable exceptions). I found the mainly English Officers of the 7th Paras very friendly and welcoming.

My room mate at Bulford was the gentle Bill Bowyer who played the trumpet in the battalion dance band and knelt by his bedside every night to say his prayers. There was Bertie Mills our Academic Intelligence Officer . . . and Richard Todd, a repertory actor . . . There was old Etonian Nick Archdale, barrister Bernard Braithwaite . . . London solicitor Nigel Taylor and my old friend Stephen Theobald, a great all round sportsman, a schoolboy international rugby stand-off.

In February 1944, Colonel Barlow had been posted to the 1st Airborne Division, and was succeeded by Geoffrey Pine-Coffin, a tall, quiet, inspirational leader, with a fondness for pipe smoking. He continued Barlow's good work in the build-up towards D-Day.

*

Now under the command of 5 Parachute Brigade for the operation, on 2 May Major Howard was briefed by Brigadier Poett and provided with typed orders that detailed the targets and their whereabouts. Paragraph 9 stated, 'It is vital that the crossing places be held, and to do this you will secure a close bridgehead on the WEST bank, in addition to guarding the bridges. The immediate defence of the bridges and of the WEST bank of the canal must be held at all costs.' A green pass was supplied that allowed him entry to the Divisional Intelligence HQ building at Brigmaston House, a mile north-east of Bulford, where he subsequently analyzed models of the bridges, aerial photographs and all of the available intelligence information.

As he became more familiar with the detail of the task, Howard realized that although the gliders would take off in a set sequence, the order in which they were going to land could not be guaranteed, nor the distance from the targets. Also, in the worst case scenario, if only one glider arrived in the correct spot, that particular party would still have to attempt the task. And so everybody had to be able to do each other's job and capture their bridge alone if necessary. He therefore decided that specific training was required. Howard spoke to his men. Nobby Clark, 24 Platoon:

He called us all together and said our job during the invasion, wherever we were going . . . and whenever it took place, would be to capture bridges at night, which filled us with gloom straight away because we knew that the chances of surviving crash landings in gliders at night was pretty hopeless. We thought 'Oh my God, what's he let us in for?' As soon as the meeting was over, we had to go in the field at the back of the barrack room. We taped out bridges and we started practising getting out of mock gliders that weren't there and capturing bridges.

This entailed marking out both bridges, waterways and obstacles using rolls of heavy cotton tape in order to better comprehend the actual distances involved. Corporal Bill 'Smokey' Howard, 23 Platoon:

John Howard was saying, 'Glider's landed here!' There'd be thirty-odd blokes dash forward towards the 'bridge'. Then he'd say, 'There's a glider landed over there!' then another thirty would dash. We all treated it as a huge joke of course, attacking tapes, but of course, it was a sensible idea.

Bill Gray, 25 Platoon:

We did it for days on end, morning and afternoon and then in the evening . . . we set them out at Stonehenge. The times we attacked Stonehenge was nobody's business.[10]

Nobby Clark:

We had to practise being first, second and third, and this went on incessantly, for days on end. We used to dream about it at night. And this went on for a week or so, maybe slightly longer.

Major Howard learned valuable lessons from the exercise:

Lengths and distances have imprecise meanings written on a page but look a great deal different when set out on the ground in front of everyone. For one thing, I realized immediately that it would be impossible for me to command the attacks on both bridges once I saw what the distance between them really looked like, bearing in mind that the assault would take place at night. I had suspected that this might be the case and had been letting Brian Priday [his 2i/c] take control of one bridge assault already in training. Now I realized that Priday would be taking command of the attack on the Orne River Bridge by himself.

On one occasion the rehearsals were interrupted by Richard Gale arriving to give a lecture to the officers. Lieutenant Wood, 24 Platoon:

General 'Windy' Gale got all the officers together there, in a barn or something and said, 'Soon, you'll be going into action. And when you do, thank God for the opportunity to kill one of the Boche. Get down on your knees and thank God!'

Major Howard:

After the lecture, I was given permission to brief my 2i/c Brian Priday on the operation, and I found it an immense relief to be able to share my knowledge and the burden with my fellow officer and friend.

The importance of the task gradually began to dawn on the men. Lieutenant Wood:

We saw more than our share of VIPs, always an ominous sign . . . Perhaps most significantly of all, we suddenly started finding transport much easier to get, and German uniforms and weapons on which we had to train, began to arrive. Clearly someone somewhere was giving us priority.

While Howard continued his visits to analyze the intelligence information, Captain Priday took over the training.

Bill French

*

The 7th Parachute Battalion had to pass through the Oxf and Bucks force and establish its bridgehead west of the canal, even in the event of the failure of the *Coup de Main* and the destruction of the bridges. Brigadier Poett had prepared a contingency plan for the battalion to cross the waterways by dinghy, further to the north. And so the 7th Battalion had carried out such training at Exminster, over two bridges closely resembling those in Normandy: the Countess Wear Bridge over the Exeter Canal and a road bridge over the nearby River Exe. Sergeant Bill French, HQ Company, 7th Parachute Battalion:

The training really was river crossing at night, in collapsible boats. The boats would have to be dropped from the air . . . get them to the river, and assemble them and cross in batches. Somebody would stay in the boat, take the boat back, get some more across. It was a shuttle service more or less.

At its conclusion the battalion was allowed into Exeter for a drink. Lieutenant Nick Archdale, OC Mortar Platoon:

Our boys pinched the moosehead out of a pub, my 3-inch mortar men. It was a tremendous joke and I don't know why but they stuffed its nose with cheese!

Brigadier Poett informed John Howard about these bridges and ordered him to get his troops down there as quickly as possible. Howard immediately travelled to the location to inspect the bridges and liaise with Colonel Pine-Coffin. Major Howard:

I could see immediately that the area would make a good training ground, although the bridges were a little smaller than those we had to capture in Normandy, and the distance between them was only 150 instead of 500 yards.
The following morning I took the opportunity of talking to Colonel Pine-Coffin, and Major Dick Bartlett, commanding 'C' Company of the 7 Para who, once they had landed and mustered were detailed to come straight to the bridges to relieve my men.

On 21 May Howard's men moved to billets in Exminster and training began at 0800 hours the following morning. They were taken to the bridges in three-ton trucks, and to represent the exit from the gliders, jumped from the rear. Nobby Clark:

Then we practised in all seriousness on real bridges with blank ammunition and things like that, thunderflashes, lots of noise, day and night. It made the local villagers' life hell,

19

but we were only there for three days, three nights, but we were dead beat at the end of that session.

In the course of twenty-four hours we would have done it at least twenty-four times each day, practising the different attacks, first over the bridge, then second over the bridge, and then third. The third platoon had to dash over the bridge to reinforce the first platoon, so that the bulk of the force would have been on the western bank of the canal. God knows how many times we attacked that bridge, but we were thoroughly sick of it.

To cover the scenario of the bridges being blown before they could be captured or the canal bridge being raised, the Oxf and Bucks also prepared for a cross-water assault. Bill Gray:

Me and Charlie Gardner, because we were the strongest swimmers in there, John Howard made us swim across. 'If ever we went on operations, you might have to do that,' he says! We might have to swim across with ropes or something.

The ropes would be fixed on the opposite bank and used by the men to pull themselves across, or pull the boats that were also to be taken.

They had been joined for the exercise by Engineers of 2 Platoon, 249 Field Company, led by Captain HRK 'Jock' Neilson. Sapper Cyril Haslett:

We all had our own little jobs. Some of us had to go and have a look on top of the bridge for explosives, others had to go underneath. I had to go underneath on the girders.

They were to tear away any wiring, then clear possible mines on the roadways across them. If the bridges had already been demolished, they were to help ferry the Oxf and Bucks across the waterways and then establish ferries for the arrival of the 7th Parachute Battalion.

At the end of this period of training, Howard also gave his men a night off. Doug Allen:

Doug Allen

They paid us out and gave us permission to go into Exeter. Biggest mistake they ever made in their bloody lives! Some of us were arrested, nearly everybody was drunk and disorderly, fights going on everywhere.

Many of them ended up in police cells. Lance-Sergeant 'Tich' Rayner:

I went with Danny Brotheridge because he took all the sergeants out. He got paralytic. Course his wife was expecting and he was supposed to be in charge of us! The police phoned up John Howard at the Headquarters we were staying at and told him about it, and John rushed down there in a jeep with Priday to sort things out. He saw this officer there in the police, he was a superintendent and he had war ribbons on from the First World War. He told the police officer we were doing some special training and he let us all loose. The police escorted us back to our barracks!

The men may not have realized it, but Howard knew that this had been their final chance to let off steam.

Chapter Three

The Divisional Plan and Deadstick Training

In Operation Overlord, five stretches of beach had been chosen for landings along the Normandy coast. The Americans were to land on the two most westerly beaches, code-named UTAH and OMAHA, while to the east the Canadian beach, JUNO, was sandwiched between two British areas, GOLD and SWORD.

At the easternmost point of the proposed invasion area lay the small port town of Ouistreham. It was here that both the Canal de Caen and the River Orne met the sea. These waterways led directly to the city of Caen, six miles to the south.

The area east of the Orne consisted of agricultural fields, punctuated by small villages and woods, and so was ideal for an airborne landing. Dropping and Landing Zones were duly chosen, DZ/LZ 'K' being to the south of Escoville, DZ/LZ 'N' between Ranville and Breville, DZ/LZ 'V' at Varaville and LZ 'W' just to the west of the Caen Canal.

A mile north of Ranville, the vital ridge of high ground began, running through the villages of Hauger, Le Plein, Breville, Le Mesnil and through the Bois de Bavent to the outskirts of Troarn. On this ridge, to the east, lay the River Dives valley, much of which had been flooded by the Germans to deter an airborne landing. However, this was to be put to good use by destroying various strategic river bridges to hinder the possible arrival of German armoured reinforcements from the east. A fortified gun battery at Merville, which had the capability of firing on SWORD Beach, also had to be silenced. These were two of the Division's three primary tasks for the early hours of D-Day and were the responsibility of Brigadier Hill's 3 Parachute Brigade.

The first task was the capture, intact, of the two bridges. These were three and a half miles inland from Ouistreham, along an 800-yard section of road running east from the small village of Benouville. Being the only crossing points before reaching Caen, failure to capture the bridges intact would have enormous repercussions for the Division. General Gale:

The administrative problems resulting from our operating away to the flank of the major armies were obviously immense . . . If we captured the bridges intact over the canal and river, and if the 1st Corps attack went according to plan, all would be well. But we must reckon on the possibility of the enemy blowing the bridges before or even as we got to them. The 1st Corps might be delayed and in the area of the bridges indefinitely held up.

The conclusion of course, was that we must be prepared for some time to rely on re-supply by air, and it was important as well to appreciate that evacuation of casualties might be indefinitely held up.

We of course had to work it on the worst case: that the bridges over the river and the canal would be destroyed and that no satisfactory maintenance link with the 3rd Division would be possible for some time. In our plans we therefore arranged for supply by air. A proportion of the air effort on D-Day must thus be devoted to flying in supplies. This meant that we would not have enough aircraft for the whole of the Airlanding Brigade.

Therefore, all but one Company of the 12th Devons was to land by sea on D+1.

Intelligence received on the main possible German forces immediately opposing the Division or that could be brought to bear within a few hours identified the 716 Infantry Division's 736 Grenadier Regiment and Ost Battalion 642, plus elements of the 21st Panzer Division. Ost Battalions consisted mainly of Poles and Russians who had been recruited or forced into service by the Germans. There were also miscellaneous troops on the northern outskirts and in the village of Ranville, but little was known about their strength. The city of Caen had a garrison of around two battalions of local defence troops that might be used in any counter-attack. However, it was predicted that no size-able force would be sent until a reconnaissance had been performed and the general picture around Caen was understood. Therefore an armoured attack was not expected until three hours after first light at the earliest. It was calculated that such a counter-attack would develop from a small-scale battle group consisting of a Company of infantry plus a few tanks and self-propelled guns. General Gale:

Looking to the south, the bridges form the apex of a triangle one arm of which, the River Orne, runs south-west. The other arm, running south-east, is the line of villages and orchards from the bridges through Ranville to Herouvillette.

The river of course, gave a considerable degree of security on that flank. The towpath and river run much lower than the rest of the country, and as might be expected, were studded with trees and orchards. A drive up this by enemy infantry and tanks would be a very restricted affair and should not be difficult to stop.

From the south-east the line of the villages, orchards, gardens and walls leading up through Herouvillette to the bridges would lend itself admirably to defence.

Looking across the front or base of the triangle, from Longueval on the river to Escoville, south-east of Ranville, ran a long, low and bare ridge. Within the three sides of this triangle the ground is completely open. Movement across this by armour or infantry would be most hazardous; it was in fact an ideal killing area. Thus, though there would not be much depth to Poett's position, by holding the village and the line of the river he would be in quite a secure position to deal with any immediate counter-attack of the type and strength which I had anticipated.

Brigadier Poett's 5 Parachute Brigade was to land a mile to the east of the river on DZ 'N'. While the 7th Battalion was to form its defensive bridgehead beyond the Caen

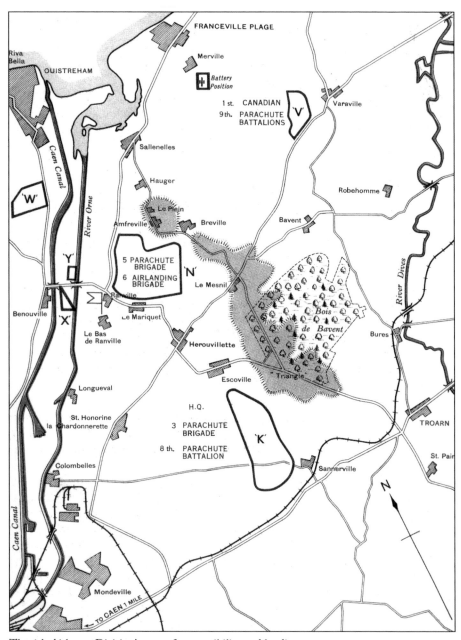

The 6th Airborne Division's area of responsibility and landing zones

Canal, the 12th Battalion was to secure the approaches to the River Orne Bridge by taking up position at a road junction on the high ground a few hundred yards to the north-east. It was also to capture the village of Le Bas de Ranville and occupy a feature called the Ring Contour, which was the high ground to the south of the village. The 13th Battalion was to take and defend Ranville itself. The Brigade also had to clear and protect LZ 'N' for the initial glider force of some seventy Horsa gliders carrying Divisional HQ, anti-tank guns and further heavy machine guns to strengthen the Division's capability to resist the expected armoured attacks from the south.

The Commander Royal Engineers, Lieutenant Colonel Lowman, had examined the problem of the anti-glider landing poles with Lieutenant Colonel Chatterton and decided that two landing strips were required, each 1,000 yards by 60 yards. Lieutenant Colonel Lowman:

This would involve the demolition and removal of one complete row of poles in each strip. Each strip would then take thirty-five Horsa gliders.

In order to take the main glider force of some 140 gliders due to land at 2100hours on D-Day under the revised plan two strips further to the east would be needed. As this force also included some of the much larger Hamilcar gliders carrying 17-pounder anti-tank guns, the strips would have to be increased to 90 yards in width. This would involve the demolition and removal of two complete rows of poles in each 1,000 yard strip. In addition each landing strip would need an approach funnel 120 yard long in which the poles would have to be dropped but need not be removed to the side. All strips would be marked with a landing 'T' of lights by night and ground strips by day and this would be for the [22nd] Independent Parachute Company to do.

With one RE Troop working on each strip, target timings were ninety minutes to clear each night strip and two hours each day strip. The two night strips had to be ready by 0320hours, when the glider force was due to land.

This force was bringing in sixteen 6-pounder anti-tank guns belonging to the four Troops of 4th Airlanding Anti-Tank Battery, and four 17-pounders of 'A' Troop, 3rd Airlanding Anti-Tank Battery.[1] Lance Sergeant George Brownlee, 4th Airlanding Anti-Tank Battery:

The Commander of the Artillery in the Division, Lieutenant Colonel Jack Norris, was told that twenty guns were to take off for Normandy but two 6-pounders would be on the Merville operation and would he therefore select eighteen positions east of the Orne River . . . which must defend the two bridges over the Orne River and Orne Canal and the area between 'to the very muzzle.'

After choosing these positions he worried about the considerable number of trees and the extensive areas of water. At first he assumed he would arrive at 0300 hours on DZ/LZ 'N' and that he could go to 5 Para Brigade HQ and check that the Paras were in their planned positions, but then he realized that General Gale was also arriving with Div staff at the same time and place and would be with the Brigadier very quickly.

Colonel Norris appreciated that this would seriously restrict his access to the Brigadier. He was also very worried about the possibility of his men arriving at the pre-arranged positions and finding no Paras there. George Brownlee:

He thought about it and then remembered that in the 3rd and 4th Anti-Tank Batteries about twenty-four officers and NCOs were Para qualified. He therefore spoke to the Brigadier and asked if any places were available for a few of his men to go so that they could verify routes from their RV to the chosen gun positions. Brigadier Poett said he would check and very soon told the CRA that eight places were available. [He] chose a Captain and three NCOs from the 3rd Battery and two Lieutenants and two NCOs (of whom I was one) from the 4th Battery.

These parachute-qualified artillerymen would check the gun positions and adjust them in accordance with the areas occupied by the 12th and 13th Battalions. As anti-tank artillerymen were trained to do each others jobs, be it gun member, NCO or officer, everybody was capable of making these decisions. The guns had to be in position by dawn.

The majority of the anti-tank guns and the Vickers medium machine guns were to be facing south, protecting the fields across which the Germans were anticipated to attack. Brigadier Poett and the Brigade MMG Officer, Captain Anton Bowler, had decided upon the precise machine-gun positions.

*

Relief for the bridge defenders was to come in the shape of the 3rd Division's 8 Infantry Brigade, which would advance from SWORD Beach in a systematic fashion, and was not expected to arrive until H-Hour plus five at the earliest, H-Hour being the commencement of the seaborne invasion at 0725 hours. However, after landing behind the initial assault waves, Commandos of Lord Lovat's 1 Special Service Brigade comprising Numbers 3, 4 and 6 Army Commandos and 45 Royal Marines Commando, had the task of punching through the German defences, fighting their way to the bridges and advancing north on to the high ground of the Breville ridge.

There were also to be various Engineers employed to satisfy another contingency plan, whether the bridges had been destroyed or not. 17 Field Company Group RE was tasked with initially establishing ferries and also the erection of Bailey Bridges. Major David Willison commanded this Group which comprised 17 Field Company (less 2 Platoon), 71 Field Company, detachments of 106 Bridging Company, 15 Field Park Company RASC and 9 Infantry Brigade Workshops REME. 17 Field Company, transporting the folding ferry boats in trucks, were to land between H+2 and H+6 on SWORD. 71 Field Company had the task of erecting the Bailey Bridges across the waterways. The two Engineer Companies formed advance parties that were to land on SWORD before their main bodies and head straight for the Canal Bridge. They were to report back via radio on the status of the bridges and the enemy resistance in the area, and then prepare for the arrival of their respective Companies. Travelling in a White's Scout Car, 17 Field Company's advance party comprised two officers, Lieutenants HC Clarke and BJ Dixon, while that of 71 Field Company comprised five men including the Company Commander, Major L.E. 'Tiny' Upton. They were also travelling in a White's Scout Car.

All parts of the Group, once ashore, were to get to the bridges as quickly as possible. Reinforcement would come later with the arrival of 246 and 263 Field Companies.

*

Knowing the difficulties in getting the *Coup de Main* gliders to their minute LZs in darkness, Colonel Chatterton also realized that specialist training was essential. For this he called upon Flight Lieutenant Tommy Grant of the Royal Aircraft Establishment, Farnborough, who for a number of years had been involved in the development of equipment for the Airborne Forces. In 1943 he had flown as a tug pilot on the Airborne part of the Sicily invasion in order to assess the equipment and procedures involved in glider operations. The flight from North Africa had been long and extremely hazardous and on arriving at the coast, a wing was hit by flak and caught fire. However, he continued to fly slowly, as was the requirement, at a relatively low altitude over a defended area, with navigation lights on so as to be visible to the pilot of the following glider. After delivering the glider at the correct height and location, that of two bridges, he turned and flew the 400 miles back

Tommy Grant

to base. Unfortunately, the overall operation was a disaster. Many men drowned due to gliders being released too early and landing in the sea. Grant's courage had been recognized by the glider troops and his superior officers, but what had really brought him to prominence was his subsequent detailed report about the whole operation, which was highly critical of the training that the pilots had received.

Although the operation was officially called *Coup de Main*, Tommy Grant gave it the training title Deadstick. The full *Coup de Main* team consisted of the overall commander, Air Vice-Marshal Leslie Hollinghurst, Colonel Chatterton, Squadron Leader Lawrence Wright, dealing with intelligence, maps and photographs, Tommy Grant, his assistant Keith Miller, Lieutenant Godman, communications, administration and flarepath, Staff Sergeant Stanley Waring, driver of the glider pilots 30cwt truck, and the sixteen glider pilots, Wallwork and Ainsworth, Boland and Hobbs, Barkway and Boyle, Lawrence and Shorter, Pearson and Guthrie, Howard and Baacke, Macdonald and Mowat, and Baker and Winsper.[2]

With the wooden gliders not appearing on radar, it was realized that German suspicion might be aroused if the tug aircraft were detected at such a relatively low height and after crossing the coast just turned around without appearing to do anything. Therefore as added disguise, the first changes to the operation were for the tugs to continue on to bomb Caen, and to increase the required flying altitude to 6000 feet. Staff Sergeant Geoff Barkway, 'B' Squadron:

All the other operations, you were towed at about 2,000 feet in a big stream of all the other gliders . . . and it was up to you to release. You'd been shown on maps where the Landing Zones were, and you knew that your tugs were going to come up towards them and as soon as you thought you could get in, you released and went in and landed, whereas we were doing something entirely different. We were going up to 6,000 feet,

27

we were going to be told when to release and when we were released we were to be given particular courses to fly which would lead us into these small areas.

This change in altitude caused another logistical problem. Staff Sergeant Freddie Baacke, 'B' Squadron, Glider Pilot Regiment:

It was found that the Albermarle towing us could not reach the height required, so on May 1, we were temporarily transferred to 'C' Squadron at Tarrant Rushton, where the tugs were of the Halifax species.

RAF Tarrant Rushton was a large airfield and the base for two Halifax Squadrons, 298 and 644. Staff Sergeant Jim Wallwork:

Here, for the first and only time, we were crewed with our tug and stayed together through the training and the final run-in. This was a most important move, as we developed confidence and friendships in a sometimes dangerous and more often hilarious training period. My tug skipper was Wing Commander Duder DSO, DFC, enough to give anyone plenty of encouragement as he obviously knew quite a bit about flying and was indeed the proverbial ace.

The training duly began.

It was all a bit half-arsed at first. A daylight tow was made at various times, apparently when Tarrant Rushton airfield was not too busy, which, as two operational squadrons were based there, was not too often.

Leading Aircraftman Bob Randall:

It was realized, not by our level, but the upper levels [of command] that this was going to be a night exercise, landing in total darkness. Tarrant Rushton was not going to be a good place to do the landings because it was a very busy airfield at night time. There were an awful lot of SOE operations going on and also aircraft coming back that had run out of fuel, you'd get emergency landings, so most nights there were lights on the airfield and the runways were busy. So it didn't make it practical to send up six gliders, fly around for an hour and land back on the airfield because for one thing they were going to see lights which would defeat the object of the exercise.
It was decided that they would take off from Tarrant Rushton . . . fly for an hour and go to Netheravon and they would land back at this Holmes Clump.

Holmes Clump was an L-shaped patch of trees half a mile east of Netheravon. The hour of flying time was necessary for the Halifax bombers to tow the gliders to the required height. Using the line of the trees, a triangular LZ had been marked on one side and a rectangular LZ on the other. Jim Wallwork:

Two separate courses and times developed. Gliders 1 to 3 to fly a three-sided path, and 4 to 6 a dog-leg pattern. We were towed in line astern at one minute intervals. The drill in flight was to cast off at 90mph while turning onto the decided course. Immediately I was 'On', the co-pilot operated the stopwatch and timing started, countdown by Ainsworth, 'Five, Four, Three, Two, One, Zero', and I made a controlled Rate One [90°] right turn to course two, and when I was 'On' again, Johnnie restarted the watch. Another countdown and at zero, another ninety degree turn right and the target lay ahead. Broadly, 1 to 3 flew a downwind leg of 180 degrees at 90 mph for three minutes forty seconds, then a 90 degree Rate One turn on to second course for two minutes five seconds, and a last 90 degree turn right for the run-in; by which time the target should be directly ahead. Gliders 4 to 6 cast off at the same spot, operated half, then full flap, and in a dog-leg course flew straight into their target.

Staff Sergeant Roy Howard

We flew this pattern the first few times by daylight wearing night goggles, and then by night with two flares. By then we had about a quarter moon, so we discarded the flares and began to take things seriously. We landed each side of the wood; the first three landing roughly north, the other three coming directly towards us flying south, with the trees to halt either if necessary, which encouraged concentration.

Staff Sergeant Roy Howard:

Three gliders would land in each of these two very small fields. RAF ground crews were there each day to somehow get the Horsas back onto Netheravon airfield and service them. This meant that we could only do one landing each day.

By this time we were training at night. At first with a few lights on the ground, but as our landings became more precise these were removed and we were told to do spot landings in these small fields with no lights or aids of any kind. At first I thought that it could not be done, but after one or two hairy missions we found that it could.

Both Grant and Miller oversaw the detail of the training. Staff Sergeant Stan Pearson:

Flight Lieutenant Grant made all the decisions regarding the positions of the gliders and the glider pilots in the stream, Wallwork and Ainsworth still always flying Number 1. Tommy flew with every glider crew and made suggestions about means of improving their flying technique.

Jim Wallwork:

These two organized everything, all briefings and calculating courses and timings — which varied, as did the winds on every flight.
A pattern quickly developed. Briefing at say, 2215 hours, all glider and tug crews.

Take-off 2300 hours, cast-off say 2350 hours and into Holmes Clump flying set courses and times. Debrief there by lamplight with cold cocoa all round, then a two-hour drive by truck back to Tarrant for a meal and bed. Up and into the truck at midday, and drive back to Netheravon, where the gliders had been recovered and assembled on the airfield for take-off. With our own tugs, tow back to Tarrant by perhaps 1500 hours, then take what's left of the day off until briefing a bit later at say, 2230 hours, as the moon moves around a little, requiring small course/timing changes each night. Our time off was the few days between moon periods, so it was not too hard as we had a truck and driver for recreational purposes as well as flying.

Stan Pearson:

Hollinghurst and Chatterton waited on the LZs watching the practice through night binoculars, and handing out cocoa to the pilots. Surely the only time in the history of warfare that an Air Marshal and a Brigadier [sic] stood in a field in the early hours to give cocoa to sixteen young NCOs.

During this training there were inevitably a few mishaps. Geoff Barkway:

Our three gliders were supposed to land, one two, three [line astern] 'cos the field was triangular. They said, 'If you get there and find that Number 1 hasn't arrived and you're Number 3,' which is what we were, 'you will roll up into their position and do their job. And Number 2 can come up and do your job, or whatever.' So we landed in this field. I couldn't see anything in there. All I could see was the line of trees and then suddenly, as we got a bit nearer, out of the darkness this great big fin and rudder of a glider already there. But that was black, the trees were virtually black, so I slewed to one side and just sort of knocked our wings together. It didn't do much good to the glider but it didn't do us any [harm]. That was the beauty of a glider, you could smash them up and get out and brush off the bits and pieces! We always reckoned it was a good landing if you could walk away from it.

Jim Wallwork:

One night Number 6 was late. Numbers 1 to 3 were in safe and sound, as were 4 and 5, and then we heard Mac coming. We heard him from a long way off, and he was coming very, very quickly. So we all took refuge in the long leg of trees and crossed our fingers. He landed, or touched down, in the right place behind 4 and 5, but to avoid them at that speed he lifted over both gliders and trees, but only just, and stalled and dropped on 2 and 3 with the most horrific noise of tearing plywood. We were all out quick to search for bodies, but despite the complete wreckage neither Macdonald nor his co-pilot, Mowat, was badly injured. There were odd broken bones and bruises . . .

However, their injuries were sufficient to rule them out of the operation. Jim Wallwork:

Staff Sergeants Len Guthrie
and Stan Pearson

*We flew as long as there was any moon at all, and about halfway through training
adopted Gee, a sort of magic beam machine in the tug which allowed us to fly and release
above cloud. So Deadstick flew regardless of weather. One night the Germans rather
unsportingly bent the magic, but we pressed on in ignorance, released as arranged, and
then at about 2,000 feet above Shaftesbury* [thirty miles to the south-west] *realized
that someone had moved Holmes Clump! But all flew their courses and all landed among
the cattle and corn intact.*[3]

Stan Pearson:

*Three were down intact in the grounds of a large private house. The other three gliders
landed near Spettisbury, also without damage to the pilots or gliders.*

Bob Randall:

*We were all patiently waiting at Netheravon and sort of gave up hope for them when
we got this call to say they were at this field up at Shaftesbury. All landed successfully,
no problem, but it gave you the idea that you could have problems if you were using radar
navigation . . . with them being diverted off somewhere else.*

The operation was performed thirteen times at night without any lights. Gradually,
Tommy Grant fine-tuned the detail of the flying and the differing approaches to the
LZs. The gliders also gradually increased the ballast carried to half-load, then full-load.
Bob Randall:

*During the training we ballasted the gliders with bits of Bailey Bridges. Any old parts
of Bailey Bridges we strapped into the gliders, these lumps of iron stuck down the fuselage. One night Jim Wallwork said, after the episode of hopping over the trees and
landing on top of the other gliders, that it wasn't a very good idea having these pieces of
Bailey Bridge. When they were sitting in the pilot's seat, if they had a sudden decelera-
tion and the moorings broke, this angle iron would come through and chop their heads
off. . . So we sort of agreed with him and went back and later on we took the Bailey*

31

Bridges out and fitted concrete slabs. In the Hamilcar glider we used to have three wooden boxes to ballast. These contained concrete slabs. They were about three-foot long, about two foot deep by about three inches thick. Part of the concrete was missing through the reinforcement iron so you'd got sort of lashing points . . . So we got these slabs, loaded them down the centre of the glider, lashed them to the floor and as you can imagine, concrete is very dense, so the three ton of concrete, running the length of the glider, only came up a few feet off the floor. And that night, Jim said he wasn't very happy about the ballast that we were using instead of the Bailey Bridge. He said, 'It might be alright, it's not going to chop our heads off, but if we stop suddenly that lot's going to come shooting under the seat and take our legs off at the knees!' At which stage we sort of said, 'Well, you've got to be careful the way you land, because you can't ballast three ton of feathers!' Anyway, it was accepted as a necessary evil.

No 'live load' training was carried out because as someone said, 'It was far too dangerous for the 'live load'!' Jim Wallwork:

Air Vice-Marshal Sir Leslie Hollinghurst, who exercised overall command of the Air Transport Groups, had expressly forbidden any live-load or passengers on Deadstick for any reason whatsoever. He was the only one to break the rule, jumping into my glider a moment before take-off time one lovely full-moon night. He enjoyed the trip, standing in the cockpit until seconds before touchdown, so that night we managed a 'perfect' for him.[4]

This whole training period was memorable for the pilots. Staff Sergeant Oliver Boland:

That was a glorious existence. We were the most pampered very small group of people in the British Army at the time.

Chapter Four

Benouville

Information about the defences of the Normandy sector of the Atlantic Wall had been arriving via the French Resistance since 1942. Vast networks of men, women and children had risked their lives on a continual basis in order to gather detail of any kind that would be useful to the Allies. This had begun at a time when there was no prospect of liberation, and even when the possibility increased, they knew that the invasion might never occur in their area. The ingenuity in gathering this information had known no bounds, and despite the heavy German security measures, the results had been staggering.

In the area of Caen the seeds of French resistance were sown as soon as the Germans arrived. Acts of minor sabotage and anti-German propaganda activities had been carried out by a group that called itself *L'Armée des Volontaires*. This had evolved into the region's most successful intelligence gathering organization, *Le Réseau Centurie*, the Century Network, part of *L'Organization Civile et Militaire* (OCM). Marcel Girard, a native of Caen and the former manager of a cement works in nearby Mondeville, had set up the OCM, which had direct links with *Le Deuxieme Bureau*, General de Gaulle's Free French Intelligence Organization in London. Besides members of *L'Armée des Volontaires*, Girard also recruited friends and former business acquaintances and through these business dealings knew the ideal person to coordinate the intelligence gathering activities. His name was Eugene Meslin. Meslin was the *Ingénieur en Chef des Ponts et Chausées*, responsible for the canal, river and port of Caen itself. He was a bachelor who lived in the Rue de l'Arquette in the Cavée area of Caen and worked in offices situated at *La Fonderie*. The importance of the job and his age had exempted him from military service or being deported to Germany as forced labour. At a very early stage of the occupation he had decided upon his stance and had been an active

Eugene Meslin

33

member of *L'Armée des Volontaires*. He was extremely discreet, and only his devoted secretary, Jeanne Vérinaud, knew of his resistance work.

The system that *Le Réseau Centurie* employed was to assign areas to agents which were then divided into sections. These were regularly monitored during their normal daily duties and any changes reported upon. Small maps were also produced of each specific section, noting anything from minefields, gun emplacements and sea defences to cables, signs and nationality of troops. Meslin's actions had been to coordinate this information and supply the small maps to a cartographer, Robert Thomas, who amalgamated them. Meslin then arranged for the resulting maps to be couriered for onward transmission to England.

Eugene Meslin's job also gave him access to the areas along both waterways, and enabled him to gather information from various trusted inhabitants.

*

Prior to the construction of the Caen Canal, the River Orne had met the sea in a wide estuary, but with the expansion of the city and its industries, it became necessary to

Winter 1943. Jeanne Verinaud (right) with colleagues Christiane Jamin, Simone Leveque and Jacqueline Parris outside the offices of *La Fonderie*. The first two windows identify Eugene Meslin's office

improve access to the sea by a waterway that was both deeper and non-tidal. Consequently, in 1838 work commenced to build the canal and redirect the river straight out to sea at the point where it curved towards Benouville. This work was completed in 1850. Two bridges were therefore built to link Benouville with the villages to the east.

Eugene Meslin knew the Benouville Canal Bridge very well because in 1933, work had begun on a replacement and he had been in overall charge of the rebuilding project, which was carried out by the DAYDE Company. The old structure was replaced with a bascule bridge, one which pivoted at one end to raise the other into the air. This was designed by his colleague, Jean Racine, the Chief Engineer, and was completed during the following year. The bridge was raised by an electric motor. If that failed, a rescue engine was available and finally, if necessary, a dozen men using cranks could also be employed.

With the canal being used for commercial purposes, its bridge was all the more important to the Germans and therefore possessed most of the defensive measures such as trenches, dugouts, barbed wire and machine guns. Ironically, in October 1939 an emplacement had been constructed on the south-eastern bank to house a 50mm gun to protect the bridge from a land assault. It had since been put to good use by the occupiers. The bridge itself had been prepared for demolition in the event of an assault.

The bridgekeeper, Auguste Niepceron, had been responsible for the operation of the bridge since completion of the rebuild. His sixteen-year-old son, René, had watched the replacement of the bridge from the digging of the foundations to the finishing of the

The western bank of the canal during the replacement of the bridge

The Caen Canal Bridge. In the background is the church at Le Port

steelwork, and he considered it to be *his* bridge. The Niepcerons had lived in a house beside the structure on the north-eastern side, in fact René had been born in the house, but in April 1944 the Germans demolished it to give the gun a field of fire up-river. The remaining part of the house, the cellar, had been reinforced with concrete and converted into a pillbox.

The bridge was garrisoned by around twenty Germans along with several elderly Frenchmen who were paid to perform minor duties such as acting as extra unarmed guards. They were known as the *Hilfsgendarmerie* and were identified by a green brassard bearing their title in black.

The bridge across the Orne River was narrower than that of the canal, in fact it was more of a footbridge. The bridge could open by pivoting about its central pillar, and so was known as *Le Pont Tournant*. A few houses lay at its eastern end.

*

Benouville was an old village with a population of nearly 600. A narrow-gauge railway ran parallel to the canal and connected the village to Ouistreham, Ranville and Caen. At the end of the bridge was a small station with a cooling tower for the steam engine. Behind the station was the *Café Picot*, owned by Louis Picot, which had a terrace and a low wall. Next door was a small garage and beside that, a distinctive house bearing the date of its completion, 1909. Behind the 1909 house was an orchard and an underground bunker which had around thirty steps leading down to it. Next on that side of the road was a bar, *La Chaumiere*. Beside this building was a house which the Germans had

The Benouville area showing the two bridges

commandeered as a HQ. Behind *La Chaumiere* was the building to which the Niepceron family had been forced to move.

Across the road from the *Café Picot* was the *Café Gondrée*, which had a petrol pump outside and behind it a small set of steps leading down to a covered spring. The owners, Georges and Thérèse Gondrée had bought the café in 1934 and lived there with their two young daughters, Georgette and Arlette.

Georges was a connoisseur of wine and champagne and had not wanted to let the Germans have his large stock of bottles, so in the summer of 1940 he and his friend Pierrot had buried them beneath a big pear tree in the garden. Fortunately the Germans had not found the stache, but times were extremely hard as there was no lemonade, beer or coffee to sell. Barley could be bought from farms, but they just made do with what they could get. In fact they sold homemade liquor to the Germans which Thérèse brewed from rotting marrows and the remains of a dusty packet of half-mouldy sugar. This concoction was drunk with avidity by the Germans who paid 25 francs a glass for it!

The canal bridge area in March 1944

Life had gone on, as it had to, with as much normality as possible, but Georges and Thérèse slept in separate rooms to prevent soldiers being billeted on them.

*

The Canal Bridge was not the only reason that Benouville was so important. The main Caen to Ouistreham road passed through it, making it vital to the Germans for direct access to the coast.

On the T-Junction where this met the route to Ranville, stood the town hall, *La Mairie*. Jean Deschamps was the Secretary of the *Mairie* and lived upstairs in the building with his wife Marie. They had not been as fortunate as the Gondrées with

Jean and Marie Deschamps

regard to soldiers being billeted on them, but the two Germans they had were not Nazis, or even enthusiastic soldiers. They just wanted the war to end.

The northern part of Benouville was known as Le Port because on the original route of the Orne, fishing boats and others loaded with stone from quarries further down-river would moor at the foot of the village church before heading off to England. Consequently, the old chapel in the church was known as the fishermen's chapel. The building had now been extended and the grounds included the local cemetery. This faced onto a small square with a row of houses directly opposite, several of which were shops.

To the west of the *Café Gondrée* a ridge of ground ran parallel to the canal for around 300 yards. A thousand yards further south was the Benouville Chateau, a magnificent eighteenth century mansion with a pillared façade within walled grounds that contained areas of woods and lawns. The Chateau itself was now a Maternity Hospital, but there were also three external pavilions beside and in front of the building for the care of orphaned and abandoned children. The *Directrice* of the hospital was Madame Léa Vion whose rather small appearance belied an extremely determined, authoritative but calm character. Like Eugene Meslin, Madame Vion's opposition to the Germans had commenced from the moment of their arrival and she joined *L'Armée des Volontaires* prior to the *Réseau Centurie*. Her job allowed her the freedom to make regular visits to Caen in the hospital's ambulance, the driver of which was Albert Lebourgeois, an escaped prisoner of war. In the previous four years she had hidden shot-down Allied

Looking north at the front of the Benouville Chateau with the canal to the right

pilots before transporting them to Caen prior to their onward journey to a neutral country. Any information gained was passed on at the same time to the leader of her Group, Henri Le Vieille, whom she had actually recruited in October 1940. All information gathered on the bridges and the immediate area was fed back to Eugene Meslin.[1]

The vehicle had also proved useful for picking up the contents of parachute supply drops. Léa Vion also hid members of the Resistance being sought by the Germans, sometimes in the cellar beneath the chapel, a separate building just to the south of the Chateau, or by obtaining false papers and employing them on the estate. In February 1944, a French Intelligence agent, Capitaine Jean Renauld-Dandicolle, had arrived in the area, and Madame Vion employed him as her gardener until May when he was summoned to form a Resistance group to the south of Caen which became known as *Le Maquis de St Clair*. Others being sheltered were members of the Communist Resistance, and although she had no love of communism, she placed *La Resistance* above everything else.[2]

*

As 1944 progressed and the possibility of an invasion heightened, the Germans had become more difficult. An incident occurred when they began to build a quay opposite the *Café Gondrée*. Georges kept some small fishing boats there, so Thérèse sent Pierrot to bring the boats over to the café side. However, she saw him in an altercation with the German sentries and so went to try and explain, but they marched her to their HQ building for interrogation and held her for quite some time. She was left traumatised but unhurt.

The worst incident had occurred when a group of soldiers came into the café and sat at a table in the corner. Thérèse served in the café most of the time and one of these

Léa Vion with one of her nurses, Louise Moulin (IWM B8088)

men was rude to her. When she refused to serve him, the German grabbed her by the throat, and if Georges had not arrived from the cellar in time, she would have been strangled.[3]

Serving did have its merits, however. She had overheard a most important detail. The switch to blow the bridge was situated in the pillbox on the opposite bank. This information had been duly 'passed on'.

The information provided by people such as these, all along the coast of France, was of inestimable value to the Allied invasion plans.

AERIAL VIEW OF LE PORT

41

Chapter Five

Final Planning and Transit Camps

On 24 May the Oxf and Bucks were informed that they would be moving to their Transit Camps. Nobby Clark:

We were warned that as soon as we got up the following morning we had to pack all our personal gear and get battle order ready . . . All the stuff you didn't need to take with you was put in your kitbag. We had to deposit them in the Company stores.

The bulk of the battalion was going to Harwell, but the *Coup de Main* party had to travel elsewhere. They boarded a convoy of trucks. Lieutenant 'Tod' Sweeney:

It was rather interesting that the Regiment turned out to watch us go because they knew we were going on some special operation. They didn't know what. It was very unusual to see them poking their heads out of windows and coming up to the doors of barrack blocks to see you motoring round the square and out. They obviously thought 'We're probably not going to see that lot again!'

The party arrived at the Transit Camp without any idea of its location and took up residence in seven-man tents. The camp was actually near RAF Tarrant Rushton.

On 27 May Brigadier Kindersley visited the camp and informed Major Howard that he could brief his platoon commanders. He therefore summoned them to a room in a Nissen hut within a heavily guarded and wired off enclosure. On the floor in front of them, an object lay covered. 'Tod' Sweeney:

There were maps all around the wall but they were all covered up with white drawing paper. John said, 'Right, now this is it. You're going to get your briefing.' Up to that point we'd known that it was two bridges, we'd known they were so far apart, we'd known they were obviously somewhere in Europe. We had ideas of dimensions, we had worked out ideas of how we would land and how we would attack these bridges, but we didn't know where they were.

John said, 'Alright now, we'll have a little bet. Everybody will put in five shillings,' or some small sum, 'into the hat and the person who guesses where we are going to land gets the lot.' Well we knew it was a river, you knew that in Europe there must be a series of rivers come out to the coast, and at that stage most people thought the main landing would take place across the narrowest trip, by the Pas de Calais . . . I said somewhere in the Antwerp, Scheldt area . . . we weren't asked to specify exactly. Someone said Le Havre I think, and two people, Sandy Smith and Dennis Fox said, 'The Cherbourg Peninsula', without necessarily knowing there were any rivers. So John said, 'Now which side of the Cherbourg Peninsula are we going to land? The east side or the west side?' I'm not sure which one won . . .

Then John said, 'Alright, now strip off the paper.' We took all this drawing paper off the maps, we lifted the paper up off the model, and he said, 'Now that's where we are going to land, the River Orne and the Caen Canal.'

No-one had heard of Caen:

It wasn't a place that was known to the British. If you'd said Deauville or Calais or one of the other places along the coast, but Caen wasn't very well known.

They then began to study the plan. Major Howard explained the theoretical order in which the gliders were to land and why each platoon had been trained to do each other's job. At the Canal Bridge, the first glider to land would carry Lieutenant Brotheridge's 25 Platoon, the second, Lieutenant Wood's 24 Platoon and finally Lieutenant Smith's 14 Platoon. Major Howard would travel with 25 Platoon.[1]

For the Orne Bridge, Lieutenant Hooper's 22 Platoon would land first, followed by Lieutenant Sweeney's 23 Platoon and finally Lieutenant Fox's 17 Platoon. The second-in-command, Captain Brian Priday would go with 22 Platoon.

To avoid the possibility of the two forces being cut off from one another, they were to land on LZs between the waterways. 'Tod' Sweeney:

There were some reasons why it might have been beneficial to have landed outside the rivers, but John was determined that whatever force he'd got, he would get them within those two rivers. Now that might have proved to have been difficult because he might have had them between the two rivers with the bridges blown on either side in which case they couldn't communicate with their own troops. But he decided that to have them together was more important than perhaps landing in a better position. He put the options to us and said, 'This is the reason why I am doing it this way.'

The other point that John made was that the important bridge was the Canal Bridge. 'If all else failed, we'll forget about the River Bridge, let the Germans have that, but let's hold the Canal Bridge because that is the way the seaborne troops are coming and that is the one bridge we must capture and hold, or rebuild first of all.'

We sat and talked and John then went through his plan again of how we were going to do it, where we were going

Lieutenant 'Tod' Sweeney

to land and what we would do, and that went on for two or three days.

After we had all been briefed you then had an opportunity to bring in your own platoon and do exactly the same thing with them with the Company Commander listening.

For most of them, the location was almost irrelevant. Frank Bourlet:

Normandy to us, kids as I always thought we were, was a million miles away. We had Army educations . . . we didn't even know where Normandy was. It was somewhere in France as far as we were concerned.

However, the detail of the intelligence was very impressive. Lance Sergeant 'Tich' Rayner:

We had photographs pinned up every night more or less, after they'd been over and photographed. We had a big sand table there and John Howard allowed any Private to go in and look and decide, give his opinion of the operation. We used to do our little planning on the sand tables ourselves more or less.

Thanks to the information obtained by Thérèse Gondrée about the location of the bridge demolition switch, Major Howard emphasized that the most important task in the initial assault was putting the pillbox out of action. This was to be the first task of the three specific platoon operations. Two men were detailed to drop grenades through the slits of the pillbox while simultaneously the remainder of the first platoon crossed the bridge. If Howard and Company Headquarters, this being his radio operator, Corporal Tappenden, landed first as planned, they would be waiting at the end of the bridge to direct the following two platoons. Captain Neilson and his sappers would immediately search for explosives beneath the bridges. The Scout section of 25 Platoon was tasked with knocking out the pillbox. Frank Bourlet, 25 Platoon:

Scout Section consisted of Jack Bailey the Section Commander, Paddy O'Donnell, sniper, myself, sniper and Private Parr. We could have a Bren gunner allotted to us and that was Gus Gardner.

Bill Gray was a Bren gunner in 1 Section, 25 Platoon:

It was my job to be first out of the glider to supply the all-round protection while everybody else got out.

Barbed wire had been laid below the bank of the road, thereby providing the first obstacle for them to overcome. Accordingly, the signal for the other two sections to get across the bridge was either a Bangalore torpedo (an explosive charge on the end of an extendible tube) to clear the wire, or a grenade in the pillbox. The second platoon would go for the trenches and machine guns beyond the pillbox, along the east bank, while the third platoon would cross the bridge to support the first platoon. Lance Corporal Arthur

Roberts was a member of 5 Section, 24 Platoon led by Corporal Copperthwaite. Arthur Roberts:

Den Dancey was my Bren gunner, two Clarks, Nobby Clark was one of them, another Clarke, a little bloke Pepperall. Our job was to go across the road, irrespective of what was flung at us, and clear the trenches on that side of the road, on the other side of the pillbox . . . and clear the two machine-gun posts.

Another section of 24 Platoon would clear the trenches in the area of the gun emplacement.

The procedure would be similar for the River Bridge. To avoid shooting each other in the dark, a simple method of recognition had to be agreed. Lieutenant Sweeney:

We had this idea of shouting a codeword as we went across, 'Able', 'Baker', 'Charlie', 'Dog', 'Fox' and 'Easy' and that would say this is such and such a platoon rushing across.

Communication would be maintained by type '38' radio sets carried by each platoon and Company HQ. Brigadier Poett, who had decided to jump early with his small Command Post party, also had a set. This was necessary because if the capture of the bridges failed, he wanted to control his contingency plan and adjust the deployment of the Brigade. Later, Colonel Pine-Coffin's 7th Battalion HQ would arrive with a set. Depending on what happened at the bridges, Lance Corporal Tappenden had various codewords to transmit. HAM meant that the Canal Bridge had been captured intact, JACK meant it was captured but destroyed. JAM was for the capture intact of the Orne Bridge, LARD captured but destroyed. Major Howard also had a whistle to blow the 'Victory V' signal, if appropriate.

Dropping at 0050 hours, 5 Parachute Brigade had its own Signals Section which was responsible for providing wireless communication from Brigade HQ to all its battalions, plus a link back to the UK. Major Guy Radmore, OC 5 Parachute Brigade Signals:

The 5 Parachute Brigade Signals consisted of myself, an excellent subaltern called Gordon Royle who was around twenty. I was then twenty-three and I had something like seventy, all ranks, of whom there were a few despatch riders who rode these lightweight motorcycles. And there were a few linesmen. We had a jeep and trailer to lay telephone line which was supposed to come down by glider and the rest were all wireless operators and each wireless detachment for local communication from Brigade to battalion we had '68' sets which were sort of souped up '18' sets which were very easily smashed and not very accurate, and they'd drift off frequency. And we had a thing called a 4G which was only on morse to work back long distances to England and everywhere else.

They were a super lot of chaps. They were all volunteers. Major Guy Radmore

45

We were all actually very good friends. There was a lot of leg pulling and terrific morale.

I had a very good corporal who was a bookie's clerk in peacetime and one day I sent him up to Windsor races with his wireless set . . . And we had a whole days racing at Bulford to Windsor on the Army wireless. General Gale got to hear about this and was actually quite amused!

*

During the night of 29 May the glider pilots left Tarrant Rushton for a forty minute flight with wing tip and tail lights switched off, flying on station and formatting by lining up on the glowing rectangular boxes of the tugs' exhausts.

They released six miles from Netheravon and timed their glide down to 2,000 feet. Staff Sergeant Stan Pearson:

There was one flare on each field clearly visible. With no flap and a long shallow glide, then flap on at around fifty feet, slowly back with the stick till the main wheels touched down with the nose wheel and a smooth run down the field . . . Cocoa from George, the practice had gone perfectly – all six gliders down in the right place inside six minutes.

Tommy Grant subsequently told them that it had been their last practice flight before the invasion and that the order in which they had flown was to be that for the forthcoming operation. For the Canal Bridge, first would be Wallwork and Ainsworth, followed by Boland and Hobbs, and then Barkway and Boyle. For the Orne Bridge it would be Lawrence and Shorter, followed by Pearson and Guthrie and then Howard and Baacke.

The following morning the glider pilots had joined the Oxf and Bucks men for the first detailed briefing and were informed which platoon they would be taking. Staff Sergeant Jim Wallwork:

At last we were told where, how and why the two bridges over the River Orne and Caen Canal had to be taken intact and held. Gliders 1 to 3, flying the three-course path were to take the canal, while 4 to 6 would drop straight down and take the river.

We saw and studied the most magnificent relief model of the coast up to the bridges, covering every lane, bush and house – the full catastrophe. Intelligence was superb. Daily overflights by photographic reconnaissance Spitfires brought the target up to date, even to such details as when a house by the canal was demolished stone by stone and the pillbox across from it reinforced stone by stone. We could almost see the Germans working at it. Such attention could only generate supreme confidence in all of us. In fact, one of the crew remarked, 'Someone's taking an awful lot of trouble over this operation, so we'd better not cock it up or the King will be rather cross!'

Staff Sergeant Freddie Baacke:

Then followed a week's intensive briefing on the military side of the matter, a briefing which was outstanding in its thoroughness, the aids being a sand model complete to every detail, and a colour film which even simulated the flight from cast off to landing under night conditions.

This film, shown to them at RAF Tarrant Ruston, had been produced by Squadron Leader Lawrence Wright using a camera on an angled wire above a sand table of the area. As the camera passed down the wire it gave the pilots an idea of what they would be looking at during their actual descents. As the pilots became familiar with it, they viewed the film with either tinted glass over the projector lens or through pilot's darkened glasses. The LZ for the Canal Bridge was a field of around 500 yards length on the south-eastern side of the structure. The embankment, upon which ran the Benouville to Ranville road, emphasized the end of the field. In the right hand corner was a pond and marshy area, the remnants of the old river, effectively making the ideal landing positions within a small triangle, with the apex touching the road. Thus, the relevance of the triangle marked out at Holmes Clump. This was designated LZ 'X'. These three gliders, designated chalk numbers 91, 92 and 93, were planned to be released first because they had a longer glidepath to reach their target. Jim Wallwork:

Staff Sergeant Freddie Baacke

It early became evident to Johnnie and me that to get up to the bridge embankment in order to leave ample room for the following 2 and 3, we had to be prepared to arrive there a bit faster than normal and, knowing such, we reckoned on a broken leg each for our pains, for which we would calculate ourselves lucky. Howard thought I was going to hit the embankment and take out the barbed wire so his chaps would have a nice tidy run across the bridge with no annoying obstacles to delay them, but in truth we had to get well up to avoid being rear-ended by Number 2, who in turn would be tupped up the arse by Number 3 and would all finish with a dose of whiplash, if nothing else.

These three Horsas also had to have a particular modification. Staff Sergeant Geoff Barkway, pilot, Glider 93:

Because we were flying right-handed turns it was suggested that the first pilot flew on the right-hand side of the glider (he normally flew on the left). Down under the perspex front of the cockpit they cut a second panel and put some perspex in it so that you could almost look vertically down at the ground and you had this extra window to look through.

Bob Randall, 15th Glider Echelon, RAF:

The command pilot was going to be in the right-hand seat because on this operation they were going to be descending at a rate of 2,500 feet a minute at the angle of about forty-five degrees, so that the pilot in the right-hand seat, doing right-hand circuits would have a clear view of the bridge . . . The co-pilot had a very small torch so that he didn't interfere with the vision of the pilot, and a stop-watch, and they had to put a direction finder [gyro-compass] *in the aircraft because the standard compass at the angle of forty-five degrees wouldn't have been effective.*[2]

After casting off, the theory behind the Canal Bridge approach was to pull the nose up and kill the airspeed down to about ninety miles per hour. When required, the second pilot would state the elapsed time and the pilot would then do a Rate One right-hand turn on to the next course. Following a shorter time on the second leg the second pilot again called out the timing, the pilot would then do another Rate One right hand turn. At this stage they should be able to see the bridge ahead of them. Bob Randall:

Once you cast off, the person at the front of the glider and one at the back of the glider had to get up and open the doors because the doors slid upwards and if there was any distortion on a heavy landing the doors would be jammed so they couldn't get out.

The Orne Bridge gliders were assigned chalk numbers 94, 95 and 96. Their approach to the target also entailed a forty-five degree dive. They would gradually lose speed, making three changes of course, again by dead reckoning. This all had to be done in six minutes. Their LZ, 'Y', was a field which was around a hundred yards wide and approximately 800 yards long, but the landing distance was reduced by a belt of trees fifty-feet in height, that ran across their glidepath at the start of the field. As at the Canal Bridge, the end of the field was accentuated by the high embankment which carried the road at either end of the bridge. Therefore, undershooting meant running straight into the trees, and overshooting, being crushed against the embankment. Staff Sergeant Roy Howard, pilot, Glider 96:

The operation required that the three gliders which were to attack the River Orne Bridge had to shed their 6,000 feet as quickly as possible, whereas the three gliders attacking the Canal Bridge were to carry out a longer, more orthodox approach. Our three gliders had only about half the distance to fly although from the same height of 6,000 feet. In order to lose so much unwanted height in sufficient time we had to apply full flap as soon as we released. This would make navigation extremely difficult but it had been decided by those formulating this brilliant and audacious plan that the height was necessary to deceive the Germans into thinking it was a bombing raid. As soon as we cast off, the Halifax tugs were to continue on to bomb Caen.

All of the pilots would be flying blind, using only their gyro-compasses, air speed indicators and altimeters. Most importantly, they were praying that it did not rain.[3]

*

During one of the early briefings John Howard had asked if there were any questions. One response had been 'Can we have a doctor?' Brigadier Kindersley therefore went to see the Assistant Director of Medical Services (ADMS) of the Division, Colonel Malcolm MacEwan. Doctor John Vaughan of 224 Field (Parachute) Ambulance, RAMC, was among the Divisional doctors subsequently summoned to a conference:

After a brief pause at the bar for a whisky and soda the Colonel abruptly emptied his glass and claimed our attention with this startling request: 'I want a volunteer for a forlorn hope.' After an uneasy silence, and pressed for more details about this desperately sounding assignation, he indicated that a medical officer was required to accompany a Coup de Main *party of Company strength . . . There was a further awkward period of silence as we all assimilated the basic facts of this perilous assault in which one of us would be taking part.*

Then as the great man's piercing gaze swept the room, most of those present muttered his willingness to accept this dubious honour (in terms of survival) of the job. The fact was that frightened though each one of us was by the horrendous prospects, our motivation was decisively influenced by the probability of our Commander's scorn for anyone who didn't volunteer.

The Colonel thanked us saying that of course he expected this favourable response, that he would decide later which officer it should be and then with a final, 'Goodnight, gentlemen,' he departed, leaving us all in a state of considerable discomfiture and apprehension.

About a week later I received an order to report to Divisional HQ . . . With mounting excitement and curiosity I presented myself at the office of the ADMS. 'Well, you wanted action,' said Colonel Mac, 'and now you're certainly going to get it. You will be the MO for that Coup de Main *force I told you about last week. You will report to Tarrant Rushton airfield after a week's leave starting now. Colonel Harvey* [CO of 225 Field (Para) Ambulance] *will take you down there and will give you all details of your responsibilities when you get there and not till then.'*

I was exultant, and curiously enough it never occurred to me that I was going to be in the slightest danger. The daring nature of the enterprise wholly intoxicated me and I was sure that I would come through it unscathed, especially as the very best fighting men were of the party.

After a few days at Tarrant Rushton, Colonel Harvey informed him of the details of the operation and his responsibilities. John Vaughan:

As MO I would be provided with six medical orderlies (one per glider) and basic medical equipment, enough in fact to initiate treatment for casualties before evacuating them to the medical teams, with their surgeons and equipment, landed by parachute at appropriate points within the Divisional Dropping Zone. Once landed, I would set up an RAP at a place to be decided upon, probably somewhere between the bridges. I would have to cope with the situation until the two Field Ambulances, 224 and 225, dropped about an hour later, were able to reach us and take over responsibility of attending to the casualties.[4]

It was felt essential that Airborne units should have surgeons embedded within them because they were

Doctor John Vaughan

inevitably going to be isolated and therefore devoid of any immediate possibility of evacuation. Therefore, three Field Ambulances were attached to the Division. 195 Field Ambulance was gliderborne, while both 224 and 225 were parachute trained and very similar in configuration. 224 was attached to 3 Parachute Brigade, and 225 to 5 Parachute Brigade. 225 Field Ambulance's Lieutenant Colonel Bruce Harvey was an ex-Grenadier Guard and keen disciplinarian. He was supported by his second in command, Major Pat Hewlings, and a small HQ staff. The Ambulance was around 120 strong and consisted of two surgical teams, each having a fully qualified and experienced surgeon, these being Arthur Macpherson and Peter Essex-Lopresti. In the months leading up to D-Day they had each worked out very good surgical teams of about ten people. There was also a dental officer.

The bulk of the Field Ambulance comprised four sections, each of twenty men and commanded by a medical officer. The main purpose of these sections was to assist, in any way they could, with the bringing in of wounded and to make sure that this went well. Also, when required, they would go out and assist the battalions if a very heavy number of casualties was sustained. Captain Tommy Wilson commanded Number 1 Section attached to the 12th Battalion, Captain John Wagstaff's Number 2 Section to the 7th Battalion and Captain David Tibbs' Number 3 Section to the 13th Battalion. Number 4 was a Reserve Section.

Many members of the Division's Field Ambulances were conscientious objectors. Captain David Tibbs, 225 Field (Para) Ambulance:

Back row L to R: Captain Nicholson (QM), Major Daintree Johnson (Surgeon Specialist – injured so did not jump into Normandy), Captain David Tibbs (MO), Captain David Clark (MO), Captain Leslie Hill (RASC Transport Officer), Major Peter Essex-Lopresti (Surgeon Specialist). Front row L to R: Captain Bill Briscoe (Catholic Padre), Captain Holland (Dental Officer), Major Dennis Thompson (2 i/c – went to command 224 Fd Amb prior to D-Day), Lieutenant Colonel Bruce Harvey (CO of 225 Fd Para Amb), Captain Maitland (2i/c on D-Day), Captain John Wagstaff (MO), Captain Tommy Wilson (MO)

When they were forming the 6th Airborne Division they were getting very few volunteers from the RAMC. Colonel MacEwan, he was the ADMS for the Division, he was very astute. He realized that there were a whole number of conscientious objectors who had been working on bomb disposal, not a safe occupation by any means, who might be willing to come along as paratroop RAMC. So he put it to these conscientious objectors who were mostly brethren, people of religious orders like that, very fine men, most of them educated, intelligent, hard working. He put it to them that would they come with us as RAMC to help look after the wounded and they said, 'Only on certain conditions, and the conditions are that you don't ask us ever to carry arms or to handle ammunition, and we can treat German wounded exactly as we treat the British wounded.' The reply was 'That's fine, that's our policy anyway.' So they came along. I think altogether there were about 190 joined the Airborne Division. 225 Field Ambulance had about one third [who] would have been conscientious objectors. They were excellent men, they weren't allowed to have any rank other than private, they could not have been any more exemplary. They would do what was asked of them, there was no need to sort of bark orders at them, indeed probably Christian names were used. You just asked them to do what was required. They managed to get on very well with the other non-conscientious objector people and they were a huge asset to the Division.

The surgeons snapped them up very quickly. They made in fact the majority of the people who worked in the surgical teams just because they were so competent. Many would have had scientific training, medical training and so on, so they were a great asset.

We all trained pretty hard for a year beforehand and lots of very valuable skills emerged as it always will do amongst the men.

*

On 30 May a problem was realized regarding the overall weight of the gliders. Balance for a glider was achieved by maintaining a steady centre of gravity, which meant calculating the exact loads and their positions, in effect the men themselves, everything they carried and anything else taken in the aircraft. Major Howard:

It began with the leader of the Sapper's group, 'Jock' Neilson, weighing one of his men loaded for action. He found to his horror that the man weighed nearly 300lbs instead of the allowed 240lbs. Neilson reported this concern immediately to me, and I quickly got one of my troops to dress and load himself ready for action. We found that he weighed 250lbs instead of the average allowance of 210lbs for an infantryman.

Every man was then individually weighed with his weapons and belts of ammunition, and the average weight found to be way above the allowance. Staff Sergeant Jim Wallwork, Glider 91:

We could not make the distance at what would be a much-accelerated rate of sink, nor could we land a Horsa so grossly overloaded in such a confined space at a speed which would be well over 100mph. So we decided to cut down what was not vital. Should we drop a sapper? No, all Engineers were vital to dismantle the bridge demolition charges.

Every man was already carrying 20lb extra ammunition and Howard would not part with that. We could drop an assault boat. Two of these were carried in case the bridge was blown, though God only knew what good we could do then. Still I insisted that another 600lbs had to go.

Lieutenant Sweeney:

The other reason why of course John was very worried about the weight of the glider is that Tarrant Rushton is an airfield on the top of a hill and at the end of the runway is a sheer drop where the cliff falls away. And he was very much afraid that we wouldn't get off the runway in time and you'd have an awful accident.

And so the platoon commanders each had the extremely difficult task of choosing and then informing several men that they were not going. Lieutenant Wood arrived at a solution:

I think it was the last man to join the platoon. I think that was the kindest way. Nobody wanted to be left behind and John Howard said they were in tears when they were told they were to be left out. We never considered whether somebody was married or not.[5]

However, having done this, the gliders still remained too heavy. Bob Randall:

It was also realized that getting seven tons, which is the three ton load of troops and three and a half ton glider, getting that down into a small field from six thousand feet and stopping it was going to be quite a problem. Although the glider was very successful in short landings using the full flap, you were still going to have a problem getting three gliders, let alone one glider into that field and have its landing run, but you've got another two coming in behind it. So it was decided to fit the drag chutes.

This was the idea of Flight Lieutenant Grant, who had seen the Americans using them during trials in the United States. Jim Wallwork:

It must have been June 2 when the loading/discarding decisions were taken . . . That night a group of Airspeed engineers, complete with mobile workshops, arrived at Tarrant and started operating on our six gliders. An arrester parachute was fitted in each tail. Now, arrester 'chutes were not new, but in a glider? It developed into a superb example of British engineering.

Bob Randall:

To unload the Mk 1 Horsa glider there was a double bulkhead aft of the trailing edge of the main planes and in the double bulkhead you had six quick release bolts to undo to drop the tail of the glider out of the way. Well, that section had a panel on the lower piece of that fuselage that you could lower to stick on a rifle or a weapon of some sort if you wanted to use weapons on landing, from the air.

52

The parachute, connected to the bulkhead, was laid in a box on this panel which could be operated from the cockpit using toggle switches in the centre of the instrument panel. One opened the trap door for the chute to fall out and deploy, and the other operated the release attachment to discard the parachute:

The pilots were a bit concerned because obviously with this thing lying on a loose panel on the floor, any turbulence might cause the panel to be sucked out. Then the parachute would deploy while being towed across the Channel. It was decided then that the Oxf and Bucks or the Engineer that was sitting on the rear seat of the glider, he would have this parachute on his lap during the time over the Channel and once they had cast off he would lean over the back of his seat and drop this parachute onto this panel so that it was in position ready for when they deployed it.

Even if the parachute worked correctly, it was still a very risky option. Jim Wallwork:

We did not like it at all. Our suggestion that we do a dummy run with perhaps one glider here at Tarrant was overruled in horror. The reason given was that it was far too dangerous, which was hardly encouraging.

Bob Randall:

Bearing in mind the theory of flight and the effect of objects on an aircraft, the pilots felt that if you deployed the parachute while you were still in the air, which obviously you would have to, it would affect the trim of the aircraft, pull the tail up, push the nose down, and finish up with a serious problem of stalling out of the sky with just the nose going down first.

There occurred another cause for concern. Jim Wallwork:

Confidence took a deep breath and paused around 3 June. The fields around our target area were all being prepared for poles, wires, mines, etc. as anti-glider/parachute obstacles, but not our two fields, which were obviously far too small to even dream of trying to land a glider in. But then the holes for poles began to appear in our own backyard. John Howard was most concerned. We glider pilots were petrified, but we had a gut feeling that after all the preparations we would be going regardless. So how were we to regain that touching faith in our flying ability which 'D' Company had somehow developed? Howard knew if we did not get them to the target intact they may as well all go home and wait for demob.

'Not to worry, Major' says I, 'I can slip between the poles quite easily and by losing a wingtip off the port and

Staff Sergeant Jim Wallwork

53

a bit off the starboard, it could quite handily help slow us down.' To my utter amazement he believed me, no doubt because he wanted to, but to my horror he asked me to address the Company parade that afternoon, allay their fears and restore their confidence. Which I did, and I was not struck by a bolt of lightning, which I surely deserved.

Lance Sergeant 'Tich' Rayner:

We knew we were going on a dangerous operation, in fact at times we thought we were going on a bloody suicidal mission, especially when he told us about the poles being put in the ground to stop the gliders. We didn't believe what the bloody glider pilots had told John Howard! The bloody nose of the glider could have hit the pole and killed you or all sorts of things. But we were very keen to do it.

*

On 26 May the 7th Parachute Battalion had moved to its Transit Camp at Tilshead on Salisbury Plain. Lieutenant Colonel Pine-Coffin:

A briefing room was set up in which the Intelligence Section, under Lieutenant Mills, worked day and night preparing models and displaying the photographs and other exhibits to the best advantage and in making large scale maps for use at the battalion briefing.

Lieutenant Ted Pool, 'B' Company:

There on May 27 all officers were briefed by the Colonel, helped by excellent air photographs and a wonderful model of the area and our objectives for June 5. My only criticism was that, in contrast to the excellent UK ordnance maps with which we had trained, the maps of France were of poor quality. Once we had moved out of the briefing area, they became a mild handicap.

Subsequently, the whole battalion assembled in the garrison cinema and was briefed by the CO on the Divisional and Brigade plans, although no mention was made of the individual battalion tasks. Lieutenant Bertie Mills then described the topography of the area, information of the known and suspected enemy positions, probable attitude of the civilians and a number of other relevant points. Then Colonel Pine-Coffin took to the stage once more and with the aid of a large scale map, explained the 7th Battalion tasks and then ran through the battalion plan in outline, being careful not to name any specific Company this time.

Briefing of the Companies began during the following days, when each Company was allotted time to spend in the briefing room. Major Nigel Taylor, Officer Commanding 'A' Company:

Each platoon commander was briefed by his Company Commander . . . and the platoon commanders briefed their platoons and you're down to thirty-two men now with the Company Commander sitting in to make sure he got it all right. That went on day after day. It was done thoroughly, thoroughly, thoroughly.

Lieutenant David Hunter, 'A' Company:

We now understood the reason for the rehearsals at Exeter. Three gliders were to land alongside each of the bridges half an hour before the paratroopers dropped. The glider-borne troops were to capture the bridges before they could be blown up.

Therefore, as Colonel Pine-Coffin put it, 'The capture of the bridges intact was very desirable from the battalion's point of view'. The battalions of 5 Parachute Brigade were to commence jumping on DZ 'N' at 0050 hours. The distinctive Ranville Church, which had a detached tower, was to be an orientation point. The 7th Battalion was then to make for a Rendezvous at the northern end of a copse situated beside the Sallenelles road, approximately a thousand yards from the Orne Bridge. The control point of the RV was the north-east corner of the copse. After forming up, the battalion was expected to arrive at the bridges at sometime after 0130 hours. For the potential water crossings, thirty J-Type dinghies and twelve recce boats were to be taken, together with the necessary ropes to make the ferries. The recce boats were being carried in kit-bags on the legs of men in 'B' Company, and twelve dinghies in those of 'C' Company; the remaining eighteen dinghies would be jettisoned on chutes usually employed for dropping folding bicycles. As rehearsed during the training, Major Dick Bartlett's 'C' Company was tasked with reaching the bridges as soon as possible and to attempt assault crossings if the bridges had been destroyed. Colonel Pine-Coffin:

The equipment carried by this Company was stripped to the minimum so that they could move fast once they reached the ground. They carried none of the extra kit bags and their haversacks were loaded into containers to be dropped from the bomb racks. It was hoped that they would be able to form up much faster than the rest of the battalion and could be sent off at the double, to carry out their rôle before the rest of the battalion had arrived at the RV. 'B' Company, under Major R. Neale, had a special rôle connected with the water crossings. They were the ferrying experts and as such, carried the bulk of the heavy boating equipment. 'A' Company, under Major N. Taylor, was to be the first over the obstacles and so carried their normal equipment and a smaller proportion of the dinghies.[6]

By whatever method, having crossed the waterways they were then to set up defensive positions beyond the small perimeter created by the *Coup de Main* force. These positions were to be amongst the buildings of Benouville. Colonel Pine-Coffin:

The lay-out of the battalion in its own bridgehead to the west of the canal was designed to cover the main infantry approaches to the Canal Bridge. Outside the battalion perimeter were a number of battle outposts, each consisting of only a few men but posted at likely approaches. Their job was to take on all comers and to delay them long enough for Major Roger Neale *any necessary adjustments to be made to the main position for their reception.*

The defence of the area between the bridges was entrusted to Howard's Coup de
Main *party; here they would form a very useful reserve and with any luck, would get
some rest too.*

The battle outposts were to be set up at a road junction south of Benouville, in a wood
to the west of the T-Junction at *La Mairie*, another on the south-west approach to the
crossroads at the entrance to the Benouville Chateau and at a battery position just over
a mile up the canal bank towards Ouistreham.[7]

'A' Company was to take up position in the southern end of Benouville, 'B' Company
at the northern end in *Le Port*, and 'C' Company would be in reserve. Lieutenant David
Hunter, OC 3 Platoon, 'A' Company:

*After crossing the bridges we had to clear up the main street of Benouville then turn right
at the top of the village and get dug in in a field in front of a farm at the south end of
Benouville. It all sounded very straightforward, but I warned them that it wouldn't be
like that. They had to be prepared for the unexpected and all sorts of disasters.*

In 'B' Company, Lieutenant Tommy Farr's 4 Platoon was to clear *Le Port* while
Lieutenant Pool's 5 Platoon had to move through and hold a curved, wooded spur about
500 yards to the south-west. Lieutenant Dan Thomas' 6 Platoon was to establish a
strongpoint at the western end of the Canal Bridge.

The battalion was to have Naval gunfire support. A Forward Observer Bombardment
party of two Royal Artillery spotters and two Royal Navy telegraphists known as
'sparkers', all parachute-qualified, would be accompanying them. Commanded by
Captain Francis Vere Hodge RA, his team comprised Lance Bombardier Ted Eley RA,
Leading Telegraphist Alex Boomer RN ('wacker'), and Wireless/Transmitter operator
Wilf Fortune RN. Their system of operating had proved very successful in the Sicily
Campaign when a map reference was sent in Morse Code to a ship. Captain Vere Hodge:

Lance Bombardier Ted Eley
RA

*The Tel had to contact the Headquarters ship and request
to be attached to a ship to fire. There was a code for doing
that. Then he was allocated one. I think it was a three letter
code you were allocated A, B, C and so you didn't know
what ship it was unless the Tel happened to know, they did
know some of them, but not all. Might be a destroyer,
might be a cruiser. The ships that were going to fire had an
RA officer on board who would interpret the information
that was sent. It was very simple clock code. The target was
the centre of the clock. You took twelve o'clock as north. If
you said, 'Twelve o'clock, 300,' the chap knew that it was
300 yards too far to the north. Very simple for us but he had
to translate it. What amazed me, these ships were not only
moving as the sea moves they were actually moving in
order not to stand still and be shot at. And to do all that*

and still bring the guns to fire on the correct place seemed to me incredibly clever.

Jumping half an hour in advance of the Division's main drop, 4 Platoon, 13th Parachute Battalion led by Lieutenant Stan Jevons was to act as the DZ protection force and establish itself at three road junctions in the area.[8] Due to the urgency in Pine-Coffin's men reaching the bridges, two sticks of the 7th Battalion were to secure the Battalion RV.[9] Meanwhile, Pathfinders of the 22nd Independent Parachute Company were to set up the various navigational aids such as fluorescent holophane lights and EUREKA beacons to identify the DZs. Also with them was a further detachment of five men of the 7th Battalion led by Lieutenant John Rogers. These were Privates Wing, Moran, Starke and Styles. Jim Moran, 6 Platoon, 'B' Company:

Jim Moran

I was selected and trained to drop with the Pathfinders which simply meant I was to set up a signal lamp which transmitted a signal to be received on the EUREKA [sic] set in the planes carrying the rest of the battalion. This meant I had to calculate the amount and direction of drift encountered on the drop so that when I set up the signal lamp, it would cause the lads to drop in the middle of the DZ.[10]

Another travelling before the 7th Battalion itself was Lieutenant Ian Macdonald, who was to go with the *Coup de Main* party for liaison duties between Major Howard and Colonel Pine-Coffin. He would travel with Lieutenant Sweeney's 23 Platoon.

*

On 3 June the officers of the *Coup de Main* party travelled to Tilshead for a co-ordinating conference in the camp cinema. Lieutenant 'Tod' Sweeney:

We listened to the briefing of the 7th Parachute Battalion by their Commanding Officer, Colonel Pine-Coffin. We were round one of these big models with seats in tiers around four sides of the room and there were about fifty or sixty officers there because there were the Parachute Battalion officers, and then there were ourselves . . . some of the Brigade officers and some of the Artillery officers and so on. At the end of the briefing the Commanding Officer looked around the room and said, 'Sweeney?' Now I'd been known all my life in the Army as 'Tod' Sweeney, [after Sweeney Todd the demon barber of Fleet Street]. So anyone whose name is Sweeney is called Tod'. So I thought this Commanding Officer must know me, so I leapt to my feet, and at the same time, a really good-looking man on the other side of the auditorium leapt up to his feet and he wore the light blue parachute flash on his shoulder strap. So clearly the Commanding Officer was addressing him. But I thought 'Well that's unusual, I don't often meet people in this country with my name.' I went up to this rather good-looking young man and I said, "I'm pleased to meet you because I think we've both got the same name. I'm Lieutenant

Sweeney and everybody calls me "Tod". He said, 'Well actually, I'm Lieutenant Todd but everybody calls me 'Sweeney!' I said, 'Well, I'll see you on D-Day . . .'

This was Lieutenant Richard Todd, the 7th Battalion's Assistant Adjutant and Reserve Mortar Officer.[11]

*

The routine at the Tarrant Rushton Transit Camp continued for the *Coup de Main* party. Lieutenant David Wood:

We were still doing rehearsals of every kind. The area had been taped out and we ran about doing it in the day and in the dark. There was the business of constantly checking our weapons and equipment and making sure they were all in order, firing our weapons . . .

Lieutenant Sweeney:

In our Transit Camp we had some other officers, mostly these Canadian officers who had been sent to us quite recently, who were all dying to get in on the act. But they were there as first reinforcements, so if you suddenly got appendicitis at the last minute, you had a lot of officers waiting to take over. One of them almost tried to bribe John, a chap called Morgan Allcroft . . . to take him somehow, even as a private, a rifleman in the platoon!

At some point a General Crawford came down from the War Office. He was the Director of Land Air Warfare . . . He came down just to see what our morale was like. We never saw Major Generals from the War Office . . . You saw your Divisional Generals and your Brigadiers but a staff officer from the War Office was a very unusual sight. Down came this very dapper man wearing Service Dress which again was very unusual and we all went in and he looked at the model and he talked to the soldiers and said a few encouraging words. Then he turned to John Howard and he said, 'You know, this is the one single Company operation of the war, which to my mind is one of the best planned and greatest operations that we are going to have throughout the whole of the war.' In fact he said, 'I wished I was going on it myself!' Whether he meant that or not, I don't know. He really thought that this was a unique type of Company operation and that it was the sort of thing that a Company Commander doesn't get the chance to do, all on his own, at the head of the invasion and so on.

For security purposes, it was the responsibility of the platoon commanders to censor the mail, and in these last few days before the operation, Sweeney noticed a distinct change in the tone of the letters:

They all became quite emotional, quite patriotic and in some cases, quite religious too. Chaps who I am sure never used the word of God normally, except as an oath, would say, 'God bless you my dear,' and 'May God be with us all,' that sort of thing. I remember one soldier whom I never thought of as being an intellectual or academic, quoting Rupert Brooke's poem . . . 'There is a corner of a foreign field that is forever England.' It is quite extraordinary how it brings out inner feelings in men who are usually just tough, rough and so on. So there was a great deal I think, of soul searching in that respect.

Wally Parr:

We couldn't wait to get into action. We'd been held back and held back and held back so long, we were absolutely frustrated with just going through exercise after exercise, rigorous as it was and entertaining as it was and instructive as it was. The thing was, we wanted to get there. The overwhelming feeling was sheer excitement. We'd been trained so hard and were so full of energy.[12]

They continued to wait as the recent good weather began to deteriorate. Major Howard:

Every morning at Transit Camp a Don R came down from Headquarters with a sealed envelope containing a codeword to tell me if we were to prepare to go that night. After about a week we were getting a bit edgy because the weather was becoming unsettled. Then out of the blue on the 4th June I got the codeword 'Cromwell' which meant that we would be going that night.

The six platoons immediately began their final preparations, checking weapons, ammunition and kit. However, soon after lunch Major Howard received another message stating that *Cromwell* was postponed. The weather had further deteriorated. Brigadier Poett:

We were very disappointed, naturally, and you were anxious because we at the top of the thing knew that unless it took place very quickly . . . we would be in a very difficult position indeed.

For the men it was just enormously frustrating. Lieutenant Wood:

We had been geared up for this operation over a series of weeks. We'd got to the point where the Company Commander had said, 'Right, it's on!' gone through the drill which was to black our faces, check our weapons and test fire them, everything ready for us to go into action. Then suddenly it's postponed. We were all absolutely shattered by this, and for some reason we decided to drown our sorrows . . . I went to the NAAFI and we got these two bottles of whisky and we demolished them, which was not like me. I'm not saying I never drank, but I wasn't that keen on whisky!

Dennis Edwards:

At 1700 hours we had tea and strolled over to a large tent to see a film show. There was little else to do because once our mission had been disclosed the camp had been sealed. No one could get in or out.

Ironically, the film being shown was *Stormy Weather*.

Afterwards we rushed to the NAAFI tent and queued for a glass of beer but became fed up with the long wait, gave up, and returned to our tent where we played cards and turned in at around 2200 hours.

It was hot inside the small tent and I suspect like me, few of the others slept soundly. On my mind was the thought that the task that had been allocated to us seemed so great and our force so small. Although it would only be for a short time, the thought of being the only Allied unit in France facing the might of the German Army seemed a daunting prospect.[13]

*

The 7th Parachute Battalion had continued with its own preparations and paid a visit to Fairford Airfield, their point of departure. Colonel Pine-Coffin:

The next couple of hours or so were spent on the airfield itself where there was much to be done. Parachutes were drawn and harnesses adjusted carefully to fit over the equipment which would be worn, aircraft were examined and the pilots and aircrews met for the first time.

Major Eric Steele-Baume was second in command of the battalion:

It was an odd feeling, quite different from that experienced before an exercise. Most people had, naturally or artificially, acquired an air of indifference as to how well the parachute had been packed. This time it was a little different. Everyone seemed to be inspecting their chute minutely; every tie, every buckle, was tested and re-tested. Our fitted chutes were then packed in a warmed store to prevent them getting damp.

We returned to our camp and organized a concert for that night. Despite the general tension and the fact that everyone was looking constantly at the sky, trying to assess the weather, the concert was a great success. The wind was rising, and it became apparent that we should get some pretty rough falls if we jumped in it. It was not long before the anticipated postponement arrived.

There was nothing to do. It was no use trying to go through the briefing again. Everyone had been keyed to the highest pitch and it was irritating in the extreme to have a postponement. It was interesting to walk around the camp and watch the reaction of individuals. At one point I came across a man surreptitiously practising his leap into space off three steps; at another I came across a very bloodthirsty creature who was grinding his fighting knife on a step and declaiming his intention vis-à-vis the Boche in a particularly gruesome and telling manner.

Most people were writing one more letter to be posted after we had gone.

The following morning the weather had improved but was still far from ideal. There was some rain, but the wind was not as strong. To Major Howard's surprise he again received the codeword *Cromwell*. Nobby Clark:

John Howard called the Company together and said, 'It's on for tonight.' He said, 'Check all your gear and make sure everything's primed, get your heads down. We'll get up and have an early meal, then we're off to the aerodrome.'

*

In the early evening, the Oxf and Bucks Padre, Captain Nimmo, arrived for what they called the 'Padre's half hour' because it lasted for more like an hour! Corporal Ted Tappenden:

> *This Padre was the kind of man who would say to the Company, or the men who were interested, 'Say what you like.' I heard real arguments going on . . . 'I don't believe in God,' and there'd be no offence taken by this Padre. They'd argue and argue about religion and he was well respected.*
>
> *Just before we left to go to the aerodrome, we had a Service . . . He got a cross and he stuck it in the ground, it was pretty muddy, and he said, 'We don't need a Church,' and every man that was there was on his knees, praying.*

Afterwards John Howard asked the acting CSM, Sergeant Pete Barwick, to order the platoons on parade. Major Howard:

> *I addressed my men for the last time. I wished them luck and thanked them for all their hard work and untiring co-operation during training. As I ran my eyes over the faces of the men before me, I was immensely pleased to see that all of them looked confident and excited and I knew that every man under my command would give of his best.*

Up to this point Frank Bourlet had been pretty matter of fact about everything, but Howard had also made a statement that brought home the reality of the situation:

> *He said, 'Of course, you realize that we will be the first there and if we are in the air and cast off and the landing is called off again, you will be on your own.'*

At around 1900 hours they began boarding the trucks taking them to the airfield. The vehicles were marked in accordance with the particular glider chalk number beside which they would stop. At the last minute Lieutenant Wood realized that he was not wearing a tie:

> *I thought it was really important to have a tie when you went into action. It shows how ignorant and inexperienced I was. We had a Canadian officer with us who was a reserve . . . and I asked him if he would lend me his tie. He very generously took off his tie which to my horror was a tie which was already made up and had elastic and a clip on the back, but I put it on because I thought I must be seen going into action properly dressed!*

Frank Bourlet

The small convoy and escort pulled out of the camp and headed up the road to the airfield.

*

With Tilshead being some fifty miles from the airfield, to avoid any snags arising during the journey, the 7th Battalion had left for a tented camp in a clearing of a secluded wood known as Fairford Park, only two miles from Fairford itself. Captain Vere Hodge RA:

There was hardly any traffic . . . but under every tree, every barn, every bit of hedge that was overgrown, was a vehicle. They were all lined up everywhere. In an orchard, every sort of apple tree had a vehicle under it . . . One realized, this is quite something.

They arrived in time for a hot midday meal and then began their final preparations. Colonel Pine-Coffin:

At 2000 hours the sleepers were roused and a final search made of all pockets and wallets for envelopes or other indications of the unit identity. Few were found as everyone was very security conscious but those that were, were duly burned.

They then had another hot meal, followed by a short Service. Major Guy Radmore, OC Brigade Signals:

We had a very impressive service given by our Padre Parry . . . he was the Padre of the 7th Battalion. We'd all blacked our faces and you could just see a little top of the white in his dog collar sticking out above his tunic.

The extremely well-liked George Parry was fondly known in the battalion as 'Pissy Percy, the Paratrooping Padre'! After the Service the Colonel made a final address to his men. They then boarded the trucks. Geoffrey Pine-Coffin:

The mental attitude at this stage was interesting to note. There were no hysterically exaggerated high spirits, no wise-cracking from lorry to lorry, as was usual in an exercise, there was a certain amount of singing, as there always will be, but for the most part there was an atmosphere of quiet confidence not unmixed, let us admit it, with a certain amount of honest funk.

At 2130 hours they left for the airfield. Ron Perry, HQ Company:

As we were en-route going in convoy, nose to tail in these 3-Ton trucks we came to one little village. There was a pub there, summer's evening, all the local men sitting outside watching us. They must have guessed what was going to happen, all camouflaged up, camouflage cream, armed to the teeth, looking like we did. There were some kiddies around the pub, and in the lorries ahead of us these blokes of ours were throwing their change. They didn't need it did they? They were throwing it down to the kids and it caught on, so when the truck got there, any English money we had, we were throwing it. The kids must have thought it was Christmas.

At 2130 hours the trucks transporting the *Coup de Main* party arrived at Tarrant Rushton and headed straight towards the gliders. WAAFs and NAAFI girls lined the runway, waving. Many were crying. Bill Gray:

> *Obviously they knew something was afoot because Tarrant Rushton was absolutely jam-packed with aircraft, like Halifax bombers and Horsa gliders.*

The *Coup de Main* gliders, with tow ropes attached to their tugs, were parked off the runway, three on each side pointing inwards. The men dismounted from the trucks beside their appointed gliders. Staff Sergeant Roy Howard, pilot, Glider 96:

> *I think everyone knew on the airfield what was happening except one of the ground staff from the Air Force, who came up to me and said, 'Are you bringing this one back tonight, Staff?' I said, 'No, I don't think so!' He walked away looking dazed.*
>
> *We'd met the Oxf and Bucks lads a few days before and they were a very good bunch. However, on the night they all arrived blacked up, loaded with arms and ammunition, they looked a right bunch of cut-throats. I think I was more afraid of them than I was of the Germans!*

Staff Sergeant Jim Wallwork, pilot, Glider 91:

> *It made a fellow feel a little safer to be so surrounded, as we pilots had been expressly forbidden to fight in Normandy, not that we had any intention of arguing against such wisdom. We had, in fact, received a pass signed by God Himself directing 'All Concerned' to help in every way possible to 'speed this glider pilot back to UK'. Our first reaction was 'At last, someone, even Montgomery, realizes our importance and value.' But alas, the reason for this quick return trip was so that we would be handy for flying in a second wave should it be necessary. So Howard could not use us as infantry.*

They drank tea containing a liberal dose of rum, chatted and waited. [14] Lance Corporal Tom Packwood:

> *John Howard was going around and saying, 'Your face isn't black enough, you've got to get some more on.' So people were sticking their fingers up despatch riders motorbikes* [exhaust pipes] *who had escorted us, getting the black soot for their faces.*

Private Leslie Chamberlain, 25 Platoon:

> *Just before we left he said, 'You can now write to your wives, sweethearts, whatever and tell them, 'By the time you receive this card, you'll be in France.'*

Tom Packwood

Major Howard:

Before ten o'clock everybody went to their gliders to check the equipment was all tied alright, platoon commanders checked the equipment on the men . . . Mike Roberts was there, our Colonel. I wondered if we'd get any more Brass there, but . . . there was only Mike. He was due to take off the next evening of course, and he came over to wish us all the best.

In fading light they began to board the gliders. Each man had been allocated a seating position according to his rôle in the operation and to a lesser extent, his weight. In spite of the weighing and the reduction of men, it was with growing concern that Staff Sergeant Barkway surveyed the men:

The lads said, 'A couple of magazines, Bren ammunition and Sten ammunition won't hurt,' and 'A couple of extra Mills bombs in my pocket might be handy,' so they all over-loaded themselves.

Lieutenant David Wood, 24 Platoon:

If you fell over, it was very difficult to get up without help. We were so convinced that we wouldn't have enough in the way of ammunition and so on to last us for the period we expected to be on our own. I decided that it was going to be a major battle and that the amount of ammunition, particularly grenades that we could take, were not sufficient. So I got a canvas water bucket which was part of an officer's washing kit and took some spare grenades.

Paddy O'Donnell, sniper, Scout section, 25 Platoon:

The standard equipment for a British platoon is three Bren guns, three section commanders, three Sten guns, plus the platoon commander's got a Sten gun. The platoon sergeant for some reason carries a rifle and then the rest of the platoon is made up of riflemen plus two snipers. We had to carry four magazines for the Bren guns as well, and then I had all my own ammunition. In addition to that I had tracer bullets . . . I had incendiary bullets as well.

Paddy O'Donnell

He liked to take as much as possible, but found it very difficult to carry all the grenades:

I got the bottom of a sandbag, cut it off, tied the corners with a bit of string and therefore I could take six grenades. It was a very crude way of doing anything, but it worked.

Nobby Clark, 24 Platoon:

I had two bandoliers of .303 around my neck . . . a smoke grenade, two little black plastic grenades. They were egg-

shaped, and they were black Bakelite things that just made a bang . . . they were more as a frightener. We had two of those each. I had six Mills grenades with the levers in my belts and they were primed, I made sure the safety pins were well split . . . In the back of our pack we had a Hawkins anti-tank mine which was a little flat thing, probably about an inch thick, probably six or seven inches long and about five inches wide. If we captured the bridges and the tanks came along, we could put a string of them across the road and hopefully stop the tank. We also had the PIAT. It was just like a piece of scrap metal. If it got any sort of a knock it was useless.

Corporal Bill Bailey of the Scout section, 25 Platoon, took up position in the tail of Glider 91 and so had responsibility for putting the arrester parachute on to the trap-door:

We had our cigarettes . . . tucked down the sleeves of our smocks which were elasticized. We had our berets tucked down our back. What we did with our smocks was to cut the double lining, and we used to carry a towel, a grenade in there and anything that might be of use to you that wasn't strictly to be carried.

Sitting in the middle of the glider were the 249 Field Company Engineers. Sapper Cyril Haslett:

We had a rifle or Sten gun, we had 5lb of explosives, 808, in case we had to blow anything up, and fuse wire. We had plenty of equipment like ladders and rope.

There was also everyone's small packs, containing such things as washing and shaving gear. Geoff Barkway:

At the last minute they chucked in what they called an assault boat . . . It was a wooden frame and a wooden bottom and waterproof canvas all round the sides. And there were some bits of wood which you put on the bottom and lifted the top of the boat up and wedged them in so they made the canvas taut. Well that wasn't accounted for in the weighing lists! We were all grossly overloaded.

However, it was too late to worry about it.

Wing Commander Duder, leading the six tug aircraft, came over and advised John Howard not to worry about the flak. Major Howard:

Then he explained to me about this gap that they'd been using to feed the Maquis, the Resistance and what have you for several months before. It was a gap in the German flak defences somewhere near Cabourg and therefore when I went round to say goodbye to my chaps in the gliders, and wished them well, I was able to give them this good bit of news about this flak gap. And then walking from one glider to the other, sort of bucking up courage to go and do it again each time, and finishing up at the front with my own glider. I started at the back with Number 6 and came forward to mine, Number 1.

As Howard got into the glider, Colonel Roberts called out, 'See you on the bridge tomorrow, John' and the doors were shut. A green signal flare was fired and the Halifax engines burst into life. On board Glider 91 they were singing. Dennis Edwards, 25 Platoon, Glider 91:

At 2256 hours the steady hum of the bomber engines suddenly increased to a deafening roar. My muscles tightened, a cold shiver ran up my spine, I went hot and cold and sang all the louder to stop my teeth from chattering.

Suddenly there was a violent jerk and a loud twang as the slack of the 125-foot tow-rope was taken up by our tug plane. The glider rolled slowly forward and my throat tightened as the plywood flying box gathered speed, momentarily left the ground, set down again with a heavy thump and a final jerk as, with a loud roar, the bomber's engines reached full thrust and we were airborne.

It was 2259 hours.

As I had climbed aboard and strapped myself into my seat I felt tense, strange and extremely frightened. It was as if I was in a fantasy dream world and thought that at any moment I would wake up from this unreality and find that I was back in the barrack room at Bulford Camp. Whilst we laughed and sang to raise our spirits to show the others that we were not scared, personally I knew that I was frightened to death.

Yet at the moment that the glider parted company with the ground, I experienced an inexplicable change. The feeling of terror vanished and was replaced by exhilaration. I felt literally on top of the world. I remember thinking, 'You've had it chum, its no good worrying any more – the die has been cast and what is to be will be, and there is nothing that you can do about it', and sat back to enjoy my first trip to Europe.

Staff Sergeant Oliver Boland, pilot, Glider 92:

Perfectly smooth take-off, got up to the height and started on our journey. Just the three of us on this particular bridge which was the prime target, were setting off on an adventure as the spearhead of the most colossal army ever assembled in the history of mankind virtually. I found it very difficult to believe it was true because I felt so insignificant.

Captain Brian Priday, with 22 Platoon, Glider 94:

We got into the air safely and although I spent all my time until it was dark looking out of the cockpit I saw nothing of the others. I allowed smoking, since most of us were in a state of intense excitement.

Glider 96 transporting 17 Platoon was the final Horsa to take off. Lieutenant Dennis Fox certainly noticed the difference that the extra weight made:

I sat immediately to the left of the door, with Tommy Clare my soldier servant sitting beside me. I thought we would never get off because normally the glider would lift straight off, long before the tug aircraft, but this time, we still lifted off before the tug aircraft but not until right at the end of the runway.

The tugs were not in any particular formation, but the gliders assumed positions above their tails in order to avoid the turbulence. To keep in station, the pilots concentrated on the exhaust flames from their particular Halifax.

Lieutenant Sweeney, 23 Platoon, was sitting at the front of Glider 95, beside the pilot's doorway.

It was rather like being picked to play for your country at Lord's. The exhilaration buoyed us up and kept us going. We were all scared stiff of course, but we'd been waiting and waiting for this stage from 1940 onwards and none of us had ever been in action before. My platoon whom I'd known for two years had trained and trained and now, at long last we were going. The men were in good humour, singing songs like 'Roll Out the Barrel' and we had some rations and a thermos of tea.

Corporal Bill 'Smokey' Howard, 23 Platoon:

One which everybody in our Company knew was "Abie". A very old song, it's a Jewish song, and we all found the Jewish sense of humour very funny. It was 'Abie, Abie, Abie my boy, vot are you vaiting for now? You promised to marry me some day in June, it's never too late and it's never too soon. All the family keep on asking me vitch day, vot day, I don't know vot to say, Abie, Abie, Abie my boy, vot are you vaiting for now?'[15]

Nobby Clark, 24 Platoon, Glider 92, was sitting on the port side, fourth along from the front door:

For a good ten minutes it was dead silent in the glider, there wasn't a sound. And suddenly, whatever it was, and I'm sure it wasn't the rum because there wasn't enough of it in there, this sort of growing confidence returned, it sort of crept up on you. You suddenly didn't give a damn. We were singing all the bawdy songs you could imagine.

Lance Corporal Ted Tappenden, Glider 91:

The lads were singing in our glider and as we went out over the Channel it was a sight I shall never forget. As we flew over the top . . . it looked like you could step from ship to ship the whole way across the Channel.

Dr John Vaughan, Glider 93:

As we in the third glider continued our climb into the air behind the Halifax I became appalled by the realization of our helplessness in this flimsy contraption. It was, moreover, my first ever time in such a device and I longed for my parachute with which I had initially been trained to go to war. Here we were entirely at the mercy of those two pilots up front and if the enemy were to see us and had had time to get their guns within range, we would be blown out of the sky. Sandy Smith interrupted these nervous trains of thought by deciding to stimulate morale generally by leading in a verse or two of such bawdy military favourites as 'Immobile'. It was well supported at first but gradually petered out as each man became preoccupied by his own thoughts. Everybody in his heart knew that anybody who survived this day would be very lucky.

The pilots were chatting in a relaxed manner and one of them, Sergeant Barkway on the starboard side and in front of me, goddamit, was smoking a cigarette which glowed alarmingly to my way of thinking. We could surely be seen I thought apprehensively – ridiculous of course, as we were already some seven thousand feet above the ground.

There was no singing on board Staff Sergeant Roy Howard's Glider 96. They mostly sat there smoking, and it felt not unlike a training flight. On board were twins Cyril and Claude Larkin, both Engineers of 249 Field Company. Cyril Larkin:

For most of us this was our first time in action and there was almost no conversation in the blacked-out interior of the glider. No lights at all were permitted.

On board Glider 92, 24 Platoon's singing also gradually died down. Lieutenant Wood:

Somebody passed the word up from the tail of the glider that they thought something had gone wrong with the parachute that was there to slow us down on landing. So I became all platoon commander-like, got a torch and went to the rear. I could see nothing that was amiss and so reassured everybody that everything was alright and came back to my seat.

Major Howard:

I didn't undo my safety belt, we were under strict instructions to do that and although I wanted to go and stand up behind the two glider pilots, looking into the cockpit . . . my desire was to want to do that, I thought it was a bad example to the rest of the men and sat tied up as I was supposed to in the safety belt.

The men of 25 Platoon were expecting a usual event:

It was a Company joke that I was going to be sick, and some bright lad at the back of the glider shouted, 'Has the Company Commander laid his kit yet?' which of course caused a lot of mirth amongst the men.

However, for the first time, it didn't happen:

I was sitting next to Den and although one would think that on those occasions you might talk to take your mind off things, we were curiously quiet, we hardly talked at all. Going through my mind apart from the plan and was what was going to meet us the other end . . . one couldn't help thinking of your family.

*

Taking off at the same time as the *Coup de Main* Party were aircraft heading for DZ 'N'. These contained Brigadier Poett's party, the Pathfinders and advance parties of the 7th, 12th and 13th Parachute Battalions, some Divisional men plus Engineers of 591 Parachute Squadron. Brigadier Poett:

The people in my aircraft were my Brigade Headquarters, a small party, only ten in the Albermarle aircraft. None of us had ever seen an Albermarle aircraft in our lives before. Never seen one let alone got inside one! When we got into our aircraft, loaded as we were, there was every conceivable problem in physically getting into it. You had to push and push and push to get in. It was a very, very tight squash indeed. I had to sit with my back to my men.

Acting Sergeant Fraser Edwards, an interpreter of 317 Airborne Security Section, had been ordered to be at the Brigadier's 'disposal' until informed otherwise:

There were six Albermarles and I was in the sixth one. Brigadier Poett, he was Number One to jump, I was Number Nine, so I was at the opposite end of the plane from him. You jumped out through a hole near the back of the plane, so you were facing the back of the plane. No seats, you just sat on the floor. I didn't know anybody in the plane, nobody at all because they were Pathfinders, a unit I'd never come across before. It was rather an awkward trip because Numbers Nine and Ten, we were leaning our backs against the air gunner's turret and he kept on turning round and round and of course we were leaning against this thing and were cursing him for not leaving us in peace!

*

At Fairford airfield the 7th Parachute Battalion had arrived. Major Nigel Taylor, 'A' Company:

Fairford was an extraordinary sight. I mean it was jammed packed with aeroplanes and gliders, absolutely packed. We went into a hangar and drew our parachutes.

Lieutenant Hunter, 'A' Company:

We then filed past the WAAF parachute packers who handed us our parachutes. 'I hope that's not your dirty washing in there', I said to the attractive girl who handed over my bag. Then it was out to the waiting aircraft, lined up in rows in the darkness like large black silent birds of prey. Before enplaning we blackened our faces.

Colonel Pine-Coffin:

The time was spent mostly in smoking final cigarettes, drinking final cups of tea or putting camouflage paint on faces. This paint was carried in tubes, like toothpaste, and

Fraser Edwards

69

was of about the same consistency but dark brown in colour. It was found that on drying, which it did very quickly, it came off again in flakes so most abandoned it and used soot off the bottom of the tea kettles instead.

They were being transported in Stirlings, another aircraft from which there had been no opportunity for the men to perform any practice jumps. Captain Vere Hodge RA:

One of the things that really surprised me was seeing these white lines painted on all our planes. Even though it was a day late starting, there were still fellows painting lines.

The Mortar and Machine Gun Platoons were split equally between four aircraft in order to minimise the loss of capability if one was shot down. The FOB Team was split between two of them. Wilf Fortune RN:

Captain Hodge and Alec boarded one Stirling and Ted Eley and me another. We had already been issued with Free French Liberation paper money, so on one of my five Franc notes, I had some of the stick sign it. One of the signatories was Reverend Parry, the battalion chaplain.

Colonel Pine-Coffin wanted one of the teams near him, so Vere Hodge and Alex Boomer were assigned to his Stirling.

Two other sailors had reported to Major Guy Radmore, OC 5 Parachute Brigade Signals and informed him that they were going to provide support via contact with *Roberts* and *Warspite*.

His Signals Section was also split between Stirlings taking off from Fairford. Lance Corporal Bob Milton and Signallers Bert Shea and Harry Leach were together on one of them. Harry Leach:

Bert turned to me and said, 'Harry, I can't go.' I said, 'Bert, you've got to, you could be shot because it's cowardice in the face of action. What's the matter?' He said, 'I'm Number Thirteen.' I said, 'Look Bert, will you swap?' He said, 'Yes' and we swapped places, so I became thirteenth in the aircraft. It was my thirteenth jump and the aircraft had chalked on the nose the number 169 . . . thirteen squared!

Lieutenant Hunter, 'A' Company, 7th Parachute Battalion:

My platoon was divided between two planes with eighteen men in each. In the plane, which was a Stirling bomber converted for our purposes, the first job was to hook up our parachutes to the static lines which were fixed to the inside of the plane. This meant that when we jumped out, the bag containing the parachute was ripped off and the parachutes opened automatically without us having to worry about it. We did worry of course, but we didn't have to do anything like pulling a rip cord.

Ron Perry, HQ Company:

There were a lot of WAAFs standing around where I was. It didn't help when they told us to emplane, and I was the second one into that plane . . . one of these WAAFs started crying. 'You poor boys.' It really did my morale a lot of good!

The plane we were in was called 'The Yorkshire Rose'. The master navigator was in our plane and because I was Number Twenty and Bill French was Twenty-One, we were forced right up into his cabin. When you were going to take off, everybody got as far forward as they could because of the weight thing, you didn't want too much weight down the tail to allow it to get off the ground.

Major Taylor, 'A' Company:

Auguste Niepceron

The engines started up and we moved round the perimeter track, got to the end of the runway, and it was dark by this time, it was certainly dark inside the aircraft. Huge fuselage, and no trouble about moving around, very comfortable, no seats, nothing like that of course.

The plane failed to take off the first time which was a bit worrying. I thought it was going to go through the perimeter fence, something wrong with the magneto or something, but he got round into the queue again, and eventually we got off. We all circled about over southern England for what seemed like a hell of a long time.

The whole of the battalion was airborne by 2330 hours. They were fully expecting the bridges to be blown and so their minds were set for an assault across both waterways.

In a short while the whole of 3 and 5 Parachute Brigades would be on their way to Normandy.

*

In Benouville, the bridgekeeper, Auguste Niepceron, heard a knock on the door of his new home behind *La Chaumiere*. It was one of the *Hilfsgendarmerie* who told him that the bridge needed opening to allow a fishing boat returning from the sea to continue on to Caen. Afterwards Niepceron returned home. This isolated occurrence showed that for all the planning and preparation, the *Coup de Main* party still needed that final element, luck.[16]

Chapter Six

The *Coup de Main* Operation

The *Coup de Main* party continued on its way unmolested. Captain Priday, Glider 94, carrying 22 Platoon:

At 2350 hours, thirty minutes before we were due to land, I stopped smoking and had the lights put out for fear of enemy fighters. We checked our equipment and weapons, and I wondered whether our grenades would explode if we had a heavy landing. I said nothing of this. I stressed the importance of shouting as we came in to land, since I did not want deaf men to deal with when we reached the ground. I again went into the cockpit and kept a running commentary going of all I saw. I didn't see very much, for it was a dark, cloudy night.

At this stage, about 0005 hours, I ordered safety belts to be put on and gave a reminder about holding on to one another and lifting the legs clear of the floor for the landing.

The tugs began to approach the designated cast-off point on the Normandy coast. Due to cloud, the Halifax towing Glider 91 was at 4500 feet. Staff Sergeant Jim Wallwork, Glider 91:

The tug pilot said, 'Weather's good, the clouds are at 600 feet,' a couple of minutes before we cast off, 'and we all wish you the best of luck.' Thanks to our tug crew we were dead on time and dead on target, and saw the French coast in plenty of time to get set. Five, four, three, two, one. Cheers! Cast off! Up with the nose to reduce speed whilst turning on to course. That was when the singing stopped and the silent flight started.

Major Howard was once again going through the operation in his mind:

Amongst those main worries was of course, that one of surprise, which was one of the salient points throughout the whole of our training and that question of the machine-gun, any enemy machine gun pointed towards one glider, wiping us out all together in one fell swoop before we could have a chance to fight back. Going through the things again, there were the poles, the explosives we carried in the glider, whether they would explode on landing, and of course whether we would be the first there.

About ten minutes before reaching the coast, Glider 95, with 23 Platoon, had run into cloud but subsequently crossed the coast by the River Dives. Warrant Officer Peter Bain, the tug pilot, asked through the intercom, 'Can you see the Orne estuary?' The glider pilots said they could and Bain turned to starboard. [1] Lieutenant Sweeney, 23 Platoon:

> *I said, 'Good luck lads. Now don't forget, as soon as we land, we're out and no hesitating . . . and all the very best . . .' The pilot turned back to me and said, 'I can see the mouth of the River Orne,' and then there was a certain amount of anti-aircraft artillery. I don't think it was very close but there was that sort of 'CRUMP, CRUMP'.*

On Glider 96, carrying 17 Platoon, one of the pilots invited Lieutenant Fox into the cockpit:

> *He pointed out first of all, where we were going to land. I could see the shining on the river and the canal, and we agreed between us that that was the right place . . .*

Lieutenants 'Sandy' Smith
and Dennis Fox

He turned round, gave a thumbs up to the men, sat down and strapped himself in:

We all had our rifles pointing downwards . . . for fear of it going off up your chin. 'Wagger' Thornton, without being asked or anything, walked up and down, made sure everyone, as I should have done and never thought to do, was buckled in.

Staff Sergeant Roy Howard, pilot, Glider 96:

Paddy O'Shea, the tug navigator came up on the intercom which ran down the towrope, and told me what to set my gyro compass on. He gave me 'Three minutes to cast off.'

The glider cast off at 5700 feet above broken cloud and the drone of the tug was replaced by the hiss of the glider sliding through the air on its descent towards the River Orne Bridge. It was travelling at 120mph:

To reduce us to our planned gliding speed of 80mph, I immediately applied full flaps. But I realized at once that she was nose heavy, and even with the control column pulled right back against my chest I could not get her to slow below 90mph. We were dropping like a streamlined brick and I knew at once that we were not only incorrectly loaded, but overloaded.

Howard yelled at Lieutenant Fox to quickly move two men from the front to the back, and fortunately this had the desired effect. They were now back on the planned descent rate of 200 feet per minute and their first course of 212 degrees. Freddie Baacke was navigating using the Sperry Gyro Directional Indicator and a stopwatch lit by his tiny hand-held light. They then turned on to 269 degrees before finally turning to port on 212 degrees for the run-in. Roy Howard:

As we made our third change of course and were down to 1200 feet, I could suddenly see the parallel waterways of the Caen Canal and River Orne glistening silver in the diffused moonlight glowing from behind the clouds.
I was afraid that we were still going down too fast, so I took off the flaps for a moment to flatten the glidepath. I just managed to miss the tops of the fifty-foot trees at the beginning of our field and immediately deployed the parachute brake, wheel brakes and full flaps to prevent us careering into the embankment at the far end.
There was our final, unexpected, hazard; no one had mentioned that there would be a herd of cows. I am sure we hit a cow, which knocked off our nose wheel. It was nine minutes past midnight when, with a rumble and final chatter, I came to rest six yards from our allotted spot, less than 100 yards from our objective of the bridge. There was the briefest moment of total silence. 'You are in the right place, sir' I announced to a pleasantly surprised Mr Fox, and before I could even leave my seat he and his men had flung open the door and alighted in a stampede of boots.[2]

Lieutenant Fox:

We jumped out and Tommy Clare who jumped behind . . . had unfortunately got his Sten gun on fire, not on the safety thing, and on automatic too . . . He landed on the ground and his Sten gun hit the ground and shot off a burst of fire straight into the air. I thought, everyone thought, that we were being fired at. We made this arrow formation under the wings which we had practised and practised and practised, and then absolute silence. We then discovered what had happened.

They could see the bridge, and immediately began to move towards a hedgerow on their right. Sapper Cyril Larkin:

I had been detailed by Major Howard earlier on to check that everybody had got out of the glider. The reason I suppose was obviously if someone had come to grief and got caught up behind. I had to feel my way around the glider if there were any personnel

Cyril and Claude Larkin

hanging around but there wasn't. So then I realized I had to jump out of the rear side door . . . The drill was to get out as quickly as possible, flatten yourself on the ground and observe around, and there wasn't a soul there! I quietly searched either side of me and there was no other glider, so I thought 'Well I seem to be alone here somewhere.' All I could see was about half-a-dozen cows and they'd got their heads down wondering what on earth I was doing! There was no movement, no sound. So I assumed that perhaps the glider was pointing in the right direction, so I ran past that . . . Beyond I could see a dark object which I presumed was a hedge, so I ran to that and there were a few Oxf and Bucks lads there and they were kneeling on one knee . . . I enquired of them if they were the Scout party because as an Engineer, I was in the Scout party. The pleasant reply came back to 'Shut up.' I left them and went on and found a few more fellows.

The leading section, led by a corporal, moved towards the road but came to a halt about fifty yards from it. Lieutenant Fox and his HQ Section, followed by the other two sections, bunched up behind. Fox went forward to the corporal to find out what was causing the hold-up:

He said he could see someone with a machine gun. So I said, 'To hell with it, let's get cracking.' So at that stage I did in fact lead. Not through any heroics or anything like that, but just to get on, and this machine gun opened up. It was a Schmeisser and it wasn't a very effective fire . . . Dear old Thornton, as quick as ever, had got, from way back from his position, a mortar trained and he put a mortar slap down on that bridge, a fabulous shot.

Cyril Larkin:

Then we all started to move again. We made a left turn at the hedge and there was a huge bank on the roadside, I didn't realize the road was so close, but there was a ditch too alongside. So we dropped down into this ditch, ran a few yards along the ditch and then up onto the road and just ahead of us was the bridge.

Lieutenant Fox:

We just rushed the bridge. I had assumed that 'Tod' was already there . . . as he should have been, as indeed should Brian Priday, and that I would have just been the back-up, but it was obvious pretty quickly that no one had been there otherwise we wouldn't have been fired at, and there was no-one around. I went across yelling, 'Fox, Fox, Fox, Fox,' and the soldiers came with me. We got to the other side and there seemed to be no opposition at all.

Cyril Larkin:

We had an aerial photograph on the Saturday before we went over and there was a disturbance or something, alteration in the road, just about seven or eight feet from the

76

actual beginning of the bridge. My Engineer Officer had detailed me to check that out. What I found was a light-hearted thing. A horse had stopped there and deposited its job there!

I ran over the bridge. I got off the bridge and down onto the river bank and you could hear people running away from the bank and that was the defenders there, whoever they were and how many there were, running off.

Lieutenant Fox:

O'Shaughnessy, I remember, as a precaution, went around all of the trenches he could find dropping a hand grenade down it and then up came Sergeant Thornton and said that he'd set himself up on the inside of the bridge . . . He thought that was the best place for him to be at the moment so he could cover us if anything was needed. He suggested to me that we 'Spread out a bit and not all stand clumped up at the end of the bridge,' quite rightly, which we did.

Lieutenant Jack Bence's section of Engineers began their tasks. Cyril Larkin:

I went down underneath the bridge and there was a well-worn path down the grass bank . . . Then I looked up into the girders of the bridge and I could see a scaffold board . . . and that ran all the way through the bridge as far as I could see in the dark. Right under the middle of the bridge was a dark object . . .

His immediate impression was that it might be a barge containing explosives:

And then in a bit of moonlight I thought, 'It isn't that,' there seemed to be some brick-work somewhere. So I got onto the bridge, underneath. Just before getting on, actually I thought 'I've got to have some assistance here' and I quietly called out, 'I want some help here . . .'

His twin brother Claude appeared. Cyril Larkin:

I said, 'I'm going to check along this scaffold board and see what's the other side because to me, that's where the explosives will be, in the middle of the bridge.' Crawling through the girders with rifle and backpack was no joke, and the water rushing below me was not inviting either. The 'dark object' turned out to be a huge brick pier containing the bridge opening equipment and thankfully, no explosives. Obviously in past time it had been an openable bridge, but it had been dismantled and all the cogs, wheels, stood up on end against the outside brickwork. So that was a relief 'cos I realized that the bridge couldn't open.

17 Platoon now had sections at either end of the bridge, but there was no sign of Gliders 94 and 95.

*

Glider 91 had cast off and headed for the Canal Bridge. Staff Sergeant Jim Wallwork:

Alter course, air speed right, John Ainsworth with the stopwatch, I'm checking the compass, he's checking the air speed. The downwind leg at 185 degrees for three minutes forty-five seconds at ninety miles per hour went smoothly as Johnnie checked the stopwatch . . . We cruise along and then 'Five, Four, Three, Two, One, Bingo,' right turn to starboard onto course. Halfway down the crosswind leg, I could see it. I could see the river and the canal like strips of silver and I could see the bridges; visibility was awfully good.

Major Howard was sat immediately opposite the front door:

Sitting on my left, was Lieutenant Brotheridge my leading platoon commander, and he undid his safety belt, leant forward, I held his equipment one side, his platoon sergeant on the other side, and he leant forward very precariously and opened up the door which lifted up into the roof.

Ted Tappenden:

We couldn't get the door open at first, that was sort of stuck, but we eventually got it open before we hit the ground. It took two or three of us to wrench the door open.

Wally Parr, assisted by Corporal 'Cobber' Caine, opened the rear door. Major Howard:

When Den Brotheridge slunk back into his seat and put his safety belt on, I looked forward at the fields of France and it had an amazing tranquillising effect on me and those near to me who could see this, because there you had that amazing stock of horses, cattle grazing very, very quietly, with all these bombers going over. They were taking no notice of it at all and it was so quiet it was like being on an exercise in England.

I knew exactly where we were because I had been studying the aerial photographs until I was starry-eyed. I recognised from the shapes of the villages, the churches and crossroads that we were absolutely on course. In any case one of the glider pilots had been giving the thumbs up ever since we cast off!

Glider 92 had approached the coast at 4800 feet with the men still singing so Staff Sergeant Boland, shouted 'Casting off. Shut up!' Oliver Boland:

Pull the button, like a bath plug, and you're on your own. Dead quiet, floating towards and over the coast of France, and know that there's no turning back whatsoever.

The third combination, involving Glider 93, had been through cloud several times at 4000 feet but managed to climb to 5800 feet. Sergeant Peter Boyle:

The navigator said something like 'The target's coming up,' and he gave us the wind speed and wind direction. Then he said, 'You can pull off when you're ready and good luck guys.'

78

Dr John Vaughan:

There was now complete silence for a space of a few minutes. Then, 'We're over the Normandy coast' Sergeant Barkway shouted back, and looking forward over his shoulder and through the Perspex windshield I could see two strips of silver in the moonlight. We were right on target, the Caen river and canal were directly below us. Then 'Stand by for cast off' from Sergeant Boyle. There was a jerk and the nose of the aircraft rose and dipped suddenly.

Geoff Barkway turned Horsa 93 onto its course and went into cloud for fifteen seconds.[3] John Vaughan:

I looked around at the men. They might have been carved in stone. The tension was palpable. Suddenly there were flashes of light from the ground and lines of red balls streamed past to the left of us. An aircraft was probably getting some attention from flak.

Down we dropped with an increasingly loud swishing sound which developed into a high-pitched squeal as we gathered speed. Muttered remarks came from the pilots; Sergeant Boyle was doing his stuff with the stop-watch.

Ahead of them was Glider 91. Jim Wallwork:

By now we could see the twin waterways of the river and canal like silver in the moon-light – which was a little better than half, and more than we had hoped for – and the bridges now showed clearly. It was tempting to fly the rest by the proverbial seat-of-pants, but we resisted and flew the courses and times meticulously.[4]

His co-pilot Johnnie Ainsworth counted 'Five, four, three, two, one, zero. Now.' The right wing dipped as the Horsa did its steady, shallow turn. Major Howard:

As we did that turn I could see the River Orne and the Caen Canal reflected in the half-moon, running down towards Caen. We came to what we knew was going to be the toughest moment of the lot, the crash.

On the left, looking through the glider, I could first see the trees that flanked the left-hand side of the Landing Zone and then halfway down, these tall trees, and we knew we weren't far from the ground.

Corporal Bailey was waiting to put the arrester parachute in place:

My worry was that I would miss the signal to do it because he didn't come back to tell me. I had to watch for Ainsworth to put his arm up.

Sergeant Peter Boyle

79

He was duly given the thumbs up and so dropped the chute into the compartment. Jim Wallwork:

We were a little high, so half flap and steady in at 90 to 95 mph. There was a feeling of the land rushing up . . . Full flap and touchdown.

The glider hit the ground with a colossal crash and bounced back into the air:

I landed probably at about 95 instead of at 85, and ten miles per hour in the dark looks a lot. I hit the field and caught the first bit of wire and so I called 'Stream,' and by golly, it lifted the tail and forced the nose down. It drew us back and knocked the speed down tremendously. It was only on for two seconds, and 'Jettison' and Ainsworth pressed the tit and jettisoned the parachute. Then we were going along only about sixty, which was ample to take me right into the corner.

The Horsa's skids were throwing up a shower of sparks from the rocky ground. The immediate thought of the men seeing these passing the doors was 'Tracer bullets!' Major Howard:

It must have been seconds of course, there was another touchdown but this time it was much louder. It shook the glider tremendously because we were on these skids . . . Then we were airborne again for a second or so and then the final crash came.

Jim Wallwork:

We got right into the corner of the field, the nose wheel had gone, the cockpit collapsed, and Ainsworth and I went right through the cockpit. I went over head first and landed flat on my stomach.

The right-hand undercarriage had been lost but the left was still in place and so the glider was lying at a distinct tilt.[5] Dennis Edwards:

The noise from the landing had ceased very suddenly and was replaced by an ominous silence. No one stirred, nothing moved. My immediate thought was 'God help me – we must all be dead.'

Major Howard:

Everything went dark and I felt my head had been knocked rather badly and my own feelings were, 'God, I'm blind. We'd been training and waiting for this all this time and now, when the moment comes, I'm going to be bloody useless.'[6]

Corporal Bill Bailey, Scout section:

Bill Bailey

In spite of how we had been taught to react there was a slight hiatus. It would have been seconds . . .

Wally Parr:

When it finally stopped, it went silent. It just went silent. There was dust and then there was a moan and then someone blasphemed. And then 'Out, everybody out.' I got out of the side door, I was supposed to go out after Corporal Caine's section. He went out, but a man behind him, his feet had gone through the deck and nobody could get past him. So I shouted to Charlie Gardner 'Come on Charlie, go.' We jumped three foot onto the ground and I dashed forward.

Corporal Bailey:

I went down on one knee as I dropped out and it was wet, wet under the knee. There was a noise up front, breaking. There was quite a bit of splinter.

Paddy O'Donnell, Scout section:

Cobber Caine went out first, Wally and Bill more or less went out together, and I shot off my seat and I think went more or less over the top of the two of them. I turned round the tail and up the other side. Now I reckon from the time I got off my seat to the time I got right up to the nose of the glider could be no more than twenty seconds.

Immediately, I got down on one knee and if anyone had come up over that little prowl in front, because I was a bit lower and had a good line on the sky, I'd have put a shot into him. I could hear the schemozzel going on, on the other side. Now what caused the slight delay in getting out, when the nose of the glider went through this fence, it pushed a part of the fence I understand over the door and it sort of delayed them.

To John Howard's immense relief he found that he had not been blinded:

All that had happened was my head had bumped on the top of the glider and my battle bowler had come down over my eyes! Once I realized that of course, I eased up the helmet and the first thing I saw was that the door had disappeared. It had completely telescoped. I could hear the glider pilots on my right moaning in their cockpit, which seemed to have been smashed, but I was conscious that everybody in the glider was moving. You could hear the click of safety belts being undone and I knew that men were getting out of the glider and people pushing in front of me to get through the broken door. I let Den Brotheridge and his platoon get out first because if indeed they were the first platoon, their job was absolutely one of speed.

Dennis Edwards was at the front:

The exit door had been right beside my seat. Now there was only a mass of twisted wood and fabric across the doorway and we had to use the butts of our rifles to smash our way out.

Bill Gray heard the order from Den Brotheridge 'Gun out', which meant him:

Out I jumped, stumbled on the grass because of the weight I had and set the Bren up facing the bridge, and the rest of the lads sort of jumped out.

Paddy O' Donnell could see Jim Wallwork lying in the wreckage of the cockpit:

The whole front was smashed up and he was 'shot through.' There's a strut that comes across the front of the glider, I suppose about four inches wide something like that, and his hands were over the top of it. He said to me, 'Undo my belt.' So I put my hand through the hole, undid his belt and I said, 'Come on, I'll get you out.' I could see he was cut and that. 'No,' he said, 'don't bother about me, get over the bridge, get over the bridge.' Well, I couldn't move at that moment because the drill for the assault was 7 and 8 Sections . . . line up for the assault. Corporal Bailey with his four men . . . they were to line up and go behind them, right on their heels . . . Brotheridge would miss the little gun on the bridge, the anti-tank gun, we would deal with that if it was occupied. If I were to move forward I would only get shot at by my own people, so I had to hold tight to fit into the drill.

Major Howard emerged from the glider:

I suppose that was the most exhilarating moment of my life . . . I could see the tower of the bridge about fifty yards from where I was standing. The nose of the glider was right through the wire fence where, almost facetiously, I'd asked the glider pilot to put the glider on the model back in the UK, in order that we would not have to use the Bangalore torpedoes which every glider brought with them for this purpose . . . Above all, and this was the tremendous thing, there was no firing at all, in other words we had been a complete surprise. We had really caught old Jerry with his pants down.

Corporal Tappenden:

The front of the glider was completely demolished. We didn't know what we'd hit. We thought that both the pilots were dead because when I looked at one of the pilots, just before we left the glider, his face was covered in blood. They were both unconscious. It was absolutely silent, there wasn't a bit of noise at all.
I stayed with Major Howard. The platoon lined up, ready to go forward to the bridge.

The right wing of the glider had obstructed Wally Parr's route from the rear door because he could not get beneath it:

I started to go around it. I was up to my knees in swamp water. We went back around the other side. By this time John Howard had got most of the fellows out of the glider and they were kneeling down facing the bridge, and it was no more than thirty to forty yards from us.

82

Lieutenant Brotheridge whispered, 'Corporal Bailey, get those chaps moving.' Bailey, Parr, O'Donnell, Bourlet and Gardner moved towards the embankment and the road. Wally Parr:

I looked up and saw this damned thing towering above me, and my mouth went dry. I couldn't spit sixpence! My tongue was stuck to the top of my mouth. I thought I was going to choke.

Corporal Bailey:

We ignored everything else left, right and centre and we went straight to the pillbox which was on the other side of the road. We moved up to the wall, pins out and shoved them through. The second noise of the night was Wally Parr saying, 'Pick the bones out of that you bastards,' or words to that effect. My mouth was absolutely dry.

Wally Parr:

I just took a great big deep breath and I screamed at the top of my voice, I don't know what made me do it, 'Come out and fight you square-headed bastards', and then all the saliva came back into my mouth.

Bill Bailey:

We used two '36' grenades there, that's Wally Parr and myself, which we put through the apertures and there was really a terrific explosion, simultaneous explosions almost. And there were great clouds of dust.
    Frank Bourlet was behind us, Gus [Charlie Gardner] . . . he was my Bren gunner, he and Paddy O'Donnell were what we called covering the road, loosely.[7]

As the Scout section had gone for the pillbox, 1 Section led by Lieutenant Brotheridge, had headed for the bridge. Lance Corporal Tom Packwood:

We could hear Danny Brotheridge shouting, 'Come on 25!'

Bill Gray:

Tom Packwood, who was my Number Two, had got in front of me and he stopped and said, 'Come on Bill, you're supposed to be in front of me,' because of the Bren gun. My job, as the Bren gunner, was to rush the right-hand side of the bridge.
    We dashed towards it and I saw a German sentry with what looked like a Verey light pistol in his hand. I fired and he went down, but at the same time he pulled the trigger of the Verey pistol and the bright light went up. I still kept firing going over the bridge and at the other side there was another German, he went down.[8]

Their boot studs thudded loudly on the bridge's metal grills as they ran across. Light

Bill Gray

fire came back at them from the area of the *Café Gondrée*.

Major Howard had followed the section up the track leading to the bridge:

Up to this moment it had all been done in complete silence. These were my orders, that if we had surprise, we had to keep it. Nobody was allowed to fire unless they were directly fired at by the enemy. Well as soon as the pillbox went up, of course with a hell of a bang, that was the signal to fire.

Corporal Webb's 2 Section, which was to cross the bridge on the left-hand side, was a little distance behind 1 Section, while Lieutenant Brotheridge had charged on across the bridge. Dennis Edwards:

Major Howard was already up ahead, and not wishing to be left behind in this exposed place, I made haste to join them. Major Howard was already on the approach to the bridge and shouted, 'Come on boys. This is it!'

A machine gun, firing from trenches to the north, forced Howard and Tappenden to dive for cover. Bill Gray:

Once we'd got over the bridge I was to turn half-right where there was a barn, a building. It was probably a bus shelter [sic]. My job was to clear it. I went to the door of the barn, slung in a '36' grenade, gave them the rest of the magazine and went inside. There was nobody in there. But when I was round there I was breaking my neck for a slash! You wouldn't believe it but I was, I just couldn't wait. Put the Bren up against the side of the building, done a slash . . . There was a lot of firing going on outside and on the other side of the bridge, and when I came out someone started firing from down the road, the unmistakable sound of a Schmeisser. So I let rip with the Bren and then dashed across the road where I saw Danny Brotheridge [lying there] . . . A phosphorous bomb was alight and part of his smock was smouldering. I dashed up this small slope to a little field where there was a German gun pit which was designated as our place to defend.[9]

This large round gunpit was up on the bank on the left-hand side of the road.

At the pillbox Scout section had moved on to a second door and repeated their drill. Wally Parr then came back and passing the first door, heard groaning inside:

The door was wide open, I pulled out a '77' phosphorous grenade, if the shrapnel didn't get them, this phosphorous would. It was undone by a tape with a lead weight on the end. A couple of whirls undone it and threw it in. It went off a treat. I slammed the door shut, Charlie and I scrambled back up onto this end of the bridge and Major Howard

BENOUVILLE — La Gare

Electric Photo Caen

The buildings at the western edge of the bridge

was there and he turned round and pointed a Sten gun at us. 'Say who's that?' So I started to shout, 'Ham and Jam, Ham and Jam!' And he stared at us, 'Right. You cleared those?' 'Yes, sir.' 'Right, run, run, run, get across that bridge.' We did and on the way over Charlie said to me, 'You're not supposed to shout Ham and Jam.' In the excitement I'd shouted out Ham and Jam which was to be the success signal for the capture of both bridges, but I wanted to make sure he knew who I was. I didn't want to be blasted down by John Howard!

Bill Bailey:

We then moved across and the next thing to remember was not to trip over the railway lines. There was a tramline running up the side of the Café Gondrée and from Caen up to the coast . . . on what we would loosely call the towpath there.

During the final approach to the LZ, Glider 92, carrying 24 Platoon, had been close behind Glider 91. Staff Sergeant Oliver Boland:

I said to my troops in the back, 'We may land short.' I knew we weren't going to land beyond, 'All you've got to do is go straight ahead because we are running parallel to the towpath. I'll stretch the glide as far as I can,' when suddenly the bridges came into view and I'm quite low now, trying to see whether there were any trees. I said, 'We're here, we shall be landing any second now,' when suddenly there was gunfire right in front of my nose which meant, Jimmy [Wallwork] they'd seen him. And we then literally

85

crash-landed . . . The landing was very rough indeed. We did the parachute there, then let it off. It's one of those things that you don't know why you do what you do, because you're having to make decisions in a split second and the shit, shot and shell are around, is how I can get down, not run into Jimmy, not run into the pond and I see another bloke coming down from my right, which was the third glider. So I'd got nowhere to go. I can't veer off, there's another bloke, so I drop in on the ground with a mighty crash and we crash along, not very far, managed to stop and break the back just before the pond. I said, 'We're here, piss off and do what you're paid to', or something to that effect.'

Boland was unhurt, but Sergeant Hobbs suffered cuts about the legs.[10] Lieutenant Wood, 24 Platoon:

We had a very bumpy ride, a lot of sparks flashing, which we took to be at that point the enemy opening fire on us, but I'm glad to say that it was simply the flints in the ground on the skids underneath the glider. The next thing I knew, I was literally on the ground under the glider, still clutching my bucket of grenades.

Nobby Clark, 24 Platoon:

It suddenly stopped dead and we all shot forward. To this day I don't know whether I went out the side of the glider or whether I went out the door. All I know is that I was the second man in a pile of bodies on the ground and there were two other blokes on top of me.

Many were knocked unconscious for a few seconds, but then their training automatically made them think about taking up positions of all-round protection. Private Fred Weaver was sitting towards the centre of the glider:

Our glider, we had to swing to the right, and swinging round, it cracked open. Instead of getting out the front and back doors, we just all stepped out. It had broken its back. When it cracked open, all I'd got to do was pick my gun up and just go through the side of the glider. Most of them followed out that way. All we could hear was Major Howard, 'Come on lads, up here, this is it!'

Lieutenant Wood:

I pulled myself together and I could see in the dark, just enough to see that the other glider was where it should be and that I was Number Two, which was my role. We assembled under the wings of the glider, section commanders reported that they were complete and then we moved off at the double to report to John Howard who was leaning by the barbed wire.

Nobby Clark:

We quickly formed up and when we thought we had enough men we moved off at a sort of fast walk, semi-trot, towards the bridge. When we got level almost of where the cockpit of Jim Wallwork's glider was, there was a flare went off on the bridge. Then all hell broke loose and firing broke out on the bridge. We quickly ran to the bridge, forty yards, so many seconds, less than twenty seconds probably, and David Wood approached John Howard who was laying against one of the ends of that bridge.

Major Howard:

When David Wood came up so quickly afterwards, he didn't say whether he was all right, he said, 'Everything OK?' And the order was given without him stopping. I just said, 'Number Two task' and he automatically went to do it, the one that he had expected and the one from the training point of view, I hoped he would do. He didn't have to issue any orders, he just said, 'Number Two' to his leading section . . .

One half of David's platoon went straight through that to clear the defences that were beyond the pillbox, while the other half wheeled, kept on our side of the pillbox and cleared that side. And the skirmishing started immediately. And of course with the others shouting on the other side of the bridge, he immediately started his call of 'Baker, Baker, Baker!'

Nobby Clark:

Dropped some more bombs in the big pillbox, grenades, and then dashed down and cleared all that bank for about fifty, seventy yards, which we accomplished within minutes. We went in there like cats out of hell and anyone who was in front of us were dead.

Lance Corporal Arthur Roberts, 24 Platoon:

We went straight across, we didn't have time to think. You know what you've got to do and the quicker you done it, the better it was. That was practically an impossible job

Arthur and Veronica Roberts

because the moon had gone in and it was pretty dark. They'd been laying mines in the trenches so if you jumped in there you might have jumped on a mine. We just tossed grenades in, we tossed these Norwegian grenades that just made a big bang. We didn't toss '36' Mills grenades about because you'd hit your own blokes in the darkness. When you flung a grenade you automatically went to ground normally. So any grenades had to be these egg-shaped, black, Bakelite grenades. I actually saw some [Germans] running down towards Ouistreham . . . but they were very vague in the dark. They just bolted.

Lieutenant Wood:

Most of the enemy, by the time we got over the other side, seemed to me to have run away. I found an MG34 for instance, intact with a complete belt of ammunition on it, which nobody had found. There was a lot of firing going on, a lot of shouting, it was part of John's thing that we all shouted our platoon name . . . There was more firing in retrospect than there needed to be, but we were new at the game and it was easier to let off rounds than not.

In the front bedroom of the *Café Gondrée* the two young daughters had been in bed with their mother. Thérèse and the girls had been awake and had heard the noise of the landing made by the first glider. She had gone and woken her husband. Georges Gondrée:

She said to me, 'Get up. Don't you hear what's happening? Open the window.' I was sleepy and it took me some little time to grasp what she meant. She repeated, 'Get up. Listen. It sounds like wood breaking.' I opened the window and looked out.

He could see nothing in the moonlight, but he heard 'snapping and crunching sounds'. Then the sounds of firing and flashes began. He believed it to be a crashed bomber and so immediately took the family down to the cellar which had been their air-raid shelter throughout the war:

Then I heard a knocking on the front door and a voice in German calling us to come out and walk in front of them. This, my wife and I refused to do.

They remained silent and continued to listen to the firing. Thérèse was only wearing a nightdress and was shivering with cold. She said to her husband, 'Go upstairs and see what's happening'.

Before David Wood's men had reached the bridge, the Scout section had crossed to the western side. Bill Bailey:

When we got to the other end of the bridge, and we are talking in seconds at this stage of the game, there was quite an amount of smoulder and phosphorous where they'd been used on that end.

Wally Parr:

There was a dead German, he had no equipment, no uniform, just trousers and what appeared to be a jumper or possibly a shirt. He was lying dead in the middle of the road, a big stout chap.[11]

Georges Gondrée opened a window:

There were two soldiers standing in front of the café with a corpse between them. It was Pere Delaunay, a neighbour of mine, who had been shot I found afterwards, by the Germans. I said 'Qu'est ce-que c'est?' They replied as near as I can remember, 'L'Armee de L'Air.' I still thought that they were part of a crew of a crashed bomber, but I was worried by the clothes they had on and also by the fact that they seemed to be wearing black masks. I did not realize at that moment that they were not masks but camouflage paint.

Delaunay was a sixty-seven year-old member of the *Hilfsgendarmerie*. Corporal Bailey had looked up and saw Georges Gondrée at the window. Pointing his Sten at him, Bailey asked, 'Are you French?' but did not receive an answer. Bill Bailey:

The Café Gondrée prior to the family's purchase of it

Georges and Therese Gondrée

I gesticulated and shouted out, 'Get your bloody head down' or words to that effect and didn't shoot him.

Wally Parr:

And then I began shouting 'Where's Danny Brotheridge? Where's Brotheridge?' We were supposed to RV with him, thirty yards past the café in a ditch on the left-hand side of

Georgette & Arlette outside the Cafe Gondrée

the road. They were milling around there. There were spare shots going off, grenades going off. There was a certain amount of confusion, and I started to run up the road and as I did so, there was another chap laying in the road and I ran past him thinking it was another German and then realized it wasn't. I stopped, turned round and came back. It was Lieutenant Danny Brotheridge. He was lying on his back with his head towards the bridge, his feet towards the T-Junction. I knelt down beside him, put my rifle down, put my hand behind his head and lifted him up. He was conscious and he said something. I couldn't hear what he said. I said, 'I'm sorry sir, I can't hear you.' He started to speak again and he just closed his eyes, gave a big sigh and laid back. My hand and the road was covered in blood.

Bill Bailey:

There was a body laying near enough alongside the petrol pump that was there . . . Wally and I went past and then came back to look at who this was. It was Dan Brotheridge, and he was obviously bleeding from the neck, he was bubbling away, he was gurgling, so I couldn't understand what he was saying anyway.

As Oliver Boland had seen, Glider 93 had not been far behind him. Staff Sergeant Geoff Barkway, Glider 93 carrying 14 Platoon, 'B' Company:

Peter suddenly said, 'There it is!' and I looked across and there it was, 'cos I was watching the instruments and generally flying the thing, the speed and everything. And when I looked I saw that big water tank on the end of the bridge. And so from then on it was just a case of judging where we were going to get down.[12]

A German flare then went up and illuminated them clearly. Due to the overloading, the glider's speed was high, ninety to one hundred miles per hour. Sergeant Peter Boyle:

We were landing rather fast . . . He swung her round and straightened up for the target and I just kind of waited to see what was going to happen.

Lieutenant Smith, 14 Platoon, 'B' Company:

My glider hit what can only be best described as a snipe bog and then took off again. And then crashed rather badly in what you might call static water and smashed its whole front up. I was myself flung through the cockpit of the glider and ejected onto the ground only to be overrun by the glider when it slithered to a halt, and I had my knee rather badly damaged . . . The wing ran over me, all the undercarriage having been smashed up.

Peter Boyle:

I seem to remember somebody coming through the doorway and going straight past me, and I went down . . . under the window.

The glider had come to a halt within a hundred yards of the bridge. The two pilots were lying in water, still strapped into their seats in the wreckage of the cockpit. Geoff Barkway:

I thought 'There's not much future in this' and struggled out. Fortunately the front had disintegrated so that the harness wasn't attached to anything, so there was no problem in getting free.

He then tried to assist his colleague. Peter Boyle:

I didn't know where I was apart from the fact that I was in the wreckage of the glider. I ached a bit somewhere . . . I was thinking, 'Oh God' . . . I remember Geoff pulling the wreckage from me and pulling me out. It was pitch black.

Lieutenant Smith:

I had a Lance Corporal Madge . . . and I remember groping around in the dark, covered with mud and water and shock, and he said, 'What are we waiting for, sir?' And so I tried to find my weapon and couldn't and found somebody else's Sten gun and ran towards the bridge, or rather, hobbled.

Peter Boyle:

I moved round the glider, or round the wreckage, and I can remember seeing a body across the undercart. There was a chap there and I put my hand on him and he was just hanging there. And although there was a kind of half-light and things were happening, I was still thinking, 'I've got to do the job I was there to do.'[13]

This was to find the PIAT and take it across to the other side of the bridge.

The Engineers of 2 Platoon, 249 Field Company had reached their appointed locations above and beneath the bridge to search for explosives. Sapper Cyril Haslett, on board Glider 92 had followed Captain Neilson, met up with the five engineers from Glider 91 and rushed down to the bank of the canal:

It was just mud. We just had to scramble on as best we could, because the bridge came over the road, into the bank. Underneath, you had to feel your way around.

Sapper Harry Wheeler had followed 25 Platoon across the bridge and then double-backing over the southern abutment, saw a large wire running along the side. He readied his wire-cutters:

Harry Wheeler

It was the only wire I could see. I didn't know what it was;

hoped for the best. It blew me off my feet, and the wire-cutters, blew them out of my hands! I reckon it was for lifting the bridge; must have been, the amount of power that was there.[14]

Although firing was going on, none of it was directed at the Engineers. Major Howard:

After a bit of a pause, Number 3 Glider came up, Sandy Smith with his platoon, and he seemed to be limping very badly. He confirmed that they had had quite a few casualties in landing, but his boys were all right and I said, 'Number Three task.' Their arrival of course increased the shouting of the codewords all the way round and what with the firing, the shouting and the skirmishing going on everywhere, it was like hell let loose I should think for about ten minutes.

Lieutenant Smith:

I found a Spandau firing right down the centre of the bridge, so I ran left down the catwalk running along the side of the bridge to avoid this machine gun. I arrived at the other end of the bridge to find Brotheridge dying. And then in the flurry I remember a German throwing a stick grenade at me and then I felt the explosion and my right wrist was hit. I was extremely lucky because the grenade exploded very close to me and hit various parts of my clothing but not my body, although there were holes in my flying smock. That was the first German I actually shot. Having thrown his grenade he tried to scramble over the back of one of the walls adjoining the café, and I actually shot him with my Sten gun as he went over.

Smith then looked at the outside of his wrist in the moonlight:

I was rather shocked because it had scooped up all the flesh up to the bone and your wrist bone is very flat as I then discovered, and it was white. I could still at that time operate my finger trigger, which was fortunate.

Having shot this German, he immediately looked up at the café, only to see a figure looking down at him. It was Georges Gondrée. Lieutenant Smith:

Well we'd been told in our briefings that the Germans had used the café a great deal when they came off sentry. They used to go and have a cup of coffee there and they were quite often, in the café as a result. And so I wasn't taking any chances because this German had nearly killed me. And so I fired my Sten gun straight up into the window . . .

Fortunately he missed, although one bullet ricocheted off the ceiling and through the headboard of the bed, while another penetrated the bathroom door. Georges Gondrée then went downstairs:

I then had a look out of the kitchen window which faces the canal. Directly beneath me I saw two soldiers and when they saw me they lifted their weapons and pointed them at me. By then there were quite a number of flares in the sky so that I could see quite plainly. One of the soldiers said to me, 'Vous civile?' I replied 'Oui, Oui.' The soldier answered, 'Vous civile?' and after a moment I realized that was the only French he knew. I was for twelve years a bank clerk in Lloyds Bank in Paris and I therefore spoke good English but I did not wish that fact to be known at that moment for I was not sure who they were. One of them put a finger to his lips and made a gesture with his hands, indicating that I was to close the shutters. This I did and went back to my cellar.

With Lieutenant Brotheridge severely wounded, Wally Parr had begun to look for Sergeant Ollis, next in line to command the platoon. However, unable to find him, he went back across the bridge and met Major Howard, who he informed about Brotheridge. Major Howard:

It was just after I'd sent Smith off that I was informed that Den had been hit in the neck by the machine-gun fire and was badly wounded. My natural feeling was get across that bridge to make sure that things were all right and to see if Den, if anything could be done for him, but common-sense prevailed. I knew that my job at that juncture was to stay at the Command Post and to tell the remaining platoons what to do and there was of course the River Bridge, although that wasn't much in my mind at the time.

Two of the gliders at the Canal Bridge. The nearer is the Horsa of Wallwork and Ainsworth (IWM FLM 3840)

Corporal Bailey and O'Donnell of 25 Platoon had moved forward and left, beyond the café, to the ridge where Bill Gray and Tom Packwood's gunpit was situated and proceeded to dig in. Bill Gray then heard someone climbing up the ridge behind them:

We all immediately assumed it was a Jerry. Because I was a gunner, my own personal weapon, apart from the Bren gun, was a pistol, a 45 Colt automatic. I just took it out of my holster put it on the edge of this cliff because the gunpit was that close to it, and the top of a helmet came up and I was just about to pull the bleedin' trigger and it was one of our blokes. What he was doing climbing up that side of the cliff . . . but he was one of our platoon.

Sergeant Boyle also arrived at the position with a PIAT. Bill Bailey:

I was a little bit aggressive at times y'know, because he said, 'I've brought the PIAT over.' And I sort of said to him, 'Where's the bloody bombs?' He said, 'Well, what bombs?' 'What the bloody hell's the good of a PIAT without any bloody bombs?'

Peter Boyle:

I went back to the wreckage of this glider to find what I should have taken in the first place and heard Geoff shouting that he'd been hit.

Geoff Barkway:

I was concussed and staggering around in the dark. I was challenged with the password by one of the fellows on glider protection and failed to give the right reply quickly enough, so the Oxf and Bucks bloke opened up. At least that's what I think happened. He might have had his Sten on single shot, but I suddenly had this awful pain in my wrist.

Along with Jack Hobbs, Peter Boyle went over and found him close to the glider:

I got him to a bit of a bank and there were two other glider pilots . . . Somebody had found a stretcher, this was within minutes, where this stretcher had come from I don't know. We put Geoff on this stretcher and took him to where we thought the Aid Post was. We were right and there was a medical orderly there, just in a ditch amongst some trees.[15]

Boyle returned to the glider, found the PIAT bombs and took them to Bill Bailey.

The two pilots which Boyle had seen at the RAP were Johnnie Ainsworth and Jim Wallwork. When Wallwork had regained consciousness he had seen Ainsworth trapped below him:

Staff Sergeant Geoff Barkway

He seemed to be in bad shape. I said, 'Can you crawl?' and he said, 'No' With the aid of a medic I managed to crawl free of the debris, but it required two of us to drag Ainsworth out. I asked if I lifted, could he crawl out and he said, 'I'll try.' I lifted the thing and I felt that I lifted the whole bloody glider when probably all I lifted was a small spar, but I felt like thirty men when I picked this thing up and he did manage to crawl out. Nothing was broken except for one ankle and a badly sprained pair of knees for Johnnie. The medic took him to the ditch which had been designated the Regimental Aid Post in briefing.

I had taken a header through the Perspex nose and was bleeding from a head cut. It had congealed quickly in my right eye socket.

Wally Parr had still not found Sergeant Ollis and so went to re-cross the bridge when he was stopped by another member of 25 Platoon:

Stan Watson came up to me and said, 'Look, I've just been down underneath the gun pit . . . I think I can hear a movement down there. Have you got a torch?' I said, 'No, but I'll borrow one off the REs.' At that moment someone got a Sten gun tangled up with a respirator and it went off and there was a shower of bullets and Corporal Webb received bullets through his leg and out through his shoulder.

Watson and I made our way down into the gun pit. As you turned right, the ammunition [was] on the right but along on the left hand side there were two big dugouts . . . they weren't just slit trenches. They were covered with curtains. The first one was empty, I shone a torch in the second one and looked around and was about to go when I looked at the bed, and the bed was literally shaking.

I went over and tapped him on the head . . . There was no response except he shook even further, so I grabbed hold of the cover and dragged it down and there was a young soldier, couldn't have been more than seventeen, and I told him to get up. He couldn't even stand up, I had to drag him up off the bed and I gave him to Watson. I said, 'Get him upstairs.' The chap was shaking so much he couldn't stand up properly. Stan Watson helped him with a painful kick up the arse.

*

Stan Watson

At the Orne Bridge, although Lieutenant Fox's Platoon had seized it, events had not gone totally to plan. Dennis Fox:

I remember standing on the bridge with Clare, on a beautiful moonlit night, with a walking stick type of thing, looking at the river, wondering what to do next. He was trying desperately to get through on the radio to John Howard.

There had been no sign of the remaining two gliders. Glider 95 of Staff Sergeants Stan Pearson and Len Guthrie carrying Lieutenant Sweeney's 23 Platoon had had a problem when coming in to land. At 4,000 feet the pilots realized that due to overloading they would not reach the bridge on their present course and so headed straight for the target on a new bearing. At 3,000 feet the pilots could see flashes from the area of the Canal Bridge and informed 'Tod' Sweeney that an action was taking place there. At a thousand feet Sweeney stood up to open the door, but again it was such a struggle that two others were needed to raise it. He then sat down and was looking out the doorway:

You could see the moon shining on the river as we went down along the river . . . saw the bridge in front of me . . . So I went and strapped up and then I heard the glider pilot say with an oath, 'Oh damn it, we've dropped!'

Their speed was still too high, and at 200 feet Stan Pearson decided that the field immediately in front of them would have to do. When level with the tree tops he allowed twenty feet of height between the glider's main wheels and the ground, Len Guthrie put on half, then full flaps. Pearson pulled on the control column, the nose wheel rose and the wheels touched down, while Guthrie pulled the line to release the arrester parachute. After a short run the Horsa came to a halt. Corporal Bill 'Smokey' Howard, 23 Platoon:

Out we clambered, did our all-round defence of the glider as we had all been trained to do. Lieutenant Sweeney called an Orders Group, that was section leaders, platoon sergeants, glider pilots, to try to make up his own mind what he was going to do.

I remember huge hedges all over the place, loads of trees in the dark, completely lost. Of course the glider pilot knew where the bridge was. Our glider had landed 600 yards from where we should have landed. It took them about a minute to decide which way to go.

They moved to the western side of a hedgerow about eighty yards to their right, while the glider pilots began to unload the ammunition from the glider. It was also their task to drag the boat down to the towpath of the river. 'Smokey' Howard:

We went along the ditch . . . At the same time there were fireworks coming from the other bridge. Tracer up in the air, you could see that, and gunfire.

They came to the end of the hedgerow and with Lieutenant Sweeney leading, began charging up the road towards the bridge. 'Tod' Sweeney:

I got my leading sections on either side and we assaulted the bridge shouting the code-word [Easy] . . . I hadn't really cottoned on to the fact that the bridge had already been seized at all, but as I was beginning to go across I suppose it was beginning to infiltrate into my mind, someone was in fact there before me. So I went racing across with my two sections leaving one section on the rear side. I saw some shadowy figures but I didn't pause because the great thing was you had to get across to the other side. I went racing over with my heart in my mouth, expecting the bridge to go up, shouting out my code-word with these chaps thumping along beside me. Then when we got to the far side, there were clearly British figures there because they were shouting back their codeword and so we came to a halt, rather disappointedly! We had been all worked up to kill, bayonet the enemy, be blown up or something, and there on the other side of the bridge was the unmistakable figure of Dennis Fox . . . who had been there about five minutes before. I rushed up panting and always on these exercises the one person you were looking out for was the umpire, because he was going to assess you . . . They were the chaps you had to deceive into making them believe you'd done a good job! So I went rushing over, and said, 'Dennis, Dennis, how are you? Is everything alright?' And he said, 'Yes, I think so Tod, but I haven't seen the umpires yet!'

So I said, 'What's happening?' He said, 'I've sent a couple of men up the road just to wait on the corner so that when the parachutists drop, they'll make contact up there.' So we both stood there talking for what was a matter of a few minutes.

Before heading off for the RV, the 7th Battalion Liaison Officer, Lieutenant Macdonald went to find out the situation at the canal.

Being the senior officer, Sweeney assumed command for the defence of the bridge from Dennis Fox. 'Tod' Sweeney:

The two River Orne gliders. Glider 95 is in the top right hand corner.

RANVILLE (Calvados) - Le Pont

The Orne Bridge and the cottage that 'Smokey' Howard knocked at

So after a few minutes he pulled his men in, back across the bridge, leaving me in sole charge of the Orne Bridge. And so we began digging our little shell scrapes. I then sent out my patrol up to the end of the road to replace Dennis' patrol ... Then I got the sections out, one on either side of the road and told them to take up their positions and got a message to the rear section telling them to take up position on the innermost side of the bridge.

'Smokey' Howard approached the cottage on the north-eastern bank:

It was my section's job to knock anybody up in that house. If it was Germans, have them out, if it was French, be careful. It seemed to be an open porch and a big door in front. On the left-hand side the ground actually dips down.

I suppose the Bren gunner was there and one or two others ready to chuck grenades in. We banged at the front door and if a French person answered, it was 'Ou est la Boche?' The door opened and an old man came there, he must have been over sixty, that sort of age. I had the impression I could see in the background a bedroom and a light on, a candle, an old lady in a nightdress. But all he did, the old man, was to look at us, turn round, put his hands in the air and go back to bed!

All of the few cottages there were investigated, but no enemy discovered. Corporal Howard then reported back to Lieutenant Sweeney. 'Smokey' Howard:

He took my Bren gunner, he took him away from me and had him down by the side of the road leading up to Ranville. Johnny Murton took a place on the right-hand side of the bridge, there was a path down there ... We were just told to stay where we were. I was down by the side of this farmhouse [that he had knocked at] *in the dip. I thought it was a good place to be and old Buck Read and I had a cigarette there. We were quite expert at it. You'd undo the zip of your flying smock, put your mouth inside and pulled your sleeve over your wrist and no-one could see it. Everybody went to war with a fag in their mouth.*

Corporal Jimmy Jennings' section had been placed at the western end of the bridge, on both sides of the road. Private Peter 'Rocky' Bright:

We weren't actually dug in, we just found a bank and got down behind it. It was marshy, it wasn't difficult to push some earth down. We got pretty wet, but it's survival . . . you do what you can.

Major Howard had become somewhat concerned about the bridge. Corporal Tappenden had been trying to contact the Orne Bridge party for some time and had begun to wonder if the set was actually working. John Howard:

I couldn't see any signs of firing over there, there were no radio messages and that didn't surprise me because the radios were pretty frail and with the crash landings, we didn't expect them to survive.

Another part of my orders was, because of the radio being a bit uncertain, a runner from each platoon would report to my Company Headquarters by the Canal Bridge, but no runners had arrived. I was beginning to consider whether I should have to send a platoon or half a platoon over to the River Bridge to try and capture that, but then all the luck turned.

The Captain of the Royal Engineers, 'Jock' Neilson, reported to me that there were no explosives under the Canal Bridge.

Sapper Cyril Haslett:

We discovered that somebody had disconnected the explosives, so all we had to do was take the leads off, leading to the explosives. The explosives were on the side, but the leads were still on the bridges, we had to cut this cordite cord.[16]

Major Howard:

So that was the first bit of good news, and then we picked up, to our surprise, a radio message which said that one of the platoons, Number 6 Platoon under Dennis Fox had captured the River Bridge almost without firing a shot. And Number 5 Platoon under 'Tod' Sweeney had reached them and so there were two platoons over there.

Well that was tremendous news to get, that the other bridge had been captured intact. Of course knowing there were no explosives under this, I didn't think there'd be any explosives under that bridge either, we weren't standing to and we were able immediately to start sending out our 'Ham and Jam' radio call.

There was radio silence at the time and my main reason for doing that was I knew that my Brigadier, Brigadier Nigel Poett, was dropping round about the same time as we pranged . . . and also that he had a '38' set on our wavelength so that he could follow the chitter-chatter between me and my platoon and would be aware of what was going on. So I hoped that he would immediately pick up our 'Ham and Jam' signal and be as relieved as we were to know that the first part of the operation, everything was OK.

However, there was no sign of Glider 94 transporting the 2i/c, Brian Priday and Lieutenant Hooper's 22 Platoon.

Beyond Howard's pillbox, 24 Platoon had cleared the trenches, encountering little opposition. Lieutenant Wood:

We'd been through the area we had to clear, got as far as the canal bank and so on, and thought we'd cleared it, so far as you could tell in the dark.

He then relayed a message via the radio that they had performed their task successfully:

I heard my runner say, 'Sir, 'Ham and Jam' and I knew that both bridges had been captured, and that was within ten minutes of the landing. Then I was ordered to report back to John for further orders.

He set off with his batman Chatfield, and Platoon Sergeant Leather, and approached the road. They did not get very far. Lieutenant Wood:

All three of us were hit by a burst from a Schmeisser machine pistol, which in my case, hit me in the left leg. I had heard lots of stories about heroics and how you went on as if nothing had happened when you'd been hit in the leg, but it wasn't like that with me. I fell to the ground and I couldn't move, in fact, I was frightened. Obviously the enemy were there and I thought somebody would come and finish me off and I shouted . . . There were two privates in my platoon who were trained as medical orderlies . . . Radford and Cheesely. They came up first and shoved a rifle on as a splint [and administered an injection of morphine].

In my hip pocket I had a flask my brother had given me and I had a swig of that. Of course, I didn't know that the others had been wounded or indeed anything at that stage, except that I was lying on the floor, quite useless.

A runner informed Major Howard of David Wood's wounding.[17] Major Howard:

Number 2 Platoon, poor old David's platoon, were leaderless inasmuch as they'd lost their platoon commander and sergeant, and the platoon was commanded by a Corporal Godbold . . . Godbold was a good old 52nd from India corporal, and one I had full reliance on. He was one I had earmarked to be a sergeant in the Company . . . You Lieutenant David Wood *earmark people for jobs once you get casualties and I was happy that the platoon was in his hands.*[18]

In the darkness, Nobby Clark was unaware of what had happened to his platoon commander:

I didn't know until Godbold came up to me. He was the senior corporal, so he became the platoon commander. 'Harry,' he said, 'I've got some bad news for you'. I said, 'What's that?' He said, 'You're my runner and you've got to carry the '38' set!' I said to him, 'Sling it in the bloody canal, I don't want it!' because you know the radios had a huge aerial on them. You'd stand out a mile and the Germans would see these radio aerials moving along a big hedge, and they'd just drop down and fire at the bottom [of the aerial], *and they'd hit the radio operator. It was a dead giveaway.*

We took up a defensive position in the area that we'd captured.

On board Glider 93, Doctor John Vaughan had been knocked unconscious in the heavy landing:

The first impression made upon my returning consciousness was the sound of light automatic fire. The initial feeling that I was abed in the Officer's Mess at Bulford was quickly replaced by the harsh and disturbing realization that the time for leisurely discussion was over and this was it, and furthermore, that I was actually in a locality bristling with offensively disposed Germans.

I then heard the sound of horrible groans as I sat up and rubbed what appeared to be mud from my eyes. I had actually been lying face downwards on marshy ground. I remember next finding myself back in the glider trying to get a man out. He was, however, hopelessly tangled up in the wreckage and after giving him a shot of morphia from a syrette which I had automatically and half-consciously retrieved from a side pocket containing a packet of these pain killers, and attempting to reassure him by promising to go and find a stretcher-bearer. I then staggered off in search of my medical orderlies, pursued in spite of the injection by those frightful groans which I shall remember as long as I live. I was sufficiently clear-headed by this time to note that we had landed close behind the second glider and in front of that I could see the nose of the first glider buried in the barbed wire of the bunker in front of the anti-tank gun on the east side of the bridge.

At the bridge I found dead and dying lying about, but there was John Howard standing in a trench near the pillbox, now his Command Post, issuing orders in every direction and obviously well pleased with the situation. He was gratified to see his MO back on the job having feared the worst, and greeted me warmly, offering me a swig from his whisky flask. I was staggering about, so I'm told, and was clearly not fully recovered from that blow on the head sustained during the landing. He looked at me doubtfully for a moment – I was also covered from head to foot in mud of offensive odour absorbed from the marshy ground around the glider – and then told me to go and find Den Brotheridge . . . I moved off straight up the road to the T-Junction and still uncertain as to my whereabouts. Frantic shouts of 'Come back, Doctor, people wearing the

*wrong uniform up there' made me turn back. I found Den
lying near a low stone wall at the west end of the café. He
was looking at the stars, bewilderment on his face and a
bullet hole in the middle of his neck below the chin. I got the
stretcher bearers to help me to carry him to the RAP.*[19]

Lieutenant Smith:

Lieutenant Ian Macdonald

*I took over Brotheridge's platoon and put them in a defen-
sive position round the far end of the bridge . . . and gathered
what was left of my platoon, because of my platoon, only
seven or eight of them were able to get out of that crash. Although they weren't badly
hurt, they were very, very shocked and bruised. One man was killed . . . I put them in
together with Brotheridge's platoon. Then I went back to the other side of the bridge only
to be told that David Wood's platoon were leaderless because he'd been shot through the
legs, and also his sergeant.*

Major Howard decided that it was time to bring one of the Orne Bridge platoons
over to the Canal Bridge. Major Howard:

*In our training, although every platoon was prepared to do any other job, the two 'B'
Company platoons were more trained to do the fighting patrol jobs out beyond the Canal
Bridge than my own platoons . . . Fox was told to come across for the fighting patrol job
that he'd trained to do.*

*And so Godbold, having cleaned up the inner defences and made quite sure there was
nobody left there, I issued him orders to go through Smith's platoon before Fox got there
to clear these houses. And at the same time the Liaison Officer, Ian Macdonald, the parachutist who had landed with us, having got the picture from me first-hand, went off to
cross the River Bridge and to report immediately to where the 7th Para Battalion RV
was to be. Now this is all happening before the Para drop of course, due half an hour
after we landed at 0050 hours. I was quite happy that he'd got the full story and would
give it to Colonel Pine-Coffin as soon as they met up. I watched Macdonald steal away
into the night and as I did so, two stretcher bearers came past carrying Den Brotheridge
to the CCP. They told me he was still unconscious. I bent over and felt for his pulse and
tried speaking to him, but Den was mercifully completely insensible, although still alive.
I watched them carry him away with a lump in my throat.*

Claude Godbold took 5 Section, 24 Platoon across the Canal Bridge and moved
towards the *Café Picot*. Lance Corporal Arthur Roberts:

*I see something move . . . shouted out the password, my Bren gunner turned round and
shouted and let fly and I let fly and all. But we didn't bother to go down and see who it
was, a German or a Frenchman, well you couldn't, it was asking for trouble. Your job
was to stay alive as long as you could.*

The casualty was actually Louis Picot himself. Nobby Clark:

He came and stuck his nose out to see what was happening. He probably didn't answer a challenge or something like that. I was laying against the railings of the house where he was. He was in a nightdress and if I remember rightly he had some sort of nightcap on his head and he was laid sprawled out in his garden. I actually saw him falling over.

In the house behind *La Chaumiere*, the Niepceron family heard a bang on the door. René Niepceron:

My father opened the door slightly, when a booted foot jammed itself into the door. I saw from my bed the muzzle of a Sten gun, so I hid under my blankets. I heard English. We thought maybe they were Boches disguised. Then the soldier entered, he had a blackened face, and gave me some Players cigarettes and chewing gum. I was hesitant, but got dressed in a hurry to go and see outside. Another surprise was to find a body with a hole in the forehead laying there. It was Monsieur Sohier, his blood still running into the gutter. Also his mate, Delaunay who was on duty; also Monsieur Picot the owner of the Bistro opposite the Café Gondrée.

Seventy-four year-old Alexandre Sohier was another of the *Hilfsgendarmerie.* Godbold's section then took up position further along the towpath, where another path led up to Le Port.

La Chaumiere

Having marched in regimental order, Lieutenant Fox's platoon arrived from the Orne and met Major Howard:

I sent them over the Canal Bridge to form a fighting patrol out beyond the perimeter defences facing west, in order to detect any enemy reconnaissance parties, or to stop any enemy forming up to counter-attack.

However, they did not have a PIAT. Dennis Fox:

On the way I would be passing Sandy Smith's platoon . . . so I was to pick up Sandy Smith's as I went. I had a chance to speak to Sandy then, who had been wounded in the foot or the leg, or something like that, and off we went up the road, Sergeant Thornton leading this time.

The Oxf and Bucks settled into their positions to await the arrival of either the Germans or the 7th Parachute Battalion. Major Howard:

The operation had been completed much quicker than we expected and in fact, much easier. They really had been caught by surprise.

Sergeant 'Wagger' Thornton

Chapter Seven

Arrival of
5 Parachute Brigade

Simultaneously with the bridge operations, Brigadier Poett and his Command Post Party had jumped at 0020 hours with the Pathfinders for DZ 'N'. Being the first to jump from the aircraft meant that Poett had the problem of opening the doors in the floor of the cramped Albemarle, but having done that the aircraft crossed the coast at 400 feet. Nigel Poett:

We went straight over the Merville Battery . . . and we expected to be shot at, but we weren't.

The red light came on, 'prepare to jump', then green, 'jump', and I was out in the night air and almost immediately, in fact some twenty seconds, a big bump. I had arrived safely on the soil of France.

It was all much too quick. I had done none of the things I ought to have done such as identifying Ranville Church, or pulling on my lift webs to get a good landing, but I was down and I had not landed on top of one of Rommel's asparagus, anti-airlanding poles set to catch us.

I had no idea where I was. I looked round and I couldn't see a thing because I was in a bit of a hollow. I could see the exhaust of the aircraft disappearing and I knew that it would be going over Ranville. I knew my direction therefore. All was black and still, not a shot had been fired.

While looking around for signs of the enemy, he got out of his parachute harness and almost immediately heard the sounds of fighting to the west. Knowing that it must be coming from the bridges, it confirmed his thoughts on the direction to take.[1]

The Brigadier's temporary interpreter and for now also his 'bodyguard', Sergeant Fraser Edwards of 317 Airborne Security Section, jumped last:

When it was time to jump, out we went and we must have been flying very low because I swung forward, back and forward and hit the ground. There was no wind. I immediately stood up and it was a cornfield, I couldn't really see where we were. I got my Sten gun and I had a pistol as well, a Colt 45. I loaded them sitting down (I took off

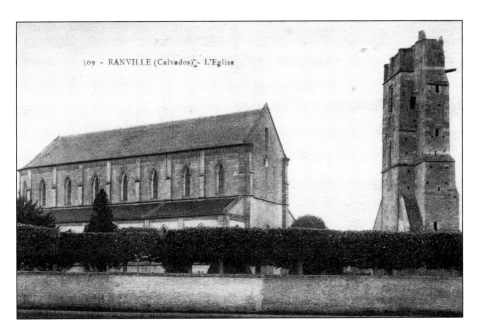

The distinctive Ranville Church with its separate tower

the parachute) and then I had noted the direction that the planes had gone. The instructions were to go to the road from Sallenelles, that is as we were coming down, facing Ranville, if you turned right you'd land on the road between Sallenelles and down to the bridges. So that was what I did, cautiously creeping, bent double until I came to the road. Brigadier Poett was Number One and so he had been further to the north. I hung around at the roadside until he came along. It was probably five or ten minutes.

Poett had spent a short while looking unsuccessfully for other members of the stick and then headed for the bridges:

I would have liked to have found my wireless operator and set, but it was more important to get to the bridges at once. The RV for all my stick was the River Bridge and my wireless operator should meet me there later. I now had some 1200 yards to go across country, typical agricultural land, much of it standing crops, but several roads to cross and it was very dark.
Sure enough I came across one of my men and he and I set off in the same direction.[2]

Also jumping with the DZ 'N' Pathfinders was the 7th Battalion contingent led by Lieutenant Rogers whose task was to rally the main body of the Light Infantry towards the RV. For this purpose he carried an Aldis lamp with a green filter. Jim Moran of 'B' Company had the job of setting up one of the EUREKA beacons:

I was going out at Number Ten which meant I had to wear the intercom and pass on the orders relayed from the navigator, ie 'RUNNING IN', 'RED ON', 'GREEN ON!' Everything went well until we approached the DZ and I realized that after the order 'RUNNING IN', I only had ten seconds to remove the intercom and put on my helmet. Unfortunately, during the rush to take off the intercom, I got the flex tangled up with my kitbag which was fastened to my right leg, and by the time I had cleared the tangled lead, the navigator had popped his head down to see that we were all clear, I realized we must have cleared the DZ. So I signalled for the pilot to do another run-in which he did and he dropped me in the middle of a cornfield.

I crouched on my knees for several minutes to get my bearings. It was very quiet until I heard the noise of someone coming towards me through the corn. I realized all the weapons I had been carrying were in the kitbag, which had broken from my belt during the drop, and all I had was my fighting knife. The corn parted and I jumped to my feet and found myself facing the officer who had dropped with my stick.

Moran then began searching for his kitbag containing the EUREKA beacon.

The two sticks of the 22nd Independent Parachute Company with the task of setting out navigational aids on DZ 'N' were led by Captain I. Tait and Lieutenant M. Moore. These landed across the south-eastern edge of the DZ and immediately began their work.[3]

Brigadier Poett and Fraser Edwards had continued their journey to the Orne Bridge. Nigel Poett:

You don't move as fast at night, even on an ordinary night, as you do in the day when you can see where you're putting your foot. You're crossing ditches and it takes a bit of time and I was getting very anxious about the time factor.

We saw no one. All I did know was that the people guarding the bridge and possibly the people who had been pushed off the bridge, would be round about. Sporadic shooting and explosions were continuing and I didn't know whether the bridges were in enemy hands or ours.

Soldiers can be rather trigger happy about men approaching their posts at night. Almost at once however, I identified our own men. The password was exchanged. I was soon with Lieutenant 'Tod' Sweeney who recorded the time as 0052 hours . . . They were naturally very thrilled with their achievement and were busy organizing their defences. They told me that John Howard's assault on the Canal Bridge had gone equally well and that he was established on both sides of the canal.

As I entered the bridge area I heard the roar of aircraft behind me, a comforting sound in the night sky. It was the main body of my Brigade beginning to come into the DZ I had just left.

Major Howard:

Bombers had been crossing the coast of course all the time, going off on various missions, the programme that night was as usual . . . stepped up quite a bit of course, but we'd come over amidst all those bombers. And the time of the Para drop at ten minutes to one, we heard all these bombers coming in low, that was the difference, the others were high, these were low, and we knew where the Dropping Zones were, and we had a first-class view of them dropping from about five hundred, as we thought, feet, and the air absolutely full of parachutes.

We saw these searchlights coming up and lighting up the chutes, and there was a bit of firing going. You could see tracer bullets going up into the air as they came down to the ground and no doubt shooting up some of the Paras before they even hit the ground. But it really was an inspiring sight and above all, it meant that we were not alone.

*

Lieutenant Rogers had not been able to locate the 7th Battalion RV in time for the drop, and therefore decided to rally the men from where he was by flashing his Aldis lamp and, once formed up, search for the RV. To compound matters, Jim Moran had not managed to find his kitbag containing the EUREKA beacon.

The Stirlings carrying the 7th Battalion duly began their run-in to the DZ. Lieutenant Richard Todd was jumping with a kitbag on each leg. The one on his right leg contained a collapsible boat, and that attached to the other, on a twenty-foot line, held various pieces of equipment:

Lieutenants Richard Todd
and Anton Bowler

My own batman couldn't come with me because he'd had a foot problem . . . I had the Padre's batman! I needed help because jumping from a Stirling was a great big coffin shaped aperture towards the tail, which you straddled, and I didn't have a hand to hold on, I was having to hold my kitbags to my legs. So when we started to take evasive action I was bloody nearly falling out, the Padre's batman behind me, hanging on to me.

It so happened that, and certainly not by choice, I was Number One of the first aircraft, which meant I was on the ground before anyone else, a slightly lonely prospect.

Lieutenant David Hunter, 3 Platoon, 'A' Company:

Anti-aircraft flak exploded around us causing the plane to shudder. The red light went on in the plane. This was the signal to get ready to jump. Each man had to check the man in front was properly hooked up to the static line. We had to be dropped at 500 feet so that we didn't drift off the DZ and we landed fairly close together. It must have been a daunting task for the pilot to fly slowly at such a low height through the anti-aircraft fire.

Finally the green light came on and one after another we plunged through the large hole in the floor of the plane. The RAF despatcher was at hand to urge us on and get us out as quickly as possible after each other. As I jumped I felt the sudden swish of the plane's slipstream and before I had time to panic, the sudden tug on my shoulders as my chute opened. It wasn't the WAAF's underwear after all! As I floated down I could briefly admire the view, and quite dramatic it was as lines of red tracer bullets shot through the darkness criss-crossing in different directions. Beautiful it was too, if you could forget these were bullets fired with deadly intent and you were one of the targets. I landed in a ploughed field without mishap. I was on foreign soil for the first time in my life.

As Colonel Pine-Coffin made his jump he was also amazed by the sheer amount of flak:

The German uses tracer ammunition considerably and the sight of this criss-crossing over the ground presented a rather pretty picture to the descending parachutist. The jump was made from 300 feet and in some cases from considerably lower, so there was only about ten seconds in which to admire the display before it became much too personal to be appreciated.

He landed on a road, causing him to bruise a heel, and subsequently became the first man to rally to the green light of Lieutenant Roger's Aldis lamp.[4] Captain Vere Hodge, the FOB officer, jumped from the same aircraft:

Our plane was caught in searchlights before we dropped, and there was a good deal of tracer flying about. When my parachute opened, I looked around, quite a lot was happening. I saw one parachute on fire and bullets started coming my way. I don't remember landing. I must have been knocked out for a few seconds because I found

110

myself being dragged along the ground, the canopy being still filled with the stiff breeze. I caught the rigging lines, pulled them, collapsed the canopy, twisted the quick-release box on my chest and threw off the harness. I had lost my helmet, surprising, as it was firmly strapped on with chin-piece as well as strap. I put on my red beret. I found later that my dagger, strapped in its leather scabbard on my right leg, had pierced the leather and my trousers and made a small but annoying hole in my leg.

There was no-one near me, but I sussed out where I thought I was, and made towards what I hoped would be the pre-arranged Rendezvous for my party, along with part of 7 Para.

One of his colleagues was RN Telegraphist Wilf Fortune:

As we stood up prior to jumping into the darkness, I well remember the wee chap in front of me. The stretcher tied to his leg was taller than him! He had a Red Cross

Wilf Fortune, Alex Boomer, Francis Vere-Hodge and Telegraphist KF Moles *(IWM B5863)*

armband. He told me his reason for being there with us. I had great admiration for that man, he was a conscientious objector who wanted to help the injured soldier. Qualified for his wings too. A very brave lad.

However, red on, green on, and out into the night.

I remember landing in a cornfield, releasing the 'chute and looking for the light.

I started to run for the array of bloody lights and heard this rustle in the cornfield behind me. Thought I was being chased, whipped round with my .38 revolver in hand, to find my sodding gas cape had come away from my webbing. Relief and calmness beyond belief!

Phillip Crofts, 5 Platoon, 'B' Company:

As soon as I jumped out the plane, or fell out the plane, my chute opened, the ack-ack was coming up. The idea just with all kitbags, when you're airborne, you put your right hand through the sleeve to slow the kitbag down as it goes down, with the left hand you pull the quick release. I pulled the quick release and the kitbag was so heavy, possibly the occasion as well, anticipation, nervousness, being fired at, the kitbag just broke away on the rope that attached it to my harness, and the rope was as thick as my fore finger. It usually hangs twenty or thirty feet below you . . . We had a pair of silk gloves and a pair of woollen gloves to stop the friction . . . All I could see was a white painted kitbag vanishing below me.

Just before jumping, Lieutenant Archdale, commanding the Mortar Platoon, threw out the stuffed moosehead 'liberated' in Exeter. It was intended to 'Put the fear of God into any German it hit!':

We weren't over the coast more than a minute or two. Then out we went. I glided across the river, for one moment I thought I was going to land in it . . . I landed almost on the east bank of the river, about a mile down the river from the bridges. I was jolly lucky that I didn't go in the river actually. I rather expected the Germans to be shooting at me as I landed but in fact found myself standing quite peacefully with my feet on French soil. 'Bloody hell, I'm in France!'

Ron Perry was on the same aircraft:

The chap in front of me was Ray Dye and the chap in front of him was Percy Fear. The plane seemed to be diving. I saw 'Pokey' Dye spent over as a starfish as he jumped. There was red and green tracer criss-crossing. The air seemed to be full of this. So when I went out I saw these two in front of me silhouetted against this criss-cross. And almost immediately, something I thought hit me, both on my back and one of my hands, startled me. I must have been at a pretty low height . . . I had a momentary look at the plane going on, didn't see any other planes, just that one, didn't recognize anything actually. I was much more concerned with the fact that as I was dropping, this machine-gun fire was being directed towards what I thought was me personally. This tracer was running through the edge of the parachute . . .

there were little flames flickering off of my parachute. My parachute was actually, to that extent, aflame. That sort of attracted attention.[5]

Just before reaching the ground his chute caught on some telephone wires and he landed in deep ditch amongst a mixture of bushes and tall nettles that stung his face:

Despite the camouflage, I could feel my face burning . . . My feet didn't go to the bottom of this [ditch], I was sort of suspended and that took me a little while really to get out of the chute.

The drop of signaller Bill Le Chaminant was another that did not go according to plan:

I lost my kitbag off my foot, wireless set, weapons, everything went down. The rope broke, snapped off with the pressure, the slipstream and that. I saw a plane cut a parachute and the occupant in half. It went right through his parachute, caught him up and dragged him up to the wing tip and snapped him off. The chap went down and landed and came up in flames after, because he was carrying phosphorous bombs.

Le Chaminant landed in the middle of a cornfield.[6]

Lance Corporal Eddie Gurney, a sniper in 'A' Company, was carrying an inflatable rubber dinghy on his right leg:

I heard the crack of the chute developing, slowing my descent. I grabbed the rope holding the kitbag on my leg and pulled the quick release, then lowered it to its full length. I had a quick look round, noting the pretty patterns made by the searchlights and tracer bullets. Then in the distance I saw a church with a detached tower silhouetted against the lighted background, which I instantly recognized as Ranville Church. I heard a thump as my kit-bag hit the ground. Then for a full minute I was violently sick from the fear and the release of tension.

'Stand with your back to the church and run forward and slightly left. There you will find a road leading to the bridges.' These words were imprinted in my brain and I blindly followed instructions.

Ron Follett, Anti-Tank Platoon, HQ Company:

I missed my landing and hit the ground with an awful thump. We were landing in a cornfield and I'd gone to land on top of the corn. I thought that's where the land was, it looked solid in the moonlight, but in effect I had another three or four feet to go! I thought 'That's a great start!'

I gathered what kit I could up together. My PIAT had had a heck of a smack and was bent. It had a metal guide which the bomb rested in and that was all bent so it was of no use at all.

I joined up with some Royal Engineers. I found some 7th Battalion people, including the second-in-command. We gradually got more together.

Captain Jim Webber, 2i/c, 'A' Company:

I landed in the right place on the DZ. Our CO had decided that everyone should keep their jumping jackets on after landing. Usually we discarded them. We all had a large green triangle painted on the back as a recognition sign; officers and sergeants had a circle painted around the triangle, a lovely aiming mark!

Bob Tanner, 'B' Company:

I didn't know where I was, apart from somewhere in Normandy. Although it was a few minutes before I located our chaps, it seemed like eternity. I heard bugles going, then a noise, and I froze for a second or two. Was it ours or theirs? If theirs, I had to shoot them. Would I be able to do it? I cocked my rifle in readiness and it seemed to me that the sound was deafening, until a good old Cockney voice bawled out, 'What bleedin' unit are you in?' I can't explain the relief on hearing that voice.

In spite of having passwords, much of the initial contact was made in this 'colourful' language.

Lieutenant Ted Pool, 5 Platoon, 'B' Company:

I was all right because as soon as my parachute developed there was a gun flash or something and I saw the separate towers of the Ranville Church. We'd been frightfully well briefed. I knew exactly where I was when I landed. I put this bloody great sack on my shoulder and started trying to run towards the RV.

Phillip Crofts also landed on the DZ, but without his kitbag or weapon:

The first thing I wanted to do was to find a weapon. They had good methods of providing secondary weapons to people like myself. Underneath the planes they carried containers and in the middle of the stick they would have a pause. The plane would release a number of containers, like giant torpedoes, that were stuffed with weapons, ammunition, all the paraphernalia of war. All had battalion markings on them. When they came down, on the 7th Battalion they had a sail come up, green. Being a night drop you would never see a green sail, but in addition to this they had a green light on the top of the sail, a triangular sail. I saw a green light, and with all the bugle playing and fire that's going on, my one concern was to get to this green light to get a weapon. I managed to get a rifle and re-arm myself.

Major Nigel Taylor, commanding 'A' Company, had had a very good landing:

Phillip Crofts

114

I got rid of my 'chute. Got my Sten gun out, put a magazine on it and started to look round. There was practically no firing at all, absolutely bugger all. There was a little light flak going up, this multi-coloured stuff and there was also a big gun firing from somewhere over in the west. I looked round and there were one or two chaps came towards me and we had a small group of us. I didn't know where the hell we were.

You come down in your parachute. You say, 'That's it, there's the Orne, I've got to make for there.' You hit the ground, you roll over twice say, pick yourself up and you can't see the Orne then. You don't know which way you were facing when you came down!

He recounted to himself the three things to look for that had been explained at the briefing:

First of all, the church tower at Ranville . . . because it's built separate from the church. 'You see that, you know you're facing south, turn right and run till you hit the road. Then you'll see the flashing light of the Reconnaissance Officer and hear a bugle sounding.' That was number one. Number two was the direction of the moon, which was in the west. 'Run towards that and you'll hit the road.' The third was the line of flight of all these aircraft, all coming in north to south. 'Stand with your back to the line of flight, turn right, run for the road.' I looked for Ranville Church but it was over the brow of a hill for me, so I couldn't see that. Then I looked for the moon and all up around Cherbourg there were searchlights up, and there was a certain amount of cloud and it was impossible to tell what was the moon shining through thin cloud and what was the searchlights shining on the cloud. That was two gone. So then I looked up to see the line of flight of the aircraft and over that Dropping Zone there were aircraft flying in every bloody direction.

All members of the Brigade were now performing their jumps. Major Guy Radmore, 5 Parachute Brigade Signals:

I helped the aircrew lift up the hatch in the floor of this Stirling. I distinctly remember seeing the surf on the beach as we passed over the Normandy coast. And then the green light came on and I shoved my bicycle out and jumped out. I think we were at about 500 feet. I don't believe we were in the air for more than about thirty to forty seconds because the parachute had opened and I had let my kitbag down. I also carried a walking stick always on jumps which I had on another bit of string because a walking stick was useful at night, and also carrying big loads it was handy for easing the shoulders a bit.

I landed in this cornfield, didn't know where I was. There were aircraft going all over and flak coming up, and I remember thinking 'I don't think I can ever shoot a pheasant again. I know what they feel like!' Not that they were shooting at me but there were things everywhere. There seemed to be total confusion and total elation on the ground. Tremendous boost to morale to everyone. 'We're here at last'.

Harry Leach, 5 Parachute Brigade Signals:

When I came out you could smell flak, smell the cordite. I landed in a tree and my chute collapsed and I sort of fell down and landed on the edge of a ditch with trees behind me and a very narrow, small lane, obviously not on the Dropping Zone. I think I was knocked out for a few seconds or a minute or so. I came to and gradually met Sergeant Bass, Bob Milton who was our lance corporal, Bert Shea and one or two others. We had no idea where we were. They told us at briefing, if you're lost, look up and the aircraft will be flying north to south. Looking up there were four norths, four souths, four easts and four wests and all points in between!

Sergeant 'Taffy' Lawler, 13th Parachute Battalion:

Harry Leach

When the green light came on, Number One jumped, followed by the remainder up to Ten, a Bren Number One carrying a very heavy kit bag. He fell across the door, preventing anyone from jumping. The only one who could help him to his feet was the RAF aircrew despatcher. This took some considerable time, during which the Dakota circled the DZ three times before I could jump. The first thing I knew when I was airborne was that my rifle, kit and shovel had fallen away from me. I landed in a cornfield and lay quite still for a moment, listening. In the distance I could hear the sound of battle, and guessed it must be the DZ. I got rid of my chute, and with my fighting knife in one hand and a grenade in the other, I made for the RV.[7]

Captain Nobby Clark, 2i/c, 'C' Company, 13th Battalion:

I was coming down into what seemed to be a large wood containing many clearings. Suddenly I was down. The trees of which the wood was composed were sufficient to subdue the wind so that the canopy of my chute subsided gently on the ground – much more gently than I had done. Planes were droning overhead. Away to the north I could hear gunfire of some sort. I remained lying down while I released the parachute harness and divested myself of the awkward enveloping jumping jacket.

It was perhaps as well that I did so. I felt a sudden obligation to cease struggling like a rabbit in a snare so that I could listen and observe. I had landed in a small clearing surrounded by, as far as I could see in the intermittent moonlight, orchards, which indeed they were. I was roughly in the centre of a field some fifty yards square. The cause of my sudden concern was that I thought I heard voices. A few seconds of absolute stillness on my part confirmed the fact. I could hear voices from just inside the orchard on the south side. Now came the crucial question, 'English or German?' I had not long to wait the answer. Three figures emerged through the hedge on the south side of my clearing. They were muttering together, but strain as I might I could not make out one syllable of their conversation. Then in that strangely capricious way that a breeze has of changing direction, it brought me their scent.

He recognized the odour, a cross between plasticine and a cheap brand of scented soap. He had smelt it on captured German uniforms during a training course the previous year:

*I think that they saw nothing although their suspicions were aroused. They may possibly have seen the flash of my arm as it described an arc in their general direction to release from my hand the '36' grenade which I dare not hold any longer since the fuse had been struck for ground before it exploded. Although I say it myself, it was a good throw. I didn't wait to see the result, but on the explosion I was up on my feet and running like a hare in the direction I judged north-west to be. After about a minute I pulled up, partly through want of breath but also, having managed to subdue my feeling of panic, to say to myself aloud, I believe, 'You ******* brave paratrooper.'*

I set off in the general direction in which I believed the RV to be, and as far as I could see I was alone in an uninhabited part of the Calvados region of Normandy. As I plodded on, suddenly from way ahead in the direction I was going came a sound as welcome as any I had ever heard, a hunting horn. It was fainter and further away that I expected to be. 'Dit-dah-dit-dit', the morse letter 'L', for Lancashire and Luard.

Captain David Tibbs, 3 Section, 225 Field (Para) Ambulance:

Just before we jumped, another plane, I was jumping Number One so I saw it very clearly, swept across our path and both planes veered heavily to one side to avoid hitting. It must have been just a few hundred feet apart. Then we went into the turbulence of this plane and our plane went all over the place but survived it all, but all my men were thrown to the floor. I looked back to my horror and saw all nineteen men behind me were wallowing on the floor struggling to get up, and at that moment the green light came on to jump. I realized there was nothing I could do so I just jumped straight away.

Holding each side of the doorway had prevented him from falling to the floor. The 12th Parachute Battalion was also jumping from Stirlings. Captain John Sim, 2i/c 'C' Company:

We had no seats. We had an aperture at the stern end of the fuselage with a couple of doors that swung open and attached to the sides of the fuselage. So you had an aperture, just a long shaped aperture about twice the size of a grave! It was easy. We queued up and when the time came, just dropped out. It was rather a nice drop because you dropped out with the slipstream behind you, so it was like going out on a chute, rather than going out of a side door as you would in a Dakota, where you had to push yourself out hard because of the slipstream of the engines.

I found myself peacefully floating down without any shooting, onto a big field where

I landed without any difficulty, next door to a horse. I got out of my harness and I was aware of other soldiers landing round me, but it didn't feel as if I'd landed in France and was involved in a live war. It was like one of our many night drops on Salisbury Plain.

Private Frank Gleeson, 'C' Company:

I had 200 rounds of rifle ammunition strapped around my chest and waist. But as I looked at my wrist watch to see if we were late, I noted that it was seven minutes past one o'clock, the lateness would have made no difference at all. Suddenly an anti-aircraft shell exploded at the side of the Stirling and I was thrown out sideways as the aircraft lurched. I lost my rifle clasped to my chest and landed alone with my only weapon: the parachute fighting knife.

Eric Barley

Private Eric Barley's landing was fine, although rather too close to the enemy:

I could hear Germans shouting orders which I understood to be instructions for the mortars to bomb the Dropping Zone.

After getting out of my parachute and collecting my equipment from the kitbag which was attached to me by a piece of rope, I took a piece of soil and squeezed it in my hand and thought 'This is France.'

Lieutenant Ellis 'Dixie' Dean, OC MMG Platoon, 13th Parachute Battalion, was jumping with the 12th Battalion:

My chute developed normally and as my body swung into the vertical I looked around. The first thing to catch my eye away to the right were two silver ribbons threading their way through the dark earth, and these I assumed were the River Orne and the ship canal running parallel together. That was good, I was over the correct Dropping Zone. To my front, but some distance away, numbers of red and orange balls were shooting up into the sky. They left the ground at speed but as they rose, slowed down and then fizzled out, and this display I reasoned was the ack-ack defences of Caen. I stared at them for too long because when I finally looked down, much to my horror it seemed I was destined to land in one of the orchards bordering the eastern side of the DZ. Away to the right I could see open fields of where I ought to be landing, so I started to pull down on my lift webs, hoping to steer clear of the trees, and it seemed at first I was going to be lucky, but finally decided I wasn't going to make it and prepared myself for a tree landing.

I had never made such a landing and had last carried out the drill on the Basic Parachute Course at Ringway in August 1942, but I remembered what to do – head down on the chest, arms crossed in front of it, and knees raised to protect my marriage prospects (as my RAF instructor delicately described that vital part of the male anatomy). Down I came, crashing through branches and foliage without as much as a scratch or bruise, but when I stopped falling and opened my eyes, I was completely enclosed by greenery. I felt around for a branch to get my feet on, but found none, so I turned the quick release on the parachute harness, gave it a bang, the straps flew apart and my Sten, which was broken into three parts, and threaded under them, fell to the ground. I slid out of the harness, keeping a tight grip on it, lowered myself to the end of the leg straps, and I hadn't reached the ground and was still enclosed in the foliage. I let go of the webbing harness and dropped, I am certain, all of twelve inches to the soil of Normandy, making in the process, the very thing which on the Basic Parachute Course, we had been warned we must never attempt, a stand-up landing.[8]

Private Ken Lang of the MMG Platoon jumped from the same Stirling:

The green light came on and of course they were all jumping. The light was where you could see it if you looked up, but we were more interested in the hole in the floor . . . Once they start jumping, you're not looking anywhere, you're not looking away from the hole . . . I was jumping after the containers . . . so after the Number Ten had gone I had to wait a few seconds before I jumped. No sooner had my parachute opened than I hit the ground. The containers were close to me when I got out of my chute.

Also jumping with the 12th Battalion was the eight-man Recce Party of the 4th Airlanding Anti-Tank Battery. Sergeant George Brownlee:

Suddenly you're stepping on nothing, you're out, and you're doing about 130 miles an hour and of course for a split, split second, you're sitting on the slipstream and it hits you. And then 'crack', you see your parachute open in front of you and you swing down under it. And first thing, your hands go up check rigging lines. No, you're not twisted or anything like that because sometimes if you went out awkwardly the wind caught you and you might get twisted which would make it awkward landing.

I was looking down, there was a bit of shrapnel flying around, but nothing very serious, nothing very near us because they were still following the aircraft. I'm looking down, I thought 'That's a track' and then as I got down I thought 'Oh, there are trees immediately there', and as I got lower 'That is not a track, that is a stone wall and I'm going straight for it, and if I don't land this side of it, I've got to land in the trees.' Kitbag hits the deck, get my feet up and I'm over this wall and down. Good old solid earth.

Everywhere, the Paras were now attempting to make their way towards their respective RVs. Lieutenant Archdale, OC Mortar Platoon, 7th Battalion:

I looked about for more of my stick; there was a certain amount of firing and after wandering round and being chased by a bull in a farmyard, made off westwards in the direction of the bridges. This direction I judged from the extra firing, my only guide to my position.

119

Sergeant Bill French had jumped from the same plane as Ron Perry without any problems, except on landing, he found that he was not on the DZ:

When I got myself together and off the ground, I picked up one of my mates and eventually we found another one. There was just three of us had got together. The first one I found was . . . Eric Truman. I said, 'Eric, we're too far south, so we'd better go for the north. We'd been flying inland too long.' We hadn't been on the ground ten minutes when Jerry opened fire on us. We heard a tank go along the road and he must have seen us, he opened fire on us, but none of us was hit and we found a sunken road. We got into this sunken road and we met another lad . . . Reg Bull. Then we saw someone walking up this sunken road towards us. We asked him for the password and he said, 'Oh bloody hell, I've forgotten it.' It was our platoon commander, so we soon put him in his place!

That platoon commander was Lieutenant Archdale. Bill French:

We got into a little huddle and had a chat and we walked down the sunken road . . . We found a little place where we could spread the maps and have a look. One of the men got out his gas cape. I got under the gas cape with a torch to look at the map, so we would not show any light. We pinpointed almost exactly where we were. We crossed another sunken road and saw a lot of lights in a field, container lights. Went and had a good look around these containers. Couldn't find our own, so we got back on the road.

Having landed in an overgrown ditch Ron Perry had had great difficulty trying to extricate himself:

I was then aware that coming across a sort of open area . . . were three or four figures. Someone opened up on them with a machine gun. They dropped down and I've no idea what happened to them. My guess is that they were probably Germans and they got in the way of one of our Bren guns.

Anyway, I sorted myself out very quietly . . . decided to prime a grenade, checked my rifle and laid it out, then became aware of a crashing in the hedgerow a little way further down and Bill French appeared. Soon after, Nick [Archdale] appeared followed by another bloke. We started to move out of this very gingerly. Then I saw Norman [Reynolds]. He'd hit the roof of a house on his way down, a building of some sort. I thought he'd been drinking! He was really concussed. He'd hit the roof and the chute had sort of flattened down but it didn't save him, he rolled down off the edge of the building. I think he must have hit something pretty hard because he was bleeding profusely.

Then I saw Freddie Fricker, he'd found two containers but they were in such a state that we couldn't get them open and then we had to move because we attracted attention.

Nick led the way . . . It was just a track, high trees either side. Suddenly a figure appeared ahead and he was a bloke from the 8th Battalion. He'd just got himself out of a tree. He joined in with us.

Norman Reynolds, Bill
Law and Ron Perry

*In a few hundred yards the [sunken] track terminated at the foot of the River
Bridge where the road ran westwards to the Canal Bridge. The battalion's call sign
was evident – a bugle call – an indication of the direction to take.*

Bill Law was a 3-inch mortar man of HQ Company:

*I landed in a tree. Being landed in a tree of course I got separated from everybody by
the time I got out of the tree. I was all on my lonesome. I finally went along a hedgerow
and I could hear one French person talking. I thought to myself 'I can enquire which
way to the bridge.' When I found out, it wasn't only a Frenchman but a German as
well. He shot me in the shoulder. It was a couple of really, spent bullets, I think from a
revolver. Anyway, it knocked me down but then as luck would have it, it must have
been somebody with a Bren gun close by who heard the shots and just fired through the
hedgerow. He either caught the German or the Frenchman.*

Colonel Pine-Coffin:

*The night was a poor one for parachuting as the moon was obscured. The wind was
strong too, but that didn't matter so much. Our first job was to form up quickly and for
this we needed a landmark. There were several we were looking for, but just one would
do. All one could see was other parachutists blundering about, lost as oneself.⁹*
    *The enemy had manned positions on the DZ itself and there was a good bit of MG
fire across the DZ which resulted in some casualties.*

Lieutenant Richard Todd:

*It was pretty dark and fortunately I landed intact on a large DZ which was raked at
the time by small arms fire. I checked on my whereabouts and decided where to go. I*

saw a sort of smudge in the moonlight of a wood . . . so I headed off into that very quickly.

I found a post, part of a small group, a dozen of us there, including the CO, Geoffrey Pine-Coffin.

Major Taylor had also found a few men:

I saw a small woodland not very far away so I said, 'Let's get in there and we'll be able to get a torch and a map and sort this lot out.' So we went over there and I got inside, and just on the edge of this wood, I met an officer of my battalion, and his job had been to drop half an hour before the rest of us with a bugler. He was to find the spot we were to rendezvous and he was to flash a light and the bugler was to sound off our Regimental call, the Somerset Light Infantry. He said, 'I've been looking for this damned Rendezvous for three-quarters of an hour and I can't find it, sir.' I said, 'Well you'd better come into this wood.' And inside, I met my CO, who had orientated himself perfectly on the way down, who also didn't know where the hell he was!

Lieutenant David Hunter:

In the darkness I could see none of my men near me. Until we got to the Battalion Rendezvous we were on our own. However, there was, fortunately, no evidence of enemy troops in the immediate vicinity, but you couldn't be sure. The 7th Battalion Pathfinder was Lieutenant John Rogers. I saw his green lamp flashing and eventually made contact with him. He told me that he was in the wrong place but he was able to direct me to the RV [sic], a small wood in a gully. Colonel Pine-Coffin and my Company Commander Major Nigel Taylor were already there.

The darkness made it extremely difficult to decide the direction of the RV. Colonel Pine-Coffin:

It was a most desperate feeling to know that one was so close to it but not to know in which direction it lay. Time was slipping by and the Coup de Main *party might well be in difficulties; everything could so easily be lost if the battalion did not arrive in time. It was impossible to pick up a landmark though, until a chance flare, dropped by one of the aircraft, illuminated the church at Ranville, with its most distinctive double tower, and thus provided the necessary clue.*

They checked their map against the church and the wood, and subsequently headed for the RV.

*

By 0115 hours Major Howard had completed his defensive arrangements at the Canal Bridge. 25 Platoon held the area around the *Café Gondrée* with some 'B' Company men of Corporal Stan Evans' section of 14 Platoon. Lieutenant Fox's 17 Platoon held the ground opposite. Beyond them a section of 24 Platoon was just along the canal bank. Lieutenant Smith remained in overall command of these parties. The fifteen sappers, having given the bridge the all clear, had moved to their pre-arranged assembly point outside the café to await further orders. The remainder of 24 Platoon held the eastern banks.

Initially, in the hope of contacting Brigadier Poett and then the 7th Parachute Battalion, Corporal Tappenden, beside the pillbox, had continued to transmit the success signal on his '38' set, pressing 'send' and then flicking the switch over to 'receive':

Ted 'Ham and Jam' Tappenden

I laid on that road for an hour, a solid hour, and all I was saying was 'Hello Four-Dog, Hello Four-Dog, Ham and Jam, Ham and Jam'. In the end I got so fed up with saying it I said, 'Hello Four-Dog, Hello Four-Dog, Ham and Jam, Ham and bloody Jam! Why the hell don't you answer?' What I didn't know was that they'd lost their wireless on their landing. Eventually, out of the blackness came a voice, 'Message received and understood.'

Brigadier Poett and Fraser Edwards had been at the River Bridge during the drop, but then moved on towards the canal. Major Howard:

The first thing of note that happened after the Para drop and the elation throughout the whole of the Company over that inspiring sight, was right out of the blue and he seemed to come out of the mist as it were, Brigadier Poett suddenly appeared right alongside my Command Post and the first thing that went through my mind, 'Somebody's going to get a bloody rocket from this on the bridge for not letting me know, either by runner or radio at least, that the Brigadier was in the Company area.'

Brigadier Poett:

He was surprised and a little put out as I walked unexpectedly into his position, but he was so thrilled with his success, and with my very warm congratulations that his platoon commander was quickly forgiven.
Howard told me his glider pilots had been magnificent.

They stood there, becoming a little anxious as the Germans, who had recovered somewhat from the initial shock of the assault, became a little more active. However, the Brigadier could not stay long. Major Howard:

After giving me a bit of reassurance and a pat on the back for the whole of the Company, he disappeared as silently as he'd arrived. But I did manage to get Tappenden on the radio to say, 'The Brigadier's coming back,' to old 'Tod' over on the other River Bridge at least. It was good to see the Brigadier there.

To the east, those who had dropped continued to make their way to the respective RVs. Wilf Fortune RN:

> *As I went to the Rendezvous I met Bombardier Hooper making his way toward Ranville. "Hello my chickadee", he said. That was dear old Humphrey, an ex-Cambridge rowing blue and a gent.*
>
> *I reached the Rendezvous. Captain Hodge and Alec* [Boomer] *had already arrived, and flopped down beside them, right into a cow pat. My lucky day I thought.*
>
> *Ted Eley arrived shortly afterwards, injured. He'd followed me out of the plane and his arm had caught in the rigging lines. These jerked his shoulder out and he was in pain.*

The RV for 5 Parachute Brigade HQ was the quarry used by the 12th Battalion.[10] Major Guy Radmore, Brigade Signals:

> *I met up with the Intelligence Officer, Maurice Dolden, and said, 'Maurice, where are we?' He said, 'I've no idea.' We came to a signpost, we'd by now got a few soldiers round us, and I said, 'Well on this exercise, let's cheat.' And he crawled on my shoulders and shone a torch along the signpost. And at that moment we heard the hunting horn so we knew roughly where we were.*
>
> *I heard a vehicle and told some chaps to get their grenades out, thought it was* [an] *armoured car, and it was these two sailors* [the two that had arrived at Fairford] *in a vehicle and I stopped them and I said, 'Get out. What are you doing?' They said, 'Well you see in the Navy, no-one taught us how to march so we bumped off these Germans and we're going to motor to the Rendezvous.' So I said, 'You're going to walk from now on!'*
>
> *We heard no sound of battle from the bridges . . . which was the whole point of our operation, and we had a bit of a discussion. We said, 'I wonder if we shouldn't gather these chaps up and go and have a go at the bridge.' 'Well General Gale said there'd be confusion, we'd better do what we are supposed to do,' which was to rendezvous in this quarry, which I suppose was half a mile from the outskirts of Ranville. So we went through the cornfield and found the quarry and the first man I saw there was Leonard Moseley of the Daily Sketch. He had his typewriter there. He said, 'I wondered when you were going to turn up!'*

Brigade Signaller Harry Leach had landed near a crossroads, found a few of his stick and then approached the road:

> *There was a little cottage on this corner with a low wall and an iron bath fence. I said to the lads, 'Get down behind the wall, I can speak enough French and if I drop flat when the door opens, shoot, don't argue because it'll be a German.' So I went to this door, knocked on it. I could hear voices inside, obviously one or two female voices so that was OK. The door opened and this old man dragged me in and my French was reasonable and I told him where we wanted to go. He understood that, he understood the bridge . . . He indicated the way down to Ranville but he kept saying don't go that*

way, 'Pas a gauche. Mitrailleuse.' Well I hadn't a clue what mitrailleuse was, so I went back to the lads and I said, 'He seems to be straightforward. There something down there called mitrailleuse.' Then out of the dark came a Colonel with a patrol. I don't know who he was. He said, 'You lads join us,' and they set off down the road to Le Pont Tournant, the River Bridge and Ranville. So 'Doodle' Bass, our sergeant, whispered to us, 'Drop back, I don't like the sound of what this old chap told us.' I now know what a mitrailleuse was when a machine gun opened up on this patrol.

Lieutenant 'Dixie' Dean of the 13th Battalion had lost his Sten on landing in a tree:

I searched all around where I had landed but found nothing and thought 'What a right Charlie I'm going to look, turning up at the RV without a personal weapon. Fortunately I had packed my torch in one of the ammunition pouches, so out it came, and flashing it around in the bottom of the hedgerow, collected my Sten, piece by piece. It was in one of the trees in the middle of a bocage type hedge surrounding an orchard, that I had landed. I was still enshrouded in the undergrowth but could tell from the noise of the planes flying over the DZ which side I wanted to be, and so I carefully pulled aside the branches and found there had been a silent listener to my thrashing about in the hedge. Only a few yards to my right stood a large white French cow staring in my direction with moon-like eyes. She was tethered to a stake in the grass verge of the cornfield of the Dropping Zone. Not many yards into the corn was a shadowy figure who as I approached, paused in hoisting a machine-gun tripod onto his shoulders, and greeted me. 'Hello sir' he said, so calmly and naturally you would have thought we were in the habit of meeting each other in this particular French cornfield at one o'clock in the morning. It was Lance Corporal Harold Turner (Regular soldiers with several years experience of skirmishing on the North-West Frontier take operational parachute jumps in their stride). He continued, 'I've just been telling that cow I've come to liberate her!'

Another member of his platoon, Lance Corporal Don Jones, had got down safely, but could not find any colleagues:

I hadn't gone very far [when] I saw someone, possibly I'd say a hundred yards from me. I whispered very loudly the password . . . and he didn't reply. As a machine gunner we only carried a Colt automatic as a self-protection . . . So as he didn't reply, I thought well he possibly could be a German. So got down on the floor and let fire at him, and he let fire at me. I think I got rid of about eight bullets and I think he must have got the same. Neither of us had hit one another, so he went his way and I went my way, and that was it!

Lieutenant Jack Watson, OC 3 Platoon, 'A' Company, 13th Parachute Battalion:

I landed at the north end of the DZ in an orchard. Everything was quiet and I thought I was miles away from Ranville, the battalion's objective. As I moved towards the RV, a wood north of the village, I heard loud and shrill the sound of a hunting horn, the

CO sounding 'L' for Lancashire, and the Company calls of 'A' for 'A' Company etc.

The 13th Battalion RV was a copse on the northern edge of Ranville, and marked by an amber light:

The DZ was a real bugger's muddle, with all three battalions of our Brigade and some sticks of the 8th Battalion who had been dropped on the wrong DZ, all mixed up. But the hunting horns sounded clearly and when I reached the RV the Company was about forty strong. Half an hour later, we were up to sixty. I was missing a section and a half and my platoon sergeant.

Captain David Tibbs, 225 Field (Para) Ambulance:

I landed within about thirty feet of where I had agreed with the pilot that he would hope the Number One, myself, would land. I could see the outline of an apple tree and then beyond it, others. I realized that I was almost certainly right by this orchard that he'd agreed would be the starting point for our stick. The next five managed to get out over the Dropping Zone.[11]

I had to trudge about a mile and a half to the church. I only encountered one other person who was walking across my way. We all had passwords to give each other, but by some mutual agreement neither of us took the chance of calling out . . . In complete silence I could dimly see him hustle by me. We both sort of agreed without any spoken word that we'd do anything about the other. I'm sure it was one of our parachutists making for a different rendezvous than myself. Although many hundreds of men had dropped in the last few minutes on to this Dropping Zone, I just didn't see anyone in the darkness.

In the Field Ambulance sections it was left to us to find our way off the DZ. So I identified a particular field with a very distinct hedge just outside Ranville itself. I'd agreed with my men that that's where we'd meet.

The 12th Battalion's chalk quarry RV was on the western edge of the DZ. Their rallying signals were a whistle and a red light. Lieutenant Phillip Burkinshaw, OC No 1 Platoon, 'A' Company:

I got down OK, had a fairly good landing, I couldn't get rid of the kitbag on my leg which was unfortunate but I don't think it did any damage to the kitbag or certainly not to my leg. I'd had ammunition in that and a wireless set and one or two other things . . . and then started to hump it towards the right direction luckily, more by luck than good judgement. We moved off towards the RV to a background chorus of sirens and a frenzied tolling of church bells coming from the Ranville direction.

Lieutenant Phillip Burkinshaw

He met another 12th Battalion man and after walking north for a while, they reached a copse that he recognized from an aerial photograph:

Being fairly certain that the chalk pit, the Battalion Rendezvous, was not too far up the road, we left the copse and headed in that direction, eventually meeting up en-route with other men from the battalion coming in from the stubble field. Shortly, we found the track leading down to the pit and there found the Company Commander, Major Ritchie and the CO Lieutenant Colonel Johnson.

Captain John Sim, 'C' Company:

It appeared to me that I had been dropped absolutely spot on, so I set off with two or three men, westwards, to rendezvous by a quarry, on the Cabourg to Caen road. When I got there our CO said the Adjutant hadn't arrived and sent me back to the DZ with a flash torch to guide everyone in.

Lieutenant 'Dixie' Dean, 13th Battalion, set off across the DZ with Lance Corporal Harold Turner. 'Dixie' Dean:

Together we pushed on through the corn. It was hard going for the crop was waist high and we soon caught up with Private Bill Price who had jumped Number Three and was carrying the Vickers itself. We headed in what I thought was the right direction, listening out for the long blasts on a whistle which were to serve as a guide. Just who was supposed to blow the whistle I never did know, but he certainly wasn't doing his job just then. As the three of us neared a line of bushes, I was challenged and asked for the password. One of the Pathfinder officers identified himself to me and asked which Battalion RV we were making for, and when I told him he informed me that we were much too close to the village of Ranville, and showed me the direction in which we should be going. We turned and started off again and shortly caught up with a sizeable body of men moving in the same direction, so we tagged along in the rear.

The column halted and the signal came from the front to kneel down. After several minutes of inactivity I decided to go and find out the cause of the hold-up. We had come to a track running across the DZ and now I knew exactly where we were. To arrive at the quarry, all we had to do was follow the track until it met the road, turn left for a few yards, and there was the RV on the opposite side of the road. I now found out there was a Major in charge of the party, but I did not recognize him. He was busy organizing small groups of men to make a dash across the track together. I knew they were moving towards the coast and I informed the Major of this fact. 'Who the hell are you?' he demanded, and when I replied, 'Lieutenant Dean of the 13th' I was told in no uncertain terms to go and fight my own war and let him get on with his.

Lieutenant Colonel
Alexander Johnson

127

I went back to the tail of the column, collected my two gunners, moved up to the track and hadn't gone far along it when the rallying call of long whistle blasts was heard. Within minutes we were turning into the quarry, where Colonel Johnson and Johnny Firth, his IO, stood on a little mound directing men to their respective Company locations. All the sub-units of HQ Company were to line the northern edge of the quarry, with the 13th machine gunners down near the river, but there were not many of the 12th present yet and we were the first of the platoon to arrive.

Chapter Eight

German Reaction
at the Bridges

With the bridges secured and the Paras down, Major Howard began to blow the 'Victory V' on his whistle:

I kept on blowing that and over the night air it must have carried for miles. Paras who perhaps landed alone in a tree or a bog or farmyard, alone and away from their own friends temporarily, could hear that whistle. It not only meant that the bridges had been captured intact but it also gave them an orientation.

However, the first arrivals at the Orne Bridge were not parachutists. Lieutenant Sweeney:

A patrol came up the path from the direction of Caen, up the towpath. They were challenged by the section on that side of the road and they shouted back something which sounded German and so the section opened fire and killed them all.[1]

Private Doug Allen, the medical orderly, was wounded in this exchange of fire. Five minutes later there was another incident. 'Tod' Sweeney:

Before we saw any of our own troops, we heard the grinding of gears and the noise of what sounded like a very, very heavy vehicle coming round the corner approaching from the east. We'd been warned of course to look out for tanks and I thought 'Here we go. This is the first tank attack.' I got everybody ready and round the corner came low, dimmed yellow lights and a grinding of gears and the sound of a track running. So I sent a message quickly to John over the air . . . that something was approaching from the east, and down the road came in fact not a tank, but a half-track, open, officer's vehicle . . . followed by a motorcyclist. We were all down in our ditches on either side of the road and the road is a high-ish road, so we were looking up, and as it passed, everybody opened fire. Up to this point of course, apart from that patrol, no-one had fired their weapon in anger. To my amazement it sailed straight on across the bridge. One just couldn't believe it could get through a hail of fire and still survive, but I think

Jimmy Jennings

the driver had been hit because the section on the far side of the bridge who had been alerted by all this hail of firing, saw this vehicle coming over, swerving . . .

Now his motorcyclist came swirling off the bike behind him, he was hit by the bullets and dropped dead at my feet as I was shooting away.[2]

Corporal Jimmy Jennings' section opened fire at the vehicle and after it came to a halt further down the road, Private 'Rocky' Bright was one of the men who went and inspected it. The Mercedes contained four Germans, one of them being the officer in charge of the bridges:

We did what we could to make him comfortable . . . We thought he'd never make it anyway. He had some pretty horrific wounds . . . He'd got several bullets in him, but he was trying to talk, make himself understood.

The officer began to shout that he wanted to be shot, but when this did not happen, demanded to see the commanding officer. A message was sent to Major Howard, who took Doctor Vaughan with him. John Howard:

When we got to it there were four badly wounded occupants. Inside there was ladies' lingerie and it smelt of perfume. There was a lot of ladies' lingerie, particularly stockings, and all sorts of things like plates of half-eaten food on them and quite where the plates came from I don't know. It was certain that he'd been to a party somewhere. And there was the smell of alcohol on their breaths as well. So our only conclusion was they must have been in Ranville probably, having this party, and when the Paras arrived and surrounded the place, they shot out.

He still went on once he found out who I was, demanding to be shot.

Howard saw that he was wearing a pair of high quality binoculars and so took them from him. John Vaughan:

Peter 'Rocky' Bright

The officer, one Major Schmidt, a fanatical Nazi, was sufficiently able to forget about the wound in his leg to harangue me about the futility of this Allied attempt to defeat the master race. We were undoubtedly going to end up in the sea he assured me with complete conviction. His part in the battle over and presumably expecting to find himself reeling before a volume of abuse from his beloved Führer, he ended his lecture by requesting that I shoot him. This I did, in the bottom, with a needle attached to a syringe of morphia. The effect of this, it seemed, induced him to take a more reasonable view of things and in about ten minutes he actually thanked me for my medical attentions.

The driver of the car had badly shattered legs and one of them I had to amputate with scissors. Not however, having a couple of bottles of blood for transfusion about me at the time, I wasn't in the end able to save the poor fellow's life.

Shortly after returning to the bridge, an ominous sound could be heard approaching from the direction of Benouville. Major Howard:

I heard tracked vehicles moving up along by the Mairie at the road junction at the top. They were obviously tracked, tanks of some kind or other and we all became extremely apprehensive.

However, the vehicles did not turn towards the bridge but headed in the direction of Le Port. Jim Wallwork:

We knew we needed Gammon anti-tank bombs, which Howard sent me to fetch. I did not have much joy pottering about in the dark in a damaged glider looking for ammo, and I just could not find those bloody bombs. So I took a case of .303 instead, which made him rather cross. 'Get the bloody Gammons' he hollered, all politeness now gone. So back I went again. This time I was using my flashlight to be sure they were either there or not when I heard a sharp rapid tapping on the wooden fuselage just above me. Woodpeckers? At night? In a battle? No. It was German Schmeisser following the stupid clot who's using a flashlight. So to hell with Howard and his Gammons. I had had enough, and told him so.[3]

On the other side of the bridge, mines carried by the men were collected. Nobby Clark:

We got the Hawkins anti-tank mines together and put about six of them on a bit of string so we could draw them across the road.

*

Private John Butler of 'C' Company, 7th Battalion had landed at the southern end of the DZ. Recognizing the Ranville Church, he knew exactly where to go to reach the RV, but upon arrival found only about forty men and an officer, this being Captain Webber of 'A' Company. Jim Webber:

From the RV it sounded as though a battle was still raging around the bridges. After some time I still appeared to be the senior officer there and was just considering whether or not to go and help at the bridges with the troops that had arrived when I heard the CO's voice in the darkness. I was delighted and relieved.

Colonel Pine-Coffin was informed about the numbers that had arrived:

The system [that] had been developed within the battalion for reporting the state of forming up was for the sub-units to pass to Battalion HQ, at regular intervals, their percentage strength.

This enabled him to gauge when the battalion was strong enough to move off. The first reports stated that only thirty per cent of Major Taylor's 'A' Company, twenty per cent of Major Neale's 'B' and fifteen per cent of Major Bartlett's 'C' were present. Bartlett himself was still missing.[4] However, the bugler, Private Lambert, had arrived and began sounding the rallying signal. This was obviously a great help. Geoffrey Pine-Coffin:

Officers and men began to come in from all sides and it was good to see how many had joined up into groups to come in as formed bodies, with their own protective detachments and the senior of the group in undisputed command although there were several groups without officers or NCOs in them. The heavy kitbags containing boating material slowed the men up a lot. The normal drill of coming in to the RV at the double was quite impossible.

With the Companies so short in numbers, several immediate changes had to be made to the original plan. Lieutenant Tommy Farr, 4 Platoon, 'B' Company was due to capture Le Port:

This was slightly changed in the RV, and 5 Platoon was detailed for the clearing of Le Port and I, with 4 Platoon, was switched to the spur to the south-west; this was necessary as I had not enough chaps to tackle the village. As we had all been briefed for all these three tasks this made no real difference and I was confident that my chaps would do their new task just as well as the one which they had expected to do.

Lieutenant Ted Pool's 5 Platoon had had a good drop and nearly all his men had arrived at the RV. Geoffrey Pine-Coffin therefore selected them to move off in advance. Ted Pool:

Lieutenant Colonel Pine-Coffin changed its original task and ordered us to occupy the village of Le Port, which stood over the bridges on the road towards the beaches. It was vital to reinforce the 52nd as soon as possible, to get into Le Port as soon as I possibly could.

*

Following the movement of the tanks towards Le Port, sections of 17 Platoon, 'B' Company had moved up either side of the road towards the T-Junction and halted. Sergeant Charles 'Wagger' Thornton:

Fox told me to get up and see the situation. I was trusted with this PIAT and off I went.

Thornton, who moved up the left-hand side of the road with Corporal Lally's Section, had two bombs. He crawled forward, alongside a hedge:

A PIAT is a load of rubbish really . . . the range is about fifty yards and no more . . . even fifty yards is stretching it. It was indoctrinated into your brain, you must never,

132

never, miss. If you do, you've had it. So I thought to myself, 'I'll get about thirty yards from the 'T' Junction.' I don't mind admitting it, I was shaking like a bloody leaf!

Private Alf Whitbread went with him:

We went up to the crossroads. There was so much going on. There was a lot of firing going on to the side of us. We were in trenches which the Germans had dug at the side of the crossroads on the left-hand side. 'Wagger' sorted himself out and said to me, 'Give me a hand.' He said to me, 'Right, load the gun', which I did. 'Get yourself covered 'cos you know what these PIATs are, [it] might turn around and come back at you!'[5]

Lieutenant Smith was feeling pretty helpless:

We were without an anti-tank weapon except for the one we'd given to Dennis, with my platoon only about seven or eight strong and Brotheridge's twenty-odd people. I thought 'This is going to be it.'

Two tanks then began to come down the road from Le Port. Smith noticed that his men were looking at him for some reaction, and so said, 'Look to your front!':

Alf Whitbread
(standing 2nd from left)
with part of his section

I gave that order because they wanted some form of reassurance, although I must confess, I didn't feel that reassured myself. Anyway, a minute or two later, this rumbling of the tank was heard getting louder and louder.

Lance Corporal Arthur Roberts was on the right-hand side, next to *La Chaumiere*:

It don't always pay to take on a tank with a Bren gun and a rifle. The best thing to do is stalk it, which we could have done because it was dark. And then again, we didn't know what sort of infantry they had behind it.

'Wagger' Thornton:

Sure enough, within three minutes this bloody tank appears, more hearing it than seeing it 'cos the wheels were rattling away there. They hung around for a few seconds to figure out where they were.

Their commanders got out and exchanged words and then got back inside. I knew that I would have to act immediately.

Bill Gray, on the ridge on the left-hand side, had a clear field of fire, straight up the road:

There was more firing from our front and then the sound of a tank coming down the road. We could see it quite clearly, this big tank, German infantry beside the tank. 'Cobber' Caine, who was our section commander said, 'Hold your fire,' which we did. It was definitely a tank, a fully-covered armoured vehicle.

Thornton took aim at the leading vehicle:

I made sure that I had him right in the middle. Anyway, although shaking, I took an aim and BANG, off it went.

Major Howard:

We heard the 'ping', we could almost see in our minds the bomb floating through the air and thank God, the first bomb to hit the leading tank was a direct hit. It exploded tremendously and there was a hell of an explosion and not only that, but it must have been full of ammunition because, WHOOF, it kept on exploding afterwards just like a boxed firework display, and it went on for a long, long time.[6]

Bill Gray:

We opened up on the infantry and they just dashed back to the crossroads where they'd come from.

Two or three guys jumped out of the tank and I said to my Number Two to give them a burst from the Sten, which he did.

The driver of the vehicle was still alive and screaming in agony. Lieutenant Fox:

The other tank came to a halt undamaged, well back, it didn't come right up. It wasn't really a tank either, it was a sort of a half-track. A couple of minutes later all hell let loose 'cos there were bombs, ammunition or whatever they had going off. I had to move back a bit.

The wrecked vehicle blocked the narrow road. Lieutenant Sweeney could hear the explosions from the Orne Bridge:

This gave me a completely erroneous impression of what was going on because I thought that this was the noise of a firefight which was taking place between what sounded like at least a Company of German infantry and John Howard's platoons. I got the impression a hell of a battle was going on over there.

Lieutenant Fox:

Finally it died down, and again we heard this man crying out. Tommy Clare couldn't stand it any longer, he went straight out up to the tank which was blazing away now, and found the driver had got out of the tank and was still conscious but both legs had been hit at the knee I suppose, and he'd lost both feet.

Clare, who was immensely strong, picked the driver up, moved him away from the wreckage of the tank and sat him against the wall on the right-hand side of the road. On the east side of the canal, Lieutenant Wood had lain wounded with, although he did not know it, three 9mm bullets in his leg. Dr John Vaughan:

David Wood I found near the anti-tank gun pit, his thigh shattered by machine gun bullets. He had no thought for himself but kept on asking how Den was getting on.

David Wood:

I was picked up and taken back to a trench or ditch rather, which was at the side of a little lane that ran at right angles to the road between the two bridges.[7] And there I was looked after by Corporal Lawson of the RAMC, who was our Company medical orderly, and he did what he could. As I was carried back I saw a flaming armoured car or tank, I didn't know which and still a lot of noise going on.

Lieutenant Smith:

The tank continued to explode for a long time, over half an hour, and the Germans, or the Russian troops, they started infiltrating down through the backs of the gardens away from the crossroads to try and come into us on either side from the canal, down through the towpaths on either side. So we withdrew ourselves to a much closer defensive position around the head of the bridge and I tried to give the impression that we were much stronger than we were by moving Bren gun sections from one position to another and firing off tracer into the dark and so on, which seemed to have some effect. It kept the Germans away from us and we didn't really have any, what you might call, hand-to-hand scrapping, it was really more them trying to find out what the hell was going on.

Major Howard:

It was soon after we hit that tank that the Liaison Officer returned to me. He appeared from the direction of the river of course, the River Bridge, and he said that he'd been to the RV and couldn't find the CO.

However, some Paras were getting to the bridge. Lieutenant Sweeney:

Parachutists began to arrive, but not as we'd hoped in a formed body all ready to take over, but in dribs and drabs because they'd been scattered all over the place.

Corporal 'Smokey' Howard had been ordered to take up position at the eastern end of the bridge on the right-hand side of the road, facing Ranville:

I remember seeing these chaps coming out of the gloom, as it would be at that time of the morning, with all their gear, staggering along. I was delighted to see them, frankly. I didn't take them across, I sent them across, I suppose it was sort of a PR job, 'You alright boys?' They were probably petrified too! They were coming across in ones and twos. They were all chaps who had these funny helmets on, all covered in camouflage with things hanging down below their legs, and big boots.

Major Howard gathered these odd parachutists and kept them by the Canal Bridge, waiting for the 7th Battalion HQ to arrive.

*

The 13th Battalion MMG Officer, Lieutenant Dean, had arrived at the 12th Battalion quarry and waited for members of his Vickers gun teams to arrive:

Numbers only increased slowly, but I was not too concerned since only the gun numbers were to report direct to the RV, while the ammunition carriers rallied to their section commanders before searching for the containers. Among the early arrivals was Lance Corporal Arthur Higgins, Number Four of my stick, who had landed with a kitbag containing a tripod still attached to his leg without sustaining any injury, and Andy Fairhurst, when he

Bill 'Smokey' Howard

arrived, told that he had been suspended in telephone wires at the road-side. But he brought the platoon wireless set with him, and opened up a listening watch. Sergeant Kelly clocked in with only a few of his section and no ammunition, and the same applied to Sergeant Osborne, no ammo, but he did have a complete section. However, we could only mount two complete guns. The canvas sleeve through which the rate of descent of the kitbag was controlled, had proved ineffective, hence some had broken loose and the contents of the bags lost. Apart from two complete guns, there were also three liners of ammunition.

Dropping had long since finished and so a vehicle coming along the road from the direction of the coast was clearly heard by all. It slowly topped a small rise fifty or sixty yards away and there halted. An armoured car was silhouetted on the skyline, with its engine ticking over.

It began firing in the direction of Lieutenant Firth, the Intelligence Officer, who was still flashing the red torch to attract stragglers on the DZ. 'Dixie' Dean:

For several minutes it remained stationary before I heard Johnny Firth saying, 'The CO wants a patrol to go out and deal with that armoured car.' I thought he was addressing members of the 12th nearer the road than we were, but thought I would get a little nearer the road to see how they dealt with it. I kept my eyes on the vehicle and noticed that it was starting to move slowly forward, so I quickened my pace. Suddenly the armoured car accelerated. I was at the roadside by now, and I thought 'It's going to get away.' Quick as I could I pulled a '36' grenade from my pouch and had the pin out and my arm back about to throw it, when a restraining hand was clamped on my shoulder and a voice said, 'Hold it, a party of our men have just gone to ground across the road, you might hit them.' It was Arthur Higgins, who seeing me set off, had followed. 'That's another cool head in the platoon,' I thought. Further on towards Ranville, the vehicle turned off the road onto the DZ, where it was destroyed.

Just like the rest of the Brigade, the 12th Battalion had suffered a widespread drop. Lieutenant Phillip Burkinshaw's 1 Platoon, 'A' Company, was typical, being at about half strength, around eighteen men.

In advance of the battalion move, the Company Commander, Major Gerald Ritchie, ordered him to take his men and occupy the copse on the road a few hundred yards to the south, which was subsequently to be the Forward Brigade HQ.[8]

Shortly after reaching the copse, a German staff car and an escorting motorcyclist came speeding down the road from the north.

Just to the south, Lieutenant Archdale's 7th Battalion group had moved towards the River Orne Bridge. Private Ron Perry:

When we got on the road that runs between Ranville crossroads where the Calvary stood and goes on to firstly the River Bridge . . . we could hear a roar of engines, got down on the side and suddenly a motorcyclist appeared. They waited for him, he went about twelve feet in the air when they fired at him, he went in one direction and the motorbike went in the other. A bloke called Hart, a Welshman, he had a Sten gun and

Major Pat Hewlings

he just let it off and caught this motorcyclist. Shot him to pieces. There was something else behind that motorcyclist, I don't know what happened to that.

The car was brought to a halt near the Brigade HQ copse. Major Pat Hewlings, 2i/c of 225 Field Parachute Ambulance was also in the area:

As we moved off in small groups from our Rendezvous to our appointed dressing station in Le Bas de Ranville, all was chaos, men of all units moving in every direction, looking for rendezvous and their own formations. One German staff car carrying two very surprised German officers drove into our midst. The German officers had to walk to the Brigade POW cage: one of our Brigade officers was delighted with the car.[9]

Archdale's group waited a short while beside the road. Bill French:

We heard troops marching down the road, so we straddled the road . . . and we halted the troops that were marching. It was our own battalion. Quite a lot of them had got together, but it wasn't the whole battalion, not by a long way.

These were men of Lieutenant Pool's 5 Platoon, 'B' Company. After a brief discussion, they all moved on towards the Orne Bridge.[10] Lieutenant Archdale:

The first person I met there was the Brigadier, who was full of enthusiasm like he always was. There was a dead German on the road, the first dead man I had seen. We crossed in between the bridges. There was quite a lot going on. Some sort of vehicle had been blown up on the far side, near the Canal Bridge.

Ted Pool:

Getting to the bridge, Poett was around . . . He'd lost some of his bodyguard and I think he tried to pinch some of my chaps so I managed to double away before he could get hold of them!

Archdale and his men halted between the bridges to wait for the rest of the battalion, while Pool's men ran towards the Canal Bridge. Phillip Crofts, 4 Section, 5 Platoon:

When we were going to the bridges there was a hell of a do going on where we thought the bridges were, and I thought 'What a battle!' and all it was, was a tank blowing up. We ran over the second bridge, the Canal Bridge, and immediately went off the road and went across ground to Le Port. We were going off the road and we were crossing

138

some Dannett wire, into the rolls of wire and somebody said, 'Halt!' Our sergeant, a chap called Vic Bettle said, 'Who is it?' because we anticipated the Oxf and Bucks were somewhere, though I never saw any Oxf and Bucks as I ran across the bridges . . . he most likely thought as I did, 'Halt', this was just the Oxf and Bucks just wanting to see who we were. Old Vic gave a mouthful of Fs and Bs and the next word came, 'Halten!' So we fired into where the voices came from and just swept through them into this Le Port.

It remained extremely difficult to see anything in the darkness. Lieutenant Pool:

During our advance on the village we heard a German group behind a hedgerow we were about to cross. I tossed a '36' grenade over the hedge. After the explosion we heard the sound of running feet and cries of a wounded German soldier.

We crossed the hedgerow and then we had some stick grenades thrown at us but didn't do any damage, except make our ears ring a bit. The stick grenades were before we got near Le Port. I remember we got over the fence and I can't remember why, whether someone heard something, but we were laying flat and luckily the stick grenades went off with a bang. But after that we got up and moved very quickly, the Germans must have run away.

And then we moved up towards Le Port. There was a house and I banged on the door. It was very funny because in training one had been so careful not to damage property and things like that and a chap came down and I told him to get everyone into the cellar, we were going to take over his house. I think he wasn't too pleased. But anyway, eventually I decided not to go into that house and then Sergeant McCambridge took over on the far side of the road from the church on the corner where it was going up to St Aubin.

Phillip Crofts:

We went upstairs and we pulled the curtains off and smashed the windows and drew some furniture to put the Brens on. And I can remember one woman saying, 'Naughty, naughty! Bad boys!' She was trying to stop us doing this . . . You had to make a strong-point, you had to make your firing positions. I think this was the house we stayed in for quite some time. It was a very solid house.

Ted Pool put out his sections in various positions around the village and set up Platoon HQ to the south of the church.

In the meantime, the bulk of the battalion had left the RV. Colonel Pine-Coffin:

I decided to move off when I reached half strength, but this took so long that I gave the order a little earlier. No mortars, no machine guns or wireless had arrived, so we would just have to do without them. The Coup de Main

Lieutenant Ted Pool

party's success signal went up just as we moved off and put new life into us. Half the job had been done, the bridges had been captured.

'C' Company, although they were lightly equipped was one of the weakest of the Companies owing to several of their aircraft having dropped them wide of the DZ. Amongst those missing was Major Bartlett himself . . . Captain R. Keene, the Company second-in-command assumed command of the Company and was ordered to move off and carry out its mission at 0215 hours. He was then at approximately forty per cent strength.

The remaining two rifle Companies, at just over fifty per cent strength, with Advanced Battalion HQ, set off just behind them and at a slightly slower rate. The plan was for Rear Battalion HQ to follow in its best time so I left the second-in-command (Steel-Baume) to collect in all he could and follow us up, choosing his own time for starting.

John Butler of 'C' Company was ordered to go about thirty yards ahead as a scout, and they started to run towards the bridges. Major Taylor, 'A' Company:

We went down to the bottom of this re-entrant. We went through an archway of a building into a farmyard. Our trouble was we couldn't find the damned way out of this yard! We walked round and round, eventually we got out and came along a track. This was overgrown by woods and it was pretty dark and we were carrying a lot of weight. It was a very rough track and we knew we had to go along as fast as we could. It's very difficult to double in the dark, carrying a heavy weight on very uneven ground. We got along it eventually and hit the road that runs over the bridges.

John Butler:

When I arrived at the River Bridge, the first thing I saw was a very young and very dead German soldier with both legs blown off from the knee. Obviously the result of a grenade.[11] Being the first dead person I had ever seen, this momentarily pulled me up, then others rushed past me and I quickly joined them.

On the far side of the canal it seemed fairly quiet except for exploding ammunition from a burning armoured half-track near the Mairie. Here I joined others of my platoon and we were sent on a forward patrol.

Lance Corporal Eddie Gurney, 3 Platoon, 'A' Company:

We were about 200 yards from the first bridge when the wireless operator shouted 'Ham and Jam', the signal that the glider troops had captured the bridges intact. I immediately threw away my kitbag containing the dinghy.

Major Taylor:

There was Nigel Poett, the Brigadier. He saw me and he said, 'Come on Nigel, double, double,' in that rather falsetto voice he sometimes drops into! So we got the chaps up together, breaking into a rather shambling run and went across the first bridge, made contact with them, they were OK.

Lieutenant Todd:

We moved fast down the slope through the scrub to where the road curved in its approach to the bridge spanning the Orne. All seemed quiet as we reached this bridge and trotted over it. Men of Major Howard's force were in defensive positions around the east end, and the glider men were using the former German trenches and wire.

The very moment that I arrived on the Orne Bridge, in front of me were the remains of 'A' Company, Nigel Taylor's lot, twenty or thirty of them, and the rest behind.

Colonel Pine-Coffin:

Brigadier Poett, everyone was pleased to note, was also there and very happy looking he was too, as well he might be. Things were going well. Both bridges had been captured and both were intact. The simplest of plans could now be used and all the heavy boating equipment could be dumped. The Brigadier urged the battalion to hurry, as if he thought they had been dawdling up to then, and hurry they did for the rest of the trip was carried out at the double by everyone.

Major Taylor:

We went on down the road between the two bridges and there was a hell of a noise going on at John Howard's bridge, the Canal Bridge. There was a lot of noise of gunfire, light stuff and a lot of pyrotechnics going up. I thought John Howard was being counter-attacked, and I was going to have to commit my Company straight into battle on the trot.

I made contact with John, [was] briefed and on we went across the bridge. He was on the bridge when I met him.

Lieutenant Todd:

As we doubled along the causeway towards the Canal Bridge, a large iron structure that could be opened for river craft, it was clear that Major Howard's men were being attacked. Suddenly all hell erupted on the road ahead. Heavy explosions, flashes and tracer bullets lit up the night like a spectacular firework display. We speeded up our jogtrot. Then as quickly as it had started, the tumult died down.

Eddie Gurney:

We raced onwards and as we approached the Canal de Caen bridge I saw a number of dead bodies amongst whom was an officer, lying in the roadway. On the other side of the bridge there appeared to be a mighty battle in progress but this turned out to be ammunition exploding in a German tank that had been destroyed by the glider troops.

Eddie Gurney

Lieutenant Hunter, 3 Platoon:

'A' Company was sent over the bridges. I went first, leading my depleted platoon. It was still dark. There were a few bodies lying on the bridges. I couldn't make out whether they were ours or theirs. It was my very first experience of death. I was still only twenty-one. A tank was burning on one of the bridges and ammunition was exploding from it. I dashed past this in some trepidation. I was rushing into the unknown. I didn't know where the enemy was or when we were going to encounter them.

Lance-Corporal 'Dave' Davey, 3 Platoon:

There was seven of us, Lieutenant Hunter, Cockburn, Gurney, Pembury, Mills, Lance Corporal Jackson who crossed the bridges into Benouville. It should have been 3 Platoon, consisting of thirty-three men.

Stan Young, 1 Platoon, 'A' Company:

We came over the bridge and I remember the Oxf and Bucks blokes saying, 'Are we bloody glad to see you!'

Bill Gray:

There was a bit of rejoicing, patting us on our helmets, saying, 'Good lads, well done.'

Due to the ammunition in the tank continuing to 'cook off', the 'A' Company men had to keep away from the road, walk along the top of the ridge position held by the Oxf and Bucks and then head across the field towards the Benouville Mairie.

Major Taylor:

At this time I had very few men, only about thirty. I got another twenty on the other side of the bridges; we then cut across the back of the Mairie. After searching that, we went up the Caen road into Benouville.

This time Major Howard received a message that Colonel Pine-Coffin had arrived at the Orne Bridge, and so set off to find him. On their meeting, Geoffrey Pine-Coffin offered his congratulations on a successful operation. Major Howard:

I can remember walking along, alongside him, chatting, telling him exactly what had happened, so that by the time we got to the Canal Bridge he was more or less in the picture.

Pine-Coffin met Lieutenant Archdale and ordered him to wait where he was for the arrival of Eric Steele-Baume and any stragglers that he brought from the RV. Returning from the western side of the bridge, Sergeant 'Wagger' Thornton saw Colonel Pine-Coffin:

He and Howard were having a conference and as I came down, he stopped me and said, 'What the bloody hell's going on up there?' 'It's only a bloody old tank,' I said, 'but it was making an awful racket!' 'I should say so,' he said.

Lieutenant Todd was ordered to go and set up Battalion Headquarters:

I went across to Le Port on that little piece of high ground next to the church. That's where we established Battalion Headquarters . . . This was just a ditch and hedges and odds and ends like that. The HQ position was only seventy or eighty yards south of the church, in the field which backed [on to it].

For a short period Pine-Coffin stood by the Canal Bridge and dealt with any problems as his men passed by. Before he crossed, the Colonel informed John Howard, whose force now came under his command, that there was to be an 'O' Group at 0415 hours, when he would receive confirmation of his orders.

The lack of men seriously restricted Pine-Coffin's options, but he just had to fulfil the battalion's defensive plan with what he had. This plan was to hold the enemy on the line of the road running north-south from Le Port to Benouville. 'B' Company's 4 and 5 Platoons were to hold the southern half of Le Port and the small wood on the north side of the road junction. Lieutenant Thomas' 6 Platoon was to take up position in and around the *Café Gondrée* to cover the open ground to the south, along the canal.

'A' Company had the responsibility of preventing a large scale attack developing from the south. Colonel Pine-Coffin:

The chief problems were connected with the various battle outposts found from 'C' Company, and the best employment of the specialists, such as mortar men, machine gunners and signallers, none of whose containers had been recovered and who were therefore without their instruments or specialist weapons.

The battle outpost problem was a difficult one because each outpost was small and had been highly trained for its job. Now they were not complete and many of them were without their leader. It had been intended to hold one platoon of 'C' Company as a small reserve force at Battalion HQ; this was a small enough reserve in all conscience, but it had now to be even further reduced in order to bring the outposts up to strength.

The original orders to the battle outposts concerning withdrawal were altered as they could not be contacted due to the lack of wireless sets, and Pine-Coffin did not consider runners reliable enough for such an important message. He ordered them to withdraw on their own initiative but only if under heavy pressure. However, he did have the option of using parts of the *Coup de Main* force if necessary.

He held the small counter-attack force in the area of the HQ to cover the small wood to the south-west of the church. To augment this force, he retained a few men of the Mortar and MMG Platoons, but these were only armed with pistols. Sergeant Bill French, MMG Platoon:

We were sent out as ordinary infantry, not machine-gunners because we couldn't find our machine guns, so we were sent to different Companies. I was kept with a couple of the lads as Battalion HQ protection, but some of the others were sent out to the various Companies who needed reinforcements, because they had casualties and people had not arrived.

Lieutenant Tommy Farr, 4 Platoon, 'B' Company:

We crossed the bridges and marched up to the T-junction, turned north towards Le Port and moved to where the wood joins the road on the left-hand side. I pushed a couple of scouts up the road to the first house in Le Port and they reported back all quiet.

I then turned off the road through the wood and cleared it to the far end. No enemy encountered. I established a position at the west end of the wooded spur and had a fairly good field of fire to the west and north-west. To the south it was not so good, but at least I could see down the gully which ran down the south edge of the wood.[12]

At this stage I had about twelve to fourteen chaps, who had managed to make the RV. I had three LMGs, thanks to the idea of dropping four per platoon. I organized into two sections and a strong Platoon HQ, which was to all intents and purposes, another section. Sergeant Balding had one section and Sergeant Cherry the other; I had the third myself with Corporal Chapman as gun corporal.

It was still dark when we took up positions on the end of the spur and as it was impossible to see all the ground, we dug in fairly close together and I was able to control quite easily by verbal orders.

Lieutenant Dan Thomas, 6 Platoon, 'B' Company:

It appeared to me that a tall building in a prominent position should be occupied by our forces and denied to the enemy. The south dormer window offered an ideal fire position. Therefore, escorted by two riflemen, I proceeded to the Mairie *not knowing if the building was occupied by the enemy. We searched the surrounding area and this resulted in the 'flushing out' from some of the outhouses of some naturally frightened civilians, the staff of the* Mairie *both female and male.*

They informed me that the Mayor had departed and that the building was not occupied by the enemy. We entered the Mairie *and commenced our search. It was my intention to place my two riflemen in the high dormer window. This task was helped by a great pile of locally confiscated radio sets under the window. My conscience was briefly troubled by the sight of two pairs of hobnailed army boots clambering over the highly polished radiogram cabinets. Having written a brief note to the missing Mayor, my namesake* [Monsieur Lucien Thomas], *I departed to join my main force at the bridge.*

The 7th Battalion's arrival was a huge relief to the Oxf and Bucks. Nobby Clark:

The Town Hall (*Mairie*)

It was three o'clock in the morning when Godbold said to me, 'Make a cup of tea will you.' I got my old Tommy cooker going and a dixie full of tea and he had a flask of Irish whiskey, and we had a dose of Irish whiskey. I do what I'm told, he was my platoon commander!

*

In the wood to the south-west of Le Port, Lieutenant Farr's men had begun to dig in when suddenly there were explosions:

At first I thought we were being mortared, but as the bombs were bursting slap amongst us I could not understand how the Germans could see us if they were using a mortar. It was still dark and unless this was a target on which they already ranged, I knew that they could not hit it. At last we worked it out, they were stick grenades.

There is a small ditch running across the field from Le Port and this came right up to my platoon position. A German sergeant and one man had crawled along this with a lot of stick grenades and a machine gun. We found them about ten yards away along this ditch from where they were throwing their stick grenades in amongst us. We returned with a '36' grenade and then Private Brennan leapt up and finished them off with a burst of Sten.

Shortly after this we were under fire from a house in Le Port. The Germans had a machine gun in an upstairs window and having seen or heard our previous activity, they gave us an occasional burst. I could do little about this as 5 Platoon were some-where in the village and I did not want to fire in that direction. 5 Platoon cleared up

145

Lieutenant Tommy Farr

this trouble in time as they came through the village. I lost two men during these incidents. Private Pepper was wounded in the head by one of the stick grenades and had to be passed back, and Private Allen was wounded in the hand by the machine gun from Le Port, but carried on and stayed with us until I moved back. Company HQ was back near the road (east of my position) and I was in touch with them by runner.

Two roads ran south through Benouville, one on either side of the *Mairie*. These roads were connected by a couple of narrow streets lined with cottages, houses and gardens. The western side of the main road consisted of farms, orchards and fields enclosed by low walls or thick hedges. The lower road rejoined the main road as it followed the high curving wall of the Benouville Chateau, to a crossroads known as '*Le Carrefour de Maternité*'. The Chateau and its grounds, which dominated the area to south-east, had an entrance on the corner of the *Carrefour*, with the caretaker's lodge being just inside the gates. The Chateau's imposing wall continued south beside the main road for over 500 yards, finally turning east down a sloping lane towards the canal. In contrast, the area to the south-west was an expanse of open fields.

It was in this close environment of houses, buildings and farms that the depleted 'A' Company was to form its defence. As they had advanced along the main road Major Taylor decided to try and get what information he could about enemy presence in the village, and so went into a small cottage where he was confronted by the elderly inhabitants:

They were naturally very frightened and took a lot of convincing that we were not Germans on an exercise. But they eventually realized who we were and then the trouble was getting out, they were so pleased to see us. We did get out in the end but we got no information from them whatsoever.

Lieutenant Hunter:

I knocked on a door. Two frightened ladies appeared. 'Nous sommes parachutistes Anglais.' I couldn't think of the word for British. I then rather absurdly said, 'Moi, Ecossais.' Who the hell cared at this time of high drama, but I had some idea that the French preferred the Scots to the English. Something to do with the Entente Cordiale. 'Ou se trouvent les Boches?' Asking the question was one thing, understanding the answer was quite another. I did however get the word 'Chateau.' I knew where that was from the aerial photos.

Frank Villis

1 Platoon's officer, Lieutenant Temple, had not arrived, and so Sergeant Frank Villis was in command.[13]

Major Taylor:

We pressed on, moving with sections staggered each side of the road. I had Sergeant Villis' platoon leading, then Company HQ with [Lieutenant] Bowyer, with me and his [2] platoon behind, then David Hunter and his platoon.

The leading man had almost reached *Le Carrefour de Maternité* when they stopped suddenly. Nigel Taylor:

Lieutenant Bill Bowyer

We heard a German motorcycle start up to the right of the crossroads. He came round the corner and straight down between us. The troops of course were on either side of the road, moving up as quietly as they could, everything very quiet up to this moment.

Stan Young of 1 Platoon was advancing up the left-hand side of the road:

We'd just got to the houses when he came down. I jumped over the wall this side, and the others went into the ditch on that side.

Private Chris Tallboys:

Lieutenant Bowyer rushed into the road to wave him down at the same time someone fired and killed Lieutenant Bowyer and the German motorcyclist.

Major Taylor was moving up the right-hand side of the road:

This chap came down and they had been training for God knows how many years to kill Germans. This was the first one they had seen.

Everybody fired at him and he crashed just behind me. He crashed and he hit my leading platoon commander with his motorbike. It was one of those big BMV vertical opposed, twin-engined bikes, and went down on top of him. As he went down he must have twisted the throttle of that bike wide open, and that engine was absolutely roaring its head off after this incredible quiet, and of course he was on top of my platoon commander. Eventually we managed to get the engine shut off, but the back wheel was going round. All this time the thing was in gear and every time it hit the ground the thing was bucking, shying about. It was chaos. That platoon commander was very badly injured and unfortunately he died afterwards.[14]

We went up to the crossroads and we got these platoons into position. It was still dark, it was still quiet now. One of the platoon positions proved to be impossible because what you couldn't see on the aerial photographs was that underneath the trees which showed up on one aerial photograph, one corner of these crossroads there was a fifteen-foot stone wall. You couldn't do much about that, so we had to adjust them.

147

I ordered Villis into the houses on the south end of the village and Hunter into the farm buildings to the west. Company HQ went into the gardens of the houses on the other side of the road and the remains of Bowyer's platoon into the houses to the east of that.

Lieutenant Robin Atkinson led a 'C' Company battle outpost of nine men to the Benouville Chateau to watch the main road from Caen. Virtually everybody in the party carried extra explosives to deal with tanks. A search of the grounds began and a figure wearing trousers was observed walking from the Chateau towards one of the pavilions. A trap was laid and the figure walked right into it and was halted for interrogation, but this person, being Madame Vion, began the questioning by asking who they were! Fortunately Atkinson spoke fluent French and informed her that they were *'L'Armee de Liberation.'* Lea Vion responded with 'What! All of you?' She duly gave the location of every German quartered in the grounds, adding that there were two doctors sheltering in the cellar of the Chateau whom she had found to be particularly unpleasant types. Afterwards, she asked if there was any objection to her going back to bed, whereupon she disappeared.

Lieutenant Robin Atkinson

On the eastern side of the Canal Bridge Lieutenant Archdale had been 'collecting' men of the MMG and Mortar Platoons:

By now there were eleven out of the total mortar and machine gun platoons and we remained with Eric Steel-Baume and the RSM. [15]

Before long Eric Steele-Baume ordered me to move off to the Battalion HQ position in the bridgehead which I did, not without some discomfort because he was close behind me with a cocked pistol pointing here, there and often at me. Having arrived at Battalion HQ we took up Battle School type all-round defence and sat quiet.

The 'B' Company HQ, which had set up in the orchard behind *La Chaumiere*, had come under attack from infiltrators employing grenades and machine-gun fire. Signaller Bill Le Chaminant:

We were more concerned about getting the wireless, getting through with the communications, which was very difficult because you had to synchronise your wireless with the other wireless in the area and of course their set was beggared up, ours was as well, and we couldn't get through, so we were quite isolated. There was only about a dozen of us in Headquarters, so it was rather a bit confused.

In the darkness, there was nothing for the FOB party to do, so they waited in the 'B' Company orchard.

Bill Le Chaminant

Lieutenant Eric Woodman of 8 Platoon, 'C' Company, was another officer who had failed to arrive, and so there remained the task of dealing with the German strongpoint along the canal. Lieutenant Walter Parrish, OC, 7 Platoon, 'C' Company:

My plane, in which I was Number One, was unable to find the DZ until approximately one hour after the remainder of the battalion. When I arrived at the RV I found that what was there of the battalion had departed for an early crack at the Boche.

I gathered what there was of stragglers and went off to carry out my first task, to attack and clear houses at DZ side of the River Orne (East) and then to clear [an] area on the opposite side of the road, which was believed to contain enemy posts. When we arrived at 0315 hours these tasks had already been done.

I then crossed the bridge over the River Orne en-route for my second task, which seemed impossible to accomplish with my few men (about ten including one sergeant, some of whom were from other platoons and even Companies and were thus ignorant of the task). Nearing the Canal Bridge I was hailed by Bob Keene [in command of 'C' Company] and given by him a few more of my own men and two light machine guns; I then had two light machine guns, one 2-inch mortar and personal weapons among fourteen other ranks including Sergeant Wilkes, one Lance-Corporal and one sniper, with full equipment. The plan called for communication by wireless but we had no wireless.

The news of the enemy in the area of Benouville was sparse and I was given Eric Woodman's task which meant proceeding down the west bank of the canal, investigating an oil storage installation and positioning my platoon as an outpost, in what appeared from aerial photographs to be a battery position. It was not known though whether this was occupied or not.

I started off in what must have been bright moonlight; I remember feeling almost naked.

Chapter Nine

Arrival in Ranville

Four Platoon, the advance group of the 13th Battalion, had been tasked with protecting the DZ by holding a T-junction near the 12th Battalion RV and two crossroads, one on the DZ itself and the other on the edge of Ranville. However, the scattered drop meant that only the Platoon Commander, Lieutenant Stan Jevons, and his batman had occupied the crossroads near the village. Using his knife, Jevons had silenced the sole sentry and then waited for the battalion to arrive, but by 0150 hours only around sixty per cent of the battalion had arrived at the RV itself. However, Lieutenant Colonel Luard decided that the time was right to move, and they duly set off for Ranville:

> 'C' Company under Major Gerald Ford had been ordered to mop up the north end of the village, as soon as Major George Bristow's 'B' Company had cleared the southern end.

Only two of the 'C' Company platoons, Lieutenant Harry Pollak's 7 Platoon and Lieutenant Jack Sharples' 8 Platoon had arrived, but the northern part of the village was secured with little trouble. The expected enemy garrison in the village was known to be chiefly billeted around the Chateau de la Comte de Rohan-Chabot, south-east of the Ranville crossroads. Lieutenant Sharples:

> 8 Platoon was given the task of clearing the Chateau in the village, and tracks through the grounds indicated that it was being used by the Germans. When we left the RV (we were the last to do so), 7 Platoon were up ahead and came under machine-gun fire as they approached the crossroads. The battalion were under strict orders not to open fire until dawn; it would have been so easy in the dark to shoot friendly forces. Major Ford called me forward and instructed me to find a way round, and I went along the street trying the door handles. At last I found one that opened. In the room was a still warm bed, a German uniform jacket draped over the back of a chair and a rifle propped up against the wall. In the yard at the back was another discarded jacket. A grenade landed amongst us and I dashed into the road and called out at the top of my voice, 'Harry [Pollak], it's Jack.'

Lieutenants Harry Pollak and Jack Watson

On his route, Lieutenant Pollak, an Austrian Jew, had answered the challenge of a sentry, located the post and shot him dead. Lieutenant Sharples:

We quickly worked our way round to the Chateau, the Germans having scarpered. I left one section covering the front of the building, another inside on the ground floor, and I went upstairs with Privates Orrel and Prince, where I met Le Comte de Ranville and his wife, protesting about the intrusion of their property. I tried to tell him that it was the invasion, we were British soldiers and that they were to stay indoors. Back came a torrent of French which I did not understand, but they clearly did not believe me. Seeing the key in their bedroom door, I took it out and gave it to them saying in my best 4th Form French, 'Lock the door. I'll talk to you in the morning.'

Lieutenant Colonel Luard sounded the success signal on his hunting horn, and Rear Battalion HQ moved into Ranville and took up a position in a garden chosen previously from aerial photographs. 7 and 8 Platoons then moved into a reserve position on the west side of the village.

Captain Nobby Clark, 2i/c 'C' Company, had not long arrived at the RV when mortar bombs began to land close by:

I would have loved to go forward into the beckoning and comparative safety of the edge of Ranville village but orders said otherwise. 'C' Company HQ and No 9 Platoon were to remain at the RV as reserve, until the village was captured and then move in to protect the left flank of Battalion HQ. The only thing that had not gone more or less to plan was that No 9 Platoon was conspicuous by its absence.

Progress seemed slow. Apart from the very regular and frequent arrival of a bunch of mortar bombs nothing much appeared to be happening. Then we began to advance slowly, haltingly, into the south-west edge of the village.

Captain Nobby Clark and Lieutenant Colonel Peter Luard

As they did so, a man from his own stick, Private Bamber came towards him with a message that Ranville had been captured.

Meanwhile, on the DZ around fifty men of 'A' Company, five Engineer sections of 591 Field Parachute Squadron, assisted by a working party from Divisional Signals, had begun to deal with the anti-glider landing obstacles.

*

By 0230 hours about a third of the officers and less than fifty per cent of the 12th Battalion had assembled in the quarry RV, but Colonel Johnson made the decision to move off to Le Bas de Ranville. Captain John Sim, 2i/c 'C' Company:

After a while I was called back to the quarry and was told by my Company Commander that very few of the battalion had arrived, that we couldn't afford to wait any longer and that I was to lead the battalion off out of the quarry and to our defensive positions south of Ranville. I set off with 'C' Company but I wasn't aware of any battle going on anywhere; it was like an exercise. When we came to the south side of Ranville we had a very pleasant surprise because we found a hell of a lot of our chaps already there and digging in. They had landed in different places and instead of going to the RV had gone straight to their positions at [Le Bas de] Ranville. Major Stephens, my Company Commander, asked me to see if there were any Germans in four houses nearby, where we were going to establish our Battalion Headquarters. I took a sergeant and two soldiers and when we got to the first house I noticed there was a light on inside. I knocked, and after probably about a minute, the door was opened by a middle-aged lady, in her day clothes. At two o'clock in the morning this was a bit unusual; behind her, her husband and two kids were also dressed in their day clothes. I said, 'Bonjour Madame, nous sommes soldats d'Angleterre; nous arrivons ici par avion, parachutistes; l'heure de liberation est arrivée. Ou sont les soldats Allemandes? Le soldats Allemandes restent ici?' She looked blankly at me. I was a dunce at French at

152

school, but I thought I'd done quite well. I had another go but now she looked dazed and terrified – we were all camouflaged up with blackened faces. I then asked my sergeant, a right raw Yorkshireman, if he could speak French; he couldn't and neither could the other two, so I tried again. I'd barely started when she burst into tears, embraced me and said, 'You're British soldiers, aren't you?' So I said, 'Yes, I've been trying to tell you this for the last three or four minutes. You can speak English well can't you?' 'Yes,' she said, 'I am English, born in Manchester, and I married a French farmer before the war and settled here. I realized that no German soldiers could have acted that part so brilliantly, and that you were genuine.' So I said, 'Splendid. Anyway, are there any damned Germans around?' She said, 'No.' There were some Todt Organization men who worked on the defences . . . constructing fortifications on the beaches. She said there were quite a lot of that type of group around but no German infantry soldiers. So I said, 'Thank you very much. This is the real thing. This isn't a raid, we're here to stay. We've come to liberate you.'

Sim reported this to Major Stephens and then set off with a small outpost group to occupy a hedgerow to the south west, in front of the main 'C' Company position. This hedgerow ran at a tangent to the River Orne and was on the western slope of the Ring Contour, the feature that dominated the area.[1]

*

Captain Tibbs of 225 Field (Para) Ambulance had waited patiently for his section, but only five men had arrived[2]:

We then went on to the church, intending to use the church for casualties before we passed them on to the village.

When we first got to Ranville Church, my batman was with me, he was a conscientious objector, we were walking quietly around the church because we didn't know if there were any Germans just anywhere. We had no idea how far the troops had managed to clear the place. Then we heard on the gravel, footsteps approaching us . . . so we tucked ourselves into the shadow of this buttress. I didn't know what the hell to do. I whispered into his ear, 'Look, if it's a German I'm going to rush him and knock him down. You can do what you like, but I'd like you to come and help if you will!' As this chap came alongside there was sufficient sort of semi-moonlight to recognize it was obviously one of our chaps, so we called out to him.

They exchanged passwords and all was well.

When we reached the church it had huge oak doors which were firmly bolted. We couldn't open them. Bruce Harvey turned up while I was standing outside this church just wondering what to do about this, realizing that perhaps that we didn't need to use the church because we hadn't any casualties, and the Field Ambulance by then was being set up. He was furious that the church doors hadn't been opened and he tried firing the Sten gun at the lock with absolutely no result at all. He realized it was pretty hopeless and I said, 'Well look, we haven't any casualties so we don't need to use the church. We can see about that a bit later.'

153

Ranville showing the DZ/LZ and respective RVs

*

Having assured themselves that the 7th Battalion had arrived at the bridges, Brigadier Poett and Sergeant Edwards had moved off to see how things were faring in Ranville. Fraser Edwards:

> By this time of course, Ranville had been cleared . . . So we walked straight on to the far end of the village. I noticed a large building and there was a German car, a Simca Eight, with a flag on the front of it, and I said to him, 'There's a German Headquarters, that's one of my jobs. I have to get to the German Headquarters. Will we go in?' And he said, 'We will not go in.' So, OK. We then went to the end of the village and then we walked back and at the edge of the village he met some of his men. And then he said, 'Well look, I don't think I need you any more. You can do whatever you're supposed to do.'

Poett went off to check on the 13th Battalion and found Colonel Luard. Nigel Poett:

> He was in splendid heart. He had had little difficulty in overrunning the village and he was now in the course of 'mopping up' some of the houses which had been occupied

by the Germans. He had established his defences on the outskirts of the village. Ranville had been captured at about 2.30 am.

Having satisfied himself about their situation, Poett went over to the 12th Battalion. He found 'B' Company preparing its defences in the hedges at the southern end of Le Bas de Ranville and 'C' Company positioned on the rising ground to the south of the village. However, the battalion did not have enough men to occupy the Ring Contour as planned. The remaining two platoons of 'A' Company were deployed near the Forward Brigade HQ, east of the Orne Bridge:

We knew they had a tough time ahead. They would bear the brunt of any attack from 21st Panzer Division which had been moved close to Caen just before D-Day. 12 Para must therefore expect strong armoured and infantry attacks as soon as it was light enough for the Germans to assess the situation. The battalion had only a short time to prepare themselves and they were certainly making the most of it.

At around 0300 hours the order was given to the MMG platoons at the quarry RV to prepare to move to Ranville. Lieutenant 'Dixie' Dean:

There were now twenty-nine gunners, myself, Alf Whalley, Andy Fairhurst of Platoon HQ, leaving twenty-six to man and defend the two guns. Instead of sections of two guns we would operate as detachments of thirteen serving a single gun. Alf Whalley had to do some reorganizing of personnel ensuring equal numbers with each gun.

We were almost at the rear of the column on leaving the quarry and setting off for the 12th Battalion's positions in Le Bas de Ranville.

Private Ken Lang, MMG Platoon, 13th Battalion:

Soon after we left the Rendezvous, we passed some cottages. We'd had these leaflets given to us, a message from De Gaulle, and we were handing them to these people. They were standing outside these cottages singing the Marseillaise.

Lieutenant Dean:

Before we reached there, several great black bats came wheeling and whistling out of the dark sky above and touched down in the corn. These were the gliders bringing in the anti-tank guns we were to defend and the advance elements of Divisional Headquarters. An excited French family of a man and his wife, together with a little girl, were at the roadside in front of their house, talking animatedly about the events taking place around them.

In spite of heavy mortaring and machine-gun fire, the parties on the DZ had been successfully removing the Rommel's Asparagus and filling in ditches. Lieutenant Colonel Lowman, CRE:

Major John Cramphorn

The removal of the obstruction poles proved easier than was expected. Few of them exceeded eight inches diameter, and little more than half of them were in place in the ground. Towards the northern part of the LZ they were securely wired together with heavy gauge wire. In many cases manual removal by three men was found to be quicker than using the prepared explosive charges.

Major Cramphorn, OC 'A' Company, 13th Battalion:

The task proved easier than I had planned for. All the holes had been dug, but many of the posts were simply placed in the hole, and not yet upright and firm. In many cases then, all we did was carry the pole away and fill in the hole. We finished the job with about fifteen minutes to spare and were digging our funk holes when the gliders started to arrive. As a result we had a ringside seat for the actual landings.

To guide them in, the Pathfinders had set out two EUREKA beacons and lights on three separate landing strips. Lieutenant Colonel Lowman:

The two westerly strips were ready in good time for the gliders at 0320 hours but lighting by the Independent Parachute Company proved unsatisfactory due to lack of personnel and special equipment. As a result gliders came in from all directions.

During his journey across the Channel, General Gale, in Glider 70, had fallen asleep. He was woken when the combination ran into a small storm, causing considerable bumping. This broke the intercom line from the tug. A few minutes later he was informed by the glider pilot, Major Billy Griffith, that they would shortly be crossing the coast. General Richard Gale:

We were flying at about five thousand feet and we soon knew the coast was under us, for we were met by a stream of flak. It was weird to see this roaring up in great golden chains past the windows of the glider, some of it being apparently between us and the tug aircraft. Looking out I could see the canal and the river through the clouds; for the moon was by now fairly well overcast and the clear wisp moonlight we had hoped for was not there. Nevertheless here we were.

In a few moments Griffiths [sic] said, 'We are over the Landing Zone now and will be cast off at any moment.' Almost as soon as he had said this, we were. The whistling sound and the roar of the engines suddenly died down: no longer were we bumping about, but gliding along on a gloriously steady course . . . Round we turned, circling lower and lower; soon the pilot turned round to tell us to link up as we were just about to land . . .

The war reporter, Chester Wilmot, was on board one of the gliders:

Came in on [a] lazy glide, barely a sign of navigation lights. We braced ourselves against the bikes in front and waited for the last few seconds before she touched down. The wheels slid to earth easily, but then one crash followed another as the glider cracked into poles and bumped over the rough fields. With woodwork creaking and straining, the glider crunched to a stop.

He then heard the words, 'Thank God' and 'Hooray, we're here!'

Lieutenant Jack Watson, 'A' Company, 13th Battalion:

At 0315 they started to come in, but not from the north as expected. They appeared from all directions. It was a nightmare, and extremely frightening. I would rather be shelled any day. Some landed well, others crashed into each other. The sparks from the skids, the sounds of splintering wood and the yells from the occupants was like a scene from hell. Some of our men were hit; and it seemed like a miracle seeing the occupants get out and even drive away with jeeps and anti-tank guns.

Following the advice from the old Frenchman, Signaller Harry Leach's group had moved towards Ranville:

We made our way out onto the Dropping Zone and we were right in the middle when the 3am gliders came in and it's no great fun because you can't hear a glider coming until you suddenly hear the rush of wind and the crash as it lands.

General Gale:

I shall never forget the sound as we rushed down in our final steep dive, then we suddenly flattened out, and soon with a bump, bump, bump, we landed on an extremely rough stubble field. Over the field we sped and then with a bang we hit a low embankment. The forward undercarriage wheel stove up through the floor, the glider spun round on its nose in a small circle and, as one wing hit one of those infernal stakes, we drew up to a standstill.

We opened the door. Outside, all was quiet.

Lieutenant Burkinshaw and his 'A' Company men of the 12th Battalion were in the Forward Brigade HQ copse:

One glider, which just missed the copse, floated down almost on top of us like some giant bat and ground to a halt after a very rough landing in the field beside us. It proved to be the one which carried the Divisional Commander, Major General Richard Gale. Apparently slightly stunned and somewhat shaken up by the heavy landing, he lumbered up to me and bellowed in his customary direct manner, 'Where the hell am I?' I tried to enlighten him with my assessment of our position and told him where the CO could be found, but I must confess my confidence momentarily suffered a setback!

The ADMS, Colonel MacEwan, and his party landed in Glider 81 and were met on the LZ by the DADMS, Major Maitland, who had jumped with 225 Field Ambulance.

Work began almost immediately to clear further obstacles for the mass landing of the Airlanding Brigade in the evening, and Major Cramphorn sent a mine laying party under Lieutenant Watson to lay a belt to the east of Ranville.

Lieutenant Dean and his MMG sections passed the Ranville Church and entered the village:

I had carefully memorized the route from the aerial photographs and had no difficulty in leading George Kelly and his section to the hedge in Major Gerald Ritchie's Company area ['A' Company, 12th Battalion], and left them there to dig their position. From this point on there was 400 yards more to go before the planned location of the other section was reached, and we were on our own, myself and fourteen men.

It was quite a simple route to follow. Continue along the hedge until it ended at the road running from Ranville to Caen, cross the road, scramble up the bank on the far side and then locate a track running west towards Herouvillette. On the aerial photograph the track looked to be well used, but it turned out to be a sandy path, wide enough to take a horse and cart, with waist-high corn on either side. We turned along it and Arthur Higgins came up alongside me and we had not gone very far when ahead of us, a dark figure emerged from the corn. 'Halt, hands up' I ordered, and the figure obeyed. 'Advance and be recognized.' The shadow became substance. 'Password' I demanded. 'Punch' came the ready reply. Now 'Punch' with the response 'Judy' had been the one set for the night 4th/5th June, and a completely different one issued for 5th/6th June, 'Fish' with the response 'Chips'. I reckoned there had been an admin slip up somewhere and so a very frightened orderly from 225 Parachute Field Ambulance joined our little party.

There was still 200 yards to move along this track before arriving at a cross path junction. Here, turn right and follow the line of the hedgerow until another, yet another farm track ran off left towards La Ferme de Lieu Haras and in this vicinity I was to site the section.

The Lieu Haras was a stud farm on the northern edge of Herouvillette.

Lance-Corporal Don Jones was with this gun section:

Went through sort of one field and then another, and it was on a bit of a rise. There was a hedge and it was in the hedge that we set the gun up for camouflage of the gun and obviously ourselves.

Jones and Lance-Corporal Charlie King then began to dig a slit trench. Lieutenant Dean:

I could not fail to notice that the field of observation and fire was going to be severely restricted by the height of the corn, and in my opinion the section was incapable of carrying out its task, but I could do nothing about the problem. On the last Brigade exercise, when the platoon had operated in the machine-gun rôle, we had been briefed from the map to occupy a certain position on the ground, and given arcs of fire for the guns. However, once on the position it was impossible to carry out the task, and on my own responsibility had moved to an alternative one of my own choosing. When Captain Anton Bowler, the Brigade Machine Gun Officer gave me my detailed briefing at Keevil, I asked if I had such authority this time, and was told firmly, 'Not under any circumstances. If you do, no-one will know where your platoon are. Besides, I will be round as quickly as possible to sort out any problems you may have.'

The problem was, Captain Bowler had not turned up.

*

Due to unloading problems, General Gale was delayed on the LZ:

Whilst they were attempting to unload the glider the passing moments seemed like hours. It was still dark and this unloading was proving to be more difficult than we had anticipated. The crash we had had, though not serious, resulted in the nose being really well dug into the ground and the problem of getting the jeep out was defeating us. Eventually we had to give it up; and so on foot we set out for Ranville.

Soon dawn commenced to break, just a few yellow streaks towards the east: in a short time it would be daylight. A figure loomed up before me that I would always recognize anywhere. It was Nigel Poett.

After checking on the 12th Battalion, Poett had headed off to meet the General:

I took the main road straight through the DZ and after I had walked for perhaps half an hour . . . I met Richard Gale coming along from his glider. And so I was able to report to him that all our objectives were safely in our hands and that he'd have no anxieties as far as we were concerned.

Harry Leach's group of Brigade Signals had joined the Brigadier on the DZ and were with him when they met the General:

Somebody let off a Sten gun and all we could hear from General Gale's party was, 'The buggers have got me!' Some poor lad had a bullet through his leg, fortunately no worse. From there we made our way into Le Bas de Ranville.

Captain Anthony Windrum of the Divisional Signals then met the group:

It was near a crossroads and the General ordered a sergeant to remove the men who were gathered there, always a dangerous spot for enemy artillery. The man foolishly ignored him, saying they were not his men. So General Gale, who was of course pretty keyed-up, exploded to his companion, 'Shamus, Shamus, there's a man defying Richard Gale!' Shamus Hickie, the A/Q, hastily ordered the men away and a frightened sergeant very rapidly did as he was told.

159

In Ranville, Sergeant Fraser Edwards of 317 Airborne Security Section had got on with his usual work:

Just after leaving Brigadier Poett, I met Rene House [another member of his Security Section] *who had also been dropped. He had actually been taken prisoner and had been sat on the front of a German vehicle. However, somebody had managed to shoot to kill the driver while it was going and Rene was thrown off the vehicle. Anyway he wasn't hurt so I said, 'I know where there's a German Headquarters. Let's go and see what's in it.' So we walked back to this place, it was still dark . . . Up the steps and a door on the left, there was a light shining underneath the door. So, cocked our guns, kicked the door open, 'Hande Hoch!' There were four young Germans there. Immediately some of them started crying, 'Bitte nicht toten, don't kill us, please, please.' So we didn't. The first thing was 'Who's got the keys to the car?' because of course we were a very low priority unit with regard to transport . . . so at least we had a car. We then took their pistols off*

The German HQ Chateau that Fraser Edwards discovered in Ranville

160

them and the keys to the car and then we escorted them back to where we had left the Brigadier. By this time, there were Military Police there and so we handed these four fellows over . . . We then went back to the German Headquarters and I think on the way we stopped and we made ourselves some breakfast. We had each two 24-hour packs . . . We made ourselves some porridge and then we went and started rummaging through the documents.

*

Major Pat Hewlings and the 225 Field Ambulance men that had followed the 12th Battalion duly arrived in Le Bas de Ranville where they met their CO, Lieutenant Colonel Harvey. They went straight to the Chateau des Comtes de Guernol which had been earmarked for the Main Dressing Station. On entering the grounds they saw a number of enemy vehicles, most of which were small Citroen trucks in various states of disrepair.[3] Harvey, accompanied by Captain Wilson and four RASC men entered the Chateau to check for enemy and found three Todt workers in bed. The owners were also found, and were very welcoming. The Field Ambulance immediately began to set up their equipment.

Captain Young, the 7th Battalion Doctor, had failed to turn up at the RV, and so Major Hewlings ordered Captain John Wagstaff to take a group consisting of nine personnel of 2 Section and five reinforcements from 4 Section to form the 7th Battalion RAP in Benouville. Also with the group were a few 7th Battalion medical personnel brought up by their Padre, George Parry.

At around 0400 hours they crossed the Orne Bridge and Wagstaff spoke to John Vaughan at the Oxf and Bucks RAP.

Half an hour later the party headed for the location that Captain Young had chosen for the 7th Battalion RAP. Crossing the Canal Bridge, they turned left along the bank until reaching a track that led them to the lower road in Benouville. Captain Wagstaff knocked on the door of the selected house:

The first house we went to, I'm sure were very cagey because the Germans I believe were playing tricks on people, pretending to be invaders and when they weren't, shooting the people. We tried one or two of these houses. 'Could you get twenty people and casualties in there?' They weren't very big and had got a lot of inhabitants . . . They pointed me across to what was one of the bigger houses with the advantage that they had barns which we could make use of.

Padre Parry with Privates Anderson, Gelson, Howard, Leggett, Davis, Sleeth and Sayles set up a ward for walking wounded in Number 32, while Wagstaff and other Field Ambulance personnel moved further along the road. Opposite a large pond they walked through the stone-pillared gateway of Number 34 and entered a yard.[4] They duly knocked on the door and were greeted

Captain John Wagstaff

161

by some more wary occupants. Wagstaff explained that they were medical people and wanted to set up in their building:

I don't know how much they took in but they were all a bit stunned of course. We took most of the stuff into the house. We couldn't set up very much because it was dark.

*

Sergeant George Brownlee of the 4th Airlanding Anti-Tank Battery had met up with his officer, Lieutenant Trease and they headed for their RV near the Ranville cross-roads:

We got to the Rendezvous point. There was only the second-in-command there. He said, 'Where are all the others?' I said, 'Well I don't know.' It was chaotic. Odd men kept turning up, various guns turned up.

I went with Lieutenant Trease, who almost immediately was told he was a Captain, he and I had to recce a certain part of Le Bas de Ranville . . . We knew somebody else was supposed to go up the hill by the farm and be able to look down at Herouvillette. Another couple did that.

They then returned to the crossroads:

We were just across the road in this corner of a field. That was our little Headquarters for all the guns as they started arriving. And it was then the CRA arrived and said, 'Thank goodness you people had got in early, because you've already given me a lot of information. Now you can do even more by leading guns into positions which I will give you on the basis of the information you've given me as to where the Paras are. Some of them are not where I hoped them to be, so you will have to find other positions.' This all took time.

*

At the Canal Bridge the condition of Lieutenant 'Sandy' Smith's wounds had deteriorated:

I went back to Howard and said, 'Look, I'm sorry but I'm not able to be of much use at the moment because I can hardly move my leg and this wrist is being quite a nuisance.' By this time it had blown up into quite a nasty sight and I had a big lump under my arm, in sympathy with it I suppose, and I couldn't anyway by that time operate any finger triggers. So I was pretty useless. 'I think I ought to go the First-Aid post.' He said, and I don't blame him, 'Must you go?' because I was his last officer on the bridge except for Dennis Fox. And I said, 'Well I think I ought to get it attended to.'

He therefore went and saw John Vaughan. 'Sandy' Smith:

He patched me up a bit and said, 'You'd better stay here.' So I said, 'No, I'd better get back' and I didn't because he said, 'No. You must stay put,' and I stayed there until dawn.

162

Major Howard went forward to the 7th Battalion HQ for the 'O' Group, where his orders were confirmed. At first light he was to withdraw his men into the area between the bridges. The 7th Battalion would take over their positions on the west bank of the canal, while the 12th Battalion would protect the bank east of the Orne. Following the meeting, Howard stayed up in the village to reconnoitre possible counter-attack routes:

To a certain extent I'd done this from aerial photographs in UK the same as everybody had, but I wasn't to know where the enemy were entrenched and fighting, and I got mixed up in some of the fighting up there. In fact I can clearly remember very nearly being shot by our own parachutists because the parachutists didn't know the bloody password! I'd given the password and got fired at. Luckily, when I gave the password I was behind cover and I missed it, but I could have easily been shot there. It was a very good day, so it was another bit of luck over that thing.

He returned to his Command Post and gathered the platoon commanders defending the Canal Bridge. These were now Lieutenant Fox of 17 Platoon, Corporal Godbold, 24 Platoon, Corporal Caine, 25 Platoon and Sergeant Harrison, 14 Platoon. Howard explained exactly what was going to happen with regard to the counter-attack plan and detailed the platoon areas inside the bridges. He also gave instructions that until first light, everybody was to 'Stand To', but unless they heard otherwise, after first light, half of them could stand down. This was important because no one had had much sleep over the previous two days.

Subsequently, the Engineers occupied some German trenches to deal with any infiltration between the waterways from the south, while Tom Packwood's section of 25 Platoon was brought back across the bridge and positioned in the trenches near the gun emplacement. Dennis Fox's men occupied those to the south of it.

*

Along the canal to the north Lieutenant Parrish and his 7th Battalion party had made their advance towards the suspected enemy position:

We were in two files proceeding quite slowly and stopping now and again to investigate noises which were never caused by German agency. Gathering boldness, by the time we reached the oil storage place (0430 hours) I should have been quite surprised to have been resisted although quite ready for it. The installation was in use but there was no sign of the users. Sending a recce party up a track which ran along its south side, in the meantime I had a large hole cut in the thickly meshed wire which surrounded the installation. A quick look round inside revealed only absentees.

*

In Ranville, Captain Nobby Clark of the 13th Battalion had continued to move into position with his 'C' Company HQ party:

Lieutenant Walter Parrish

The light seemed to materialize quite suddenly as we emerged from the village's southern end with its cover of tall trees, into the north-western outskirts with its church on the crossroads, conveniently close to the Chateau and presbytery, in the garden of which Battalion HQ was set up, with our Company HQ a trifle close, I thought. Our Company was though, somewhat naked by reason of the non-arrival of 9 Platoon.

Across the north end of the little orchard in which we had stopped, and separated from it by a 'Gloucestershire type' stone wall, ran the narrow country road. On the other side of this road there stood a rather long, three-storied house. From the windows of this waved hands and pieces of cloth as though tentatively offering either friendship or surrender, dependent upon which might be best received by us, the new eruption into the lives of the occupants. A section of Number 8 Platoon, having taken up position astride the road, tried their hands at making friends, but the little group of occupants were very scary. I didn't blame them after what the village had very recently been through.

Lieutenant 'Dixie' Dean had been unhappy with the specified position for one of his Vickers guns on the southern edge of the village:

Unsatisfactory as the location was, there was no alternative but to dig in at this location. The single gun was set up, sentries posted on either flank, defensive weapon slits sited, and we set to work digging. This was quite a noisy process. Every man carried either a short-handled pick or shovel, and in addition each detachment had a two-foot length of one-inch steel piping. Once trenches were spit-locked (marked out and the top sod removed) the length of piping was hammered with the flat side of the pick, down into the ground, twice in each slit. The piping was removed and a half-pound charge of plastic explosive attached to a slow burning fuze dropped into each hole, and the explosion loosened the earth, but the noise alerted the Boche in the farm to our rear, and a few shots were fired in our direction. But the firing was wild and no serious attempt was made to interfere with our presence there.

The defences were dug, camouflaged and occupied, but there had been no visit from Anton Bowler. Andy Fairhurst kept a continuous listening watch on the wireless, but orders were to maintain radio silence unless contact was made with the enemy. We stood in our slits and waited. I wasn't at all happy with the situation, unable to carry out my task, one belt (250 rounds or two minutes firing at the normal rate) of ammunition and an unknown number of Boche no more than one hundred yards to our rear.

However, there was a possible answer to the ammunition problem. From their position they could see many containers that had been dropped:

Since there were three different coloured lights, the area in front of us resembled a railway marshalling yard, with red, yellow and orange lights twinkling away. In the daytime these were replaced by flags, one colour for small arms ammunition, another for sapper stores and the third indicated medical supplies.

With an NCO and half a dozen men to search the containers for any Mark VIIIZ, I set off for the low crest of the Ring Contour, south of Ranville. [5] If all had gone well *for the 12th they were to have a force up on this feature and I wanted to know their exact location in case we had to open fire. Both parties were to be disappointed, no machine-gun ammunition and no sign of the 12th, but I had been able to have a good look at the surrounding countryside, especially to the south-east, the direction from which the Panzers were expected. To the immediate south, the industrial complex of Colombelles dominated the area, and further to the left of the village of St Honorine la Chardonerette slept secure within its stone walls, and all was quiet and peaceful as any morning in rural England. But those vast open fields looked ideal for armour to manoeuvre across. I turned and looked back over towards the DZ and several gliders were clearly visible. These and the little coloured flags of the containers were the only signs of the largest airborne operation the world had ever experienced.*

Chapter Ten

Coup de Main Glider 94

Major Howard still had no idea of what had happened to Lieutenant Hooper's 22 Platoon, including Captain Priday, in Glider 94. The landing by Staff-Sergeants Lawrence and Shorter itself had been fine, although they touched the ground rather more quickly than Brian Priday expected:

> We hit it very hard, for it was extremely dark and the pilots could hardly see, and bounced up into the air again. We seemed to poise for a minute with our nose in the air and then we came crashing to earth once more, tearing along the ground at terrific speed. The wheels must have come off, for the floor of the glider broke up and the seats came adrift. We came to a standstill, the people on my side almost lying on their backs.
>
> With difficulty we got out of the wreckage. We were all out by 0022 hours. Instead of recognizing my surroundings, they were completely strange to me.[1]

It had been a magnificent piece of flying because the glider had landed beside a waterway, only thirty-five yards from a bridge:

Glider 94 only yards from the River Dives bridge. Varaville is to the west

The fuselage was resting in a ditch that ran parallel with the waterway, the right wing tilted down until it nearly touched the water. As the men had got out, they too realized that we were at the wrong place, and they took up all-round protection of the machine. I moved them away in case the enemy decided to open up on us from anywhere, when they would surely aim at the aircraft with its white stripes showing up in the darkness. I sent Lieutenant Hooper off to have a look at the bridge, and after another look round the men, where I found Sergeant Barwick looking after our rear, I joined Hooper. There was a swampy bit of ground and a fairly wide ditch with high banks, then an embankment leading up to the road and bridge. When we reached the road we could see a German steel helmet on the walls of the bridge, but no enemy. I decided not to break the silence for fear of spoiling the element of surprise for the others, who I hoped would be at the correct place. Withdrawing, I left the road, hoping the enemy would think us a crashed bomber as they had done at Syracuse, and made off to work out my position.[2] I remembered to collect my maps, binoculars and a signal pistol from the aircraft, for we were wearing light assault order, all else being left in the glider for collection afterwards. I wasn't able to do much salvaging, for the enemy on the bridge had gathered their senses and had returned to put a few bursts into the machine. We came to a deep, dry ditch and I decided to take up an all-round defence in it. Patrols were sent off after a brief 'O' Group with instructions to go off so many hundreds of yards in certain directions, to look out for landmarks, and I settled down to question the pilots on what they had seen as we came in to land.

Gradually I pieced things together and decided we were at a point south-east of Cabourg by a road running east from Varaville where it crosses the River Dives and another waterway. The two bridges were close together and in the darkness from the air could easily look like the Orne and Caen Canal bridges. The pilots were again most profuse in their apologies, and although the error meant that I should not see the fruits of my labours of the last few months and the careful planning of the last weeks, for I had been privileged to take a full share in it, I knew it wasn't their fault and gave them what consolation I could. I now made two main decisions. One was to have a little battle at this bridge, for I thought a few live rounds in this area would add to the deception plan which up to now was silent, and the second was to get back to my Regiment as strong as possible. The Regiment had a task to perform and I knew we should need all the men we had to carry it out. I gave orders to this effect. After sufficient time had elapsed to allow the proper bridge party to get going, I again moved towards my bridge. I sent Lieutenant Hooper on a small patrol forward to have a look round and I followed him closely. Two enemy sentries must have heard us and they came over to see what was happening. With a 'Comment ca va?' Hooper opened up and as they ran away, one went down. We closed to the edge of the road and a few stick grenades were thrown. We returned with small arms fire and threw grenades including No 77's, and their fire did us no harm. I was in a slit trench at the side of the road by now, with the senior glider pilot, and unfortunately a No 77 landed in our trench.

The pair of them got out of the trench and joined the others in charging across the bridge:

It burned our clothes a bit and I smiled to see his luminous feet running across the bridge. I gave the enemy a final burst from my Sten and then I brought up the rear. I was told afterwards by Lance-Corporal Lambley, who was watching from a different angle, that this last long burst of mine had fetched down a couple of enemy who were moving towards the machine gun. Presumably they were going to replace the original crew who must surely have been knocked out by the weight of our fire. It was sheer luck. I couldn't see for myself because of the smoking No 77 in my pit, but I was gratified to hear it. We got down at the side of the road as planned to check up, and I now discovered about ten or twelve of the party had failed to cross. I sent someone to the bank to tell them to cross under cover of our fire and the necessary guns were placed to cover them. This wasted a good deal of time and I sent Lieutenant Hooper and two men [the glider pilots, SSgts Lawrence and Shorter] *to have a look at a little wood I wanted to get to. I then went down to the river bank to try to make touch with the other party. No answer came to my shouts. They must have withdrawn from the bridge, but I had confidence in Sergeant Barwick, who was with them. The next thing that happened was when the men from the wood came back to report that the wood was clear and that Lieutenant Hooper was waiting for me there. Before we could move we heard voices coming out of the darkness and footsteps down the middle of the road. Very soon I recognized Lieutenant Hooper's voice. He was talking very loudly and I soon knew why. He was being marched along with his hands in the air and a Boche escorted him. I was wondering what to do when Hooper edged over towards the spot where only a few minutes before he had left me. This gave me a view of the German against the skyline.*

Lance Sergeant 'Tich' Rayner:

Coming back to us with his boots off, round his neck, weapons taken away from him, maps taken away from him . . . As he got about ten yards from me, myself and Captain Priday shouted, 'Jump Tony!' Tony Hooper jumped in the ditch away from the German, left the German exposed on the road. As he jumped, we fired. The German  *fell down dead, but as he fell down . . . he pulled his trigger and shot me through the arm. It went straight through* [the bicep area]*, never broke a bone. It burnt, my fingers went all tingly, couldn't control them much. I could lift it* [the arm]*, but very painful.[3]*

Another round had hit Captain Priday's map case:

Apparently a few minutes after dispatching the two men to report to me, a party had moved into the wood and he walked up to them, thinking it was I. They were, in fact, a party from the other bridge coming along to see what the fuss was about. The issue was obviously confused to them because of the lone escort being sent to the bridge from which all the firing had come. Guns from the enemy in the wood now opened up, and very obligingly, the gun from

Pete Barwick

168

the bridge we had just crossed fired back at them. Hoping they would fight each other, I thought it a good time to get out. Lining up on the side of the road, I gave the order, 'Go', and we dashed across the road. Unfortunately, Private Everett, my radio operator, was killed at my side and we had to leave him behind.

'Tich' Rayner also saw him:

Captain Brian Priday

He was running over there, he was our wireless operator, he got hit straight through the head. He fell down dead immediately. We tried to get his wireless off of him but unfortunately we couldn't. We were under so much fire we had to leave it, and him, there. Only about sixteen of us got across, that includes the pilots.[4]

We jumped over the hedge, found we were nearly drowned! All the area there had been flooded, so the boys got a toggle rope around my waist to pull me along. I couldn't swim much with a wound in my arm.

They had continued on through the water. Captain Priday:

During our withdrawal across the fields an aircraft roared low overhead and a stick of parachutists floated to earth. They were approached. Sergeant Lucas was in charge, and he and five others joined my party.[5] The remainder of the stick must have landed on the other side of the river. We later found another parachutist, who was suffering from concussion and did not even know his own name. He too, joined the party.

For about two hours we swam and waded, going south. In places we had to get the non-swimmers across on toggle ropes.

'Tich' Rayner:

We saw a lot of Paras drowned in this water. They had so much equipment on, they didn't have a chance, poor buggers. There were a lot of Paras who did join our party.

Captain Priday:

Then we came to a farm. It was isolated on a piece of high ground in the middle of the swamps, just what I wanted. There had been some heavy bombing going on and we saw a plane crash to earth in flames. The next day I found the pilot and brought him back with me. Leaving the platoon a little way off, I went forward with a couple of men to have a look at the farm. On rounding a corner I almost shot at a head sticking out of a window, but it spoke to me in French and I held my fire. The platoon was called up and I went inside. The Frenchman, his sister and his daughter were up and about because of the bombs. They were pleased to see us, and I had to explain how we had arrived. They fired many questions at me and I'm afraid my French was rather

Lieutenant Tony Hooper

overtaxed. I pulled out my cigarettes, but they were wringing wet and useless. The farmer asked for them 'pour manger'. He was welcome. One of my men had kept a packet dry by carrying them in his helmet, so we had a smoke. With the aid of my maps, which although soaked were serviceable, I confirmed my position, and I learned of enemy garrisons in the neighbourhood. I was told that the two bridges we had just left were guarded by fifty men. They were Russians and had German officers. Hooper came and joined forces with me. The Frenchman obviously coveted our 'fusils automatiques'. He picked one up that had been put down on the table. I must confess I covered him with mine which I was still holding, but he meant no harm and merely stood it up on its butt on the table. Before we could make him understand he had put a burst through the ceiling. No one was upstairs in bed and no damage was done. The night was cold and the wind blew. We were soaked to the skin up to our necks and some of us who had been finding the way had stepped into deep water without being ready for it and had gone right under. I decided to rest a while. I was shown to a loft which contained hay. We moved into it and pulled the ladder up behind us. Settling into the hay we got gradually warmer and the water was soaked up out of our clothing. Lookouts were posted.

'Tich' Rayner:

We went into the sheds of the farmhouse where we pushed a hole through the thatched roof and we could see Germans walking about, ten yards from us, and we had to keep quiet . . . Eventually, they did go away, but we told the farmer that if the Germans find out that we were staying in his house they would have shot him. We told him to say he didn't know we were in the farm buildings.

Rayner's wound was deliberately left unattended:

I didn't have it dressed for six hours, I had to leave it, couldn't dress it, everything was wet through and you couldn't put a wet dressing on it. I lost a lot of blood.

The men ate their K rations, giving some of their own as extras for 'Tich' due to his loss of blood.

Tich Rayner

Chapter Eleven

The Morning at Benouville and the Bridges

Following their meeting on the LZ, General Gale and Brigadier Poett had headed for Le Bas de Ranville. It was getting light by the time they reached the Chateau du Heaume, the chosen location for Divisional Headquarters. There they found that some of the Signals Section had already arrived and dug in. Captain Anthony Windrum, Divisional Signals:

> *General Gale knocked on the french windows and the startled occupants let in the unexpected visitors. Being of humbler occupation, I went to the outhouse where the Signal Office was to be set up.[1]*

The Chateau du Heaume

General Gale:

The poor people inside had not the remotest idea what it was all about. They were, I think, doubly mystified because the Germans, by all the coincidences in the world, had apparently been carrying out an anti-invasion exercise that very night. Rommel, they told us, was in the area of the German Headquarters in Le Plain! [sic] They were very frightened, these people, but very kind. They did not know at the time whether this was just a raid or the real and long waited for invasion.

Brigade Headquarters was temporarily set up in a farm a few hundred yards to the south. [2] Brigadier Poett:

I suppose I got to my Headquarters . . . about half past five, perhaps six o'clock, where I was able to pick up a wireless set and check up on everything generally. As far as I was concerned I was then OK, got all of the control again . . .

Just along the road from Gale's Headquarters was the Chateau des Comtes de Guernol, where 225 Field Ambulance had established the Main Dressing Station (MDS). Two upstairs rooms in the Chateau were converted into operating theatres while a barn was prepared for the wounded. The MDS had opened at 0400 hours and surgery commenced five minutes later.

During the night, the unit's RASC Transport Officer, Lieutenant Leslie Hill, had captured a supply truck containing such things as bread, cheese, sugar, tinned meat and tobacco, which would all be very welcome in the forthcoming days.

*

In Benouville, 3 Platoon had been ordered to take up its allotted forward position. Lieutenant Hunter, OC 3 Platoon:

We proceeded up through the village to the south end and turned to the right (westwards) along a track which was hidden from the open field to the south by a high hedge. I suddenly heard German voices from somewhere beyond the hedge. I asked McCara, who was a very small man, if he could see anything through the hedge. Dawn's early light was just on its way. Before I could stop him he squeezed through a small gap in the hedge. There was a burst of fire and he was killed. Oh God. I'd sent the brave wee man to his death.[3]

A grenade was thrown over the hedge into a slit trench that the Germans occupied. David Hunter:

When we got beyond the hedge and to the front of a detached house, we had arrived at the place where we were to dig in. I then saw to my dismay that a long line of German infantry was advancing towards us over the field. They were not much more than 200 yards away. Could we get cover in the house? I hoped it was empty. No such luck. A man within shouted 'J'ai peur, j'ai trois enfants.' Oh hell! Why do civilians have to get in the

172

way of battles? In front of the house was a small wall no more than one foot high. I ordered my men to get down there and not to open fire until I gave the order. Before that order could be carried out, all hell let loose. Grenades exploded among us, thrown by Germans from the corner of an orchard a few yards away. One of my men was killed. I got hit in the ear, but it didn't seem too bad.

Lance Corporal Eddie Gurney, 3 Platoon:

A machine gun then opened fire from inside the Chateau gates, wounding Private Whittingham, who later died of his wounds. A German stick grenade exploded near the head of our officer who started to bleed from his eyes and ears, which gave us the impression that he had a fractured base of the skull.

The platoon returned fire and gradually things quietened down.

At the Le Port end of the village the 'centrepiece' was the church which faced on to the small square. This was part of an important intersection between the Caen to Ouistreham and Benouville to Colleville roads. Along one side of the church was the cemetery and on the other, a lane with several houses and cottages running down towards the canal.

It was also at first light here that some German armour made a tentative approach from the north. Lieutenant Pool, 5 Platoon:

Le Bout du Haut. Lieutenant Hunter's men advanced up this lane from the crossroads, just beyond the carriage. Private McCara was killed after getting through this hedge

Two motorcyclists and six tanks came down [the] *road from St Aubin. We shot two motorcyclists with* [the] *Bren. The commander got out to have a look and we shot him too, so* [the] *rest of them withdrew! This job* [was] *done by 1 Section.*

This section, commanded by Sergeant McCambridge, was in a large house on the north-east corner. They had allowed the Germans to get within yards of the village entrance before opening up.

As it became lighter, the Paras began to be sniped from the church tower. Lieutenant Pool, who was dug in behind a wall on the cemetery's southern edge, took two men and ran across to the building:

We got through a door and there were steps up pretty soon, they were more or less straight in front of us. I tried to rush the tower . . . but we were driven back down the narrow staircase by stick grenades and Schmeisser fire.

The narrow entrance to the tower stairs

The tight, winding, stone staircase did not give them the slightest hope of getting to the bell tower, and so they ran back towards their position. As they scaled the wall, a bullet shaved the skull of one of the group, making him the first of Pool's men to be wounded.

John Butler and members of 9 Platoon, 'C' Company, had been sent on a patrol to the west of Le Port and had reached the far end of the wooded spur:

> At dawn we ran into a patrol of Jerries about twice the size of ours. After a bit of a fire-fight, with one man wounded, we were forced back to our perimeter where we joined the other defenders. On the way back to our main line at one point we were able to see Paras lying on a bank near the village of Le Port in an obvious ambush position, but with their backs towards us and also to the Jerry patrol that was coming towards us. The Jerries were passing a farm and an orchard at that time but once past they would be able to see the Paras with their backs towards them. The platoon sergeant then ordered a rifleman named Mortimore to run out and warn the Paras. This Mortimore did, but after running about half way to them he was hit by fire from the Jerry patrol. He lay still for a bit and then began to painfully crawl on. He was still being fired at by Jerry and may have been hit again but he kept on crawling until he was about 200 yards from the Paras when he reared up on his knees and shouted and warned them and in doing so was finally shot and killed by the Jerries.[4]

9 Platoon then took up position on the roadside between the T-junction and Le Port.

As it had slowly grown lighter, Captain Vere Hodge's FOB party in the orchard behind *La Chaumiere* could vaguely see the Paras around them lined up along a hedge and a ditch. Vere Hodge realized that for observation purposes the position was of little use. And so looking around he noticed the distinctive house on the T-junction and thought that it would make a decent vantage point. Before moving off he went to see Major Roger Neale, the Officer Commanding 'B' Company. Neale advised him that he expected the Germans to attack from the fields to the south-west, just across the road from the house itself. Captain Vere Hodge:

> I said to him, 'You'll let me know if you have to withdraw won't you?' because he knew I was going out on a limb, and he said, 'Yes.'

The four members of the party then made their way towards the T-junction. Vere Hodge:

> It was getting light . . . I tried the front door, it was locked. Around the back, two steps down, was another door. No answer there either, so with Wild West films in mind, I drew my revolver and shot at the lock. I missed, but inside the house a woman screamed. I was horrified. It never occurred to me that the house was occupied. The

John Mortimore, who gave his life for his colleagues

175

place looked slightly run down . . . It never crossed my mind to call out 'We're British soldiers. Can we come in?' In my best schoolboy French I called out 'Pardon, Madame, nous sommes soldats Anglais.'

The door opened and they were faced by a man of around sixty years of age and two young women:

'Allemandes' the man muttered. They were terrified. I suppose at 5.30 in the morning, in full kit and with blackened faces, we were hardly love's young dream!

In spite of the efforts of Vere Hodge and Alex Boomer, the family continued to believe that they were Germans. The FOB party went upstairs. Vere Hodge:

At the top of the stairs in the house was a bedroom and a little window and it was looking out on the hillside opposite which was the direction I wanted to look in . . . where the Company Commander thought the attack would come from. Alec got the 18 set, set up in the bedroom.

*

In the *Gondrée* café the family were still sheltering in the cellar when Georges heard the sound of digging:

Dawn was just beginning to break, and looking through a hole in the cellar wall (the hole is about a foot square) I saw vague figures moving among the vegetables in my garden. There was a wonderful peaceful air of dawn coming up over the land. The figures seemed peaceful enough and to my astonishment I could hear guttural orders which I always associated with any German working party. I said to my wife, 'Ils ne

The FOB house on the corner of the T-junction

176

quelent pas comme d'habitude.' The light grew stronger and I then began to have serious doubts as to whether the people I could see were in fact the crew of the bomber. Their behaviour seemed to me to be very strange. I told my wife to go to the hole in the cellar, listen and tell me if they were talking German, who said presently that she could not understand what they were saying. Then I listened and my heart began to beat quicker, for I thought I heard 'All right.' There came to my mind the thought that this was indeed the arrival of the English, but I said to my wife, 'Don't move because this may not be the real invasion. I have not heard what the BBC has said.'

Lieutenant Dan 'Tommy' Thomas

He then heard a sound at the front door. The 7th Battalion officer, Lieutenant Thomas, had decided to break into the building:

In the pitch darkness one of my men stumbled over a table and let forth a stream of language, which indicated his Cockney origin. Immediately a trap door was opened and a very frightened patron, Georges Gondrée, appeared.

Georges Gondrée:

They looked around the room. I then led them towards the cellar and invited them to go down. Reluctant at first, they were finally reassured by my friendly manner and followed me down the steps. At the bottom I showed them my wife and two children. For a moment they were silent. Then one turned to the other and said in English, 'It's all right chum,' wonderful words to me because I knew then that they were British. They had come at last. I burst into tears and there followed hugging and kissing on both cheeks in the continental manner, laughing and crying by Madame and the children and soon their faces were as black as those of the soldiers. We talked in English and they gave chocolate to the children.[5]

*

Between the waterways *the Coup de Main* party was further consolidating its position. Major Howard:

By now it was first light and I was able to move into the pillbox. It had been cleaned up, it was rather like a butcher's shop before they could do it, and they cleaned it up beautifully, found a very large Nazi flag in there which we immediately commandeered . . .

Lieutenant Sweeney's 23 Platoon had held the River Orne Bridge all night without any problems, although there were still plenty of Germans scattered around the immediate area:

177

It took about two or three hours before we had enough parachute troops there, that John was able to say to me, 'Give up your position and come into the inner perimeter.' In fact it was very nearly dawn by the time I felt safe enough to hand over to the paratroopers.

Responsibility for the defence of the bridge was passed to men of 'A' Company, 12th Battalion. Sweeney's Platoon moved into the area between the bridges. Corporal Bill 'Smokey' Howard's section was ordered to defend an area beside Dr Vaughan's RAP:

Walking from the Orne Bridge to the Canal Bridge on the left hand side, probably about a hundred yards down that road was a small orchard and we took up position there. I wasn't very happy about it because of the mortar shells hitting the trees. Not very nice.

They took cover behind an ivy-covered stone wall about three feet high:

We made ourselves as comfortable as we could. We didn't have a chance to dig in, there just wasn't the time to do that. So we just waited there to see if any infiltrators came through.

Lieutenant Sweeney:

I went down to see John [Howard], which was the first time I'd seen him since Tarrant Rushton, and he had got himself pretty well organized down in that area. He was just in fact beginning to search through the dugouts and the underground chambers, because there was quite a big fortified area. There were a lot of Germans all sitting around who were captured and about another half-dozen suddenly appeared. I saw them all being doubled away with their hands on their head.

Sapper Harry Wheeler was one of those searching the dugouts:

There were tunnels right underneath the banks coming from the bridge. They had cast iron doors on them. I crawled along one tunnel and bloody met a German! He didn't open fire, I didn't open fire, but he was gone in a flash, so he must have been to[wards] the end of the tunnel. I heard machine-gun fire afterwards so I expect he must have copped it.

Lieutenant Fox's men were on the south-east bank:

I again should have checked for any enemy in the trenches but I assumed because they were so near where John Howard had landed . . . I assumed they were empty. However, Sergeant Thornton as ever, came up to me and told me that there were three Germans asleep in the trench. We went down in this deep dug-out and even further down and came to this well dug out bunk room with three bunks in it, one on top of *the other. He took me down to show me and there they were, three Germans fast asleep with their rifles neatly stacked in the corner. This is all by torchlight. Of course we were covered in black camouflage and so Thornton said he'd take the rifles out before I did anything, and he did. I shook the nearest German, the middle bunk, which was level with me and I ripped the blanket off him. I shone the torch on my face and I just said again . . . 'Komm, komm.' The German looked up, looked at me and reached for the blanket and said whatever the equivalent in German is 'Oh f*** off!' and went back to sleep. Thornton cried his heart out. He laughed and laughed, lay on the floor laughing his head off. So I said, 'Oh to hell with this' and 'take over' and left him to do all the work. It was done so naturally, this German presumably thinking one of his friends was having a joke on him or something. It never occurred to him that it was the enemy or anything like that. It took the wind right out of my sails. Here was a young officer, first bit of action, first German he'd seen, giving him an order and to receive such an expression, taking no notice of, was a bit deflating!*

Thornton put his Sten on automatic and fired beneath the bunks. The Germans moved.

These were not the only people having a problem comprehending what had occurred during the night. Lieutenant Sweeney:

There was an Italian slave worker going along and he had brown battledress type uniform on. By the side of these holes were the poles where they were going to stick them . . . John and I walked over to him and I don't know how we communicated, but we said, 'What are you doing?' He said, 'Well, I work here and this is my job. I've got to put these poles up.' And so we said, 'Isn't it a bit late, we've already landed!'

Wally Parr decided to take a look in the gun emplacement:

Charlie Gardner came with me with two other fellows . . . It was getting slightly light and we could see what we were doing. The only way into the gun pit was to go down a flight of concrete stairs. The gun pit itself was covered with a large umbrella, a brown and green painted camouflaged corrugated tin. We got in there, the space between the lower part of the lid to the gun pit itself was no more than eighteen inches, so you had to go in down these stairs. Turning right as you went down the stairs, two of the chaps went in there. I didn't bother, I just went straight into the gun pit and climbed in and looked at this thing. I'd never had any experience of one of these before. We knew it was there, we knew its calibre, we knew a lot about it. I climbed onto the seat, I sat there and looked. In front of me was a telescopic sight, there was an elevating handle, a traversing handle. I tried them out, the gun swung up and down, and it was gorgeous. It traversed left and right, we got the thing going. The chap behind me had opened the breech, somebody was bringing up ammunition. They had a very large shell . . . I'd say just over two foot, two foot six . . . We slammed one up the breech. Right, all we've got to find out, how to fire the thing. Charlie was stood next to me. Now I worked out that if you're elevating and rotating this side, the firing button must be on the other side. I walked round there looking for it, I climbed up onto the base of the thing, and was

Charlie Gardner

looking around and Charlie said, 'Hang about, I've found something here Wally . . . There's a button here.' I said, 'Well press it and see what happens.' He did. The first shell from that gun was fired by Charlie Gardner by accident! They took off in the general direction of Caen and I turned a somersault backwards! I thought both my eardrums had gone. Charlie clambered back, turned round and said, 'I want nothing else to do with it. It's all yours.'

Two of the glider pilots, Oliver Boland and Len Guthrie, had carried out a reconnaissance along the towpath towards the sea. Oliver Boland:

Coming back from that reconnoitre, we were walking along and there were some dead Germans in the grass at the side. Fortuitously, I kicked one for no particular reason. Turned out to be the best thing I ever did 'cos they got up! They'd been waiting, playing possum. They'd come out of the hedge, heard us, couldn't get back in cover and they'd thrown themselves on the ground on the basis of being dead, until we go past and we'd have probably been dead instead. But in the bravado of my ridiculous youth I belted one with the boot, in case. I nearly fell down dead when they got up. So we took them prisoner.

*

By 0510 hours Lieutenant 'Dixie' Dean had returned to his MMG position on the southern outskirts of Ranville:

Once back at the section position, H-Hour for the seaborne assault was fast approaching, and my binoculars were focused on a solitary Halifax bomber loitering about in the direction of the coast, when suddenly all hell was let loose. We had been warned of the barrage which was to precede the actual landings, but I had never imagined it would be of such a ferocity, from dead quiet to indescribable bedlam in the matter of seconds.

Lieutenant Richard Todd, HQ, 7th Battalion:

The vibration of air and ground, the magnitude of that destructive assault, was far beyond anything I could have imagined. From our grandstand positions on the slope of the knoll at Le Port, the sights and sounds were literally breathtaking. The ground shook beneath us, and I felt sorry for the poor sods I could visualize cowering in those German bunkers. How could they possibly emerge and fight back?

Phillip Crofts, 'A' Company, 7th Battalion:

Even at this distance inland, my eardrums were going in and out. I thought they would burst. On top of that there were obviously huge shells coming over, they were passing over us and it felt like they were tearing the skies apart.

Colonel Pine-Coffin:

It was music to the battalion and spirits rose with the rumbling of it. The sense of fighting a lone battle passed completely, even fatigue was forgotten.

'Dixie' Dean:

As the minutes passed, the uproar rose in fearsome crescendo, and it seemed that no one could survive such a battering. It also meant that I could at last break radio silence and inform some higher authority of our plight, but try as he may, Andy Fairhurst could not contact Brigade, nor was there any response to our calls from other Machine-Gun Platoons of the 7th and 12th Battalions.

*

Towards Ouistreham, along the western bank of the canal, Lieutenant Parrish, having found the oil installation empty, had sent a patrol along a track on its southern side:

The reconnaissance party returned and reported that the track joined a road, that there were no Germans about and the wire did indeed surround the storage tanks.

Time was running short. The ground was tricky with wire fences and ditches and it was with a sense of urgency that I began the last leg of our approach to the outpost position.

Mistaking in my haste the position of the gun site, we began to penetrate a tangle of bramble bushes which lay on the left of our line of approach. This was, to date, the greatest enemy we had met. By the time we were extricated the war was a distant thing, the drop was forgotten, the enemy a vague thing and officers, especially me, were an anathema.

Luckily the objective was next door and we occupied it – it was deserted.

Just as dawn was rosily flushing the east . . . Wilkes took a section to face the road which was about 350 yards distant and the lance corporal faced the sandpit bounding the north of my position and overlooking a bend in the canal. I further placed two men close to the canal bank, while I had a small HQ in a pit in the approximate centre. An LMG was placed to cover our rear as I expected to be cut off from the battalion.

These dispositions were hardly made when D-Day was heralded by long and large explosions from seawards (I could just see the tower of the church at Ouistreham from my Command Post). Clouds of dust and smoke, tinged gently to roseate hues by the fading dawn, towered high above the church, showing how close we had approached to the coast.

This Naval bombardment continued until 0615 hours when it became even more intense as thirteen destroyers added to the cacophony. Just over half an hour later, seventy-two guns of the 3rd Division's artillery began the 'run-in shoot' from their LCTs. It was to the backdrop of this exhibition of immense firepower that just before 0700 hours the rumble of tracked vehicles became apparent in the southern part of Benouville. Lieutenant Atkinson's battle outpost in the Chateau grounds saw a number of tanks coming up the main road from Caen and begin to form up to attack the village. However, they halted and the crews got out and began a discussion. Some then started to move forward on foot to try and obtain a better view of their objective. Atkinson's men opened fire and the survivors immediately ran back to their vehicles and withdrew.

*

At 0630 hours the Germans attempted to probe the Divisional perimeter from the south-east. Lieutenant Colonel Alastair Pearson's 8th Parachute Battalion of 3 Parachute Brigade, which had begun to establish itself in the Bois de Bavent, had set up a PIAT detachment on the Escoville to Troarn road, at a road and track crossroads around a thousand yards forward of the main junction known as the Triangle, where it met the Breville road. Six half-tracks drove up from Troarn and each was hit by a PIAT. The enemy crews dismounted and took up position on the side of the road. A fire-fight ensued, but the Germans eventually withdrew. This was another vital interruption to the initial German reaction in the area.

*

In southern Benouville further German armour became apparent in the shape of SP guns and armoured cars. Attacks began with heavy calibre fire straight down the road. Major Taylor, 'A' Company:

> They'd brought up self-propelled guns which were able to shoot at us at a range we couldn't touch . . . and we hadn't got any radio to get in touch with the battalion. So what the chaps did who were in houses on the edge of the village was to pull back into the houses, they just left one or two men to keep look out, and then when infantry actually came in, they re-manned the windows and the garden.

Major Taylor moved Company HQ to a zig-zag trench which the Germans had dug at the side of the road to avoid aerial attacks. This was around a hundred yards north of *Le Carrefour de la Maternité*.

The Germans subsequently tried to penetrate the village with tanks, supported by SP gun fire.[6] Eddie Gurney saw several approaching:

> They stopped near the Chateau gates and the one to my right opened fire. The shell hit a wall about three or four yards to my left.

One tank started to move down the street. Major Taylor:

> I had alongside me our only PIAT, with a splendid, splendid soldier who was a typical Somerset Light Infantryman, a big round-faced countryman. We heard this tank coming. People were shouting to us where it was, how near it was and there was a high wall. I said, 'Now don't fire until I give you an order to fire. Aim at his sprocket wheel.' So he was all loaded up . . . and he crept round the corner. I said, 'Now wait, wait, FIRE!' He pulled the trigger and there was just a click. He turned round, looked at me and said, 'It's bent, sir!'

182

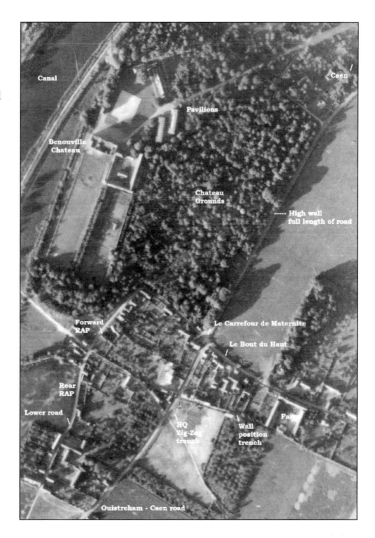

The area of Benouville that 'A' Company occupied

Labels on the image: Canal · Caen · Pavilions · Benouville Chateau · Chateau Grounds · ----- High wall full length of road · Forward RAP · Le Carrefour de Maternite · Le Bout du Haut · Rear RAP · Lower road · HQ Zig-Zag trench · Wall position trench · Far... · Ouistreham - Caen road

The tank was only four yards from the zig-zag trench. Private Michael McGee stepped out from behind a wall and began walking towards it, firing a Bren from the hip at a range of ten yards. The tank stopped and two Paras ran out and attacked the vehicle with Gammon bombs. Another bomb blew a track off a second tank which then attempted to escape, but could only turn in a circle, so the crew baled out and were dealt with by McGee. The remaining tanks fell back.

Shortly after, the SP guns moved forward and began firing into the village. Major Taylor:

The houses on the forward edge (south) of the village became untenable because we had nothing with the range to keep the SPs quiet, so Villis had to be retired into houses farther back.

Michael McGee

183

Infantry were again attacking Lieutenant Hunter's 3 Platoon, which was also forced to withdraw:

'Get the hell out of here!' I shouted and led them up a track leading back northwards to the back of the farm. This unfortunately allowed the Germans to come through the farm under cover. I thought we were very vulnerable but we couldn't retreat any further.

I spotted a German up a tree about fifty yards away trying to get a better view of us. I grabbed Pembury's rifle and shot the German who fell from the tree. I had a Sten gun which was only effective at very short range – about three feet in my case.

Lance Corporal Eddie Gurney:

We set up a defensive position astride the main Caen-Ouistreham road on a bank of earth bordering a sunken cart track that was about ten feet wide. On the opposite side of the track and immediately in front of us was a seven-foot brick wall with a wooden door at one end.

Major Taylor:

The position then was that we were holding a sort of reverse slope position behind the village. It was remarkably effective. The Germans couldn't get at us, but if he tried to infiltrate we had snipers in odd houses who gave the general run of the battle by shouting so that most could hear (we were in an extremely tight locality). Mortar fire was not particularly effective against us.

Private Chris Tallboys:

A tank started to come down the road so I tied four or five tank mines together on a string and pulled them across the road. The tank driver must have noticed them and started to fire shells at them. The shells hit the road and skimmed up, knocking the tele-graph pole down, but they couldn't get by.

Major Taylor was lying on a bank of the zig-zag trench, watching what was happening to David Hunter's Platoon:

On my right as I was lying down on my face there was a wooden telegraph pole. This damned gun fired and it hit this telegraph pole about four feet above me I suppose, and a fragment came down and got me on the inside of my left thigh. It was a damned close run thing I can tell you, because it must have gone over the back of my right thigh and into my left.

Major Nigel Taylor

The shell caused a number of casualties. RAMC personnel administered a shot of morphine and dressed his leg, but the wound made it impossible for him to command the Company and so Captain Jim Webber assumed responsibility. Webber had been just across the road from Company HQ:

I occupied a house and did a bit of sniping from there. I let off one or two shots and moved. I went right back behind the wall. I thought I was fairly safe behind this wall and I was a bit lazy and went back and stood in the doorway. Luckily I did because a bullet hole appeared through the wall.[7]

Crossing the road in itself was very dangerous because of the SP gun targeting the road, but around half an hour later Webber managed to return to the zig-zag trench and report his experiences. Major Taylor:

He had been up in the bedroom of this house because he got a good view up this village street and a German armoured car came right up the street. The armoured car commander had been stupid enough to open his hatch and stick his head out to have a look round. Jim had a sniper rifle which he had picked up off one of our dead snipers, with a telescopic sight on, and he neatly shot him through the head.

Jim Webber:

About fifty minutes later [following the pole incident] *I was sitting in the same spot as Nigel had been, when the* [SP] *gunner got a hit on the corner of a house and I got a shell splinter in my lung.*

However, he continued carrying out his duties as if nothing had happened.[8]
To the west of the zig-zag trench Stan Young of 1 Platoon tried to advance with a few men behind the area of the houses and farm:

There was a wall all down in front of us . . . then it went out into the fields. There was a bank and we were looking across the bank. We were right up the far end of it.

Some Germans came through the bushes and the Paras killed two or three, but then they heard a tank coming and jumped over the wall. Two men ran into a cowshed on the corner of the lane. The tank, which had come across the fields from the south, turned towards the wall, fired a shell and demolished the shed, but then for some reason, retired. Although relieved, the remaining Paras could not understand why it backed off.
On the lower road Bill Law, who had been wounded in the shoulder, arrived at the RAP at Number 32:

The first person I saw actually was Reverend Parry. He was mostly at that time looking after the wounded. He said, 'We've got no room here,' 'cos they were all laying about. Of course they couldn't even get them under cover, so they built up part of it with

The Reverend George Parry

a canvas, like a tent, and they had a lot of them in that. He said, 'Could you become walking wounded?' Yes, I can walk but I've got a couple of bullets in my shoulder.' He said, 'They won't be taken out here.' I thought 'What did he say that for?' 'Well in that case you can be taken back to England.' I said, 'Are you joking?' He said, 'No, there's a hospital ship waiting out there to take you back to England.' They had no more room there, they had so many wounded.

A great friend of mine, Pete West . . . he had his ankle smashed, so I said to him, 'Do you reckon you can make it Pete?' Yes, I think so if I could get a stick or something, something to hold on to.' I propped him up with a bit of a stick and we went off.

They left the Aid Post, but had to wait until a link was established with the seaborne forces before heading towards the beach.

A few hundred yards behind 'A' Company, Lieutenant Tommy Farr's 4 Platoon, 'B' Company, was on the edge of the wooded spur that ran west from the area of the T-junction:

At first light we noticed a lot of movement in the open ground to the west of our position. We were attacked soon after this. The attack started by machine-gun fire from the end of the hedgerow on our right front; we returned this and nothing much seemed to be happening. We then noticed a couple of sections of Germans approaching from the west along the gully at the bottom of our spur (south side of it). They had not seen us and we were able to let them come right up to us before we opened fire. Unfortunately the cover was good, and although we got quite a few, some of them went to ground. The attack now developed from the direction of the original machine-gun position and the Germans were advancing in ground which was dead to me. I reported the position and was ordered to withdraw to the road, which I duly did.

I lost a couple of chaps in getting out and one of them was a Bren gunner, but thanks to Sergeant Cherry, his weapon was not left. The enemy was now in the wood between us and Company HQ but by keeping on the Le Port side of the wood we were able to get back to the road where we consolidated with Company HQ. The attack did not develop and although a few shots were exchanged, the enemy did not attack Company HQ from this direction.

Trouble at this time was coming from the Benouville direction (south) and there was a lot of activity at the T-junction on the south side of Company HQ.

At 0730 hours Captain Wagstaff and his RAP party were treating about half a dozen wounded in the forward Field Ambulance building when they realized that the sound of firing was getting uncomfortably close. He went up a central wooden staircase, turned left and from a bedroom window saw Germans coming along the road. Rushing back downstairs he ordered everyone to move the wounded upstairs. John Wagstaff:

Looking north along the lower road in Benouville. Captain Wagstaff's RAP was in the house behind the telegraph pole

We kept quite quiet. Two Germans came into the courtyard, inspected our equipment and spoke to the owners of the house. They apparently diverted their attention. I think they sort of saw the odd-Red Cross flag strewn about, so it all looked a bit deserted . . . Shortly afterwards an armoured recce vehicle approached and was shortly followed by a Tiger [sic] tank. But we didn't gawp, we were far more concerned with keeping the chaps safe.[9]

The Germans continued up the road and entered the other RAP house. A fight ensued, during which several medical people and wounded were killed. Having put up a terrific struggle, the Padre, George Parry was also killed. The patrol then moved on towards the Mairie.

At the T-junction, Captain Vere Hodge and his FOB party had begun to receive attention from snipers. This had occurred when the telegraphist, Alec Boomer, had by necessity put the aerial out of the window. Wilf Fortune:

Alec was trying to get a ship attached by radio and Vere was scanning the area when he saw some Germans coming into view over this sloping cornfield [to the south-west]. He called me to have a look. 'They're riding little motorbikes,' I said to him. He agreed, it looked like that, but soon you could see they were running [with knees bent due to the slope]. Captain Hodge then sent Ted and me back to the platoon to which these Germans were heading, to warn them. He was also afraid of the OP being overrun. Ted and I made our way to the orchard, arriving just before the attack came.

187

Lieutenant Malcolm 'Garth' Hill

'B' Company men saw the German armoured patrol emerge from the cover of the houses on the lower road and begin to move towards the *Mairie*. Private Dennis Fox ran forward with a group of men towards the garden of the T-junction house, where they could clearly see the tank:

It wasn't very far, just across the road. We dove in this garden . . . about six of us in the garden of that house. It had a wall between the house and the next house, only a small wall, but a gateway was in there.

In their rush to get into position the group was split into two by the wall. On the opposite side of the wall to Fox were Sergeant John 'Paddy' Armstrong of the Signals Platoon, the MMG Platoon Commander, Lieutenant Malcolm 'Garth' Hill and his batman, 'Dinghy' Sutton. Armstrong saw the tank about a hundred yards away, its turret pointing away from the Paras:

The earth was banked up against the wall and we could see over it. The Lieutenant had an anti-tank gun [PIAT]. I crouched down beside them as he put it on his shoulder and fired. I saw the shell hit the turret and bounce right off. The turret came swinging round and . . . BANG! The next thing I knew I was flying through the air with pieces of the wall.

This shell killed Hill and Sutton.

The half-track travelled past the *Mairie* and turned down the road towards the bridge. Madame Marie Deschamps was still sheltering under the covered part of the school playground when she saw the vehicle being hit and begin to burn. Terrible cries emanated from the wounded.[10] The tank turned left and began to go back down the main road towards Benouville. Major Taylor:

I could hear the battle going on in 'B' Company's area and, on one occasion, a German Mk IV tank came through from that direction. This was slightly shaking, but we got it with about four Gammons and were pleased to see him on fire.

Wilf Fortune and Ted Eley had slowly moved back during the attack. Wilf Fortune:

It was fierce, and what Paras remained retired to the next hedgerow. We (on the strategic retreat) had to scale a wall of the orchard. Poor Ted with his painful shoulder was having difficulty, even with my help (he was a big lad, Ted). This sergeant (I think) started giving us 'a bottle.' So, in my best 'Geordie' language suggested he should have seen my 'oppo' had hurt his shoulder. I shall never forget his calm reply. 'Look sonny. We're the only ones left.' We BOTH heaved Ted over that wall.

John Butler, 9 Platoon, 'C' Company, was dug in on the roadside, just up from the T-Junction:

The road was elevated and I was at the base of an eight or ten foot slope. It was not a good position and Jerry was able to get quite close before we could see him and fire at him. Our bacon was saved a couple of times by Bren gun fire enfilading down the road from the T-junction and the village.

There were very few of us, and the nearest person was about ten to fifteen yards from me. An attack had come in, which I assumed was from the platoon of about thirty that we had bumped earlier on patrol. It was mainly broken up by Bren fire from either the T-Junction or Le Port.

John Butler

I was kneeling back looking at the top of the slope with my Sten gun pointing. Suddenly a Jerry came in view with his rifle pointing towards me and I pressed the trigger of my Sten, but to my horror the man didn't fall down as I expected and just stood looking at me, and I was in absolute terror. Then the magazine ran out, it had been about half full, twelve to fourteen rounds, and probably took about two to two and a half seconds to fire off. And then the man came at me, collapsing on top of me and his bayonet pierced my left thigh, hit the bone and flipped out again, and the left side of my smock was covered in blood.

Now all of this had taken but two or three seconds, though it seemed like minutes that the man was standing at the top of the bank leering at me. He was of course dead, and the thud of bullets in his chest had held him for those few seconds, though at the time I did not realize this. All I could see was this big Jerry who seemed to be immune to my bullets and was going to shoot or bayonet me, and I was in a state of abject terror until I pushed his body off me and realized he was dead. Then recrimination set in. I felt that I had been guilty of cowardice because of those moments of terror, and to a nineteen year-old in his first day of action, this seemed to me to be a cardinal sin, something I had to hide and never tell anyone. I even hid the wound on my thigh.[11]

In the garden of the T-junction house, Dennis Fox's sergeant was pinned down by enemy fire from the *Mairie* and shouted 'Can you see them?':

I said, 'No I can't, they're not interfering with me. They can't see me obviously.' So I went across there to try and get them out. I went out the gateway, flitted across the road, got around the back. As I went through the gate I heard this noise by the back door. A couple of Jerries dragged me in the house. I was here for a few minutes, they took the belt out of my trousers and dragged me out [of] this house.[12]

Private Dennis Fox

Captain Vere Hodge and Alex Boomer were still inside the T-junction house. Vere Hodge:

Alex continued trying to get a ship, without success. There was a knock on the front door and the occupants spoke with a German soldier. Alex and I held our breaths, but they didn't give us away and the soldier left.

A sort of eerie silence fell and I thought it was time to think of leaving. So I said to the family in my broken French, 'If I don't find my friends we'll come back here. Ici.' They didn't say anything. They were absolutely terrified, poor things. It was terrible for them having two British soldiers in the house because they'd have got shot no doubt, if they'd been found out. Anyway, lying in the road was a dead man, don't really know if he was a German or one of ours, and one or two other things. There was one of our Airborne tin hats which I took and put on 'cos I'd had mine knocked off in the landing, and there was a German rifle and a bandolier of rounds for it, both of which I picked up. And then I said to Alex, 'I think this is where we exit, fairly briskly!'

They followed the line of a hedge on the *Mairie* side of the road, down towards the bridge, where they met the men of Lieutenant Thomas' Platoon on the knoll of ground west of the *Café Gondrée*.

The Airborne troops tried to deal with the wounded of both sides. From her place of shelter Marie Deschamps could see that one of the half-track victims had been dreadfully burned and a Para shouted to her, 'Do you have any medical supplies?' When the answer was negative, the wounded man was mercifully shot.

Paddy Armstrong's leg was full of shrapnel but he managed to crawl through a gate to safety before passing out. When he regained consciousness he found himself lying on a kitchen table in a farmhouse. He was offered a glass of Calvados by the elderly farmer's wife and then taken to the First-Aid post on a jeep.

*

At Battalion HQ Major Steel-Baume ordered Lieutenant Archdale to go and check on Walter Parrish's Platoon. Archdale gathered ten men from the vicinity of the HQ. One of them was Ron Perry:

He led us all down the towpath. We didn't get too far . . . We were fired at from these sort of cottages [running parallel to the towpath], *rifle fire. So that stopped us. Fired back, left the towpath, which was elevated anyway, dropped into this lower ground. That was a mistake, it was marsh, you sort of sank into it halfway up to your knees. It was difficult to move but we kept going and we cleared those cottages and went through them. We shot one or two there. In the cottage I went through at one point, there was a woman dead, with a rifle laying there. A lot of these French women were consorting with the Germans. I reckon she'd been shooting that bloody rifle. She'd been shot right through the head, right through the skull, and she was just laying there.*

Passing beyond the cottages they continued through an orchard and up a lane towards the main Caen to Ouistreham road. Perry and Nick Archdale approached the corner of a building on their left. Lieutenant Archdale:

There was a little alleyway and I looked round the corner and the bullet literally hit the wall [an inch from his eye] *and completely blinded me with brick dust . . .*

Ron Perry:

He'd got round, just, and I was immediately behind him, about to turn. The stonework between Nick and I, it just splintered it in bits.

They fell back from the corner and Archdale went into a house:

There was an old French lady in one of these houses who washed my eyes out, and she had one of our boys, who was wounded, on her kitchen table.

Lieutenant Nick Archdale

His men waited in the alleyway. Ron Perry:

I noticed this door in a high wall, typical French building, Normandy style, quite high, steep gradient on the roof. I had some vague idea of getting under cover and I kicked the door . . . There was a stairway immediately off to my right, leading up into the darkness. There was a hell of a lot of banging and clanging going on, firing in all directions. I thought if I got up there on the upper level somewhere, I'd be able to look out, see what the picture was . . . When I got to the top I was confronted by another door right at the top of the stairs, there wasn't a landing of any sort, and I burst in there and there was this couple. They were quite naked, laying on the bed. They were both spark out and the girl suddenly sat up, pulled a cover round her. This bloke didn't move at all. When he did, he looked, [and said] *'Sale Boche,' dirty German. I must have looked a sight, I was bleeding, bloody camouflage running in all directions. Other than that I was probably as white as a sheet! 'Non.' 'Vous êtes un aviateur?' That's what he thought I was for the moment, when he realized I wasn't German. And then he woke up to what was happening around. He got out of the bed, ran through this door, down the stairs and disappeared. He reappeared moments later with a bottle. So we had a swig from the bottle. Then of course I had to get back. When I got back they were digging in.*

The group had taken up position in the orchard. The Germans were on the opposite side of the main road:

Hayward [the RSM's batman] *was tucked in the verge there with a Bren gun. Behind him, the bank went up and there were all orchards there.*

A sniper shot Hayward through the heart. Sergeant Freddie Fricker, Mortar Platoon, HQ Company:

Freddie Fricker

Many French women braved the whizzing bullets to give us cider and drink. They were very grateful to us. I saw one of my men kill a sniper who had just sniped our RSM's batman. The French people had seen it too and before he could do anything to protect himself he was being kissed from all angles by women and men.

Archdale then decided to again try and reach Lieutenant Parrish via the canal bank:

By that time there was fighting all over the place, the sound of battle all around Le Port and Benouville. Our attention here was quickly drawn to a small shack on the canal bank by a burst of machine-gun fire hitting the wall between Fricker and myself. Our subsequent attack fell through as the occupants of the shack made off and were apparently covered by a Spandau from the north-west. I was a bit puzzled here. Should I push on regardless, or should I report to Eric Steele-Baume and suggest that a patrol to Walter was, for the moment, likely to be expensive, if not impossible. This was an awkward moment as I was terrified of failing in my duty, and experience could not tell me the correct path.

He decided to report back:

We then returned to Battalion HQ and were ordered by Eric S-B to prepare quickly to defend Battalion HQ as it appeared that he deemed an attack was imminent. I remember, with Mr Johnson the RSM, setting up a Bren gun and having a bit of fun with one little attack, but this massive attack did not take place.

After brewing up, he went to see Colonel Pine-Coffin who ordered him to go and find out what was happening in the areas of Major Neale and Lieutenant Pool. Nick Archdale:

I had to keep the Commanding Officer informed. He had no other means of knowing what was happening. I left Sergeant Freddie Fricker to establish a defensive position for Battalion Headquarters and went to try and head off these small German attacks. It was like playing cowboys and indians, only we were better at it than they were. I took two men with me and we had quite a lot of fun getting into the cracks, looking over walls and doing a bit of shooting.

I found him [Lt Pool] sitting quite gaily under the southern wall of the church with Private Miller, having a sniping match with a Spandau. There was a good deal of blood splashed about [on the wall]. I remember Ted and I sitting under a wall, sort of chatting there.

There wasn't continuous shooting, there never is. You had long spells when nothing was happening at all. Of course the men, inevitably, were playing cards. Vingt-et-un was the game . . . pontoon.

From him I went south down the road ditch and met Roger Neale, who told me of Garth Hill's death and that there was no contact with 'A' Company.

The piecemeal but varied attacks around the village had isolated 'A' Company from the rest of the battalion.

*

At the bridge Major Howard had ordered Wally Parr to 'Get the strips out.' Wally Parr:

These were fluorescent strips. They were in a very bright greeny-yellow colour and a sort of chaparraly pink, and we weighed them down with weights all across the bridge. Just after dawn, sweeping out of the sky came the first fighters and it was a most emotional experience. They turned in the sky . . . they came down and peeled off and as they came over the bridge, and they couldn't have been more than two or three hundred feet above us. Each one did a 'Victory Roll'.

Major Howard:

As they did so, I estimated that they were about less than a mile away, they dropped something which could have been I thought, reserve petrol tanks. Anyway, I sent a section out to find out in case it was messages and when they came back, believe it or not, it was the early morning papers. The RAF's contribution to us. There was no mention of course of the invasion.

They all went for the Daily Mirror *because it had a wonderful cartoon strip that portrayed a girl named Jane who was always in her undies or nudity and of course very popular amongst the troops, indeed everybody!*

At around 0800 hours Corporal 'Smokey' Howard received orders to take a farm cart with all of their spare ammunition from their position near the Orne Bridge up to the Canal Bridge. He and 'Buck' Read pulled it along the road and Howard, concerned about the sniping and open ground to the south, used smoke grenades to cover them:

We got the ammunition across to the other side to John Howard's Command Post. I went in there, it was the first time he ever called me 'Smokey', it was always Corporal Howard. 'Smokey, there's some lovely bottled water in this place if you want any!'

Coming out he was greeted by Wally Parr shouting 'Have a look at my gun 'Smokey'!'

Further along the canal bank, since their arrival at dawn Lieutenant Parrish's platoon had not been bothered by any German activity:

The first incident to concern us was the arrival, all unknowing, of three civilians with one bicycle. They approached to within 100 yards before they saw us and then began to depart. A shot over their heads brought them back and the usual emotional scene followed. I was kissed on one cheek, but managed to save the other one. These

193

The three Horsas at the Canal Bridge. To the left the German vehicle can be seen strewn across the road. To the right, on the road, is the Mercedes staff car

Frenchmen had no news, so I parked them in the small quarry which was behind my Command Post and forgot them until very late that day.

Then something important happened. Driven inland from the bombardment, three vessels of the fishing type, came up the canal. The decks were armed with what was either an AA LMG or a light shell firing piece, manned by men in the uniform of, I believe, the GAF.

As the vessels came level with my canal bank post, my men there raked the decks with Sten fire; four or five enemy were seen to drop and it is difficult to see how they could have escaped death from that range. It was about thirty yards. The ships went on up the canal towards the bridge.

Still without any knowledge of how Parrish and his men were faring, Colonel Pine-Coffin ordered Lieutenant Todd to gather a patrol to go and find out. He rounded up about eight members of the Mortar Platoon. Richard Todd:

We set off along the line of the canal towards Walter Parrish's position . . . Along the way, in the rough ground between the Ouistreham road and the canal, I could see a glint of metal and I thought 'sniper'. So I got my chaps to get down, take cover and give me cover, and I went down to the canal, underneath the height of the bank until I got parallel with whatever it was that I'd seen. I started to crawl towards it, there was no sign of any movement, so I stood up and walked and it was one of our own chaps. He was shot [in the middle of the forehead] *and I recognized him . . . about eighteen,*

194

nineteen. No blood, no mess, no nothing, just a hole in his head, dead. He'd fallen forward on his rifle in a sort of firing position . . .

I got to Walter, found that everything seemed to be in order although he too had a skeletal platoon.

*

The Forward HQ of 5 Parachute Brigade had been established in the copse a few hundred yards east of the Orne Bridge. Lieutenant Guy Radmore, OC Signals Section:

Certainly by seven in the morning everyone was more or less coming in and I distinctly remember listening to the BBC News to say we'd landed, the seaborne chaps had landed. In the meantime a corporal and two men had gone down a manhole which I'd spotted and disconnected this telephone line.

This cut contact between the bridge and the German Battalion HQ.[13]

Lieutenant Burkinshaw's Platoon of 'A' Company, 12th Battalion that had initially been in the copse were ordered to move to Le Bas de Ranville:

On the way I was told to stop and take up a position on the side of the road there and to dig in, which I did commence doing.

Their position was on the Ranville-Benouville road facing north and east to protect the DZ, 'N'.

*

In spite of all the problems encountered, 5 Parachute Brigade and the Divisional troops were now in their defensive positions, although not in the planned strength. Brigadier Poett:

We were just absolutely thrilled that these plans, which we had been chewing over for two months, they really had worked, and worked one hundred per cent. My main anxiety I thought was going to be the 12th Battalion on the left because the ground was very vulnerable up there. The 7th Battalion had behind them the extra Company of John Howard's, they were close up to the bridge, they had something behind them, whereas the 12th were rather on a limb out there.

General Gale outside his HQ, the Chateau du Heaume (IWM FLM 3450)

Gale's only reserve was the 22nd Independent Parachute Company.

With Divisional HQ established, at around 0900 hours General Gale set off to see how things were faring at the bridges.[14] Lieutenant Sweeney was at John Vaughan's RAP:

There was my old pal Den Brotheridge with a bullet mark

195

through his throat, dead by this time, together with the German officer who was white-faced and unconscious, having been given his injection of morphine, together with two or three other chaps, some of whom had been hurt in the glider. One of my soldiers got shot in that first fire-fight when the patrol came up the path, Private Allen, who was my medical orderly and he was there and David Wood who had been shot in the leg and Sandy Smith . . . They were all lying there with the Doctor in charge, up a narrow track . . . I stayed there for a little while and I think I then brewed up a cup of tea because we'd had nothing since the day before, and it was at that moment that I saw General Gale and Brigadier Poett with their red berets.

Doctor Vaughan also saw the party marching briskly along the road towards them:

They were General 'Windy' Gale, commander of the 6th Airborne Division, Brigadier Kindersley, Commander of the 6 Airlanding Brigade, Brigadier Poett, Commander of the 5 Parachute Brigade and Colonel 'Technicolor' MacEwan, the Chief Medical Officer, looking even more conspicuous than the others with his heavily be-ribboned chest. It was a remarkable morale booster, albeit rather foolhardy under the circumstances as enemy sniping was by this time keeping our heads down.[15]

'Tod' Sweeney:

Gale was wearing a pair of sort of pinkish brown jodhpurs and a cravat round his neck, his red beret and a rather smart airborne jacket . . . He'd always preached that the Projector Infantry Anti-Tank could not take on a tank full-face because the armour is heavier in the front, and it must always be sited to a flank. I'd dropped this PIAT of mine at the road junction where I'd gone up the track to the RAP, so the guy was there facing either up that road [East] or down that road [West]. And as I was hovering about he called me over and gave me a rocket and said, 'Now look, I've always said you must never site your Projector Infantry Anti-Tank to the face the tank, it must be to a flank.' So I said, 'Yes sir' and moved it away.

Gale and his small entourage then walked on towards the Canal Bridge. As they approached, the password was requested, only to find that they had forgotten the reply. Corporal Ted Tappenden:

I remember one of our lads saying, 'You were bloody lucky sir, you nearly got your head blown off.'

After warm greetings to some of the men, they stopped to talk to Major Howard at his Command Post. Colonel Pine-Coffin subsequently saw two figures walking nonchalantly across the bridge:

They seemed to possess charmed lives and to be confident in this knowledge as they showed no signs of hurry although there was plenty of reason to do so over that unhealthy spot. Look-outs with glasses reported them to be General Gale and the

Commander of the Airlanding (gliderborne) Brigade, Brigadier the Honourable AKM Kindersley . . . They were seen to stop and chat to Thomas' men and then swing right-handed and walk slowly down the canal bank.[16]

Pine-Coffin and RSM Johnson moved off to meet them, arriving on the bank about fifty yards ahead of the General. Gale's position gave him a good view down the canal, and he noticed two boats coming towards them. He could not quite see what they were and so shouted to Pine-Coffin to take cover. Geoffrey Pine-Coffin:

The two boats, each about twenty foot long, chugged slowly past the party and on towards the bridge, keeping an interval of about a hundred yards between them. There was no sign of life to be seen on either, but there was a closed wheelhouse aft where the crew were presumably watching events just as closely. Each had a pom-pom gun in the bows but these were apparently completely unmanned. It was obvious that they did not know what the situation was and had come down to try and find out. Not a sign were they given however, although everyone in the area was watching intently for an opportunity. The opportunity arose when the leading boat was within a hundred yards of the bridge.

One of the boats opened fire with its heavy machine gun on the 7th Battalion HQ, and the Paras responded. Nobby Clark of 24 Platoon was positioned behind some large rocks on the bank, north-east of the bridge:

We heard the 7th Battalion about two hundred yards down on the other side, firing at them. One turned tail and went back off towards Ouistreham and this other one got in the middle of the canal and it started to drift down. You couldn't hear the engine, it must have been geared down as low as possible to cut out the engine noise. We wondered whether they'd killed some people aboard and it was just drifting. Because we weren't sure if it was an attempt to go down and blow up the bridge or something, we decided to put a PIAT bomb into it and if there was anybody in the wheelhouse, it would get them. When it got level with us, we were probably fifty yards down on that side, on the bank, myself, Corp Godbold and Jess Cheesley, Godbold it was, he fired the PIAT . . . We fired at the rear end of the wheelhouse, where we thought the engine might be. It went off in the boat internally and it immediately swung in, came into the bank. . . [17]

The boat's occupants were taken prisoner and Claude Larkin searched the vessel for explosives but none were found. The prisoners were given to Nobby Clark:

They were the only two on there . . . a little swarthy looking bloke, could have been a Russian or a Pole and a tall arrogant bastard who was probably a German. He was a bit bolshy till I thumped him on the shoulder with my rifle butt. He realized he wasn't in charge any more. Claude Godbold

197

Nobby Clark

Lance Corporal Arthur Roberts:

A right arrogant perisher of a German officer in command, right nasty. 'My Fuhrer will do this . . . my Fuhrer will do that . . .' Claude [Godbold] said, 'One more bloody Fuhrer out of you and I'll put the bayonet up you!'

Nobby Clark:

I took him to John Howard and he said, 'Take them down to Brigade Headquarters.' When I got to the River Bridge, on the south-east side of the bridge was a paratrooper, only a short bloke, laying there in agony. He reckoned he'd got a bullet that had smashed his spine and he asked me to shoot him. I said, 'I can't do that old son. I'll get someone to you as soon as I can, I'm going into Ranville, but there's people over here on the bridge.' I shouted something to three blokes on the opposite side, 'Come and do something with this guy will you?'

Walking between the bridges was of course certain death. I'm glad I had two German prisoners 'cos I got in the middle of them.

In Ranville he dropped them off at the prisoner of war pen which had been hastily erected by the Airborne Military Police.

*

At their meeting, Brigadier Poett joined Pine-Coffin, Kindersley and Gale. Geoffrey Pine-Coffin explained that he had no idea how 'A' Company was faring in the southern end of the village because runners could not get through, but they were obviously putting up a terrific fight because of the amount of fire being given and taken. It was apparent to both Gale and Poett that the battalion would not give way, but there was still the possibility that it might be overrun. After the meeting Poett stayed with the battalion while Gale set off back to Ranville.

Lieutenant Bertie Mills

In an attempt to find out what was going on in Benouville, Pine-Coffin's Intelligence Officer, Lieutenant Bertie Mills, led a patrol into the lower part of the village and found the bodies of those killed in the RAP. Captain Wagstaff was still in the forward RAP house:

About 0930 hours Private Howard came across the road and reported that a patrol of 7th Battalion Headquarters had passed by and advised remaining RAMC personnel in the road to come back with them. Howard had come

198

across to collect his kit whilst the two others had moved off with the patrol.

Private Howard also told us that the Padre had been shot and he believed that Sleeth, Sayles and Leggett had also been shot.[18]

However, Wagstaff decided to stay where he was:

We couldn't evacuate with any speed and I reckoned the risks trying to get away were far greater than the risks of staying put. We knew that the Germans were pretty well all around us.

With the Battalion RAP being, in effect, out of action, a location had to be found to set up another. Georges Gondrée had earlier offered the use of his café for the treatment of the wounded, and it was in an ideal position for such a purpose. And so at around 1000 hours, Captain Urquhart of 225 Field (Para) Ambulance decided to establish a First-Aid post there.[19]

*

After crossing the canal, Gale had informed John Howard of the Para's situation. Howard therefore sent two sections of 25 Platoon, each of around seven men under Corporal Bailey and Lance Corporal Minns, across the bridge. These were met by Lieutenant Thomas. Dennis Edwards was a member of Minns' section:

We found a quiet spot beneath a tree to have a bite to eat. I had eaten nothing since leaving England and was glad to open my twenty-four hour ration pack which consisted of a few dry biscuits, boiled sweets and a bar of unsweetened chocolate. I chewed a hard biscuit and sucked a sweet. It was not much, but for a short time it took my mind off the thought of food, until suddenly our 'meal' was interrupted by a long burst from an enemy heavy machine gun. The stream of bullets ripped through the tree inches above our heads, showering us with twigs and leaves. At that moment the 7th Para Battalion's Commanding Officer, Lieutenant Colonel Pine-Coffin, accompanied by a young officer (Richard Todd), appeared next to our tree, crouching to keep below the line of the machine-gun fire, and busily looking all around, taking in the picture. The two of them paused momentarily, glanced up at the splintered tree and the Colonel said to his companion, 'That is not too healthy old boy. He's firing just a shade too close for comfort. We had better deal with him, eh?' With Stens tucked under their arms, they wandered off southwards in a leisurely manner and disappeared through a gap in a nearby hedge. A few moments later came the rat-a-tat-tat of two Stens, followed by complete silence.

Soon they reappeared with broad smiles on their faces, looked towards us and the Colonel said, 'Well lads, that's fixed him up.' With a casual wave they continued strolling on their way, two grand officers who gave the impression of having not a care in the world, although they must have realized that the situation was fast becoming desperate.[20]

*

Lieutenant Hunter's 3 Platoon was still under pressure on the bank position opposite the high wall in Benouville. The Germans had occupied several gardens on the

199

opposite side of the wall and began throwing stick grenades over it.[21] Lance-Corporal Eddie Gurney:

The Germans launched several counter-attacks, one of which penetrated to the far side of a wall about ten feet in front of me. A stick grenade landed close to me, which I knocked into a sunken lane in front of me and I replied with one of my grenades, which silenced things a lot.

Lieutenant Hunter:

Private Pembury, who was beside me, was badly wounded with a shattered leg. He lay on the roadway which ran alongside the wall of the farm. I took out his two large field dressings and bandaged him up as best I could. I also gave him a shot of morphine. While I was doing this I put my Sten gun down. Suddenly the door in the wall was flung open. I looked up and was confronted by a German no more than a yard away with his Schmeisser sub-machine gun pointing right at me. I was a press away from oblivion. He hesitated long enough to enable one of my men to send him to oblivion.[22]

German stick grenades were now being thrown over the wall. When they landed at your feet, you had a second or two to move like hell away from the danger. That is the course I took, but I was amazed to see my men picking them up and throwing them back over the wall.

I attempted to throw one of the grenades over the wall which was ten to twelve feet high. I was unaware that blood had been pouring out of my ear all day and I didn't realize how weak I was. The grenade didn't make the top of the wall and fell back on our side exploding on the roadway, adding to poor Pembury's problems. I also didn't have the energy to use my entrenching tool to dig a hole for myself.

The Germans tried to attack us through the orchard on our right flank but were repulsed. There was a burst of German machine-gun fire. Private Smith, a Bren gunner, lying beside me gave a mortal scream and was dead. Simultaneously, a bullet went through my armpit. I was very lucky. It went right through without hitting the bone. It did catch the nerve however, and my arm went numb.

Captain Webber continued to use his sniper's rifle from an upstairs room of one of the houses. He then came out and moved into a slit trench. While there, an enemy grenade landed in the bottom of the trench:

It's amazing how much you can think in a hundredth of a second. I ran away and although the thing went off, all it did was pepper my back with pieces. Soon after that the chap next to me was killed and I felt a bump in my back. That was a machine gun bullet.[23]

Now with several wounds, Webber carried on as if nothing had happened.

Lieutenant David Hunter

*

The fighting in Le Port had also escalated. The section commanded by Sergeant McCambridge continued to play a vital part in its defence. They were completely detached from the rest of the platoon, which had had to withdraw slightly. Their building became a target for a large amount of German fire, but he had positioned his men well. At one stage the enemy attempted to beat down the door with their rifle butts, but his men dealt with this by dropping grenades from the windows. Phillip Crofts, 5 Platoon, 'B' Company:

> *A chap in our section called 'Scotty', brave sod, he didn't seem to know fear. The Germans were passing by on the pavements down below and old 'Scotty' was putting a little piece of mirror outside the window and when they came he was just firing at them. It went on like this. There was a lot of sniping there, an awful lot of sniping.*

Lieutenant Todd:

> *'B' Company repelled repeated attacks, one of their worst problems being the large number of snipers making movement difficult as they picked off men from cottage windows, roof-tops and especially from the church tower.*
>
> *We had to be careful about any sort of movement around there. You realized you were taking a chance but you had to go about your business, otherwise you'd have sat cowering in your trench for the whole of the day.*

After receiving permission from Colonel Pine-Coffin, Corporal Tommy Killeen of the Anti-Tank Platoon and a small covering party of two officers and a private armed

Virtually the same view from which Tommy Killeen fired the PIAT at the church tower window

201

with Stens, set off to deal with the snipers in the church tower. The Paras crossed the road and got into the house on the corner opposite the church, the only one that gave a clear angle on the wooden-slatted tower window. Killeen went into the upstairs bedroom and propped his PIAT on the wall of the window. The shot was a perfect hit on the tower. They then ran across the road to try and clear the church. Amazingly, the Mayor of Benouville, Monsieur Thomas, appeared and began gesticulating to them, 'Don't hurt my church!'[24] Corporal Tommy Killeen:

We didn't do any damage to [the] church, we just knocked the top off it; and when we went inside, I did take me hat off!

The level of sniping around the bridge had also increased dramatically. Lance-Corporal Arthur Roberts, 2nd Oxf and Bucks:

We had different tasks to make sure there were no infiltrators between the bridges and each side of them, which was a very dicey assignment because it meant keep going back and forth . . . and the snipers were very busy.

Major Howard ordered him to 'Have a go with the MG34' which he duly did, aiming at muzzle flashes. However, he was forced to give up because of the amount of attention that he received in return. Lance-Corporal Tom Packwood:

You daren't go over that bridge without keeping down below the ironwork. Any heads above it, they'd fire. Fortunately for us this side of the bridge, we were sheltered from the men in the church tower at Le Port because of the bridge lifting gear . . . The water tower we kept lumping at, but they were nearly at the range of their rifles, so quite a few people got injured, but not killed.

The water tower was down on the south-west bank of the canal, and its supply fed the Benouville Chateau.

At John Vaughan's RAP, Lieutenant Wood, with his bullet-ridden legs, lay on a stretcher:

'Tod' Sweeney came along, his platoon had been given orders to try and clear the snipers and at least one man had been hit by a sniper. I was feeling pretty helpless and felt that I might well be a target. Sure enough, a few seconds after that, there was a shot into the ground a little distance from me and I thought that I was going to get it next. And there was a shot that was far too close for comfort, thudded into the ground by my head and looked up to see that the corporal had drawn his pistol to protect his patient and had accidentally discharged it and very nearly finished me off!

Lieutenant Smith was sniped while having his wrist bandaged by a medical orderly:

A sniper bullet came cracking over my right shoulder and hit this fellow in the chest, who was actually bending over me, and knocked him clear into the road. The bullet went straight through him. I remember him lying in the middle of the road and I expected the next bullet from the sniper to come and get me in the back of the neck 'cos I couldn't get down any lower. That wasn't a very pleasant moment. The sniper, as they sometimes do in those sort of situations, he shoved off.

John Vaughan:

At my RAP one of the walking wounded standing within about two feet of me suddenly dropped flat on his back. I found that a bullet had passed through the middle of his back and obviously damaged his spinal cord as he was paralyzed from the waist downwards.

Colonel Bruce Harvey, the CO of 225 Field (Para) Ambulance then arrived at the RAP. John Vaughan:

As I was applying a dressing to Sergeant Barkway's badly smashed arm, Colonel Harvey turned up crawling snake-like along a ditch leading from the roadway to my RAP, a rather ostentatiously careful performance I thought, as he was still in full view of snipers firing, I felt certain, from a building about a thousand yards away on the west side of the canal [the Maternity Home]. *The Colonel suggested that I should move the stretcher cases (some twenty of them) to a safer place on the east side of the River Bridge. By this time I was reduced to one stretcher-bearer so I sat pondering the matter. The Colonel remained crouching in the ditch, eyeing me expectantly as I hesitated (I was also thinking of the soldier who had been shot in the back). After a minute or two he shrugged his shoulders slightly and with an 'it's up to you' sort of nod of the head, turned and crawled back to the roadway to rejoin his Field Ambulance on the Dropping Zone. I thought to myself and then called for volunteers from the walking wounded. With the help of three volunteers I carried six of the badly wounded cases (including David Wood) away from the scene and deposited them on the other side of the River Bridge where they were picked up by the 225th Parachute Field Ambulance later on in the morning.*

Guy Radmore, OC 5 Parachute Brigade Signals, sent a party across the Canal Bridge to lay cable for a telephone line:

Corporal Waters, who had the only reserve wireless set, saw my line party, a corporal and two men, shot up from a Chateau about 500 yards away, and he went out, threw smoke grenades and got one of my chaps to give covering fire on to this Chateau with a Bren gun, dragged these people off and then took the telephone line across and maintained really all day without any orders from me at all. Totally, absolutely on his own.[25]

Thomas Waters

In the gun emplacement, Frank Bourlet, Gus Gardner and Wally Parr decided that something had to be done about the water tower. After receiving permission from Major Howard to fire the gun, they readied three armour-piercing rounds. Wally Parr gave the 'order,' 'Number One gun, Fire!' Frank Bourlet:

We loaded the pack gun, aimed it on, fired at the water tower, put a hole completely through the water tower. Fired another one at a very large tree that was in front of the Chateau which we thought the snipers might be up. Being armour-piercing they just whistled straight through the tree, didn't do anything at all. Fired a third shell, at the water tower again and missed! John Howard shouted out to us, 'Stop firing that bloody gun!'

After we fired at the water tower a woman appeared on the balcony of the Chateau waving a white flag piece of material and Howard forbid us to fire on to this building again.

Major Howard knew from his intelligence that the Chateau was a Maternity Home and that it was run by Madame Vion:

I was under strict orders no firing at the hospital should be made, or in anyway disturb the inmates. I became rather cross about this because we knew that there was a German OP on the top of the Chateau. You could see him through binoculars and when the Moaning Minnie mortar bombs started late on in the morning, they were so accurate round the bridges that we knew damned well that this OP was directing the fire. And so what with the snipers firing and the Minnies, the bridge became quite a hot potato.[26]

The face of the Benouville Chateau which those around the bridge could see

Although enemy pressure was being exerted against the 7th Battalion positions, Pine-Coffin was more immediately concerned about the areas he could not fill:

My weak spot was the flank immediately north of my HQ, i.e., an approach down the bank of the canal or round the south-west of Le Port. This was covered only by Battalion HQ personnel and was continually threatened by small infiltrating parties of enemy and snipers. Excellent work was done here by the Mortar Officer (Archdale) who led numerous small patrols to break up parties attempting to come in this way during the course of the day's fighting.

Due to this and the 7th Battalion's increasing casualties, the two sections of Oxf and Bucks were called upon to go up to Le Port. Sergeant Freddie Fricker led the parties to an orchard that had just been under severe mortar and Moaning Minnie fire and the Paras were bringing in heavy casualties as they arrived. Corporal Bill Bailey, 2nd Oxf and Bucks:

We filled in behind the church, having reported up to Pine-Coffin first. Pine-Coffin's Headquarters was purely and simply a fold in the middle of an orchard, underneath the church . . . They were discussing the situation down in the village and I think they were talking about 'A' Company. They were having a hard time there. We were given the task of securing the track which led from the back of the church down to the canal bank.

The situation was that we were holding the hedgerow . . . and the Germans were holding beyond the far hedgerow on the other side of the towpath, no more than 120 yards [away].

Dennis Edwards, 2nd Oxf and Bucks:

On arrival at the outskirts of the village we made contact with the Paras who directed us to defend a short row of cottages just to the south of the church. Up in the village we were having a hell of a time, for the village was spread out over an area of about a thousand square yards and we only had a very small part of it fully under our control. The Germans also had a small part to themselves and the rest was No-Man's-Land.

It was a typical small French village with winding narrow streets, houses and cottages set close together, often in small terraces, nearly all seemed to have high walled gardens, there were plenty of varied trees, hedges and cover all round the place.

Unfortunately for Corporal Joe 'Cobber' Caine, he developed a pressing problem. Bill Bailey:

He was a phlegmatic sort of a character, nothing sort of seemed to perturb him. He said to me, 'Keep me covered . . . I'm going to have a crap!' He got over this little wall near the cemetery and went to this outhouse. He came back, he said, 'I can't face that. It ain't been emptied for years!'

Corporal 'Cobber' Caine

It was just a bucket.[27]

Dennis Edwards' section was sent forward into the houses:

We only held a small part of one side of the street and they held a small part opposite and all of us were inside the solid old houses, mainly in the upper rooms. Like a Punch and Judy show we kept bobbing up and down from the windows, take a quick look at the house across the street, hurl a grenade or two, then duck quickly out of that room and down the staircase before the enemy retaliated with their stick grenades.

Not wanting to be pinned down, we regularly crawled out from one cottage, across gardens, through gaps and gates in walls, frequently stopping to listen intently for any kind of movement and always ready to fire if suddenly attacked.

It was all extremely confusing because no one dared to remain in a static position for fear of being surrounded and we didn't have enough of us to take up permanent defensive positions which would ensure all round fire and protection.

There were far too many Germans and far too few of us, so we had to keep moving around lobbing the odd grenade, firing rifles and automatics from various vantage points in the hope of kidding the Germans that there were far more of us around the village than there actually were.

Periodically, someone from our Company, the Paras or the Germans would hear movement in a house or garden. Then would come the crack of rifles, the rat-a-tat of British and/or German automatics, a few grenade explosions, followed by shouting and screaming in English and German, a sudden scamper of running feet as someone attempted to find a healthier spot and then a comparative silence.

What was really weird about our battle around this village was the attitude of the French civilians, for with machine guns, other automatics, rifle firing and various types of grenades exploding all over the place, in the houses and cottages, around the gardens and up and down the narrow streets, with everyone's nerves strained almost to breaking point so that we were inclined to fire at anything that moved. The French people were wandering around quite openly and with an air of complete unconcern, as if the war was something between the British and Germans and was nothing to do with them! One grey-haired old lady suddenly stepped out into the street only a few yards from where we were positioned and with a machine gun which at the time was firing and a German machine gun was firing back, the old lady walked slowly up the street with an air of total unconcern. A few yards further on, and as she came to a gap between two houses, she decided to cross the road and walked directly into our line of fire!

Momentarily, we were forced to stop firing but very quickly had to recommence as we realized that behind the cover of the woman crossing the street the Germans were also doing some changing around and where we had previously had them pinned down they had now smartly crossed the street and into houses on our side. This put them into an advantageous position and made our houses virtually untenable. God we cursed that old woman as she had put us into a very difficult spot. Someone pointed out that she had crossed the street without being hit and in fact, had then entered a house that we thought was occupied by the Boche. The only bright spot about that little incident was that although no one fired at her, the Germans did not get away unscathed for although she obstructed our line of fire, some other lads in another house were able to fire at the enemy and when we again looked out of our upper window there were some fresh enemy bodies laying in the road. (Later we wondered whether we had seen an old lady or a German dressed up to fool us. We had earlier been warned to expect such trickery).

Dennis Edwards

With Germans occupying buildings on either side of ours we decided to carry out a fast withdrawal by running down the back garden and out through a gate in the end wall. As we did so the garden was raked by machine-gun fire, but we all got clear without being hit.

We moved into a small field on the eastern fringe of the village and immediately to the south of the church. In our new position it would be difficult for the enemy to carry out a surprise attack as we spread out and lay down in the longish grass. We were screened from the cottages by the tall back garden wall. If we covered the gateway and the churchyard, we felt fairly secure.

Soon a German peered cautiously through the gateway. We ducked down and kept still. Then another appeared and obviously assuming that we had vacated the area, they both stepped out into the field. Despite our shortage of ammunition, all seven of us opened fire with everything we had, including even a Sten gun that was being carried by Lance Corporal Minns, who had taken over our section when our NCO, Corporal Webb, had been wounded at the Canal Bridge. The two Germans could hardly have known what hit them and they crashed to the ground and made no further movement.[28]

With two sections of 25 Platoon already supplied to the 7th Battalion, Major Howard prepared for the request of further reinforcement. Lieutenant 'Tod' Sweeney:

John Howard called Fox and myself into an orchard. We were told to await orders to carry out a counter-attack on 7 Para's position. We weren't all that happy about this. We thought we'd done our stuff. We'd got over all the alarm and excitement of the previous night and we were tired. The idea of counter-attacking a position, which a battalion was in the process of losing, didn't thrill us at all.

As we sat there waiting, Richard Todd poked his head through the bushes and said, 'Hello, I said I'd see you on D-Day.'

Chapter Twelve

The Morning in the
Ranville Area

While it had been an extremely difficult morning in Benouville, the Ranville area had also been very eventful.

The screening party of the 12th Battalion had taken up position behind the hedgerow on the forward slope of the western side of the Ring Contour. Captain John Sim:

I had a FOB, Forward Observation Bombardment Naval officer with me with his radio operator. He was linked up with a battle cruiser . . . It was dark when we arrived, not pitch dark but moonlight dark. When it became lighter he contacted the guns of the cruiser . . . and we managed to register about three defence fire tasks on positions in front of my position.

The party was around fifteen strong, armed with Stens, rifles and two Bren guns.[1] A 6-pounder anti-tank gun had also been hauled up and positioned at a distinct right-angled kink in the hedge:

It should also have had a 17-pounder anti-tank gun, four PIATs and a '38' wireless set. The flanks were supposed to be covered by medium machine-gun fire.

Although isolated, the hedge did afford Captain Sim a view to the outskirts of Caen:

When dawn broke there was little movement to be seen. The men sat motionless in their trenches, alert with their weapons ready. They were invisible, camouflaged steel helmets and blackened faces merged into the green hedgerows. In front a farmer was seen leading his horse and cart. Two local farmers were allowed to walk into the position from the enemy side and were interrogated.

Frank Gleeson was at the eastern end of the hedge:

I was on the extreme left of the position in charge of one of the several machine Bren guns with Private Andrew Gradwell, who was nineteen years old. With us was our sniper, Private Rudolph and in charge of this end of the position was Sergeant Frank Milburn, a North African veteran. It was a bright sunny morning with wheat or maize fields to the front and rear. In case we were seen during our excavations we decided not to dig in. We waited patiently for first sight of our enemy. This happened to be a single German soldier cycling towards us from the direction of Colombelles. The sniper took aim at about 100 yards and that was one Kraut less. Soon afterwards, a small black civilian car came from the same direction and stopped. A large German wearing a Red Cross armband got out of the car and looked towards our direction. The sniper was about to kill his second German, but as he was a medic I said, 'No.'

This was our first action and we realized that we had alerted the enemy as to where we were.

Behind them, the rest of the battalion had dug in. Private Eric Barley:

My first task was to accompany Major Rogers to inspect the Company's trenches. As we were walking up a lane there was a burst of machine-gun fire and three bullets hit Major Rogers' clothing. One cut his belt off, one went through his epaulette and when I saw moisture on his chest I was sure he was shot dead. From his breast pocket he took out his whisky flask. It had two holes in it. I said, 'With luck like that, you should see out the end of the conflict!'[2]

A thousand yards to the east Lieutenant 'Dixie' Dean, commanding the 13th Battalion MMG Platoon, was worried about the lack of men and Vickers guns, but still more concerned about the paucity of ammunition:

Urgent action was required, so I set off to find my CO, and since Ronnie Boylan, my batman was missing, took Alf Williams along and also the medical orderly who was to re-join his own unit. We retraced the paths through the corn until we came to one leading down into the village, and followed this until we reached a group of three houses. On the right of the path were some tall bushes and alongside one lay the body of a British soldier, whom I had no difficulty in recognizing as Private Johnson, battalion despatch rider.

There was no sign of the 13th Battalion, so he decided not to go any further into Ranville, but to carry on and report to Colonel Johnson of the 12th Battalion:

As the three of us neared the main road into the village from the south, smoke and flames were rising from the road which ran through a hollow as it entered Ranville, and I made a slight detour to investigate. Looking down from the bank I saw a burning German half-track slewn across the way, and a body of soldiers led by a corporal, busy re-laying a string of Hawkins anti-tank grenades. I stopped to congratulate them and instantly recognized the NCO as Frank McLean. In 1940 we had been members of the same platoon and the last time I had seen him was in the balloon cage, one wet morning in August 1942.[3]

Our route had taken us past at least three locations where I had expected to see 6-pounder anti-tank guns, but not one was in position. I had also kept my eyes open for an alternative site for the Vickers, and believed I had found one. Before I reached his HQ, I met Colonel Johnson and told him the platoon were dug in with two guns only, but were desperately short of ammunition. He replied that the 12th had neither guns nor ammunition and then gave me orders that I personally was to take as many men as could be spared from manning the guns, go back to the DZ and search for the containers, but I was to be back in position by 1000 hours with or without the ammunition.

I sent Alf Williams back with a message to Sergeant Osborne that all spare men were to come to Sergeant Kelly's section to help search for our containers. It must have been 0830 before we all set off to the DZ which was over a mile back to where a path ran into the centre of it.

Ken Lang, 2 Section, MMG Platoon, 13th Battalion:

Shortly after most of the section went off searching for ammunition, the Brigadier came along the hedge where we had dug in with a platoon of the 12th Battalion, looking for us. He had two anti-tank 6-pounders with him, and he took us all up the road and positioned [one of] the weapons below the crest of the Ring Contour. There was a sunken lane, then a bank, then the hedges and we were on top. The field was higher than the road.

In the meantime 'Dixie' Dean had reached the DZ:

On either side were Horsa gliders, mostly damaged where wings had smashed into the poles, and one I remember with the cockpit buried deep in a large thorn bush. There were containers galore in the corn, but we concentrated on those holding small arms

ammunition, and were not long in finding what we were looking for. We must have been twenty strong and we each slung the canvas backpack holding two belts onto our shoulders and set off back for the guns, and we really had to move to be back in the specified time.

Lieutenant Dean was not the only one roaming around the DZ. Captain David Tibbs, 225 Field Ambulance:

As soon as daylight came, myself and the five other men started as best we could searching the DZ looking for injured, and we found them. It was nearly all corn, wheat, it was about three feet high, so a man lying amongst that was very difficult indeed to see. Why did

Ken Lang

parachutists get broken legs? About 48 hours before we were due to jump they suddenly came out with a new release mechanism for kitbags. It was issued to everyone to use instead of the old mechanism, but quite a few chaps just didn't understand it. It was not all that self-evident how it should be used, and they landed with their kitbags still strapped to their legs. This just snapped their femurs . . . There were up to about a dozen chaps scattered in the corn, difficult to see. Many would find various dodges, such as finding a stick or something like that and tying something to the end and waving it, so every now and again you'd see a cloth or a handkerchief being waved on the end of a stick and you'd know there was a chap lying there.

That was hugely laborious, instead of twenty of us, to have only five of us to carry them back. A man on a stretcher's a very heavy object! We managed to get them in, one way and another.

By 0900 hours, apart from the gun on the Ring Contour, several 6-pounders were in position on the southern edge of Ranville. One gun, commanded by Sergeant Bert Clements of 'F' Troop, 4th Airlanding Anti-Tank Battery, was situated behind and to the right of Lieutenant O'Brien-Hitching's Platoon of 'A' Company, 13th Battalion, which was busy digging in, close in to a farm that overlooked the fields.

Two glider pilots, Staff Sergeant White and Sergeant Eason, were manning an anti-tank gun sited to the right and 200 yards forward of this gun, behind a low stone wall. The remaining gun was commanded by Sergeant Portman of the 4th Airlanding Anti-Tank Battery. Having got themselves into position on the Ring Contour, Ken Lang was surveying the scene to the south-east:

To our right was St Honorine and it was in the cornfields near there, at about 0930 hours, we saw the German armour assembling. They were over a thousand yards away. They stopped and then two small groups advanced, one of them in the direction of Herouvillette, but the second group drove through the corn, and the direction of advance meant they would pass immediately across our front.

There was just the anti-tank team, the three Vickers numbers, Bill Price was one of them with Sergeant Kelly, the section commander. We didn't have very much ammunition, besides our orders were not to open fire before the anti-tank guns.

The two German detachments, each of three SP guns and supporting infantry, continued to advance and the most eastern group disappeared behind some trees in Herouvillette. Everyone waited to see if they would continue along the road to the 13th Battalion's left and behind into Ranville itself, or take the more direct route to the bridges and pass across the high ground in front.

From the Vickers gun position a few hundred yards north of the Lieu Haras farm, Sergeant Osborne and Lance-Corporals King and Jones had seen infantry but none of the SPs. Don Jones:

I saw this German patrol making their way towards this farmhouse which would be a couple of hundred yards away. Like a fool I opened fire on them. I obviously couldn't have got all of them, if any of them . . .

We were sat there, sort of forgot that these Germans who had either got away or been killed, we weren't sure. Then all of a sudden there was an explosion around us and of course when we looked around we saw the SP on the brow of the hill, and firing at us.

Two high explosive shells landed very close to the Paras:

I remember Charlie King saying . . . 'Taff, I've been hit in the shoulder.' 'Don't bugger me about Charlie.' 'No,' he said, 'honest.' At that time I thought I'd scratched my leg on a bramble or something.

Don Jones

Sergeant Osborne therefore hid the gun in the hedge and they headed for the RAP.

The SPs re-appeared from behind the trees of the Lieu Haras farm, broke through a hedge on the track and entered the corn. They preferred the high ground.

Advancing slowly, these vehicles moved into formation and began to pass in front of the small field in which Lieutenant O'Brien-Hitching's men had been busy digging in. They kept low in their half-completed slit trenches as the armour and supporting infantry continued across the slope.

Lance Sergeant George Brownlee of the 4th Airlanding Anti-Tank Battery had been collecting ammunition and stores from the gliders on the LZ, before returning to Ranville:

I was going up this wall and I knew there was a gun just over the wall, but I was wondering 'Where is it?' A man appeared, it was in fact a glider pilot, sneaked through by the farm [on the forward edge of the Airborne perimeter], *they'd made a hole in the wall, and he came through it. 'Down, down, down' he said. 'Don't utter a bloody sound or attempt to look over the wall. There are four tanks approaching and German infantry. If you can, you can find a hole, a chink in this stone wall and perhaps be able to look through and see,' which is what I did.*

This Para officer, he was in charge, he had men up the trees, they were snipers but they were also watching, and their orders were 'Watch Herouvillette.' They signalled down below and the Para officer had seen them and he came along to Sergeant Clements and said, 'German tanks approaching.' Yes, I've seen them too. If they come this way, nobody moves, nobody fires. I will be the first to fire, and I will do that either when I'm spotted or that gun is very, very, very close.' As the supporting infantry were crossing a path through the corn, the officer leading them called out and pointed left towards the ridge. The armour was now 175 yards away.

Just before 1000 hours Lieutenant Dean arrived back at the position where he had left Sergeant Kelly's section, only to find it abandoned. However, the nearby 12th

Battalion Platoon Commander informed him of Brigadier Poett's action and that the gun crew was now in position on the crest of the Ring Contour.

Staff Sergeant Raymond White was on the 6-pounder near the farm:

We came under small arms fire and Sergeant Eason opened up on the Bren gun. By this time the first SP tanks were in range of the gun, but [the] gun-layer did not think he could hit the tank.

Lieutenant Dean:

We moved along to the road and I sent George Kelly's men off to join him, then we heard engines, tank engines, and they were heading in our direction through the corn-field. I don't know what I thought I could do about the situation, but I was across the road and scrambling up the far bank. Then I heard the bark of a gun being fired, followed almost immediately by the regular rat-a-ta-tat of a Vickers away to our right.

A vehicle of the second detachment, from St Honorine, had moved into view on the slope. Ken Lang:

One came first, slowly, about ten mile an hour, feeling its way across, the front one. Suddenly 'WHOMFF', away went the first round, quickly followed by two more. The shot just hit and you saw a flash as it hit the shield at the front of the gun . . . and after a few seconds the whole thing burst into flame. They had either got the fuel tank or the ammunition . . . The first one got so close, they couldn't miss it at that range.

Sergeant Kelly was behind the Vickers, firing short bursts of ten rounds or so, not the usual twenty-five rounds we were trained to fire. He only had one belt of 250 rounds.

George Brownlee watched closely as the SPs approached from Herouvillette:

At the high ground point, suddenly they were opposite Sergeant Clements and he shouted, 'Fire!' The nearest German infantry was about a hundred yards away, the nearest German tank was about 150, 160 yards away. Absolutely broadside on, hit it straight in the middle of the tracks. Beautiful shot. Clements and Portman both fired virtually at the same time. They hit separate targets.

Staff Sergeant White:

In the meantime, I had loaded a round and had a look along the sights myself. By this time the tank was almost dead ahead in front at 200 yards and needed stopping. So I decided to have a go myself.

Sergeant Eason kept the Nazis heads down with Bren fire, and I laid the gun ready to fire. The first round missed, so I immediately reloaded and this time I applied 200 yards on the sights. The tank had stopped and I was expecting them to open fire on us any minute, so I quickly sighted the gun and fired. This time it was a hit, and the tank went up in flames. During this short time, another tank had been hit by the gun on our left flank, and also one which was almost unobserved from our position, was put out of action by a gun on our right flank. From our position three tanks were seen to be blazing, and ammo was exploding in each at various intervals. The infantry, who were escorting the tanks, were then engaged by small arms fire.

George Brownlee:

Clements, because of the smoke and the flames from those two burning tanks could not see the other two. But Portman could and the other gun there could, and those two guns

The area of the tank action at Ranville

fired. Unfortunately, they hit the same tank. So the third one went up. By then Bert Clements could see the final one, Portman couldn't but that one could. Those two both fired and the fourth tank went up.[4]

Lieutenant Dean:

By the time I reached the top of the bank several more rounds had been fired, and when at last I was in a position to observe, an unbelievable sight met my eyes. Immediately to my front and not one hundred yards away three tanks were stopped and blazing merrily, with another such single armoured hulk away to my right, and it was from that direction the Vickers was firing – my war had begun.

I decided that the path through the corn was quite likely under enemy observation, and my party would make a good target, hence we moved a little nearer the village and put a stone wall between us and the Ring Contour.

Along the wall he could see one of the 6-pounder guns and its crew responsible for the destruction of the tanks, and then went on to meet Sergeant Clements. 'Dixie' Dean:

I congratulated him and his gun team on their coolness and the accuracy of their shooting. Another hundred yards and those self-propelled guns, they were not tanks after all, would have been on the road leading into Ranville, and then on to the vital bridges.

Before the remaining German armour retired to shelter among the houses in St Honorine, one of the SPs knocked out the 6-pounder on the Ring Contour. Since there was no reason to stay at this exposed position, Sergeant Kelly and the MMG crew returned to their original position.

Lieutenant Dean moved on and passed Lieutenant O'Brien-Hitching's men who had recommenced their digging:

I then turned down the path leading into the village I had moved down earlier, for it was just past the three houses I thought I might be able to re-site the gun and be able to carry out the task given to me and so it proved. It was in a sunken lane on the southern outskirts of Ranville, I found a good position.

There was no need for us all to go back to the original position, so I left Lance Sergeant Tom Donnelly with all the ammunition carriers, and just accompanied by Alf Williams, set off for Sergeant Osborne and the rest of the section. As we turned to move up the hedge towards the position, for some reason I will never know, I took a '36' grenade from my pouch and carried it in my right hand. I was moving slightly ahead of Alf as we neared the original gun site and was looking to my left where the hedge had been flattened by the armour as it drove through. Suddenly, he was alongside, hissing in my ear 'Jerry's up there.' I looked to the front and sure enough a number of Boche had come down the path from Lieu Haras and were intently gazing towards the burning SPs. 'Down' I said, pulled the pin and threw the '36', they were that close. As it exploded, we were on our feet and charging, firing my Sten as we ran. We took them completely by surprise and they turned and started running back to the farm. For once the Sten didn't let me down . . . I fired a full magazine of twenty rounds non-stop. As I ran I noticed that the Vickers had been moved from its trench and shoved into the hedge. By now I had reached the path to the farm and the Boche were still running. I called to Alf to get the gun, reloaded the Sten and carried on firing. I must have hit one of them for he stopped, clutching the back of his thigh. He called out and two of his companions came back to support and carry him. I kept on firing even when they were out of range because I didn't want them to know there were only two of us.

Alf called out that he had the gun ready. He was a big, strong lad and had the forty-pound weight tripod over his shoulders, and the partly full condenser can, another twenty rounds, in one hand, leaving me with only the gun itself to carry. We didn't hang around but started to leg it as fast as we could to where the ammunition carriers had been left. Within minutes we reached the path leading to them and here, puffing and panting, exhilarated and quite proud of ourselves, we slowed to a walk.

To the right on the village side was a high stone wall, while on the left bordering the cornfield ran a straggly hedge. We were almost back to the new section area, when I noticed a rabbit, standing on its haunches in the hedge. I motioned Alf to halt, carefully lowered the gun to the ground, took out my 9mm pistol, aimed and fired. For a second nothing happened. The rabbit was still there, and then slowly it rolled over. In triumph I said, 'I've killed it,' whereupon only ten yards into the corn a single German soldier stood up, looked at me, and then turned and started running. I dropped the pistol, grabbed my Sten and fired another full magazine at the retreating figure. I then went to collect what I intended to be the section's supper. The rabbit was dead alright, but there was not a mark on it, and I reckon I must have blown the body over with a near miss, it was almost cold.[5]

*

Lieutenant Ellis 'Dixie' Dean

On the western side of the Ring Contour, Captain John Sim's party were spread along the hedgerow, a Bren positioned at either end. At 1030 hours around two platoons of enemy troops appeared. Frank Gleeson:

From a position of eleven o'clock, a single line of Germans appeared approaching at a tangent front of our position, distance about 400 yards across flat ground. They dropped off and sited a machine gun with two men to cover their approach.

They then turned and advanced towards the hedgerow. Except for the two snipers, the Paras held their fire. Frank Gleeson:

When the infantry were about fifty yards away I told the Bren gunner, Andy Gradwell, to extend the tele-

216

scopic legs on the weapon and with me holding them and sitting them on top of my small backpack, he could stand behind me and open fire. I remember telling him not to lower the gun barrel or else he would blow my head off!

Cries of 'Mein Gott' filled the air as this lot went down. I thought at the time, what right had these Germans to call upon God with their record of murder and atrocities?

Captain Sim:

When we opened up they all went to ground in the high grass, but we carried on firing in the general direction of where they had disappeared.

One heard the officers shouting orders to their men and the voices seemed to go down to my right flank. I fired two red Verey light signals in the direction of the canal, a call for my Company Commander to bring mortar fire down on the right flank. A runner was also sent back, but the mortar fire did not materialize.

Fifteen minutes passed:

Next came the clanking of tracked vehicles and from behind dead ground two light SP guns appeared. The FOB officer endeavoured to contact his cruiser and bring down fire, but the cruiser guns were on a priority target. The two SP guns came to a halt, right in the open and about seventy yards from the hedgerow. There was no reaction from the anti-tank gun that I had in my position about twenty yards to my right.

They didn't fire at us, they just stopped there. To my amazement the hatch of one of the SP guns opened and a German officer, splendidly arrayed in polished jack-boots, stiff cap and Sam Browne, leisurely climbed out and lit a cigarette. He was allowed two puffs and was shot, but I don't think we killed him.

From behind came a line of German soldiers in extended order, passed their two vehicles and came towards us. We opened up our fire, I fired a red Verey light straight in, that was part of our battle plan, we would hold our fire until the enemy had reached a certain line.

A soldier from the anti-tank gun came crawling down the hedgerow towards me and he saluted me on his hands and knees and said, 'Sir, we can't get the gun to work. It must have been damaged in the landing.' The breech block had become damaged apparently.

The SP guns began to blast the hedgerow, trying to search them out:

It was all very frightening as there was a lot of noise, crashes and explosions around. I noticed that the man on my right had been shot through the head with his rifle at the aim and his hand on the bolt. I noticed a soldier crawling towards me, moaning and groaning, but he slumped over before he reached me and lay still.

Frank Gleeson:

Sheer instinct made us move to shift the Bren gun to a new position. So the four of us now waited again. Correction, three of us, because somehow our sniper had not come with us.

Disaster now followed because upon realizing that the sniper was not with us, Sergeant Milburn shouted out for him, 'Rudolph, Rudolph!' The Germans heard this English voice loud and clear as there was no firing after our Bren fire.

Captain Sim:

I crawled along the ditch to contact Sergeant Milburn shouting 'Have you any smoke grenades and Gammon bombs?' He said he had and I suggested he might be able to get to the nearest SP gun under cover of smoke. There was no answer and I think he may have been killed at that moment.

A stick grenade had been thrown from the area of the Bren's previous position. Frank Gleeson:

Private Gradwell and myself were in a crouched position facing the enemy, Frank Milburn was sitting upright facing us on our left, but only a yard from us.

The grenade thrown was accurate, landing just behind Frank Milburn, the blast killing him instantly. Gradwell and myself were lifted upwards a few inches and then down again. There was not a mark on Sergeant Milburn, his eyes were closed and he was still in a sitting position. As I had borrowed Private Gradwell's .45 Colt pistol because of losing my rifle on leaving the aircraft, I was about to grab the Sten gun from Sergeant Milburn. He was still holding the weapon in the high port position across his chest with the bayonet over his left shoulder. The grenade blast had caught this bayonet and I saw it had been twisted into the shape of a pig's tail, all nine inches of it.

Captain John Sim

After the stick grenade, the silence from our area must have convinced the Germans that the machine-gun crew (us!) had been killed, because I now saw to our front as we were still lying down, a pair of German jackboots slowly approaching. I nudged Private Gradwell and pointed forward. He got the message that an enemy was approaching. This German in a camouflaged cape was approaching straight for us, rifle and bayonet in his left hand and moving aside the foliage with his right hand. The last bush he moved to his right he suddenly saw us, in a crouched position with blackened faces. He gave a startled grunt of 'Ugh,' then received a Bren gun burst in the face plus a round from my borrowed Colt .45 Yank pistol. He must have been lifted backwards a good four feet onto his back.

A map of the area showing the hedge position of the 12th Battalion's 'forward screen'

Captain Sim:

Peeping through the thick hedge, I saw a German soldier standing up in another section of our hedge. I drew my batman's attention to him and ordered him to shoot the German. He did. Again we were subjected to fire but this time by mortars, the bombs airbursting in the hedgerow trees.

This went on for about half an hour, and then again a sudden silence ensued. Frank Gleeson:

I asked the Bren gunner, Andy Gradwell, 'Did we bring any dogs with us?' because I could hear a howling further to our right. I later realized that some Para had had the bottom part of his face and neck blown away including his identity discs around the neck.

Captain Sim:

One of my sergeants came to me and informed me that there were only four of us left alive and asked me what we were to do. I decided that rather than wait in the ditch to be killed, it was worth the risk to dash back to our Company position and perhaps live to fight another day.

Frank Gleeson:

Shortly after the tank fire the officer in charge of the position dashed up to where we were, glanced at Sergeant Milburn and realizing that he was dead he looked at me and ordered, 'Give us covering fire till we get back, then we will cover you.'

They withdrew along a ditch at the eastern end of the hedgerow. Frank Gleeson:

The Germans now rushed a tank along the lane to our right with infantry on the top of it. There seemed to be a lull in the firing and I began to think of our situation, which was that there were two of us left alive in the hedgerow. I decided to order Private Gradwell with his Bren gun to the rear, then I would follow him. He refused to retreat saying, 'I'm not bloody going anywhere,' and took up a firing position behind a fallen tree trunk. After several more orders to move, which he refused, I stood up and kicked him in the ribs. He then picked the Bren up and ran back along the ditch that Captain Sim had used.

Gleeson then decided to move back, but as the others had already withdrawn along the same ditch, he thought it might now be under observation:

So holding my Colt .45 in my left hand, I started to crawl back through the field of wheat which was nearly three feet high, but under a clear blue sky I began to lose direction so I decided to crawl back towards the roadside ditch. I moved the wheat stalks aside and dropped into the ditch, about a yard in front of a German machine gunner and three others who were using the cover of the ditch to advance towards our main Company position. They grabbed my Colt pistol which I hadn't realized I still had. The young Jerry machine gunner smelt the barrel, his face red with anger and pointed the weapon at my face.[6]

I sat on the bottom of the ditch whilst being searched. My tin of concentrated chocolate was taken. A German corporal with the Russian front medal was sitting to the right of me. Suddenly from the right a bullet zipped across the back of my neck. I ducked, but this bullet penetrated the right side of the Jerry on my left and must have stopped behind his left eye which nearly came out. Certainly now, I thought I would be shot. I whipped out an Army shell dressing from my back pocket and offered this to the corporal. He shook his head and said, 'He's finished.'

Just as the German corporal beckoned Gleeson to follow him back to their position, a barrage of 3-inch mortar bombs landed accurately on the hedgerow:

Suddenly, from the middle of the position two Paras dashed up to race across the wheat-field. They had hardly gone five yards when a burst of machine-gun fire brought them down, side by side.

Gleeson was led back to the German lines and into captivity.

The SP guns did not pass through the hedge but turned east towards the 'B' Company area.[7]

*

At 1100 hours Brigadier Poett arrived in Ranville to occupy the building chosen for his Main Brigade Headquarters:

When I got to my Headquarters, we'd marked down that it would be in this chateau, and in fact the chateau was absolutely chock-a-block with refugees. There were some very nice people, the Rohan-Chabots, the Comte de Rohan-Chabot, he was an old boy of over eighty and his wife was well in charge. She wore the trousers completely. And she came over and told us that she had all these people in the cellar. I said, 'That's fine, quite alright, we won't go into the chateau, we'll go into the pavillon' they called it, a little cottage by the gate. And so we established ourselves in there as our Headquarters.

Guy Radmore, 5 Parachute Brigade Signals:

The Rohan Chabot Chateau

Brigade HQ building in the grounds of the Rohan Chabot Chateau

It was really the sort of lodge of the chateau where we set our Brigade Headquarters, our wireless sets, and we got our telephone lines going and there was a hell of a lot of mortaring and shelling.

A few hundred yards to the south the 13th Battalion was still settling itself in Ranville. Lieutenant Dixie Dean:

First of all was the dreary task of having to dig a fresh lot of weapon slits, and now there were no explosive charges (we had exhausted our supply of plastic) to help. I sent an NCO and some men to check there were no Boche hiding in the nearby houses. He reported them empty, but asked me to have a look at what he had found in the nearest of the three. It was really a small cottage with a walled yard in front. To the left of the front door, another one opened into a bedroom, which from the highly scented atmosphere was used by a female. The double bed had clearly been used recently, for the covers were thrown back and the bottom sheet was heavily bloodstained. And it was only yards away from the track that Private Johnson had been killed.

When the new position had been dug and camouflaged, I decided it was time to visit Sergeant Kelly's section and find out exactly what had happened to them since I had last seen them about 0830 hours. I again kept to the line of the wall, passing the 6-

pounder, and stopped to have a word with them, and mentioned to Sergeant Clements that not all the anti-tank guns intended for our area had arrived. He agreed and said he had not seen one of his own officers since arriving in Normandy. As we talked, there came the roar of a diving aircraft heading in our direction from the coast and before we could take cover an ME109 came into sight, flying at no more than 100 feet. It was completely engulfed in flame and hit the high trees on the road side, somersaulting over, before hitting the ground and exploding not fifty yards away. Wreckage was thrown all around but we managed to find what was left of the pilot, a charred torso and head. Not a pretty sight.

Two of his men, Lance-Corporals King and Jones, who had been wounded in the tank attack, were at the RAP. Don Jones:

They sorted Charlie and then the medic said to me, 'Drop your trousers, let's have a look at what's up.' 'But I've only bloody scratched myself.' He said, 'Drop them!' Of course, when I dropped my trousers I could see that a piece had come out of my thigh muscle, and when I looked at my equipment, there was quite a bit of damage . . . We had an anti-tank mine and three or four Mills grenades in the other pocket, and I know the top, across the land mine, the cover, a piece of shrapnel had cut that. Also, I had another small wound in the inside of my left leg and some of my equipment was shot about.

The MDS had gradually filled and the courtyard was covered with men on stretchers and other wounded just laying on the ground. With all the shelling and

The front of the Chateau des Comtes de Guernol

223

mortaring going on, they had been very fortunate. Major Pat Hewlings, 225 Field (Para) Ambulance:

We were only disturbed in our work with the casualties once or twice during the morning of 6th June by a stray shell dropping near or in the garden of a house, and ultimately a shell went through our cookhouse roof, killing one of the orderlies, very seriously wounding our padre, and greatly surprising our portly Somersetshire cook sergeant, who smartly exchanged for his red beret, a steel helmet.

Chapter Thirteen

Seaborne Arrivals at the Bridges

Seaborne forces were expected to start arriving at the bridges some time after midday. Colonel Pine-Coffin had arranged a signal with both the expected relieving battalion, the 2nd East Yorks, and Lord Lovat's 1 Special Service Brigade. However, with the time well past 1100 hours, the only sign of anyone approaching from the coast had been French civilians, mostly women and children trying to escape the fighting. Cyril Larkin:

The amount of civilians that came along the river bank . . . They came on bikes, they were walking, running, everything else.

Colonel Pine-Coffin:

They did not know which way they wanted to go, but were very frightened and wanted someone to take them under control. Obviously they could not be allowed to stream across whichever way they wished as there was always the chance that they would later contact the Germans and report what they had seen. There might even be Germans concealed among them. Thomas' Platoon had the job of separating the men from the women and children and herding them into hastily improvised cages. The obvious pleasure of these civilians at meeting British soldiers on the bridge was most noticeable and gratifying, but their attempts to shake hands personally with everyone had to be discouraged as it took so long.

*

One of Lieutenant Richard Todd's duties was visiting the Companies to find out how they were faring and what losses they had suffered. While in Le Port with Major Neale there was a lull in the fighting, so he decided to check again on Walter Parrish's platoon:

I was wandering along this road, it was very much no-man's land, there didn't seem to be anyone around. I got a mile or so, maybe a mile and a half. I passed Walter Parrish's position on my way towards Ouistreham, but still no sign of the relieving force or Germans or anything else. I suddenly saw a small convoy of seven or eight soft-skinned trucks coming towards me, and they stopped. There was a very florid and sweaty RE Major who said, 'Am I on the right road for the Canal Bridge? I'm a Bridging Company and we've come to replace it.' I said, 'There's nothing wrong with the bridge, it's there, intact. I think if I were you, don't come any further because I'm not too sure about who holds what of this ground around here and particularly when you get towards 'B' Company's positions. There are Germans there. The best thing you can do would be to stop your vehicles, get your chaps down, take up defensive positions and just wait for the infantry to come through from the beaches.' I thought 'What the hell! How extraordinary that a convoy of ordinary three-tonners could get through to us without any trouble and the bloody troops, there was no sign of them!' No tanks, no troops, no Bren carriers, nothing![1]

Leaving the convoy by the road, Lieutenant Todd returned to Le Port.

Further evidence that seaborne forces were getting off the beach became apparent when the advance party Engineer Officers of 17 Field Company Group arrived at the Canal Bridge. Lieutenants Clarke and Dixon duly began their reconnaissance along the bank towards the planned location for the Bailey Bridge, but in doing so, came under fire. Clarke was hit in the arm by a bullet and Dixon by shrapnel and both were evacuated to the Airborne MDS.[2]

Another seaborne unit, 90 Company RASC, commanded by Major James Cuthbertson had a special task. 'B' Platoon and its thirty-three waterproofed Austin 3-Ton 4 x 4 trucks were to land at H+6 and move directly to the bridges, taking supplies of food, fuel and ammunition to the Airborne Division's Maintenance Area in Ranville. Cuthbertson landed in advance at 0920 hours on SWORD Beach in order to make contact with the Airborne and to reconnoitre a route to Ranville. Travelling by motorcycle, he was accompanied by a despatch rider. Major James Cuthbertson:

The beach was complete chaos. Eventually we moved inland through Hermanville and made straight for the Orne, so off we went, out into open lanes, no hedges – an open, bare landscape. There was no one in sight. We just followed our maps and pressed on for five miles. It was very eerie – where were the enemy, or our own troops? We went along on our bikes and saw no one.

At about 1130 hours, having passed through two silent villages, we went down a steep little slope and around a sharp turn to the Orne bridges ... We pulled up under some tall trees by a thick hedge and heard someone shout 'Get down, you're under enemy observation!' Looking more closely we saw half-a dozen paratroopers in defensive positions about the bridge, but no Liaison Officers. We stayed 'doggo' with the occasional recce to the bridge to see if the seaborne troops had arrived.

*

John Butler of 'C' Company, 7th Battalion dropped back towards the canal to a spot where he was able to dress the bayonet wound in his leg:

After having done this I felt very much the need of a drink, having had nothing since emplaning the night before and also feeling a little nauseous after bandaging my thigh. So I went to some buildings by the bridge to find something to drink. Just as I arrived at the bridge, a barge came into view from the direction of Caen. It appeared to be armed with a 20mm gun and a machine gun (MG39). An officer there ordered about six of us to deal with it.

On the opposite bank, Wally Parr was still manning the gun emplacement:

I was just taking a quick cigarette and I was turned sideways in the seat, it was a swivel seat, and all of a sudden one of the fellows said, 'For Christ's sake look!' And as I sort of looked up and looked round, John Howard had apparently come out for a breather and shouted 'PARR! Don't let that bloody boat get near this damned bridge.' I looked and coming up from Caen right in the middle of the bloody canal was a boat, heavily laden with German soldiers. I just couldn't believe it. I've got one up the spout, I've got the elevating handle, I've got the traverse. Over on the right-hand side of the gun pit was a range chart in metres, all written in German. It gave the range to a clump of trees on the right, a larger clump on the left, to the Chateau and to the curve in the river. So all I had to do to get between them was just calculate the difference between this and that, altered the range and I'd got everything under control. But this thing was a moving target, and I'm looking at it through the sort of telescopic sight and it's getting closer, and I started to shout 'Will somebody give me a range on the damned thing!' I was still keeping it in focus but obviously the range is decreasing as it's belting towards us. Then somebody shouted out, 'About 800, 750, it's got to be 725.' I've adjusted it and fired the first one and a terrific plume of water went up about twenty yards in front of the boat as near as I can estimate, twenty or thirty. I'd never seen a boat do a U-turn so quick! It turned across from right to left as I'm looking at it. By this time the next one's up and I hit it broad side on, just about where the railings met the woodwork and it shuddered, literally. By this time it had managed to turn and before it disappeared around the bend of the Caen Canal, I managed to put three out of four shots up its backside, and it was limping up the canal with smoke pouring out of it.[3]

John Butler:

Just as we were about to sally down the canal bank there was a loud bang from the opposite bank and pieces flew off the superstructure of the barge, which beat a hasty retreat.

He then headed back towards the Café Gondrée:

As I was going to it I saw a White Scout car and a Bren gun carrier pull up opposite. They contained a sergeant and a section of Royal Engineers . . . The sergeant told me they had kept clear of the road and followed the tramway Wally Parr *parallel to the canal without incident. Their job was to survey the area for a Bailey Bridge, expecting our bridge to have been knocked out.[4]*

*

While this had been going on, in Le Port the Germans began another assault. Dennis Edwards:

At the front, the church was separated from the road by a high wall. We could hear Germans on the other side barking orders to each other. Two of us slithered through the tall grass to climb over the low wall that separated the south side of the church from our field. Once within the churchyard, we darted from gravestone to gravestone, until close enough to the much higher front boundary wall to lob over a couple of grenades, before turning and running back to the field. As we ran back into the field the grenades exploded and we had the satisfaction of hearing screams from someone in the roadway. Suddenly, in perfect English, a German shouted, 'You English in the church. You are surrounded and cannot escape. Leave your weapons behind and come out through the church gate and no harm will come to you.' Two of the others jumped over the wall along the southern edge of the churchyard to hurl the last of our grenades over the wall, shouting, 'Have these, then. That's all we're giving up.'

With no more grenades and very low on ammunition, we shared out our remaining rounds which were sufficient to part-stock our rifles and the Bren light machine gun, both of which used the same .303 bullet. We had no idea of what was happening else-where around the village and did not know if any more of our lads were still in action and if, like us, they had run low on ammo and were conserving stocks.

By lunchtime, or thereabouts, we were beginning to become extremely worried, for this was the time when reinforcements from the beach landing were expected. Our numbers were steadily diminishing while the Germans seemed to be increasing by the hour.

Gradually the Germans were gaining more and more of the village as, one after another, our lads were killed or wounded and, with each one that we lost, our ability to hold out diminished.

*

At 0840 hours, half an hour after the initial landings on SWORD Beach, the Commandos had begun their own landing. They immediately got off the beach, waded through a flooded area and then cut across country. Colonel Derek Mills-Roberts' Number 6, the leading Commando, had followed a planned route to avoid known German defences. They *had* to get to their first objective, the two bridges, as quickly as possible, but unfortunately the fields had not been easy to cross, with minefields (some dud, although this was not known initially), ditches, uneven ground, long grass and corn that was sometimes above head height, hindering their progress. They had attacked pillboxes, been sniped and taken on anyone who confronted them directly. Trouble on their flanks was for the most part bypassed.

Finally they began to close on the bridges. Lord Lovat, with Brigade HQ and Troops of 6 Commando had reached St Aubin d'Arquenay, a mile from Le Port. With

Lovat was a piper, Bill Millin:

Lovat approaches me. 'Piper, we are leaving here now and I want your pipes playing as long as you possibly can. The Orne bridges are not far off and I would like the forces holding the bridges to know when they hear the bagpipes that the Commando Brigade is close at hand.'

Dennis Edwards, 2nd Oxf and Bucks:

After all the earlier din of battle it suddenly became very quiet. Even the Germans had stopped shouting to each other, when suddenly, in the uncanny stillness of that spring day, I heard a sound that will live with me for the rest of my days. From somewhere to the north, well beyond the churchyard and probably beyond the village, I heard a sound that made the hairs stand up on the back of my neck – a sound like the wild wailing of banshees.

A tremendous cheer went up through the village and the Germans recommenced firing. Colonel Pine-Coffin:

At 1200 hours . . . the piper of 1 Special Service Brigade could be heard in St Aubin. This was the pre-arranged recognition signal but I did not give the answering bugle call as this would have meant that the way was clear for the Special Service Brigade to come through. Until the whole of Le Port had been cleared this was not the case.

Brigadier Poett had returned to Le Port:

I was with Geoffrey Pine-Coffin when we first heard them. It was marvellous for us because of course we had no idea whether the landing had been successful or not successful. All we knew was that the troops doing the seaborne landings had a hell of a tough job.

Dennis Edwards:

For us excessively tired young soldiers, out of ammunition and in an impossible position, the sense of relief and exhilaration can only be guessed at. To know that the seaborne forces were ashore and moving inland was also a cause for enormous relief and satisfaction. We were English every one, and always ready to have a bit of fun at the expense of Scotsmen and their pipes, but those wild wailing bagpipes were like the sound of Heaven. The raucous noise came to me more sweetly than any music that I had ever heard. It was like hearing a reprieve of sentence, which in effect it really was.

Various groups of Commandos were ahead of Lovat. One of them was Captain Alan 'Dickie' Pyman's 3 Troop, 6 Commando. Trooper Cliff Morris, 3 Troop, 6 Commando:

229

The sun had by this time broken through and was shining brilliantly and was right overhead, so we knew that it must be around mid-day. There was also more noise and activity, we could hear our other Troops signalling each other by means of small hunting horns which some of the lads carried, also the skirl of Lord Lovat's piper, not to mention some very persistent machine gun, rifle and mortar fire to the front of us. This meant that the Airborne lads were still holding out and fighting hard. We all immediately quickened our pace till finally we were doubling. Just then the paratrooper's bugler answered the bagpipes with 'Defaulters', warning us that we should go round them.

Captain Alan Pyman

They moved up to the crest of the knoll that over-looked Le Port and were greeted by the sight of the canal and a bridge that was intact. Trooper Sid Dann, 3 Troop, 6 Commando:

We reached Benouville but found a small-scale battle going on there with Germans holed up in the church. We bypassed that as we were supposed to be at the bridge by midday. As we came out onto the road, about 200 yards from the bridge, we could see a small group of men. There was a short pause while we tried to decide whose side they were on, and then a long cheer and much waving of Union Jacks – the agreed signal.

Trooper Geoffrey Scotson, 3 Troop, 6 Commando:

We were in a hollow field . . . As we reached the edge of this field, on the other side a bloke blew a bugle. It was one of Major [sic] Pine-Coffin's men. Out of my pouch I took a Union Jack, which had been given to me the day before, and we all held it in front of us . . . and we met in the middle of this small field.[5]

The Troop carried on across the fields and met Brigadier Poett and Colonel Pine-Coffin:

The leading elements of the Brigade (No 6 Commando) succeeded where the Germans had failed and found my weak spot.

This was between the lower end of Le Port and the canal bank. Brigadier Poett said to Captain Pyman, 'We are very pleased to see you.' Alan Pyman looked at his wrist watch and answered 'I am afraid we are a few minutes late, sir!'[6]

Geoffrey Scotson

230

Brigadier Poett:

The Commandos weren't going to stay on, they were going to pass through, but it showed us that the thing is moving and had been a success, and by God those chaps on the beaches had done it.

As they moved on, Cliff Morris noted the scene around the bridge:

Everywhere was confusion, the area was still under heavy fire and all movement was made at the double or crawling, as Jerry snipers were taking a heavy toll and both Jerry and Airborne dead and wounded lay sprawled in the road and in trenches. The whole area was pitted with shell and mortar holes and the air reeked of smoke and cordite.

The Troop then rushed across the Canal Bridge. Gordon Fleming, 3 Troop, 6 Commando:

When I myself went across the bridge it was still being fired at with small arms fire because you could hear the bullets pinging off the metal parts of the bridge. Once over the bridge we didn't hang about . . . There was no sort of backslapping or anything like that.[7]

Phillip Pritchard, 3 Troop, 6 Commando:

I did not see or contact any of the glider party and can only suppose that they were very wisely keeping their heads down due to the sniper fire. I then went on to the next bridge that crossed the Orne River proper, where I saw Captain Pyman talking to two Airborne officers. I did not stop as the Troop was hurrying up the hill to Amfreville.

Poett then received a radio message from General Gale informing him that the situation east of the river had deteriorated. Nigel Poett:

It was undoubtedly a crisis time on the east bank of the river when he sent for me because he wouldn't have sent me a signal, 'Please come back at once' . . .

In spite of the arrival of Pyman's men, Le Port had still not been cleared. The bicycle Troop of 6 Commando, 1 Troop, was led by Captain Douglas Robinson. They had begun to approach the high ground before Le Port when a machine gun opened up, hitting one of the cyclists. Robinson ordered his men to dismount and told Lance-Corporal Peter Masters, a German Jew of 3 Troop, 10 Commando, who was attached to 6 Commando, to head towards the village and find out what was happening:

Phillip Pritchard

231

Robinson obviously hadn't seen from what angle the machine gun had been firing and he needed to know this. I asked him how many men I should take with me and he said, 'None.' That was fine by me, we'd been trained in just this kind of work. I told him I'd go round the left flank, reconnoitre the village and come back from the right flank, which is what we had been taught to do. 'No, no,' said Robinson, 'I just want you to walk down that road and see what's going on.' It was quite clear to me that he wanted was for me to be shot at by the machine gun so he could see where it was positioned. It was a bad moment for me and I began to think feverishly. I knew he had to know, but that didn't help me. We'd been trained to try and figure an angle to improve the odds. I remembered an old Cary Grant film, set in the Khyber Pass or somewhere. He had walked straight into a rebel stronghold alone because he'd had no alternative and had said, 'You're all under arrest,' which I'd always thought a very funny line indeed. So I decided to do the same, so I walked down the centre of the road where everyone in the village could see me and began shouting in German, 'All right, everybody out with your hands on your heads. It's no use fighting, you're totally surrounded. For you the war is over. Come on, give yourselves up.' No one came out of course.

It was very disappointing, but on the other hand nobody shot me as yet. I guess they didn't shoot because they were curious to see what else would show.

Below him was a parapet wall, on his left an impenetrable ten-foot hedge and unusually no ditch, just a grass border a few feet wide. There was no cover at all:

They waited and waited and I looked around and my Captain Robinson said, 'Keep going.' I kept going, closer and closer to what I knew was my execution . . .

A man popped up from behind the parapet and shot at me with a Schmeisser. He missed because he fired too quickly and perhaps because he was a bad shot anyway. I didn't see where the bullets went but assumed they went right high because that's how a Schmeisser fires. Then he ducked back and as he ducked I went down on one knee and fired. My Tommy gun fired one round and then jammed because the thirty-round magazine had caused a double feed, though I didn't know it at the time of course.

I couldn't look because my eyes were glued to where the man had been. I cleared the gun quickly, but when he popped up again and missed me again, it jammed without firing. By this time I was lying down in the grass by the verge, and I forced myself to look and see what had gone wrong and saw that two rounds were crumpled in the breech. I cleared them and thought that this time I had to get him otherwise he was bound to get me.

Suddenly Masters heard the sound of feet charging down the road. It was the rest of the Troop and as they passed him he saw a tall Irish ex-Grenadier Guard firing a Bren gun from the shoulder:

It took me a little while to pick myself up and follow on behind because I was still a bit traumatized and the [Bren] machine gunner in front was spraying the whole country-side. Suddenly I saw him swivel to the left and empty practically his whole magazine at his feet. I rushed over there and he had shot the two machine gunners that had shot the cyclist. They were extremely young, sixteen, maybe fifteen, one was an Austrian. One could not be interrogated, he was too badly wounded, the other one could talk. I talked to him and he told me what little he knew and at that moment a very strange thing happened. The Irish lad, the machine gunner who had led the charge came back and said to me, 'You know, I have never shot anybody before. How do you say, 'Excuse me, I'm sorry in German?' And I said, 'Entschuldigen Sie. Es tut mir leid,' and he repeated after me and I was very shaken by this.'[8]

Piper Bill Millin was approaching Le Port:

We marched along. At this point some prisoners came marching towards us, the first Germans I'd seen with their hands in the air. They didn't look like a very master race type of people. They were pushed to the rear. As we approached the village I could hear the sound of heavy firing, mortars and automatic weapons.

The Airborne behind the cemetery could hear the piper getting nearer. Dennis Edwards:

Shouting and cheering, we all expressed our joy together and, abandoning all caution, were up on our feet and leapt over the wall into the churchyard again, yelling things like 'Now you Jerry bastards, you've got a real fight on your hands.'

Suddenly, as if in response to our lack of caution, and from just above our heads somewhere up in the church tower, a fast-firing enemy machine gun burst into life. We dived for the cover of the nearest gravestones, but then realized that he was not firing at us, but towards the Commando.

Bill Millin:

I continued piping and as we approached Benouville, the road turned right at the entrance to the village, and we came under some rifle and automatic fire. I stopped playing the pipes as the road turned right, and joined a group of Commandos who were crouched behind a low wall on the right-hand side of the road. There were several wounded lying at the side of the road being tended to by a medic. Opposite us, sheltering behind the gable end of a house, was another group of Commandos.

I moved along the low wall, crouching down and holding the bagpipes to my chest. With the group of Commandos sheltering behind the gable end of the house opposite is the CO of Number 6 Commando,

Piper Bill Millin

Mills-Roberts. He looks impatient and keeps peering round the building and into the village.

Two DD tanks of the 13th/18th Hussars, which had attached themselves to the Commandos on their move inland, suddenly reappeared and Millin was ordered to get behind them and start playing. Dennis Edwards:

From the churchyard we could see nothing of the machine-gunner, so we ran back to the field and fired our last few rounds at the upper part of the church in the hope of keeping him quiet. He ignored us and continued to fire towards the Commando.

After a quick discussion we decided to rush the church, get inside and dislodge him from there. However, just as the decision was made, we heard the Commando in the street beyond the churchyard's front wall. They were accompanied by two Sherman tanks which halted, swung their guns over the wall and fired with a deafening crash, blasting away the top of the church tower.

When the firing stopped we went back into the churchyard, out through the front gate and greeted the Commando.

Eric Truman, HQ Company, 7th Parachute Battalion:

I remember throwing my arms around a huge Scottish Commando, his very first words, 'Well, you can go home now, Cherry Beret, the real men are here.' I must admit that I would have given anything to have complied with his statement.

Colonel Pine-Coffin met Lovat and explained that 'B' Company had been pretty well tied down by snipers, and so the Commandos began to help clear them out.

With the pressure in Le Port relieved, Corporal Bill Bailey's section of 25 Platoon was allowed to go back to the bridge. They took up position near the gun emplacement on the eastern side of the canal. He had had nothing to drink for fourteen hours:

At this stage we got the first inkling of Commandos coming through, some with bicycles, and I thought this was a good time to make some tea. So I took my 'Tommy cooker' down into the position between the gun. Little primus stove with a little block of meth and mess tin of water and a little mix of sugar and you're away. Takes six or seven minutes.

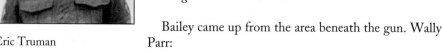

I think it was Wally and 'Gus' [Gardner]. I was sitting on this bunk watching and the bubbles had just started to come up. I'd just dropped the tea and there was a God Almighty crash over my head. Charlie Gardner was up on the gun, and they fired this bloody thing while I was down there and of course all the sand from China came crashing down on our heads!

Eric Truman

Bailey came up from the area beneath the gun. Wally Parr:

234

Le Port square, the location of the main link-up between the Airborne and the Commandos

He just looked at me and said, 'Parr, don't fire that bleedin' gun again will you till I've had my cup of tea, there's all shit falling on top of me.' I said, 'Yeah, alright, alright.' So the war stopped for about fifteen minutes as far as the gun was concerned, but they [the Germans] were creeping up and creeping up. It was over on the right hand bank, there was space between some bushes and another clump, and one shot across, [another] one shot across. Now there was already two there we knew, so that made four. And then two more came scurrying across because the gun was quiet and they were doing alright. There were six of them and I swung the gun round, I'd got six of them behind this clump of bushes. I suppose it was a ten-yard clump give or take a 'thou', and I just aimed the gun and I fired. The next thing you knew there was a terrible scream from somewhere outside and I thought 'Some poor bastard's got it.' Then, believe it or not I saw two hands, big hands . . . pulling himself up the two steps inside the gun pit. It was Bailey. His face was livid, his cup of char had just come to the boil. He'd put his powdered milk and his sugar in it and I fired the bleedin' gun and the whole of the roof fell in on top of it and turned it into mud! Bailey came into there, and I left my post and I run round the front end of the gun. He chased me round there. He eventually gave up the chase and he went off swearing and cursing, without his cup of tea.[9]

While the clearance of Le Port went on, the remaining Troops of 6 Commando duly closed up. Geoffrey Pine-Coffin:

There was plenty of time for chatting anyhow as the actual crossing of the Canal Bridge

235

was to be something of a ceremony which took quite a bit of organizing. Eventually, it was all teed up . . .

When they had formed up, they began to head for the bridges. Bill Millin was leading them:

As I start up the bagpipes and head out along the road playing Blue Bonnets over the Border, and keeping well into the side of the road, with Lovat and the others close behind, I could hear the sound of heavy firing in the distance, and the now familiar crump of the mortars. We continue round a bend in the road and I can now see a large house up ahead. The house is about 300 yards away, and our route veers to the left in front of it. I am fascinated with the house. It has a low wall round it, with iron railings on top. The door is in the centre, with large windows on either side. I find myself, as I am walking along playing the bagpipes, looking mainly at the windows for the presence of snipers.

Above the sound of the pipes I can hear the rattle of automatic fire. Glancing round, Lovat is still there, the rest of the Commandos strung out on either side of the road. Everything seems to be all right.

John Butler was still at the bridge:

Airborne troops meet members of 6 Commando outside La Chaumiere (IWM B5058)

I went across to the café which I found was being used as an RAP. I have no idea which MO came to the café at the time I was there, there was just a corporal, Para not glider rider, and one other medic, plus several wounded . . . I asked the medic inside if he had anything to drink and he told me to knock on the inner door and ask the occupants, which I did. The inner door was opened by a little man, Monsieur Gondrée, badly in need of a shave, who kissed me on both cheeks and in my best schoolboy French I asked if he had some water to drink. In perfect English he said, 'Don't drink water, I have a real drink.' He then went inside and a few moments later appeared with an armful of dirty, muddy bottles, champagne . . . He poured out two glasses and we toasted one another. He was going to pour out some more, then he grinned and said, 'You don't want a glass do you?' and gave me the bottle. Just then, one of the medics said he could hear the pipes, so I went outside with several bottles of champagne and the first thing I saw was two amphibious Sherman tanks at the T-junction by the Mairie. Then as the pipes grew louder, round the corner came Brigadier the Lord Lovat with a piper on one side and I presume his bodyguard on the other. He looked neither left or right as he marched down the street as though he was strolling through his Scottish estate. He carried no weapon but instead carried his swagger cane and wore a collar and tie. He didn't look like he had made a wet landing from an assault craft.[10]

Bill Millin:

I stopped piping immediately across the road from the café [Gondrée]. *There was a right battle going on, huge columns of black smoke. Even where I was standing I could hear the shrapnel, bullets were hitting off the sides of the metal bridge, and wounded were being carried up from along the canal banks and into the café.*

Lovat went and spoke to an Airborne officer just before the bridge. Bill Millin:

Then Lovat came back to me and said, 'Right, we'll cross over.' I put the pipes on my shoulder and he said, 'No, don't play, wait till I tell you.' So we walked over and had to duck a bit because the machine gun, snipers, were shooting from the banks of the river.

Major Howard greeted Lovat at the other end of the bridge with 'About bloody time!' Corporal Ted Tappenden:

He shook hands with John Howard and he said, 'John, today history has been made.'

Howard briefly explained the situation and then Lovat moved on, giving Millin another order:

Lord Lovat (IWM FLM 4023)

'Right, play now, keep playing and all the way along this road, about 200 yards, till you come to another bridge, and keep playing across to that, no matter what. Just keep playing.'

They gradually approached the Orne Bridge. Bill Millin:

It was a narrower bridge with open railings on the side . . . I looked across and I could see two Airborne on the other side, dug in, in a slit trench. They were going 'get back' and pointing to the sides of the river, meaning the bridge was under fire. I looked around at Lovat.

Lovat said, 'Carry on, carry on' and so Millin piped his way across the bridge:

I stopped and shook hands with the two chaps in the slit trench . . . Then, from across the road appears this tall Airborne officer, red beret on. He came walking across the road, his arm outstretched towards Lovat. 'Very pleased to see you old boy!' And Lovat said, 'And we are very pleased to see YOU old boy!'[11]

The remainder of 6 Commando began to follow across the bridges. When Colonel Mills-Roberts crossed the Canal Bridge, a man was shot in the head only a few paces in front of him:

Seconds later the big swing bridge across the Caen Canal behind us was under heavy mortar fire. Mixed with the crump of the bombs was the whine of metal fragments as they struck the steel girders of the bridge. Casualties were now increasing.

Trooper Harry Bell was in 5 Troop, the Heavy Weapons Troop comprising the 3-inch mortars and Vickers machine guns:

At that time the bridge was under fire. On the right-hand side of the bridge was a German gun emplacement which the Airborne were manning and firing up the canal to where all the flak was coming from.

On reaching the east side of the Orne they immediately turned off the road and headed towards a quarry.

3 Troop, the bicycle Troop of Colonel Peter Young's 3 Commando, had had orders to leave the main body and dash towards the bridges. Trooper Stan Scott, 3 Troop, 3 Commando:

*At Le Port, opposite the Church, a lone Para was sitting with his leg up on a chair. He had a shattered leg and was guarding a little knot of prisoners. He looked at us and said, 'Where the f*** have you been?' 'Bollocks!' is my reply as I go past, on to the T-junction and the Town Hall. We turned left past Benouville Town Hall, down the slope.*

MG Section 5 Troop, 6 Commando. Harry Bell is standing, far right

On the left hand side of the road was a garden with a little bank, and we got down by this bank. That was all right if the fire was coming from the left, on the other side of the bank, but it wasn't, it was coming from the right. We were looking down the road about seventy-five yards from the bridge and it was like a beehive. There was rounds hitting it from all sides. Most of it was coming from the Maternity Home in Benouville. Across the bridge on the other side was a gun and it was being used to try and hit them. So you were getting all the ricochets and then suddenly, WHOOMPF! Just as we realized the bank wasn't doing us any good, someone said, 'Get on your bikes, you'll probably get away with it!' We all jump on our bikes and away we go, pedalling like bleedin' mad. I shot across that bridge and on the right hand side there was a German vehicle burning and I shot behind that. That's solid; that's protection. Jimmy Synnott and the others went to the left-hand side in a ditch. Campbell, he was the unlucky one, got shot straight through the neck. Went down in one big heap, him and the bike. I suddenly realized, standing behind this half-track, there was a pong of roasting pork. It was the crew, incinerated.[12]

Lance-Sergeant Jimmy Synnott:

Stan Scott

There was an Airborne chap on the right-hand side [of the bridge], sort of looking up the road, protecting the road up to it with a Sten gun. And I just spoke briefly to him and he said, 'Bloody glad to see you people! Your lads are all over on the left-hand side. Don't hang about, there's snipers. They're sniping here all the time.' The number of Airborne, you couldn't see them, they were all well dug in or else camouflaged.

We went into the ditch on the left and it was a ditch off the road and it was all sort of bush, bocage. It was well screened. The sixty-odd Commandos were all down on the left-hand side, apart from Campbell.

There they stopped, in preparation for the move towards their coastal objective of Cabourg. The Troop Commander was Captain Roy Westley:

Lovat turned up, said, 'There's a change of plan. You've got to go up and get this village here and hold that because the parachutists, some of them, have been dropped all over the place.'

Captain Roy Westley

Lance-Sergeant Synnott:

He must have got one of our bikes or one of the bikes of 6 Commando, but he came up, and it was about ten minutes or fifteen minutes after we'd got there. He just simply came up, spoke to Westley.

The remnants of the 9th Parachute Battalion, which had carried out the assault on the Merville gun battery during the night, were hanging on to a chateau in the village of Amfreville on the Breville ridge. Short of men and ammunition, they were in danger of being overrun. Jimmy Synnott:

As soon as Westley gave the order that we were going to attack Amfreville, he just led off and we all followed. Lovat certainly didn't come with us. We crossed the Orne Bridge, there was a sentry dug in on the right-hand side. We were all spread out, but no artillery fire, no mortar fire, no machine-gun fire, the odd rifle shot but that was all.

The Troop moved on down the road, passed a few houses and took the left fork towards the village.

Further Commandos and Engineers were now arriving in Le Port piecemeal. The sections of 71 Field Company tasked with building the Bailey Bridges had landed in two LCIs, and made their way towards Benouville separately. Sapper Stan Sharman, 6 Section, 2 Platoon:

I didn't see any Commandos until I got to Benouville, and then there was a Commando already there, in position. He was just past the church. He was in a prone position, lying down, and a Bren gun he had. He was covering the road I think. He was on his own funny enough, there was no-one with him. He said, 'I'm glad someone's coming!'

We were supposed to have an infantry lot with us, but the sad thing of it all was we'd walked through like that and the infantry lot that were supposed to give us protection, they had terrible casualties.

Jimmy Synnott

Sapper Bob Heath, 6 Section, 2 Platoon:

Opposite the church there was this row of shops. One was a baker's and the other was a café. I was quite surprised to see these locals drinking outside! We passed the church and as we reached the bend in the road which went downhill towards the Mairie, *we were fired on, possibly from the church tower.*

Stan Sharman:

There was one of those moments when we didn't know what to do and then Major Willison came along. 'Oh, you've arrived,' he said. 'This is where I'm going to have our HQ for the time being,' he said, 'Go round, it's full of snipers . . . look for them.'

Major David Willison, the CO of 17 Field Company Group, had been another early arrival in Le Port and had witnessed Lovat and the Commandos marching down to the bridge.

Sharman's group went into the church, found it empty and tried the door to the tower, but it was wedged shut. They came out and took up position beside the building.

The church tower had thick stone walls and although it now had gaping holes around the window, the staircase prevented anyone from ensuring that it was clear of snipers.

*

General Gale had called for Brigadier Poett's return to Le Bas de Ranville because the situation involving the armour-supported attack, which had forced the survivors of Captain Sim's 12th Battalion outpost party to retire, became critical when armour and infantry began to infiltrate between the Company positions. This was all happening a few hundred yards in front of the MDS buildings and the Chateau of Divisional HQ.

Captain David Tibbs and his men of 3 Section of the Field Ambulance had finished searching the DZ for casualties:

When we got back to the MDS, the Chateau, it was absolutely full of wounded, seething with wounded, more than they could cope with at the time. There was a tremendous stonk of firing going on, mortars, just across the road from the MDS, [in] the Chateau there was a whole battery of mortars and they were firing at the Germans because this was their attack coming in. The Germans were firing mortars at us, and the dental officer asked, 'would I go out with him and bring in a wounded man lying in the road outside.' It was my first experience of being in real heavy fire. It was quite noisy. We picked up this wounded chap and got him in. Then I moved over to another part and saw, coming up the slope leading to the side of the Chateau, where all the wounded were coming in, was a dreadful sight of two men supporting a young officer who was limping on one leg, the other leg just trailing loosely behind him and obviously a dreadful injury. How on earth he managed to walk I don't know. He was an officer from one of the other battalions I knew a little bit, and was always astonished that he looked rather a pale, small man, who you felt he should not be quite the type in the paratroops like this, but there he was, dreadfully wounded. As he came up, to my astonishment he managed to say to me, 'Oh Doc, glad to see you, but I am sorry to be a nuisance.' We laid him on the ground and got a stretcher and carried him in.

They did what they could to move the men lying in the courtyard into the buildings, but those casualties with no hope of survival were placed in a building at Number 7, a farm across the road owned by the Lefoulon family. Tibbs was then put in charge of the stone-walled barn beside the Chateau that contained around a hundred wounded:

I was dead beat . . . and was a bit uncertain about what I should be doing about it all. I'd go round and make sure their needs as far as possible were satisfied and Pat [Hewlings] came in to see how we were getting on when he suddenly realized that most of them had not got the proper documentation which was a label attached somewhere round their necks. Essential details. Most of them had not got this and he tore me off a big strip. I apologized and tried to put things right as best I could. But he was the sort of guy who, because you knew he was doing his job well, he was probably tired and bad tempered as well. But you didn't take it to heart.

Shortly afterwards the door suddenly burst open:

A very panicky RASC driver said, 'The Germans are here, they're at the bottom of the lane,' which was about fifty yards away. There was a moments silence and then there was a sort of general stirring amongst all the wounded some of whom were very badly wounded indeed, and a Scottish sergeant levered himself up and fished out a Sten gun that he'd been lying on and pointed it at this chap and said, 'Stop yer blathering you f**** or you'll be the first to go!' The noise of battle still continuing outside, spasmodically, this RASC driver hurriedly disappeared because he was more frightened of this Scotsman than the Germans. I stood absolutely irresolute, I carried an automatic, I was a good shot, if the Germans appeared at the door, my wounded were all going to open fire at them, and would I join in or would I try waving a Red Cross flag? While I was standing there irresolute, wondering what the hell I should do, I heard somebody calling my name right at my feet, 'David, David.' I looked down and there was the Padre, Padre Briscoe, who'd been badly wounded, and he'd really been put in this barn because no one thought he'd survive . . . said, 'David, remove my pistol.' This was just sort of the fashion of the day that you carried a pistol, even Naval officers. 'If the Germans find my pistol, they'll shoot me.' So I unbuckled his belt and kicked his gun under the straw. Then I looked around and everything by then had fallen silent. I realized the battle had been won as it was and the Germans didn't actually reach our doorway. But then I reflected that it was terribly wrong for all the wounded under a Red Cross flag to be still in possession of their weapons, so I had all the weapons rounded up. I also reflected that no-one had ever discussed with us the Geneva Convention, the rights and wrongs permitted to us.

Facing determined opposition, the Germans began to withdraw at about 1300 hours, having lost 3 SP guns and one Mark IV tank in front of Le Bas de Ranville. Patrols and snipers were sent out to clear any Germans remaining in front of the position. Lieutenant Gordon Medd, OC 'C' Company, was ordered forward to Captain Sim's former hedgerow:

We went in single file up the river side of the bocage which ran south towards Caen and which intersected the western edge of the hedgerow. When we reached the intersection I assembled my little band, and we cantered along the back of the hedgerow like a lot of ninnies, not knowing what to expect, waving our weapons and ready to shoot at anything that moved – even the leaves on the trees.

By the time our momentum had taken us to the eastern end of the hedgerow it had become tragically clear that indeed nothing was moving or alas, going to move again.

There were no Germans visible, so I split my little force into two, a group for each end of the hedgerow, and with Doughty, set about making an assessment of the casualties.

Lance Corporal Hateley, one of my two platoon snipers, was leaning forward in his slit-trench immediately behind the sparse hedge and in a firing position. He was dead. The hole in his head which looked like a bullet wound (but may have been shrapnel) had hardly bled and I assumed he had died instantaneously when he was hit.

Lance Corporal Skellett, my other platoon sniper was lying on the ground behind Hateley's foxhole. He had been savagely wounded in the body and was quite dead.

243

Lieutenant Gordon Medd

About ten to fifteen yards westwards from Skellett and almost in the cornfield, I came across the FOO lying on his back. He was unable to move or speak much and in considerable distress. Doughty and I turned him over as gently as we could, to find he had been terribly wounded in the buttocks. One hip-bone was sticking out from a mass of raw flesh, which had had soil and grass ground into it as he rolled about. We had no means of cleaning him up but just clapped two field dressings on and hoped for the best. [13]

Halfway along the hedge and still moving westwards, was the 6-pounder gun, sited in a slightly thicker part of the hedge. It had a restricted arc of fire, being positioned between and to the rear of two saplings. The Gunner Bombardier was sitting propped up against the wheel of the gun. He was very bloody about the head and appeared to be blind. I tried to question him but got no sense. One dead soldier lay about ten feet from the gun. I didn't recognise him and assumed he was a gunner.

Just past the gun position and still going westwards, I found Lance-Sergeant Jones lying face down on the ground. He was in the open and appeared to have been walking or running towards the eastern end of the hedgerow when caught in the back with a burst of fire. He was dead. I came to the conclusion that the Germans had come around the western edge of the hedgerow and caught Jones with a burst as he tried to get back to the eastern end. His weapon was missing and I assumed they had taken it.

Right at the western end of the hedgerow were two well dug slits in the hedge itself with a body nearby. I did not recognize who it was immediately, and regrettably was called back to the eastern end of the hedgerow before I could find out.

I was called to the eastern end because the men had discovered a body, Sergeant Milburn, in a spit of the hedge running southwards at right angles to the main hedgerow. Further down was a dead German with no identification; however, one of the men had taken his red leather cigarette case which was handed to me. It contained an official-looking docket which turned out to be a certificate saying that Rizi, working in a Caen brothel, has passed her routine hygiene check! There was a photograph too, of some farmhands standing around a mare being served by a stallion – most odd. [14]

*

The 12th Battalion's situation remained a matter of real concern for General Gale:

The 12th Battalion had had a bad time and they were considerably under strength; if the Germans developed a second attack of similar strength and vigour, I doubted their ability, with the best will in the world, to stand up to it. I had by now also put in the Independent Parachute Company and had nothing in hand. The bridgehead was my major responsibility: this must be held.

He therefore decided to divert a Commando unit towards Ranville, and send a Liaison Officer to find Major-General Tom Rennie, commanding the 3rd British Infantry Division, to request a speed up in the relief of the 6th Airborne.

However, it had not been all bad news for him. Reports concerning 3 Parachute Brigade had begun to come in, and although like 5 Brigade they had suffered a scattered drop, all five of the proposed bridges had been destroyed and the vital Merville Battery silenced. The 8th and 9th Parachute Battalions and the 1st Canadian Parachute Battalion were now attempting to concentrate in specific areas to form the northern side of the defensive perimeter.

Chapter Fourteen

The Remainder of the Day

Tommy Farr's 4 Platoon, 'B' Company, 7th Parachute Battalion had been in action for most of the morning in the southern part of Le Port, but with the reduced enemy activity in that area their rôle was altered:

> *The platoon was then moved back towards the bridge and occupied two houses west of the Canal Bridge. Here our task was to cover the open ground to the south towards the Chateau de Benouville. 'A' Company were having a lot of trouble in this area and we were moved back to cover any breakthrough by the enemy and to assist 6 Platoon in holding the bridge itself.*

On the lower road Captain Wagstaff was still working in the original RAP. It had remained cut off from the battalion for most of the morning:

> *We'd got some strays come in . . . and one or two we'd brought in ourselves. In the interest of the wounded you very much had to keep it low-key.*
> *At 1330 hours we saw a Sherman tank about 300 yards away. It had been firing at enemy machine gun posts. About 1400 hours an armoured recce car came down and an RE Lieutenant came into the RAP. We gave him such information as we had and he set off to scout around.*

This patrol was led by a former Commando, Lieutenant Whyte of 1 Platoon, 71 Field Company. After leaving the RAP they immediately ran into opposition and a small action followed during which he threw a Gammon bomb through a house window, flushing out and capturing nine prisoners.

*

Commandos and Seaborne Engineers continued to make their way to Benouville. Emlyn Jones of the Commando Signal Troop was attached to Lieutenant Colonel Ries' 45 Royal Marines Commando, which had passed through St Aubin d'Arquenay:

> *Whilst on our way to Benouville we heard what we thought could only be a tank coming from our road. This would be a great help to us but unfortunately it turned out to be one of our bulldozers. We warned the driver to stay put as the area wasn't cleared*

yet but he insisted he'd had his orders. We were to meet up again a few hundred yards down the road, he was slumped over his wheel, a bullet through his head.

At 1430 hours 45 RM Commando reached the bridges:

A halt was called and we were thankful for the break but still we couldn't relax as the enemy were keeping up a relentless bombardment. The time came for us to cross the bridge, which was under a smoke haze. Lord Lovat was standing in the middle of the road, just a few yards away from the bridge, oblivious to enemy fire which came raining down from the Chateau de Benouville . . . Lord Lovat standing there reminded me of a policeman on traffic duty, urging us on. 'Don't run across the bridge, walk' was his order. Then it was my time to go, passing some Airborne lads dug in at the side of the bridge. 'Good luck, keep going, there's another bridge' they shouted. I think it must have been one of the fastest walks I'd ever undertaken, feeling so vulnerable with bullets pinging off the steel girders and a fair amount of mortar fire. Soon I was across and into the ditch on the other side, a slight breather. A shout: the Colonel had been hit by a sniper. Lieutenant Colonel Ries was immediately evacuated. It looked as if he'd caught it in the thigh. His second-in-command, Major Nicol Gray took over.

They then headed north towards Merville.

Captain John Hoare, 2i/c of 71 Field Company was leading a party towards Benouville and had passed through Colleville and St Aubin d'Arquenay. They then found themselves behind 3 Commando. The road ahead of the Commandos was being shelled and so they had halted. The Engineers also stopped, fell out and rested against the embankment of the road. Contact was made while the Commandos considered what to do. A Commando Adjutant and several men went forward to see if there was a chance of getting any further along the road. Captain John Hoare:

There were a few more shells coming over and they lay flat on the ground, then got up and came back. He was quite a young man, the Adjutant, he sort of sprinted along the road. He had a map case and I remember this sort of flapping as he was running along. Then one or two shells came in. They didn't land on the road itself, they were in the fields each side of the road. They didn't do much harm to personnel.

The next thing that happened was the Commandos sheared off to the left . . . There was a side turning there, a little bit of a track, and that's where they went.

It was right out in the country, it was not like an intersection in the middle of the village.

Our column was quite long. We had about 150 chaps there at least and they'd be spread out in aircraft Captain John Hoare *formation, that is a section each side of the road, alternatively, so that would have gone quite a way back, but this bank lasted quite a long distance. Anyway, we pulled them in so as to make sure there was no exposure in the rear.*

At that moment, up came the Forward Observation Officer from the artillery . . . He was on a carrier which was crossing the fields.

The officer came straight up and addressed John Hoare:

He said that he was going to deliver a counter-strike against the battery and if we hung on a bit, this would happen and then in the pause afterwards, we might be able to move further along. I decided to go firm and stay put.

The subsequent barrage duly suppressed the bombardment of the road, and so Captain Hoare's group continued straight on to the *Mairie* in Benouville:

On arrival at that site I was favourably impressed by how quiet it was. I think it was that stage we were required to set demolition charges on the bridge.

Being a steel girder bridge, there wasn't much to do in that respect, it was a question of lashing high explosive onto the steelwork.

It was also decided to find out how to operate the bridge. René Niepceron:

A British officer came to get my father to show a Royal Engineer how to work the bridge alongside him. There was so much activity, the time passed very quickly, and not seeing my father returning, I decided to risk a visit to the bridge. There was a crack, a whistle above my head. A sniper, but he was off centre. Once across the bridge I was again in the open when smack, a second bullet off target. I ran very fast towards the trench where the Paras [sic] were. A hand caught my leg and pulled me to earth, flat on my stomach and into the trench. The sniper was on a slight rise behind the Gondrée Café.

When calm returned I thought I'd visit the German Guardroom where there was a cellar of ammunition of all sorts and food, tins and jars of conserves. Very welcome! This bungalow had been the office during the rebuilding of the bridge.

*

After taking the slight detour onto the Caen to Ouistreham road, the main body of 3 Commando passed through Le Port and approached the Canal Bridge. Colonel Peter Young, OC 3 Commando, had been there a while, having raced forward on a bicycle:

We ran across the bridge as fast as we could. On the other bank in a ditch beside the road sat a row of German prisoners. Almost at once Lord Lovat appeared and told me that our advance on Cabourg was off. The Airborne

Rene Niepceron

248

troops had dropped over a far wider area than had been intended. The Commando was to move into Le Bas de Ranville, so as to protect the Headquarters of the 6th Airborne Division and to block any enemy advance from the south.[1]

And so 3 Commando, less 3 Troop, headed east.

In the area of the T-junction Major Willison, OC 17 Field Company, was organizing his men:

More and more people kept on coming in. 71 Company, who were under my command, they started appearing during the afternoon. By then I had 500 sappers there, my own 250 plus 71 Company, plus masses of RAOC drivers who were, so far as we were concerned, not really up to mounting an attack upon the Germans.

There were also further tanks from the 13th/18th Hussars:

They came to me and asked what they should do. I said, 'Well, distribute yourselves under cover as best you can around here.'

The Engineers began to dig in beside the *Mairie*.

The Germans in Benouville could see the continual arrival of these men and vehicles and this dissuaded them from making a more concerted effort until they were reinforced with further armour.[2] Major Willison:

We then were invited by 7 Para to mount a counter-attack with the tanks. I said, 'Yes, this is on, and we will support the tanks, who will shoot up the Chateau de Benouville' which was just two or three hundred yards down the road I suppose, where the German infantry had installed themselves.

He then walked up to the Troop Commander of the 13th/18th Hussars who was standing in the turret and began to discuss what to do. There was a sudden explosion and Willison was struck by pieces of the tank's armour. An anti-tank gun had managed to get the Sherman within its sights:

I was removed on a stretcher to the Regimental Aid Post which was in the Café Gondrée *just down the road from the crossroads, near the bridge.[3]*

Major 'Tiny' Upton, OC 71 Field Company, assumed command of the Field Group.

At Captain Wagstaff's RAP, Private Skelley, one of the conscientious objector medics, arrived after a very difficult and dangerous crawl from the 'A' Company positions. Captain Wagstaff:

Major David Willison

249

It took him approximately three hours although the two positions were only a few hundred yards apart. He told us that 'A' Company were still holding out and that they had heavy casualties. They required more dressings and stretcher-bearers to evacuate the wounded. It wouldn't have been any good bringing them to us, but they could work back to the Main Dressing Station. All available personnel went off, with Skelley as guide, to endeavour to reach 'A' Company. A Sapper Major stopped the party and advised them to wait until tanks had neutralized the machine gun posts and infantry had gone through to 'A' Company. The party therefore returned to the RAP.

Lieutenant Dick Harding, commanding 3 Platoon of 71 Field Company, subsequently led 9 Section on a patrol along the lower road while the tanks went down the main road.

The 'A' Company men were very happy to see the Shermans approaching, but their happiness was mingled with a little concern. After the German tank had got through earlier, they had slid Hawkins anti-tank grenades into the road. Major Taylor:

We'd skate these across the road and the whole road was covered with them. We wanted to stop these tanks, we wanted to tell them what the situation was, and we were there, and we didn't want them to run over these grenades which we couldn't pick up because we couldn't get onto the road without getting yourself killed. So we hung our berets on the rifle barrels, waved those and we held out celanese yellow triangles which we all carried, which were an aircraft recognition thing. They took not a blind bit of notice, they came straight on, closed right down, straight over the anti-tank grenades, none of which went off.

Captain Jim Webber:

We thought the seaborne troops had reached us when three British tanks raced through the village from the direction of Ouistreham. Immediately after passing us, one of them was hit and caught fire.

The Germans had three 7.5cm anti-tank guns covering both main and lower roads. One situated just inside the Chateau entrance fired at a range of around twenty-five yards. The shell penetrated the turret and the tank burst into flames. The other tank tried to manoeuvre on to the gun but was also destroyed. Captain John Wagstaff:

A Sherman tank was going in to attack as our party came up and so they waited for it to clear the road. One tank was knocked out and another Sherman tank twenty yards south of the RAP was knocked out by an anti-tank gun. One member of the tank's crew escaped and came into the RAP.

This tank had turned left at *Le Carrefour de Maternité*, moved past the RAP and was halted by a gas-driven truck owned by a local, Monsieur Hamard. He had parked it outside the house of his friend Monsieur Liot, just on a T-junction, and it blocked the road. It took quite a time to start such a vehicle and some French people had come out to greet the crew while the tank, an amphibious DD Sherman, tried to pull the truck out of the way. It had been an unmissable target for an anti-tank gun in the garden of the Chateau.

The Engineers on the lower road then became involved in a sharp fire-fight and were forced to withdraw. Sapper Bob Heath of 71 Field Company, who was dug in beside the *Mairie*, saw figures he recognized running back towards him:

I remember Barnett running past me with blood running down his head and he was shouting, 'Dransfield's had it.' That was the first I heard of Georgie Dransfield getting killed, closely followed by Jock Kerr, who was wounded in the leg.

Bob Heath

Sapper Stan Sharman:

He was protecting his officer when he got killed. The officer said to him, 'Look Dransfield, cover me, I'm going in this woods . . .' near where the hospital was, and a sniper shot Dransfield through the head.

Thirty-six year-old Dransfield was one of their RASC truck drivers.[4] The fate of the patrol proved that at this stage there was no chance of the Engineers being able to reach their designated location for the Bailey Bridge, or of relieving 'A' Company. Therefore, little could be done to clear the Germans out of Benouville without reinforcements. Captain Wagstaff:

A sniper of 7th Battalion called in to collect all available arms and ammunition for 'A' Company as he said they had expended almost all their supplies. The sniper of the 7th Battalion recced forward and found that it was impossible to get through to 'A' Company and so the stretcher party went to consult the RE Major. He informed them that his men were going to withdraw to the north side of Benouville and that arrangements were being made for 'A' Company's wounded in armoured cars. He therefore advised us to withdraw from the RAP.

For the sake of his wounded, Wagstaff again decided to stay where he was. 'A' Company had become seriously depleted. Lieutenant Hunter:

I was now very near Company HQ at the crossroads. I quickly nipped over and found Major Nigel Taylor lying at the bottom of a large zig-zag trench which had been provided by the Germans. He had a large gash in his thigh. I reported where my platoon was now located and what had happened. He told me both the other platoon commanders had been killed and Captain Jim Webber was trying to make contact with Battalion HQ. There was no radio contact. I said to Nigel, 'If this is war, quite

251

Ron Follett

frankly, I don't like it one little bit.' He asked me to try and get in front of the farmhouse. I knew this was a hopeless proposition, but I said I would see what I could do. I didn't feel like arguing with him in his present condition. I was sorry to leave the safety of the trench.[5]

Back with my platoon things were hotting up. We were at the receiving end of mortar bombs. I told Sergeant Newman that the Company Commander wanted us to try and get back in front of the farm. He agreed it was out of the question. We were down to about a dozen men and we were really pinned down.

Attempts had already been made to get in front of the farm. Ron Follett, Anti-Tank Platoon:

There was a walled garden in front of the area and a narrow farm track and one door going through. Sometime during the middle of the day, we made a little sortie through to see if we could advance in that direction and were pinned down very quickly and came back to our side of the walled garden. Then the Germans made a little sortie and we kept them away. Then soon after that, I was blown up a by a grenade that they'd thrown over the wall. I was blown into the middle of the road and much nearer the wall. It actually landed between my legs . . . [6]

This knocked him unconscious.

Having made several unsuccessful attempts to get runners through to Battalion HQ, Captain Webber managed it during the middle of the afternoon. Lieutenant Nick Archdale:

Jim Webber from 'A' Company arrived in a very tired state. He had been wounded a couple of times and informed us that 'A' Company was in a desperate situation.

Lieutenant Todd:

What we didn't realize at the time was that he was badly wounded himself, in the lung . . . His webbing and equipment covered any signs of the wound and we didn't realize he had been wounded and he didn't let on.

Colonel Pine-Coffin sent Webber back, accompanied by Archdale. It was a difficult and frightening journey up the right-hand side of the road, but they successfully reached the zig-zag trench which was by now virtually the entire Company position. Nick Archdale:

I got back with Jim, where things were pretty desperate and of course you could not get the wounded out. There were a lot of wounded men. Nigel Taylor was at the bottom of a trench, wounded. David Hunter was badly wounded and it was very difficult. We

252

were all concerned for 'A' Company's wounded. These poor, wretched men were so full of morphine that their hands felt cold and stiff.

Jim was absolutely magnificent and infused a terrific spirit into the men of that Company. Jim never gave anyone a moment to doubt that all was not well and cheerful. He had apparently been three times, by himself, into the house opposite and blasted the Germans out.

The farmhouses were quite close in front of us and were disputed territory. It was more or less no man's land, the buildings. I know we were being shot at from the upstairs windows, doing this business of one man putting his helmet up, another looking to see it, getting a shot at the chap shooting from the upstairs windows. They were very close too. And they fell for that business, bobbing the helmet up! If they had been bold enough and they had any numbers, they could have overrun us at any time.

Captain Jim Webber

*

4 Commando, along with two attached French Troops of 10 Inter-Allied Commando, had cleared the port of Ouistreham before heading towards the bridges. Having left their rucksacks on the edge of town prior to the attack, they returned to collect them and then followed the route taken by the Brigade. Major Ronald Menday, 2i/c of 4 Commando, had ordered the Adjutant, Captain Donald Gilchrist 'to go forward as quickly as possible, contact Brigade Headquarters and find out the forming up area for us. Get information and be ready for our arrival.' Gilchrist took a bike taken from a dead Commando and cycled off:

Soon I was through the tiny hamlet of Benouville and climbing the incline to the Mairie . . . I raised my hand to salute a French couple who were standing, partly shielded by a stone wall which surrounded the village hall, the Mairie, *a solid masonry building.*

He then headed down the slope towards the bridge:

A lieutenant of the Airborne Forces greeted me. I told him that Number 4 Commando, like the Campbells at Lucknow, were coming, and my purpose was to contact Number 1 Special Service Brigade. He nodded and without speaking half-turned and indicated the bridge. My eyes followed in the direction he pointed. I hadn't noticed before. I did now.

Four crumpled shapes of soldiers in khaki lay strangely silent. I stared curiously, willing them to move. Slowly I turned back to the lieutenant. In clipped tones he answered my unspoken enquiry. 'Dead – German sniper up river in the trees some-where – a sure shot – must be using a telescopic sight – we have people trying to flush him out – so far, no success.'

Hobson's choice and I wasn't Hobson. I took time off to think but the thought process

253

was disturbed as a jeep screeched to a halt. In the jeep were paratroopers, wearing their own special type of helmet and camouflaged jacket. The driver, an officer, started a confab with the lieutenant. The other three looked me over unwinkingly – hard-eyed, hard nuts. Still, there would be no harm in asking.

My youth in Paisley had not been entirely mis-spent after all. Cycling with others of my own age, I had often hung onto the rear of lorries and vans to be transported at high speed, free of charge. It had been an exhilarating experience. Here was my chance to give a demonstration. The officer driver agreed. The three hard nuts showed poker faces. The jeep backed up to get a flying start. The pilot revved the engine, let out the clutch and trod hard on the accelerator. Stones and dust smoked at the rear. I grasped a strut of the raised roof and the vehicle took off.

Careering down the slope it hit the surface of the bridge, bumping and jarring. Breathless seconds later we were over and protected by a line of trees in a road-cutting going uphill. Halfway up the slope the driver changed gear and slowed, giving me a quick glance over his shoulder. I let go and, just for the hell of it, did a little flutter with my hands, imitating a glider parting from its parent craft. The driver kept his eyes on the road, but I had success. The others grinned and gave me the thumbs-up sign.

At the top, the jeep disappeared, taking the right-hand fork. There, suddenly before me, out of the ground, appeared paratroopers. They were neatly entrenched and camou-flaged. Surprised, I found myself looking down into the large mouths of rifles. Funny, they had never seemed so big before. I shouted 'Number 4 Commando.' They raised a cheer and pointed to the left fork on the road.

The road here had a white powdered surface – probably crushed stone from the quarries at Caen. A white dust storm was approaching me now. In it was Lord Lovat, and his Brigade-Major, Michael Dunning-White, was at the wheel of the jeep. They looked as if they were having a day out on the moors.

They enquired about Gilchrist's health and the state of the Commando, and then Colonel Mills Roberts arrived. Having discovered the necessary information, Gilchrist turned back towards the Orne Bridge to meet his Commando, which had begun to cross the bridges.

Murdoch McDougall of 'F' Troop, 4 Commando, reached Le Port and spoke to the Para with the wounded leg who was still guarding the prisoners:

Captain Donald Gilchrist

We went on. Once through the village, the road sloped down to a left-hand bend, and as we rounded this bend a burst of shots spattered the trees on the right. We dropped swearing into the nettle beds by the side of the road and tried to see where the shots were coming from. This, however, was completely impossible owing to the amount of foliage round us. About fifty yards in front of us we could see figures in British uniform moving amongst the trees on the left of the road. The shots still cracked overhead, so we were apparently not the target. That was a comfort. We decided to move on up to the next corner, from which we might at least see what was going on. The leading sub-section struggled out of the nettles, and had no sooner done so when there was a red streak followed by a vicious ear-splitting crack overhead, and we dropped, ears singing, back into the welcoming nettles.

There was another hissing red streak, another ear-splitting crack and one of the branches of the next trees crashed to earth. Another crack. Again the leading sub-section dragged itself out from the nettles and lurched into a run for the next cover at the corner of the road. Once they got there they found an Airborne sergeant who said, 'Keep down the road here to the bridge and run like hell across, because there's a sniper in a pillbox who's got about twenty blokes already. You'll find an officer down there.'

We continued down towards the bridge as indicated by the sergeant and met the officer about fifty yards short of the bridge. He grinned as he saw us.

It was an officer he knew, who then gave him a brief report on what was currently happening and advised him to keep left on the bridge. They crossed the bridge and got down into the field on the left. Murdoch McDougall:

Here, we were in comparatively good cover because the road itself was raised above the fields on either side of it, and as long as we were close to the road embankment, we were safe from small-arms fire.

The edge of the field was a muddy, slippery ditch, and after about a hundred yards we came to a second mud hole running directly across our path. The first man tried to jump it, failed because of the rucksack and sank to his thighs in the slimy mud. The man behind him hesitated and the troops following up concertina'd on the leading man. The Troop Leader ploughed forward. 'Look Mac, we'll have to get on faster than this, we should be catching up on the Brigade now.'

They decided to get a man on either side of the mud hole to push and pull everyone across. This was successful and virtually the whole Troop managed it. Two officers remained to help the men across, Lieutenant Peter Mercer-Wilson and McDougall himself:

There remained but a few, and looking round for a means of getting myself over, I saw a rock in the mud some little way away. 'I'll get over down there and then we can drag the others over.'

I shoved the last man at Peter, turned, and I had just reached it when I heard a shot, and turned in time to see Peter spin round and fall. I leapt on to firm ground and raced to where he lay, my heart filled with dread. But as I bent and turned him over, I knew it was no use. He must have been dead before he fell. In straightening to pull the last man through, his head and shoulder must have shown sufficiently above the level of the road for the sniper in his pillbox to take a quick shot.

All of the Commandos had now crossed the Orne Bridge to take up their positions in the defensive perimeter.

Murdoch McDougall, Len Coulson and Peter Mercer-Wilson of No 4 Commando

*

In Benouville a lull developed. Suddenly, a couple of the Engineer's White Scout cars arrived at the zig-zag trench to collect the wounded. Lieutenant Archdale:

In the street, they'd just driven up from the beach regardless. Incredible. They were very brave.

We got out as many of our wounded as we could onto these White Scout cars. We were not shot at while we were loading them on.

When Ron Follett had regained consciousness, he had put a field dressing on his leg and used his morphine. Sergeant Fiddle, who lay beside him, had been shot in the head, and Follett could do nothing for him:

I crawled back over the road and got back into the orchard in the ditch area. There I lay. Soon after that a big Engineer's half-track came up, looking for wounded people and I was collected. Tony Sluman picked me up and this White's half-track was full of explosives. We were laying on all sorts of explosives!

Lieutenant Hunter:

For some time I had become very dopey and not capable of taking any significant part in the proceedings. Things quietened down. Perhaps my prayers had been answered.

Sometime later I found myself being lifted up and carried between two men. It was then that I realized that I was covered in my blood right down to my boots. I was taken to the café near the bridges. This was the Battalion Aid Post. I remember telling the orderly there that all I needed was a blood transfusion and then I would be okay. I didn't feel there was much wrong with me.

Stan Young had been wounded in the left side of his back:

Stan Young (left)

It must have been against the wall at the top. A sniper or something, because there were houses on the far side, over the other side of the road. There were snipers everywhere. Although it might have been a stray bullet. I bloody felt it!

With the situation the way it was, it was impossible for Young to move back for treatment, so he had just stayed at his position.

A big Red Cross truck came up. They never even fired at us, that I could make out. When I went back, I was on the bridge. I had blood all running down my back.

He had his wound dressed just outside the café. Major Taylor:

We came out in an American vehicle called a White Scout car. They drove straight in under a Red Cross flag and the wounded were all evacuated. No German fired on those vehicles when they were evacuating wounded. We were taken back to Gondrée's Café, which was our Regimental Aid Post, which had been very well chosen by our doctor who was a very good chap. He had a look at my thigh and he re-dressed it and said, 'That's OK Nigel.'

Lieutenant Archdale:

I had to go back to Battalion Headquarters to report and I said to Jim, 'Shall I go back in the scout car?' 'No,' he said, 'That wouldn't be fair.' I was frightfully embarrassed [that] he thought I was frightened to go on my own.

View north from the *Carrefour de la Maternité*. The house further down the road was the one destroyed by the M10

Made my way along the ditch on my own, feeling rather lonely, back to Battalion HQ, reported the situation to Colonel Pine-Coffin, who sent me back to 'A' Company, which I thought was rather disheartening.

On arrival back at the trench they came under fire again from the house in front. Archdale had requested some reinforcement:

This was forthcoming in the form of a composite platoon under Mac [Lieutenant Macdonald] *which gave covering fire from the houses behind the Company position, also from an M10, which came out after much persuasion and blew down the house in front of the Company.*

Jim, of course, was the last wounded man to go, by this time hit three times. I found myself in command of the Company really then, eleven men I think we had then.

I then sat quietly with the remainder of the Company and Sergeant Nobby Clarke, waiting to see what would happen.

Colonel Pine-Coffin:

The position at this stage was not very comforting because although I felt confident of holding off attacks for some considerable time to come, there seemed no prospect of relief for the battalion and I could not be certain how things would go during the night, especially if the enemy made a really determined attack with large forces.

*

In Ranville, it had been an extremely tough day for all members of the Field Ambulance. Captain David Tibbs:

As a Regimental Medical Officer, really in essence one's duty was, if somebody was badly wounded, to put them in a position where they could be transported with all speed back to the Field Ambulance. The Regimental Medical Officer . . . couldn't do very much more except give morphia to control pain, immobilize fractures; if there was a sucking wound, a hole in the chest sucking air in and out, which could quickly be

258

fatal, I could try and plug this but we had no proper materials for plugging this . . . It would need closing by bringing the skin together in some fashion. I did my best. We had no way of giving them any intravenous infusions, no plasma or blood out in the battalion to give them. When they came back to the Field Ambulance they would be assessed fully and where necessary, they'd usually be very necessary, would be given resuscitation to prevent shock they were probably already in, and getting deeper. That would mean blood transfusion. I'm sure they ran out of blood at various stages.

The two surgeons would stop haemorrhage. For instance a man might be sent in with a tourniquet on, which had saved his life but quickly caused a loss of his limb if it wasn't taken off and the bleeding point properly stopped, and that might require an anaesthetic and operation. They would almost certainly be doing amputations of limbs if it was necessary to save a man's life, because some limbs were so badly mangled there was no hope of salvaging them, and it was better to do an amputation higher up. If the guts were widely laid open, a common injury, the surgeon would, again anaesthetic necessary, repair all the guts and put them in a stable state. Head injuries . . . they would probably decompress some of them if they could. Airways, they could provide tracheotomies, in other words there was a whole range of surgical things to keep a man going, so they didn't die over the next hour or two.

Most of those casualties would have survived because they were all screened and those that were salvable were salved, those that could wait because many wounds you could leave alone and they'd be fine for hours, were just quietly left lying.

The Germans were pretty good in observing, regarding the Red Cross, letting us get on with our stuff. We looked after their wounded well and they often looked after our wounded well.

Throughout the day, the Ranville area had been subjected to heavy shell and mortar fire. Captain Nobby Clark, 2i/c 'C' Company, 13th Battalion:

There was no denying that the enemy was persistent and also that he was far from inaccurate in his fire on us. It was of course, inevitable that the reason should at last be borne in on us: the church tower, that rather strange edifice built separately from the church proper, although an integral part of it. We investigated it. The cause of the previously persistent though unexplained arrival of mortar fire coincided with the movement or gatherings on our part was made clear, but not before a sudden well-directed concentration of bombs on the crossroads had coincided with the moment chosen by various rather indispensable members of the Company, to assemble there to exchange news and views on the tactical situation. That moment cost the Company the platoon commanders of Numbers 7 and 8 Platoons, the Company Sergeant Major, the Colour Sergeant and a couple of men, all at one fell swoop.

It was too late that the offending 'spy' was located in his signalling post at the top of the church steeple. The previously unexplained ringing of the church bell at odd moments ceased forthwith.

No enemy activity had been seen on the Ring Contour since just after midday, but at around 1700 hours, 'B' Company of the 12th Battalion reported further movement

The main Ranville crossroads. 'C' Company, 13th Battalion was defending this area

The Ranville church
tower

in that area and suspected an attack. Consequently, a Troop of 3 Commando was sent forward to an area near the crossroads below the crest of the Ring Contour. About an hour later, Lieutenant Burkinshaw's 1 Platoon, 'A' Company, 12th Battalion, which had been protecting the DZ, was ordered to occupy the crossroads itself. They dug in on either side of the road on the apex of the intersection. A 6-pounder anti-tank gun was positioned on the south-eastern edge of the crossroads. 2 Platoon took over the hedgerow position from Lieutenant Medd's Platoon of 'C' Company, while 3 Platoon and Company Headquarters were set up on the southern edge of Le Bas de Ranville.

*

The Liaison Officer sent out by General Gale had duly found the Commander of the 3rd British Infantry Division, Major-General Tom Rennie, and explained the desperate need for relief. Due to Brigadier Ken 'Kipper' Smith's 8 Infantry Brigade having problems in clearing the beach and silencing several difficult strongpoints, it had not managed to advance inland as far as planned. Therefore, part of 185 Brigade was tasked with moving further east, passing through and ahead of 8 Brigade. After receiving the Liaison Officer's information General Rennie had spoken to 'Kipper' Smith about the urgency of the situation in Benouville and the use of the 2nd Royal Warwicks to relieve them. However, German activity in the area had increased after the Commandos had punched their way through to the bridge. Smith's latest information stated that the Germans held St Aubin d'Arquenay and even worse, that the Airborne had been driven from the bridges and that both were now back in enemy hands. This assumption was down in part to the amount of enemy sniper and mortar fire that was going on in the area. Earlier he had ordered the 1st Royal Norfolks to advance towards Bieville by making a wide detour to the east of Colleville and a German strongpoint codenamed 'Hillman'. The Norfolks had suffered casualties from machine-gun fire from the position and so he did not want to repeat the experience with another battalion. He also realized that a strong attack would be required to recapture the bridges and so intended to launch this attack the following morning.

185 Brigade was supported by the twenty-four self-propelled guns of 7 Field Regiment (SP) RA. Lieutenant Colonel Nigel Tapp was the Commanding Officer:

At 1700 hours the General visited Brigade Headquarters again. This time he practically ordered Brigadier Smith to release the Warwicks. The situation was getting acute as the remainder of the 6th Airborne Division was timed to land in the Benouville area before dusk. The Brigadier's hesitation was through lack of information about the village of St Aubin d'Arquenay, through which the Warwicks had to pass on their route to Benouville and Blainville. Owing to faulty information the Brigadier imagined this village to be held by the enemy. Not wishing to get the Warwicks involved in this village he was waiting until it was reported clear by 8 British Infantry Brigade. However, as the General somewhat testily remarked that, 'he supposed the village was, clear as he had just driven through it in his jeep', the Brigadier released the Warwicks.

Major JF Lister, 7 Field Regiment RA, was with the Warwicks as they advanced:

St Aubin had been reached without opposition and the battalion was in position round the village with 'A' Troop Commander manning an observation post covering the eastern approaches. 'B' Troop Commander joined us in his tank.

At 1900 hours General Gale arrived in Le Port for a brief visit and told Colonel Pine-Coffin that he had contacted the 3rd Division and stated that the relief of the 7th Battalion must be treated as a first priority task.

Shortly after, General Rennie arrived in the village. Colonel Pine-Coffin informed him of the latest situation and Rennie explained why the 2nd East Yorks had been delayed, about the confusion over the capture of the bridges and that the 2nd Warwicks were on their way.

Half an hour later, an advance party of the Warwicks arrived and Pine-Coffin gave them a situation report. A patrol of Warwicks with a few Engineers of 3 Platoon, 71 Field Company, went into the forward edge of Benouville to carry out a reconnaissance. Captain John Hoare, 71 Field Company RE:

Shortly afterwards one of the battalions from 185 Infantry Brigade, the 2nd Royal Warwickshires, appeared on the scene under the second in command. Apparently, their Colonel had got either wounded or disconnected somehow from the battalion and the second in command was there. He was a young man . . . I think it was Robin Kreyer. We got into an 'O' Group in a bit of a hole with my OC [Major Upton] and a representative from the Oxf and Bucks and also one of the officers from the Troop of Hussars and thought about making a plan to clear the front. It so happened that shortly afterwards, up the road came a Naval Officer who was a Forward Observation Officer for the fleet, available to take on various targets as required. He was a very enthusiastic officer, wearing a white helmet with FBO . . . and otherwise in a sort of Naval version of battledress. He said, 'Well if you want covering fire I can arrange it.' He was dovetailed into the plan which we were making, which very briefly was that our unit would muster all its light machine guns, the Brens. We had a lot in the Company, mainly associated with vehicles, and we took them all off the vehicles and carried them in because we thought they might be pretty useful. We must have had at least twenty-four guns.

These were put together in a group and sent down towards the bridge and then south to take up position between the lower road and the canal:

We sent about thirty men under Dick Harding with the guns, might have been more than that. They took up position to provide a sort of curtain of covering fire right in front of the entrance to the Chateau grounds. At the same time, the fleet were going to put down a strike on the Chateau grounds and meanwhile the Warwicks were then to do a right-flanking battalion attack and get right round to the south of the Chateau, and this way it was felt that the situation could be cleared. So we sent the Naval Officer off to get a forward observation position and he chose a water tower which was sticking up in the middle of standing crops, I would say in a south-westerly direction. He went over with his wireless operator, carrying all his equipment, and he climbed up the ladder and got on top of the tower. He brought down a few ranging shots and I think he must have been seen because immediately we saw him collapse his equipment, come down in double quick time, looking for an alternative place I suppose where he could carry on!

The Warwicks were by now approaching the village. Major Lister:

The battalion pushed on but was held up by snipers at Le Port, just outside Benouville. 'A' Troop Commander who was with the leading Company, commenced ranging in support of an attack on the village.

Lieutenant Colonel Nigel Tapp:

We heard that the Warwicks were held up a few hundred yards south of Benouville, so the Brigadier and I went up to see what was happening. We stopped on the crest looking down on the village, while Captain Appleby of 9 Battery completed his registration of the simple fire plan. In front of us the infantry and tanks were forming up for the attack. We were much annoyed by a sniper suspected of being in the church tower. One of the tanks, however, put a couple of 75mm HE shells into it and we were bothered no more.

Major James Cuthbertson of 90 Company RASC had managed to reach Ranville, but unfortunately both of the Airborne Officer guides he was due to meet had been wounded. General Gale had therefore ordered him to bring up his convoy after dark and off-load the stores in a nearby quarry. They then listened to the King's speech on the radio. Just as it finished, they could hear the dull roar of aircraft approaching.

Captain David Tibbs was in the MDS barn:

Suddenly a hush fell over everything. This was a dramatic moment and people were all walking outside and looking upwards . . . This was a magical moment because we realized we were not going to be left stranded there.

General Gale:

Then they came, hundreds of aircraft and gliders: the sky was filled with them. We could see the tug aircraft cast off their gliders, and down in great spirals the latter came to the Landing Zone . . . It is impossible to say with what relief we watched this reinforcement arrive.

In Le Port, 'A' Company, 2nd Royal Warwicks prepared to head south. Lieutenant Colonel Nigel Tapp:

We were all standing by waiting for the Battalion Commander, Lieutenant Colonel Herdon [2nd Warwicks], to finish his preparations, when out of the north came the most wonderful sight of D-Day, hundreds of twin-engine bombers towing gliders and hundreds of four-engine Stirlings and Halifaxes dropping supplies, the air vibrated to the roar of these engines and the sky looked as if a cloud of locusts was crossing it.

The gliders were transporting the 2nd Ox and Bucks, the 1st Royal Ulster Rifles, 'A' Company, 12th Devons, the 6th Airborne Armoured Reconnaissance Regiment, 211 Light Battery RA, 249 Field Company and two sections of 195 Airlanding Field Ambulance. As well as using LZ 'N' at Ranville, these glider reinforcements were landing on LZ 'W', to the west of the canal.[7]

A Troop of Bofors 40mm guns belonging to 318 Battery, 92nd Light Anti-Aircraft Regiment, Royal Artillery, arrived at the eastern end of St Aubin d'Arquenay. It was their task to reach the bridges and defend them against aerial attack. Due to congestion and artillery fire on SWORD Beach they had landed an hour late, at around 1430 hours. It had taken them all this time to reach St Aubin d'Arquenay. Jim Holder-Vale was a driver/wireless operator attached to 'F' Troop:

As we were coming up, so these gliders were being released and landing across this road. It was very scary because we hadn't gone very far when suddenly through the hedge burst a glider. I was sitting there watching them coming out of the gliders and they'd got all the poles stuck in the ground, anti-glider defences, but they weren't making the slightest bit of difference because they were taking off the wings but they weren't stopping anybody. They had to hit it head on to really stop them. Some of them were that close that we looked at them straight in their faces.[8]

Len Harvey, F3 Gun, 'F 'Troop, 92nd LAA:

After a glider landed, its troops had been trained to get out immediately, take up a defensive position around it and open fire. That was fine if you were landing in enemy territory but they were surrounded by Allied troops. I personally saw a few of the Suffolks who were with us go down and be attended by their mates.

General Gale:

The German reaction was quick. He mortared our Headquarters, the village of Ranville, and attempted to mortar the Landing Zone. His fire was inaccurate and ineffectual. Unfortunately, at my Headquarters poor Jack Norris, my Artillery Commander, received a terrible throat wound; none of us thought that he could possibly survive, but he did. His loss to us out there was great. Gerry Lacoste, my Intelligence Officer, was also hit. One of my provost men standing just behind me was killed. On the Landing Zones, however, we were lucky and only one 6-pounder anti-tank gun was hit.

Len Harvey

In Benouville the Warwicks were ready to attack. Captain Harry Illing, 'A' Company, 2nd Royal Warwicks:

Flak shot into the air disclosing admirably the German defences. Some gliders and tugs were hit, but more landed or crash-landed. One glider, alas, came down squarely on top of two ['B' Company] signallers struggling forward with Number 18 sets on their backs and headphones over their ears. The diversion caused by this dramatic air armada enabled us to storm into Benouville.

With the gliders down, the FOO called in the bombardment of the Chateau grounds. This was the signal for the Brens of 71 Field Company to open up and for the Warwicks to advance. Lieutenant Archdale waited with the tiny surviving party of 'A' Company in the zig-zag trench:

There was spasmodic fire from the south and west, but nothing to get worried about until a cascade of mortar bombs and machine-gun fire suddenly arrived from Le Port. [Sergeant] Nobby Clarke and I put our heads together and decided that the battalion must have lost Le Port and this was our moment for a last man, last round effort. However, none of the men, who obviously thought the same, appeared anything but cheerful and we collected all the loaded weapons we could for a final 'do'. We picked up all the dead and wounded men's rifles, so instead of having to reload spare ammunition, you could just pick up another rifle. I don't think we had a Bren gun left still working.

The attacking Company then appeared amidst the corn . . . We then realized that our assailants from Le Port had British steel helmets and amid shouts of 'It's us, you bloody fools!' managed to stop the shooting and hand over our position.

Captain Illing:

We formed up behind some farm buildings and a long high wall. Two lone Germans (the first live ones the battalion had seen at close quarters) ran towards us unaware of our presence. As we moved into view, the Germans dived into the hedge for cover, but before they could open fire a very willing Sten gunner shot them neatly in a pair from over the hedge.

We pushed forward from the burning village, along the Caen road. Almost immediately two tanks were hit, one of them the artillery observer's. One had its turret knocked clean off and bounced across the road.[9]

This vehicle belonged to 7 Field Regiment RA. Major Lister:

We pushed on through Benouville with only the odd snipers to worry about. By this time it was growing dark and we were working in close country. 'B' Troop Commander's tank, with the forward Company was hit and set on fire by a 75mm at the bend in the road [around 500 yards beyond the Carrefour de la Maternité]. Captain Gregory and his OP assistant were both badly wounded, but managed to

Jim Holder-Vale

jump clear. Nothing was found of the driver until some days later. He must have been killed outright as the first shell entered the turret where he was sitting.

It took ninety minutes for the Warwicks to clear the village, forcing the Germans to retreat south towards Blainville.

*

In Le Port, 'F' Troop of 318 Battery, 92nd LAA had arrived. Jim Holder-Vale's vehicle was parked beside a large barn at the southern end of the road:

I presume that Captain Reid [the 'F' Troop CO] had gone off to look where they were going to put the guns. Whilst we were there, I was standing, contemplating putting camouflage nets up. I didn't hear the actual shot but this bullet thumped by. I knew instantly what it was. 'I'm being shot at'. It didn't whine, it was a thump. Almost immediately someone shouted 'Sniper in the tower.'

Incredibly, after a day of having small arms fire, PIAT bombs and various tank shells directed at them, snipers were still operating from the church tower. An Airborne officer went over to the LAA guns that had stopped near the church and suggested they use one of them to fire at the tower. Gun F1, commanded by Sergeant Clements, hit it with some 40mm rounds. Finally, out came two youths of about seventeen years of age waving a white flag, although around a dozen bodies were subsequently found inside the church.[10]

Jim Holder-Vale moved down to the T-junction:

There was a burnt out truck at the top of the road there, facing towards Le Port, a German truck. It had got a palm tree painted on the side. On the other side was a dead German . . . There was all the usual litter. Where the hell all the battle litter comes from I don't know.[11]

On the lower road, after spending virtually the whole day cut off from relief and supplies, Captain Wagstaff received a message that the route to the bridge was clear, and so taking all the equipment they could lay their hands on, they walked back:

The party made its way back through the garden, through another house and back up the road where we were covered by REs.

Between the bridges, Dr Vaughan was still tending the wounded at his RAP:

At about 2100 hours the ADMS, Colonel MacEwan, came to my RAP with the grim news that his DADMS, Major Maitland, had been killed by a mortar fragment which had struck him in the back. He had thus but a few hours of war in the grounds of the

The Church Tower at Le Port after a day of having small arms, PIAT bombs and tank shells fired at it *(IWM5431)*

chateau, now being heavily mortared. I was ordered to take his place immediately. I accepted this, I hoped temporary, promotion, with mixed feelings under the circumstances, saluted the Colonel and made off towards the chateau about half a mile up the road. As I turned right along a lane the sound of a low-flying plane had slipped through our air defences.[12]

The Airborne Engineers, Claude and Cyril Larkin, were in a trench beside the canal around a dozen yards from the bridge. Cyril saw a solitary FW190 approaching rapidly at low level. Captain Hoare was also in the vicinity, on the north-west bank of the bridge:

I was talking to the OC at the time because it was getting near the time when he wanted me to do a reconnaissance of a route directly back to Ouistreham onto the beach where we landed, where the bridging equipment was supposed to come ashore, and make sure that the route was clear and that it could be used for the 'empties', because we wanted them to come up laden with the bridging equipment, discharge, go back down the other route so that it would be a complete circle.

They also saw the aircraft and took cover in a ditch. Major John Howard:

Everyone jumped for cover into the pillbox or the trenches and watched helplessly as the aircraft dropped a bomb with fatal accuracy onto the bridge. It hit the side of the bridge's tower with a dull clang, and then, unbelievably, dropped into the canal with a splash. We had all braced ourselves for the inevitable mighty explosion which would blow the bridge sky-high and were open-mouthed with amazement as it failed to explode. 'My God,' I said to Tappenden in the pillbox, 'it was a dud!'

Cyril Larkin, on seeing the bomb heading straight towards him, had said to himself, 'I've had it':

I couldn't believe that with a bomb being released so low, I could escape from it. Claude was on my left-hand side and the bomb fell on my right-hand side and I got a bit of shrapnel in my side and Claude got some bits in his back. I managed to get up and climb up the bank and just said to the colleagues, 'I've been hit', and within moments the First-Aid personnel were there, put me on a stretcher. But in a few more moments there was a French Resistance lorry was passing through, the first time I'd seen anything of the French Resistance, and I was put on top of the lorry, an open truck. I wasn't sure if Claude was on there or not. There was a lot of activity going on.

John Hoare:

It didn't completely explode because we found bits of it lying over the deck, plus a considerable dent in the road surface which we proceeded to fill up with boarding taken out of the houses, and lodged between the girders, and everything we could get in the way of filling was put over that and the roadway kept usable. It broke away the road surface and it didn't go right through, but you could see underneath, to hold the ballast in place or the foundation of the road in place, there was some thin platework between the cross-girders. It had broken open, you could see the casing, this yellow filling was all exposed.

There were also some explosives on the bridge . . . There was a bit of a fire from this bomb that didn't completely go off and there was enough to set alight to some of the charges. It was a spluttering sort of fire . . . bits and pieces. We had to tear these off and throw them in the canal.[13]

*

Captain Wagstaff reached the bridge, went into the *Café Gondrée*, reported to Lieutenant Colonel Harvey and began to help his colleagues from the Field Ambulance. Operations were being performed on the dining room table in the back room. Being a trained nurse, Thérèse Gondrée had helped in any way she could during the day and before the arrival of any medical supplies had provided sheets for use as bandages. Major Howard:

I went over to see Gondrée after it was settled up and was very, very impressed by the way Madame was running round with a black face and having spent most of the time after it was opened up, running around kissing all my chaps and the Paras and getting the camouflage paint transferred onto her face.

At 2215 hours the 2nd Oxf and Bucks who had landed on LZ 'W' had organized and begun to move towards the bridges. Upon arrival, the CO, Lieutenant Colonel Roberts, met Brigadier Kindersley and Major Howard and the battalion crossed the bridges, taking the two 'B' Company *Coup de Main* platoons with them.

In Benouville the 'A' Company survivors had finally been able to hand over to the Warwicks and move from their position. Somehow, they had held out for seventeen hours. Lieutenant Nick Archdale:

When they had taken over our rather precarious positions, the eleven or so men from 'A' Company who were left, returned to the bridges, where we were met by the Colonel who counted us off and then told us where to go.

John Wagstaff:

I set up a new Dressing Station about 200 yards from the bridge. We received most of 'A' Company's casualties who were being successfully evacuated. The Dressing Station filled up by 2230 hours when facilities for further evacuation were established by 8 Field Ambulance.

The Field Ambulance transport evacuated nearly sixty casualties to the MDS.

*

In Ranville at around 2200 hours the Germans on the Ring Contour had begun a considerable amount of shouting and firing, and the sound of tank tracks could be heard. Major Gerald Ritchie, OC 'A' Company, 12th Battalion:

The enemy started a hell of hullabaloo; first at us and then at the hedgerow where my right platoon was. First it was only machine guns but when they switched fire to the hedgerow they started putting up flares and coloured lights and they also had about six self-propelled guns . . . which were firing right into the hedges. They appeared to go right up to the hedge, and they also had some infantry with them as you could hear them shouting. Anyway, in about twenty minutes the tumult and the shouting died and all was quiet again.

When an hour later, a Company of the 1st Battalion Royal Ulster Rifles went forward to attack the Ring Contour, they found the position unoccupied. The firing had been purely to enable the Germans to withdraw without being bothered.[14]

Finally, at this stage of the day there was some relief for a few of the most serious casualties at the MDS. Contact was established with the Field Ambulance within the 3rd Division and Major Macdonald established a Casualty Clearing Post in a farm a few hundred yards east of the Orne Bridge. Captain David Tibbs:

We were able to send a group of fifteen casualties, who they thought might recover if they were given more complex medical care. I think it was after dark that they were whistled across the bridge which was very perilous at that time, there was lots of fire crossing the bridge, and got them to the safety of the 3rd Division which had then a proper line of evacuation back to the beaches.[15]

*

At around 0100 hours responsibility for the bridges was handed over to 'D' Company of the Warwicks. At long last for the Airborne troops, Benouville and the bridges had been relieved. Lieutenant Richard Todd:

We assembled as a battalion on the road by the Canal Bridge and began our march to an area just north of Ranville, where we went into Brigade Reserve.

Throughout the day, stragglers had made their way to the bridge area, and by the end of it they mustered around 250 men, having lost about 60 killed and wounded. It was a heavy price to pay, but their heroic defence had been absolutely vital.

Major Howard's *Coup de Main* party had performed its duties magnificently and fortunately with few casualties:

Thus it was almost exactly twenty-four hours after the party had been the first to land in occupied France to spearhead the invasion that I, and what remained of my men, left the bridges' area and headed off towards Ranville. I found myself glancing back at the distinctive bulk of the bridge that had come to mean so much to me. We all felt a kind of sadness at leaving this place where we had achieved so much, only to hand it over to the men of the Warwicks.[16]

However, the achievement and sacrifice of the men of Richard Gale's Division had been such that the structure would forever be known as Pegasus Bridge an Airborne bridge.

Four graves opposite the canal gliders. These belong to Fred Greenhalgh, who was killed during the landing of Glider 93; Arthur Charity of No 6 Commando; 'Jock' Campbell of No 3 Commando and Lieutenant Peter Mercer-Wilson of No 4 Commando *(IWMFLM3447)*

Appendix A

Members of the
Coup de Main Force

Glider No 1,
Serial No PF 800
(Chalk No 91)
S/Sgt Jim Wallwork
S/Sgt Ainsworth

25 Platoon, 'D' Coy
Lt Den Brotheridge
Sgt Ollis
Cpl Caine
Cpl Webb
Cpl Bailey
L/Cpl Packwood
L/Cpl Minns
Pte Baalam
Pte Bates
Pte Bourlet
Pte Chamberlain
Pte Dennis Edwards
Pte Bill Gray
Pte Gardner
Pte O'Donnell
Pte Wally Parr
Pte Tilbury
Pte Watson
Pte White
Pte Windsor
Pte Jackson 08
Major John Howard
Cpl Ted Tappenden

Glider No 2
Serial No LW 943
(Chalk No 92)
S/Sgt Oliver Boland
Sgt Phillip Hobbs

24 Platoon, 'D' Coy
Lt David Wood
Sgt Leather
Cpl Godbold
Cpl Cowperthwaite
Cpl Ilsley
L/Cpl Roberts
L/Cpl Drew
Pte Chatfield
Pte Lewis
Pte Cheesley
Pte Waters
Pte Clarke 33
Pte Musty
Pte Dancey
Pte Harman
Pte Warmington
Pte Leonard
Pte Weaver
Pte Radford
Pte Clark 48
Pte Pepperall
Pte Malpas
L/Cpl Harris

Glider No 3
Serial No LH 469
(Chalk No 93)
S/Sgt Geoff Barkway
Sgt Peter Boyle

14 Platoon, 'B' Coy
Lt Sandy Smith
Sgt Harrison
Cpl Higgs
Cpl Evans
Cpl Aris
L/Cpl Madge
L/Cpl Cohen
Pte Greenhalgh
Pte Wilson
Pte Hook
Pte Stewart
Pte Keane
Pte Noble
Pte Crocker
Pte Basham
Pte Watts
Pte Anton
Pte Tibbs
Pte Slade
Pte Burns
Pte Turner
Pte Golden
Dr J. Vaughan

Royal Engineers
Cpl Watson
Spr Danson
Spr Ramsey
Spr Wheeler
Spr Yates

Capt Neilson
Spr Conley
Spr Lockhart
Spr Shorey
Spr Haslett

L/Cpl Waring
Spr Clarke
Spr Fleming
Spr Green
Spr Preece

Glider No 4
Serial No PF 723
(Chalk No 94)

Glider No 5
Serial No LJ 326
(Chalk No 95)

Glider No 6
Serial No PF 791
(Chalk No 96)

S/Sgt 'Lofty' Lawrence
S/Sgt 'Shorty' Shorter

S/Sgt Stan Pearson
S/Sgt Len Guthrie

S/Sgt Roy Howard
S/Sgt Freddie Baacke

22 Platoon, 'D' Coy
Lt Tony Hooper
Sgt Barwick
Cpl Goodsir
Cpl Bateman
L/Sgt Rayner
L/Cpl Ambrose
L/Cpl Hunt
Pte Allwood
Pte Wilson
Pte Hedges
Pte Everett
Pte St Clair
Pte Waite
Pte Felix Clive
Pte Timms
Pte Whitford
Pte Johnson
Pte Lathbury
Pte Hammond
Pte Gardner 08
Pte Jeffrey
Capt Brian Priday
L/Cpl Lambley

23 Platoon, 'D' Coy
Lt 'Tod' Sweeney
Sgt Gooch
Cpl Murton
Cpl Bill 'Smokey' Howard
Cpl Jennings
L/Cpl Porter
L/Cpl Stacey
Pte Allen
Pte Bowden
Pte Buller
Pte Bright
Pte Bleach
Pte Clark 46
Pte Galbraith
Pte Jackson 59
Pte Roach
Pte Roberts 94
Pte Read
Pte Tibbett
Pte Wixon
Pte Wood
Pte Willcocks
Lt Macdonald (7 Para)

17 Platoon, 'B' Coy
Lt Dennis Fox
Sgt 'Wagger' Thornton
Cpl Reynolds
Cpl Lally
Cpl Burns
L/Cpl Loveday
Pte Jollett
Pte Halbert
Pte Clare
Pte Peverill
Pte Pope
Pte Whitehouse
Pte Whitbread
Pte Lawton
Pte Rudge
Pte O'Shaughnessy
Pte Ennetts
Pte Summersby
Pte Woods
Pte Wyatt
Pte Ward
Pte Starr
L/Cpl Lawson

Royal Engineers
L/Sgt Brown
Spr Deighton
Spr Guest
Spr Paget
Spr Roberts

Cpl Straw
Spr Bradford
Spr Carter
Spr Field
Spr Wilkinson

WS Lt J. Bence
Spr Burns
Spr CW Larkin
Spr CH Larkin
Spr Maxted

273

RAF Crews.

298 Squadron.

Halifax V, LL355-G	Pilot:	W/C DH Duder DSO DFC
Towing Glider No 91	Nav:	P/O JD McLaren
		Sgt E Lappin
		F/Lt GD Palmby
		F/Sgt HA Newling
		Sgt AB McAllum

Note: This was F/Lt Barren's crew. He stood down to allow the CO to fly the operation.

Halifax LL335-K	Pilot:	W/O AK Berry
Towing Glider No 92	Nav:	F/Sgt J Roberts
		P/O AE Letts
		F/Sgt EW White RCAF
		Sgt J Stewart
		Sgt KW Austin RNAF
		F/Lt WD Reevely (2nd Air gunner)

Halifax LL406-T	Pilot:	W/O GP Bain
Towing Glider No 95	Nav:	F/Lt LJ Rowell
		Sgt A Holder
		F/Sgt C Mansell
		Sgt EA Weeks
		Sgt R Beusley

644 Squadron.

Halifax LL218-N	Pilot:	W/O JA Herman
Towing Glider No 93	Nav:	F/Sgt WL Mills
		Sgt RL Duncan
		F/Sgt CC Morrison
		F/Sgt JP Walsh
		Sgt FL Waterfall

Halifax LL344-P	Pilot:	F/O G Clapperton
Towing Glider No 94	Nav:	F/O D Roberts
		Sgt GJ Hensby (A/B)
		F/Sgt WE Burness (W/Opr)
		F/Sgt VR Bareham (RG)
		Sgt FE Rolt (FE)

Halifax V, LL350-Z   Pilot: F/O WW Archibald
Towing Glider No 96   Nav: F/Sgt AJ O'Shea
                                    Sgt CO Hones (A/B)
                                    F/Sgt EW Chidley (W/Opr)
                                    F/Sgt FG Brown RCAF (RG)
                                    Sgt JT Orford (FE)

RAF Squadrons that transported the 6th Airborne Division to Normandy:

38 Group: 190, 196, 295, 296, 297, 298, 299, 570, 620 and 644 Squadrons.

46 Group: 48, 233, 271, 512 and 575 Squadrons.

Information supplied by the late Dennis Edwards, Coup de Main Glider 91.

Appendix B

Issues Involving the
Coup de Main Operation

1. Chronology of events regarding the initial German response at the Orne Bridge.

Regarding the incidents of the German patrol and the arrival of the German staff car/motorcyclist at the Orne Bridge, various publications state that these occurred prior to Brigadier Poett's arrival. However, from what we know of the events that immediately followed the *Coup de Main* landing and the time available before the Brigadier's arrival, it would appear that these actions occurred AFTER he had reached the bridges. Indeed, John Howard confirms this in several accounts.

2. The landing positions of Gliders 92 and 93 at the Canal Bridge.

For forty years the landing positions of the gliders were understood to be 91, 92 and 93 with regard to closeness to the bridge. Then at the 40th Anniversary, David Wood and Geoff Barkway were told by Sandy Smith that this was an error because he had been thrown through the cockpit into the pond and then 'run over' by a wing. And so the three marker stones are now in the order 91, 93 and 92. This was not something which I had intended to question, indeed why would I? It was only while listening to Oliver Boland's audio account, which is highly detailed, that the thought arose that something may be amiss. Therefore, the following are various pieces that I have gathered on the matter.

GLIDER 93 'JUMPING'.

The 'current thinking' on how the landing positions of 91, 93, 92, actually occurred was that Geoff Barkway's Glider 93 'jumped over' Glider 92 whilst on the final leg of their approach, while very close to the ground. When I interviewed Geoff Barkway he had no knowledge of doing this and it is surely something that would not be forgotten!

It would appear that there WAS an avoiding action, but this took place somewhere in the area where they turned into the final glidepath, and although Geoff Barkway did not see the Horsa of Boland and Hobbs, Peter Boyle stated that he did. Oliver Boland stated that he saw Barkway's glider and consequently, during the landing, knew that it should be coming down to his right and so could not move in that direction.

THE LANDINGS.

The following is Oliver Boland's statement. It begins after having seen Geoff Barkway as the gliders had turned, and then looking ahead at Jim Wallwork's Glider:

> *I had to keep to his right otherwise I'd run up his bum, and there's a pond appears, and I still haven't got down properly. So in fact what I had to do was to use the spoilers, which destroyed the lift, so I dropped the last foot.* [Note: David Brook of the GPR advised me that there were no spoilers on the Horsa. Could this piece be confusion on how he actually got the glider down, i.e. did he mean the ailerons?]
>
> *I found myself in the situation where I'm tearing along just above the ground, tearing relatively . . . , thirty miles* [an hour] *or less, twenty. I was suddenly faced with Jimmy in front of me, who was crashing through into the hedge, and a pond. I couldn't go in the pond, I don't know how deep it is, nobody's told me and I've got thirty blokes in the back, full of gear. So I pulled the spoiler and dropped the last foot or so. BASH! And then I have to swerve to the right to avoid going into the pond with enough speed, so the back of the glider broke.*

He also stated:

> *We did the parachute there, then let it off. It's one of those things that you don't know why you do what you do, because you're having to make decisions in a split second and the shit, shot and shell are around, is how I can get down, not run into Jimmy, not run into the pond and I see another bloke coming down from my right, which was the third glider. So I'd got nowhere to go. I can't veer off, there's another bloke, so I drop in on the ground with a mighty crash and we crash along, not very far, managed to stop and break the back just before the pond. I said, 'We're here, piss off and do what you're paid to,' or something to that effect!*

With the two gliders seeing one another during the turn, would 24 Platoon have had enough time to recover from the landing, organize (as David Wood states below), and then reach the bridge, all before Glider 93 landed? If 92 had landed to the far right, 93 could well have ploughed into the men exiting the glider and heading for the bridge. Also, no man of 92 has mentioned having to pass Glider 93 to get to the bridge.

Both Barkway and Boyle state that their glider was brought to an abrupt halt by the bank of a ditch. In the aerial photos it can be clearly seen that what remains of the nose of the third glider is positioned above a ditch. The centre glider is nowhere near the ditch.

Casualty-wise, it makes more sense that the glider with the broken back would have incurred the most casualties. However, perhaps the manner of the landing was also a factor, ie the right-hand glider came to an abrupt halt by hitting the ditch, and if, as described by Barkway and Boyle they were travelling at quite a high speed, then injuries could certainly have occurred.

I asked about this during the interviews with the living survivors of Glider 92, namely 24 Platoon's David Wood, Nobby Clark and Fred Weaver. The following are their recollections. Lieutenant Wood:

We had a very bumpy ride, a lot of sparks flashing, which we took to be at that point, the enemy opening fire on us, but I'm glad to say that it was simply the flints in the ground on the skids underneath the glider. The next thing I knew, I was literally on the ground under the glider, still clutching my bucket of grenades. I pulled myself together and I could see in the dark, just enough to see that the other glider was where it should be and that I was No 2, which was my role. We assembled under the wings of the glider, section commanders reported that they were complete and then we moved off at the double to report to John Howard who was leaning by the barbed wire [against which his glider had actually landed].

Nobby Clark:

It suddenly stopped dead and we all shot forward. To this day I don't know whether I went out the side of the glider or whether I went out the door. All I know is that I was the second man in a pile of bodies on the ground and there were two other blokes on top of me.

Fred Weaver was sitting in roughly the centre of the glider:

Our glider, we had to swing to the right, and swinging round, it cracked open. Instead of getting out the front and back doors, we just all stepped out. It had broken its back. When it cracked open, all I'd got to do was pick my gun up and just go through the side of the glider. Most of them followed out that way. All we could hear was Major Howard, 'Come on lads, up here, this is it!'

Although Sandy Smith told David Wood that he ended up in the pond, in his interview he just mentions being in marshy ground. He stated that he went through the cockpit, which was confirmed by both Boyle and Barkway who saw a figure pass them. Both Geoff and Peter lay in the wreckage in water, but neither was under water.

DYNAMICS.

It may be a rather unusual way of trying to deduce what happened, but by analysing the dynamics of what happened to Sandy Smith, it throws another idea forward as to what actually occurred. We know that he was sitting at the front of the glider. The only way that someone can be thrown forward is by the glider coming to an abrupt halt. We

278

know that the centre glider actually stopped after having been wrenched around to the right. Therefore, no one in that glider should have been thrown through the cockpit, but out through the side. If somehow Sandy Smith was thrown through the cockpit of the centre glider, he was so close to the edge of the pond, there is no doubt that he would have ended up in the pond itself.

Smith also mentioned that the wing ran over his leg. It can be seen that the wing of the outer glider has swung around anti-clockwise, and could possibly explain this event.

PRIVATE GREENHALGH.

The other main reason for the change in positions of the gliders is the death of Glider 93's Private Fred Greenhalgh. I have not been able to find anyone or any account explaining the exact circumstances of his death. Some say that he fell out just before landing [perhaps while opening the door or after the first impact?], others state that he drowned in the wreckage of his glider. The ground in the area of Gliders 92 and 93 was very marshy, but the worst position would have been that of the easternmost glider, on the edge of the former route of the river. Dennis Edwards recalls hearing the following morning that Greenhalgh's body had been found trapped in the wreckage, having drowned.

On a battlefield tour many years ago, a Bren gun was found in the area which was thought to belong to Greenhalgh. However, I cannot find anything recorded about where it was found exactly or how it was positively linked to him.

JOHN VAUGHAN.

I also looked for other clues wherever possible. The Doctor, John Vaughan, who travelled in Glider 93, wrote in his book, *All Spirits* (1988) (p78), that as he started off for the bridge:

> *I was sufficiently clear-headed by this time to note that we had landed close behind the second glider <u>and in front of that</u> I could see the nose of the first glider buried in the barbed wire.*

CONCLUSION.

The only way of conclusively clarifying which glider landed where is by photographic proof showing the serial numbers of the gliders. However, after extensive effort to find a photograph that is both close enough and at the right angle, nothing appears to be available. Maybe somewhere, one does exist.

3. The armoured vehicle visible in the D-Day aerial photograph.

The famous aerial photograph of the Canal Bridge showing the three gliders is usually cropped. However, in the original, an armoured vehicle can be seen about halfway down the road between the *Café Gondrée* and the *Mairie*, near the position taken up by Bill Gray.

Using the photograph and knowing the wingspan of a Horsa to be 88 feet, the armoured vehicle shown is around 20 feet long. The front end can be seen to possess long, tapered sides. I have not been able to find a breakdown of vehicles held by the 1st *Panzerjäger* (Assault Gun) *Kompanie* of 716 Infantry Division which carried out the probe, but a similar vehicle within 21st Panzer Division, *Panzerjager Abteilung* 200, was equipped with SPW U304(f) vehicles, which was the equivalent of a Sdkfz 251/10, mounting the 37mm PaK 36, but employing a P107 French halftrack chassis. This vehicle is around 21 feet long. The difference between the two is that the Sdkfz version has a rectangular profile, while the P107 possesses long, sloping sides forming its front end profile. The vehicle in the photo has long sloping sides, and so it is likely to be a P107 variant.

Appendix C

Issues Involving the 7th Parachute Battalion

1. Debate on timings – 7th Battalion arrival at the bridges and assuming defensive positions in Benouville.

There appears to be much controversy surrounding the time of arrival of the 7th Battalion at the Canal Bridge. Having analysed the various sources and discussed the matter with many of those involved, the time will never really be absolutely confirmed. It is not something which I personally think is now of much importance, because on time or late, no blame is attached to anyone. These things happen in warfare. And since, following the initial probing of the tank and its destruction by 'Wagger' Thornton, there was no further serious assault on the bridge until after the arrival of the 7th Battalion, it hardly makes any difference. I have been far more interested in getting the chronology of events as close as accurate as possible. However, the following is a list of the War Diary entries and relevant comments by those involved.

THE 6TH AIRBORNE DIVISION WAR DIARY (WO171/425):

Battalion was dropped somewhat wide of correct DZ. There was consequently delay in re-org and Bn did not reach br until 0300 hours.

This also states elsewhere: *Crossed brs at 0140 hours (of other reports 0300 hours).*

THE 5 PARACHUTE BRIGADE WAR DIARY (WO171/595):

The following was initially typed against 0330 but altered by hand to 0230:

7 Para Bn (approx one coy in strength) move from Bn RV, cross brs and est tight bridge-head on WEST of canal.

Bn occupied objective and held it against various counter-attacks, 'A' and 'B' Coys being heavily engaged.

In the remarks column it then refers to Appendix 1, written by Geoffrey Pine-Coffin on 29 June 1944. This states:

By 0130 hours I had about 50% of the riflemen and Bren gunners in . . . I could hear Howard's success signal and knew that he had captured the bridges and that they were cross-able so at 0130 hours I set off with my initial attack force.

After having positioned his forces, he then stated:

Then I judged that the position had been occupied at about 0210 hours I ordered Howard to withdraw his men over the canal.

DURING A BBC RADIO INTERVIEW WITH COLONEL PINE-COFFIN ON 18TH AUGUST 1944, HE STATED:

The night was a poor one for parachuting as the moon was obscured. The wind was strong too, but that didn't matter so much. Our first job was to form up quickly and for this we needed a landmark. There were several we were looking for, but just one would do. All one could see was other parachutists blundering about, lost as oneself. The Germans were there too; they were firing tracer ammunition. Officers and others collected parties and began to search systematically, but it was a question of the blind leading the blind. It was an hour and a half before I found the Rendezvous with my party, and we were the first there even then. My rallying signal was a bugle and luckily my bugler was with me. Private Lambert sounded off continuously and we waited and hoped. They came in as fast as they could, but it seemed desperately slow and there was practically none of the heavy gear with them. No sound came from the bridges. I decided to move off when I reached half-strength, but this took so long that I gave the order earlier. No mortars, machine guns or wireless had arrived, so we would just have to do without them. The Coup de Main *party's success signal went up just as we moved off and put new life into us. Half the job had been done, the bridges had been captured. We dashed across them and into our positions to start the long job of hanging on for the invasion to start and come up to us. The parachutist fights a very lonely battle and this one was no exception.*

This would mean arrival at the RV at around 2.20am.

LIEUTENANT HUNTER, 'A' COMPANY, 7TH BATTALION WROTE:

The delay at the RV was going to prove disastrous to our positions in the dark and got dug in before the Germans knew where we were and then be able to repulse the expected counter-attack.

We proceeded up through the village to the south end and turned to the right (west-

wards) along a track which was hidden from the open field to the south by a high hedge. I suddenly heard German voices from somewhere beyond the hedge. I asked Lance Corporal McCara who was a very small man if he could see anything through the hedge. Dawn's early light was just on its way.

BRIGADIER POETT TALKED ABOUT THE TIMINGS OF BOTH MAJOR HOWARD AND COLONEL PINE-COFFIN IN AN INTERVIEW WITH MAJOR GENERAL JULIAN THOMPSON:

They are both completely incorrect, one extreme in one thing and one extreme in the other.

I couldn't tell you exactly when they arrived, but I can make a pretty shrewd guess when they arrived because I was there myself when they did arrive! People didn't know what the times were [Howard said his watch stopped at the time of landing].

I would guess that the first chaps came up to the bridge about half past two and they didn't really take up position until about three o'clock.

Note: Poett did not arrive in Ranville until after its liberation, post 3am.

SURMISE.

From the things that happened and the necessary tasks to be performed, it would not be unrealistic to surmise that the 'bulk' of the 7th Battalion was indeed delayed in getting into position in Benouville. With a perfect drop <u>starting</u> at 0050 hours, a quick move to the RV, a rapid organization into Companies etc., and then a speedy march to the bridges, to have actually reached them in 35–40 minutes at the planned 0130 hours would have needed everything to have gone perfectly. We know that the drop was scattered, the RV could not be found, and when it was, the move was delayed due to the lack of men. Therefore, the main party would almost certainly have been delayed. However, some other scattered parties did head straight to the bridges and got there before the 'bulk' of those from the RV.

2. The Position of the RAP in Benouville.

Captain John Wagstaff supplied a written account in which he stated that the house where he set up the surgical part of the RAP was No 32 on the lower road in Benouville. However, in September 2005, when discussing the matter and looking at aerial photos plus old and new images of the houses, it became apparent that the house was further along the road. This was backed up by him making several statements, e.g. that directly across the road from his part of the RAP, there were definitely no houses. There were three houses opposite and directly in front of No 32. He had initially identified No 32 as the house because it possessed two large gate pillars. However, as we found, a house further along, No 34, also had such gate pillars. During a subsequent visit to Normandy he visited No 34 and the owners made him very welcome. He walked around the house and recalled that his RAP had a distinctive wooden staircase which went up the centre of the house, at the top of which he had turned left to look down the road from a bedroom. This feature still remained. No 32 appears to have been the house where the remaining part of the RAP was situated.

Appendix D

The Arrival of the Commandos and Seaborne Engineers

The subject of who was the first seaborne arrival at the bridges is of course another issue that has been clouded in controversy and one which was compounded by the film of Cornelius Ryan's book, *The Longest Day*. By this I mean the impression given that Lord Lovat was the first British soldier to reach the Canal Bridge from SWORD Beach. That this is incorrect is beyond doubt because other Commandos [and seaborne Engineers] arrived before him, a fact that is well recognized within Commando [and Engineer] circles.

The whole episode is hampered by the lack of detailed accounts by Lord Lovat and Brigadier Mills-Roberts. Both wrote books, but the information with regard to the approach and crossing of the Canal Bridge is hazy to say the least, especially with Lovat's March Past. Frustratingly, I have been unable to locate any in-depth interview with Lovat on this action, but hopefully one does exist and will come to light at some stage. It would certainly be a huge addition to what we already know.

Various queries arose as I got further into the detail, and the issue itself grew into one of how this 'first past the post' should be described. Should the question be 'Which was the first UNIT, as a whole, to arrive at the Canal Bridge?' 'Which Troop was first to make contact with the Airborne in Le Port?'. ' Who was first to actually cross the bridge?' and finally, 'Who were the first seaborne troops seen in Benouville?' All of the witness reports to these questions depend on where that soldier, be it Para or Oxf and Bucks, was positioned and what was happening at the time. With the amount of sniping going on, unless an actual attack came in, most were wisely keeping out of sight, thereby hindering their knowledge of what was happening 'above ground'.

I have described the arrival of the Commandos and Engineers in a more general manner than the rest of the book because of the confusion at the time and subsequent conflicting evidence, however, the description is still in a calculated sequence. Therefore, the following is my reasoning behind the order in which the text has been written. Hopefully, feedback may clear up or confirm in more detail the sequence of events.

It would appear that the first seaborne troops seen at the bridge belonged to a recce patrol of the 71 Field Group Royal Engineers. These were either Lieutenants Clarke and Dixon, the Recce officers of 17 Field Company, or the party led by Major 'Tiny' Upton of 71 Field Company. As in the text, another was Major Cuthbertson. Major Willison was high on the list of first arrivals, but even so, we know that Clarke and Dixon had performed part of the reconnaissance, been wounded and evacuated to Ranville before Willison had even arrived.

Three different Commando Troops lay claim to be the first to the bridge. Undoubtedly, the first Commando Unit to make contact with the Airborne in Benouville was 3 Troop, 6 Commando. This is backed up by accounts from Poett and Pine-Coffin, plus of course those of the Troop. However, the first to cross the bridge could have been a Commando bicycle Troop, either 1 Troop, 6 Commando or 3 Troop, 3 Commando. One thing that Derek Mills-Roberts did state, although not in his book, was that 1 Troop, 6 Commando was first across the bridge. How he knew was not stated, however, Trooper Fleming of 3 Troop, 6 Commando recalls seeing cyclists racing past them towards the bridge while the Troop was heading towards the bridge after meeting Pine-Coffin. 1 Troop ended up in the Varaville area and this is corroborated by accounts from the 1st Canadian Parachute Battalion. Perhaps the fighting that 3 Troop, 6 Commando heard in Le Port, which caused them to bypass the church area, was the 1 Troop action that was started by Peter Masters.

3 Troop, 3 Commando, also on Para bikes, had raced ahead of their own Commando. Both Troop officers, Roy Westley and Keith Ponsford, along with Jimmy Synnott and Stan Scott, are convinced that they were ahead of everyone. However, there are a couple of matters that do not 'add up'. Firstly, Stan Scott, on their arrival in Le Port, saw the Para with his wounded leg up on a chair guarding some prisoners. Before the arrival of the Commandos in Le Port, it would not have been possible for anyone to sit in the open guarding prisoners. Indeed, no Para or *Coup de Main* member mentions prisoners taken in Le Port. If there had been, prior to the Commando arrival, they would surely have been moved away from Le Port, not held within it. It is quite possible that the prisoners were either taken by the Commandos before reaching Le Port, or during their arrival in the village. Crucially, this Para was also seen by Lord Lovat and later by Murdoch McDougall of 4 Commando, who arrived much later in the afternoon. We know for certain that there was a small action to clear Le Port, but if Lovat, Scotty and McDougall all saw the Para, then there could not have been any fighting in Le Port AFTER the Para took up position with the prisoners.

Subsequent actions can also provide clues. 3 Troop, 3 Commando then crossed the bridges and halted. Lovat appeared from somewhere (which is agreed by Westley, Ponsford and Synnott (not Stan!)) and gave them a change in orders, i.e. not to go to Cabourg but head for the Breville ridge to liberate Amfreville/Le Plein and thereby help out the remnants of the 9th Parachute Battalion which were holding out in the Chateau d'Amfreville. Here is where another piece of evidence does not back 3 Troops' claim. Lieutenant Tug Wilson and Jock Byrne of 2 Troop, 6 Commando were ordered by Mills-Roberts to go up to Amfreville to find out what was going on. They got to the edge of the village and found a firefight going on between some Paras and the

Germans in the middle of the green. A Para saw them and came over. They were the first Commandos that he had seen. They went back to report to Mills-Roberts and it would appear that 3 Troop, 3 Commando, then moved up and attacked the village. There is no question that they liberated the village and were there before any TROOP of 6 Commando. However, for the two 6 Commando men to have reached the village first must surely mean that 2 Troop had also crossed the bridge before 3 Troop, 3 Commando.

Also, after crossing the bridges, 3 Troop, 6 Commando, went to the Mairie at the Breville crossroads, where they ran into heavy opposition.

Following 3 Troop, 3 Commando's liberation of Amfreville, Jimmy Synnott took up position in the house at the southern end of Amfreville, on the road to Breville. He saw no-one pass him and go up the road. Therefore 3 Troop, 6 Commando must have reached the *Mairie* before he arrived.

From all of the accounts, it is clear that after initially crossing the bridges, Lovat was back and forth across them. It is also clear that there was quite a time between Lovat arriving in Le Port and actually crossing over with Bill Millin. Therefore, it is also possible that Lovat crossed the bridge on his own to speak to Commandos that had already got across. The crossing with Millin was an 'arranged ceremony' with Ian Grant, the Army Film cameraman, in front, which, as can be read, set off from Le Port towards the Mairie. However, on reaching the bridge it was too dangerous to walk, let alone pipe across, and so this piece of *The Longest Day* film was also false. And again, Lovat was wearing a battledress, NOT A WHITE SWEATER! (Ref. photo p.237).

Parties of 71 Field Group Engineers were arriving during this period and many were there well before Lord Lovat's arrival. Major Willison witnessed the 'ceremonial' crossing of the bridge.

I have been unable to confirm where the first trucks of 71 Field Company Group were parked. These were almost certainly those seen by Richard Todd. Major Willison stated that they were in the dip between the T-Junction and Le Port, however, John Butler, who was on that piece of road, did not see any before he moved down to the canal. No Para or glider troop fighting in Le Port recalls the arrival of the trucks before that of the Commandos.

As a final thought, David Howarth published a book called *Dawn of D-Day* in 1959 (around the same time as *The Longest Day*), and it is interesting to note that he had the same problems in working out the arrivals at the bridges when matters were much clearer in the minds of the participants, albeit more than ten years after the war. Although we now know that Bill Millin piping across the Canal Bridge is incorrect, there are still things within it that certainly make interesting reading. Howarth stated (P245):

> *There are still, and always will be, rival claims for the honour of having been the first to reach the bridge. A unit of engineers drove there in jeeps* [sic] *by a roundabout route, finding no opposition on the way except from snipers. Their mission was to build a new bridge, whether the original one had been captured intact or not. Their first reconnais-*

sance officers got there at one o'clock and found the place still under shell and sniper fire; and like true technicians they set about their plans without ado. At somewhere about the same moment, the first commandos arrived on bicycles, and crossed the bridge to join the airborne forces. An hour later, the main body of the commandos under Brigadier Lord Lovat arrived at the bridge, and with a better eye for the picturesque and perhaps for history, they marched across it with Lovat's personal piper playing a cheerful tune.

Appendix E

Tank Attack on the Ring Contour – 7 June

At about 1300 hours on 7 June, the Germans made another attack across the Ring Contour, towards the bridges. This involved seven tanks and about 150 panzer grenadiers. They headed straight across the front of Lieutenant Burkinshaw's 12th Battalion party at the crossroads:

> *They were only about fifty yards from us, but they didn't try and attack us, they tried to come down here,* [west of ring-contour crossroads] *obviously to the village I suppose. If they had taken the village they knew we wouldn't have had any means of getting away.*
>
> *The six-pounder we had, the crew were killed, but obviously Hall* [an ex-anti-tank gunner] *took over the six-pounder. They were enfiladed, we were firing at the side of them. As the tanks came in he fired at them here and brewed up two of them and the third was hit by something and again blew up.*

The third tank was hit by a 17-pounder anti-tank gun situated in the 'B' Company area. This was towards the river at a hedge junction, MR 101734.

> *They* [Company HQ] *thought we'd been taken over and they put down defensive fire and the mortar bombs came down amongst us. I got out of the trench, which was hit by one of our own mortar shells. They put down defensive fire on that crossroads and started landing the mortar shells amongst us. I sent a runner back then to Headquarters to say, "For God's sake don't do any more, we're OK." Company Headquarters was just below us in the village.*

The loss of this third tank signalled the end of the German effort and they withdrew back towards St Honorine. The 12th Battalion was subsequently relieved by the 12th Devons.

Appendix F

The Defence of the Bridges by 92nd LAA

After arriving at Le Port during the evening of 6 June, the 92nd LAA contingent moved into position. Len Harvey, F Troop, 92nd LAA:

At first light, about 4am, we drove straight down to the bridges. F3 Gun was sited on the river bridge and the sergeant, Billy Fletcher, got everyone digging, NCOs, cooks, everyone, digging the gunpit and trenches. We were ready to defend the bridges by 7am. Action started at 7.30am when approximately fifty Messerschmitt fighters attacked.

Jim Holder-Vale:

On D+1 the first attack started on the bridge, the air attacks and they went on for five days. I didn't have any job there, I wasn't on the guns . . . I just watched it all happen. You saw these planes flying around trying to get in to dive and the guns were just driving them off, knocked down seventeen of them, all confirmed, in the first five days. They were bloody good there's no doubt about it. They really knew their stuff.

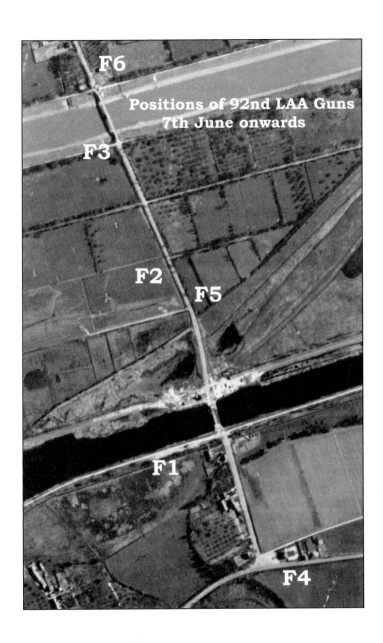

Positions of 92nd LAA Guns
7th June onwards

Appendix G

How the Naval Bombardment Capability [FOOs] Became Attached to Airborne Forces

BY *CAPTAIN FRANCIS VERE HODGE RA*

I'm a gunner really, Royal Artillery, and I was with a Light Battery which is the smallest guns in the British Army, the 3.7 howitzers which you took to pieces on the backs of mules to go to dash up [to] the chaps on the western frontier of India and that sort of thing. And when I joined them, when I was first commissioned, this was a new battery which was mechanized. We were in Bulford at the time, probably about January '43, a note came into the office that an officer had to be sent on a course to learn how to land by sea from a landing craft or something and go ashore with the forward troops and wireless back fire information to a ship by Morse Code, to bring down fire on the shore, which had been done a number of times. That was up at a place called Troon, in Ayrshire, and I hadn't been on a course for a while, and the way the things are in the Services . . . 'Right. Your turn Vere, you go off. You'd better go and learn how you do this.' We all rather enjoyed courses, I mean it made a break to the routine, so I was very happy to go. I think I had about a week there or something, ending in an exam. And one of the questions was 'Do you think it would be possible instead of landing by sea to do this, to land by parachute with parachute troops and do the same thing . . . ?' I hadn't felt too happy about one or two of the questions, but this one, broadly speaking I said, 'Yes, I don't see why it shouldn't be done.' And so I went back to Bulford and never thought any more about it. About a fortnight later the CO called me and said, 'You've got a War Office posting to send you up to Troon . . . Do you want to go?' 'Certainly not.' Anyway he tried to stop it but he couldn't and I was obliged to go up. The CO up there said, 'Very interested in the answer that you gave in our exam paper, about landing by air, so we decided to give you the chance to see if you can do it.' So that's how it began really. We had to catch hold of a few other unsuspecting officers, and get them taught to parachute, I'd already got my parachute [wings], they had to find some others gunners who were willing to be trained to parachute and do this observing job.

292

The first time it happened was in Sicily. I was given a lance bombardier [in gunnery terms, like a corporal] *and one Royal Naval telegraphist, Alex Boomer. We were put on a ship in the Clyde and carted off to North Africa and in due course we took part in Sicily, not where the main landings were, but twenty miles south of Etna, the volcano, and it was to prevent the enemy blowing the Primasole Bridge. It was quite a sort of battle really. It is one of the Parachute Regiment's battle honours. Alex was brilliant and he got in touch with these ships. I hadn't realized until it actually happened, how arduous this Morse-Coding was because there's so much mush and so much traffic on the wavelength that you had to have an expert. I and my bombardier had learnt Morse Code but it was very school-boyish really and I realized when I saw Alex at work that we could never really have done it. It's not just a question of Morse Code, it's a question of picking out one signal amongst dozens of others, all this sort of crowding on the wavelength. And also, they send so fast, very fast. Anyway, we had some shoots and it did sort of turn the tide really. That was with the 2nd Battalion, the Parachute Regiment, Colonel John Frost.*

Many years afterwards, he met John Frost:

He told me that he'd recently met the German commander he was opposed to and they had sat down over a couple of beers and re-fought the Primasole Bridge job. The German had said, 'Of course, I'd got on top of you until you had those Naval ships started firing at us and that's what really forced us to give way.'

Unfortunately John Frost's book, A Drop Too Many *wasn't actually published but was being printed, so he wasn't able to put this in . . . That was the first time that Parachute troops had been supported by Naval gunfire. It had never been done before in any Army.*

Note: The 'adopted' song for the Forward Observers was 'FOOs rush in where angels fear to tread'!

Appendix H

Building of
The Bailey Bridges

In the planning stage it was realized that if a normal floating Bailey Bridge was built over the Caen Canal or River Orne, the enemy had simply to divert water from the river, which was normally tidal, to the canal to considerably alter the water levels and consequently put both bridges out of action. The Company was therefore given the task of devising bridges which would withstand swift changes in water level. Much time was spent in experimental work and the final solution was a tidal Bailey Bridge. With the addition of pontoons and a few extra parts, robust floating bridges, capable of operating without interruption throughout very large fluctuations in water level, could be constructed across the widest river. The bridge across the canal was the first time that such a construction was used operationally.

The Bailey Bridge could take loads up to Class 70 (i.e. 70-ton tanks or 40-ton tanks on transporters). The maximum single-span capacities of the standard Bailey equipment were 190 feet for Class 40 loads and 150 feet for Class 70.

With the clearing of Benouville, at 2300 hours on 6 June, the seaborne engineers began constructing the rafts for the Bailey Bridge across the canal. A few days later the bridge was complete, the Engineers having withstood strafing from aircraft, artillery fire and an attack by frogmen.

The Class 40 Bailey Pontoon Bridge over the River Orne was 358 feet long and consisted of a 100 foot landing bay, a 32 foot end floating bay, two 42 foot floating bays and one 110 foot landing bay. The width of the gap was 313 feet. The approaches were extensive. Sommerfield track was laid across a ploughed field from the main road but did not last long and was later covered with hardcore.

From D-Day to the break out from Normandy, 10,000 feet of equipment bridges were built. The greatest obstacle was the River Orne, over which three Bailey Pontoon Bridges were built across tidal gaps of 250 to 300 feet, and fourteen fixed bridges across the river as a whole.

Notes

CHAPTER 1 - PLANNING

1   Initially the 7th Battalion was in 3 Para Brigade, but with the arrival of the Canadian Battalion, it was decided to transfer the 7th to Poett's 5 Para Brigade.

CHAPTER 2 – BUGLE HORNS AND PARA WINGS

1   Bailey decided that he would like to stay with 'D' Company and went to Major Howard and told him so. John Howard's reply was 'I'm not sure 'D' Company wants you!' Bill Bailey: *John Howard was on the periphery of the Regimental Officer's set up . . . , an outsider to the 52nd Light Infantry. I was an outsider to the 52nd Light Infantry. Within the Company, there was this feeling that we weren't really part of the 52nd, it was John Howard's Private Army. He wasn't slow in getting rid of people he thought were not 'up to tick'.*

2   Bill was given his nickname after being made the 2-inch mortar man. He received two orders: H.E or smoke. Thus 'Smokey'. Any 70th Battalion was a Young Soldiers Battalion. These contained youths between the ages of seventeen and a half and nineteen, the age at which they became eligible for Foreign Service. In reality, quite a number of them were younger than the minimum age.

3   Ted Tappenden: *I first met Major Howard in the office when he asked if I had any clerical experience. I had, and he put me in the Quartermaster's office* [with CQMS Smith] *doing the pay, the soap coupons that sort of thing. Then he said, 'Well we've got to have someone on the telephone the whole time, so you won't sleep in the barrack room you'll sleep in the office.' My bed was in the office, so as far as kit inspections were concerned, I never had any all the time I was in the Army . . .*

4   David Wood: *The training was really hard and we got pretty fit and pretty tough. We went down doing section attack exercises at Cranborne Chase near Shaftesbury and it was my job to simulate enemy fire as the section moved up the valley . . . This you did by firing your live rounds as close as you safely could to the men who were advancing, shouting that they were under fire and then they took the appropriate action. Well, during one of the spells back at the start of the exercise, because we had to go through it X number of times depending on the number of sections there were in the Company. I was standing with my weapon, fortunately pointing at the ground and I accidentally discharged a single round and it went through the calf of Den Brotheridge's leg. So we took a gate off its hinges and carted him back to the road and into Shaftesbury hospital, where I that night had to, quite rightly, go down with his kit and so-on, rather sheepishly, ashamed of what I'd done. There was a formal inquiry but accidents were not uncommon. Some people were killed on training in that very valley. I don't think I was even given a formal rocket for it, certainly no formal disciplinary action was taken against me.* Brotheridge made a complete recovery.

5   The standard 6-pounder anti-tank gun was too wide to go in a Horsa glider, so a new carriage, the Mk IV, was produced. This was not as wide, which meant that the shield was also narrower. A jeep became the towing vehicle, so the wheel base size was altered to correspond to that of a jeep.

6   The Landing Zones in the immediate proximity had limited the assault to three gliders for each bridge. Regarding the Hamilcar, it was designed to carry heavy loads into battle. It had a wingspan of 110 feet and could carry a maximum of 17, 600lbs of cargo or a Tetrarch, a 7.5 Ton light tank, or a carrier.

7   Howard chose Sandy Smith and Dennis Fox because he felt they were experienced officers who would work well with the 'D' Company officers. Major Howard: *I wanted two 'D' Company platoons on the canal bridge and two 'D' Company platoons on the river bridge. So that left one 'B' Company platoon for the others. I chose Den Brotheridge because he was the platoon commander I was closest to. He was the eldest of the four platoon commanders, in fact he was older than Brian* [Priday], *so he was the oldest officer next to me. He was about three years younger than me. Most of his platoon were cockneys and I was a Londoner myself and felt very much at home with the Companies. I very much appreciated their wit and I think that's why I chose him.*

No 2 was David Wood, he was the Young Soldier platoon, a very energetic platoon, they had more dash in them as they always seemed to me because they were that bit younger and I chose him as No 2. Sandy Smith was the Cambridge Rugby Blue and was the better of the two 'B' Company platoons, at least that's the opinion I formed during the training, so I made him No 3.

No 4 was the one that Brian Priday was to go into, so I put the youngest, the least experienced platoon commander with him and that's why it was touch and go whether it would be Tod Sweeney or Tony Hooper, but Tony Hooper had only joined my Company very late in the day, he'd only been with us about a year I think. And so I put him with that platoon. He had a very good platoon sergeant, that's what balanced those two. And Tony Hooper's platoon sergeant [Pete Barwick] *was a man I had earmarked as you always do on these occasions, to be the Company Sergeant Major in battle.*

8   There remained the problem of 'dropping' the poles and then removing them. Permission was obtained to fell 100 suitable trees in the New Forest, something that would be unheard of in peacetime, and these were then transported to Bulford Fields on Salisbury Plain where they were erected according to the pattern in the air photographs. Following trials of various possible methods a standard drill was evolved as follows:

(a) The ground around the base of each pole was excavated to a depth of 6in and about 12in out from the pole.

(b) A 5lb sausage of plastic explosive was attached round the base of the pole to be fired individually by safety fuse and igniter. These sausages were made up in bicycle inner tubes and carried down by the Parachute Engineers as bandoliers.

(c) Each pole was then removed by human porterage provided by an infantry working party and the shallow crater filled in and stamped down. Demolished poles were carried away to the side of the strip and laid at the base of a standing boundary pole and at 45° to the axis of the strip to allow gliders to turn off. Six infantry teams of twelve men were required for each strip and they were headed by an RE NCO to ensure a safe separation from the demolition parties.

9   PIAT stood for Projectile Infantry Anti-Tank and was a shoulder launched weapon which employed an extremely powerful spring to 'fire' the bomb.

10 Bill Gray came from Silvertown in the east end of London: *When I first joined up in the KRR's, my first place was a drill hall on Harrow on the Hill. The next morning after joining there, I went in for breakfast and I saw some people. Some were eating bacon and mash, some had porridge. I thought, 'Bloody hell, what shall I have here, the porridge or the bacon?' I never realized you had both! I came from a very, very poor family, we had nothing, and I mean nothing. I used to have to go to the Friar at the Catholics . . . and ask for a bread ticket and they gave you a big brass plate you used to take to the baker's to get a loaf. Many a time I've been home as a kid and had Oxo and a bit of bread for dinner. And that's it. So it was a real eye opener to get in the Army, and all the food. I'd never seen so much food in my life!*

CHAPTER 3 – THE DIVISIONAL PLAN AND DEADSTICK TRAINING

1 The 6-pounder anti-tank gun had done well in North Africa and so the War Office decided that there should be more Anti-Tank Batteries. Subsequently, the Royal Artillery began to gather men, many from other specialized artillery units to train on the 6-pounder. However, it was realized the anti-tank role must be in the front line, and not the usual artillery task of indirect fire. Eventually it became apparent that these artillerymen required infantry training. And so, rather than re-train gunners on the 6-pounder (and avoid losing specialist gunners in other areas), then give them infantry training, it was decided to convert already trained infantry battalions. The advantage was the necessity of only one lot of training, on the anti-tank gun. Consequently, six infantry battalions were converted to anti-tank regiments. 'C' and 'D' Batteries of the 14th East Staffs eventually 'went Airborne', to become the 3rd and 4th Airlanding Anti-Tank Batteries.

2 Jim Wallwork: *Grant, who made a name for himself in the Sicilian affair, was undoubtedly the magician who made the whole thing possible and gave it the training title 'Deadstick', aided by Keith Millar (a NZ or Aussie) and they made an excellent combination.*

3 'Gee' was not actually a radar system because reflected echoes were not used. A signal was transmitted from a ground station, and the time it took to reach a receiver on board an aircraft was measured and the distance between them calculated. Using further stations and signals, a series of distances were calculated and the location of the aircraft could be pinpointed.

4 There was another passenger. The Air Vice Marshal's No 2 had more of a scare when the tow rope snapped on Oliver Boland's glider: *The only time I failed to get where I should have been was when I had an Air Commodore Blaydon on board and we landed out on an aerodrome instead of in the field.*

CHAPTER 4 - BENOUVILLE

1 One evening in the winter of 1946, a very dark and cold night, he left his office at the *Fonderie*. Wheeling his bicycle along, he turned left along the Quai Caffarelli, and in the darkness mistakenly fell into the Basin St Pierre. He swam to the ramp at the Cafe à Bois, and crawled to the Garden's House where Madame le Vot, the janitor, warmed him and gave him dry clothes. He died some time later from congestion of the lungs.

2 Further to this, there is evidence that SOE agents had begun to operate in the area.

3 From that moment until she died, Therese suffered with a throat problem.

Major Howard: *I knew in my intelligence that the patron's name was Georges Gondree. I also knew that he spoke perfect English . . . Also that his wife was of German origin and understood the Germans using the café for drinks and what have you, and a lot information had been obtained and passed on to the French Resistance.*

CHAPTER 5 – FINAL PLANNING AND TRANSIT CAMPS

1 David Wood: *It was originally my job to lead the first platoon across the bridge, and John changed that and put Den Brotheridge's platoon in. He never told me why, there was no reason why he should. We were all supposed to do everybody's job anyway.* A complaint from the Devon River Board about their conduct at the Countess Wear bridges arrived in Normandy on D+14!

2 Bob Randall: *Each co-pilot was issued with one of these special electric lights that fitted into the palm of the hand. The battery was fastened to the wrist.*

3 An RAF Squadron Leader attended one of the final briefings because his squadron of Tempests was tasked with knocking out any searchlights that might appear.

4 John Vaughan's actual surname at the time was Jacob, but since it was a Jewish name, after landing in Normandy he was later advised to change it in case of capture, and became known as John Vaughan. As everybody subsequently knew him and described his actions using this name, I have therefore used it instead of Jacob. Vaughan was an ancestral family name on his Father's side.

5 Lieutenant Wood: *All the men were weighed, but not the officers. Someone said, 'We can't help it if Lieutenant Wood is X number of stone, he's got to go.'* Bill Howard thinks that three men were left out of the No 5 glider: Sandy Ferguson from his section, Colin Willcox (Sweeney's batman) and one other. Pearson, the glider pilot does not think this due to being over-loaded! On John Howard's glider, Bill Gray believes that they dropped some ammunition instead.

6 Geoffrey Pine-Coffin: *The bags that would have been carried by 'C' Company were distributed amongst the other aircraft, but were not fitted onto the legs of any parachutists; most of them had one already anyway. They were fitted with bicycle chutes and were to be kicked, or thrown, out of the aperture as the stick jumped. Folding bicycles had always been thrown out in this way so there was no great difficulty about it except for the great weight of the bags which would make them awkward in the dark, and in a hurry.*

  Once on the ground anyone locating one of these unattended bags, which were all painted in a very distinctive colour, was to bring it into the RV with them.

7 The battle outposts were to be at Map References 086736, 076758 and 093766 respectively. The battery was at Map Ref 105765.

8 These were at Map references 116749 (Junc) 125739 and 116736 (both crossroads).

9 The Copse at Map Ref 114745.

10 The receiving set on the aircraft, known as REBECCA, was in effect a cathode ray tube upon which was marked a vertical centre-line. A horizontal 'blip' indicated the reception of the EUREKA signal. To maintain the correct course the 'blip' had to be held on the centre-line and if it moved to the left or right, the navigator would advise the pilot of the necessary adjustments. A grid was laid over the screen to judge the distance and as the aircraft approached the DZ, a larger scale grid could be employed. When the blip reached the top of the vertical line, the aircraft was directly over the DZ.

11 Richard Todd of course, became a famous actor who actually portrayed Major John Howard in the film, *The Longest Day.*

12 Wally Parr: *They were so keen but at the same time so ignorant of true warfare, and this is one of the things that keep men going in battle. He can always imagine his mate being killed, he can always imagine himself getting a nice tidy wound across the head or through the leg or shoulder, but the thing that keeps most men going in battle, is despite seeing men die left, right and centre, they always seem to get the idea that it's not going to be them.*

13 The 'B' Company officers, Lieutenants Smith and Fox, had other plans. Dennis Fox wanted to see his WREN girlfriend: *Sandy and I broke camp that night. I don't think anyone knew that we did. It was absolutely forbidden. It was a horrific thing to have done, not that we realised perhaps as we should have done. It could well have delayed the whole operation if it had got to the ears of Ike.* They went into Sherborne and had dinner.

14 Staff Sergeant Freddie Baacke: *At 2130 hours on June 5 we assembled on the runway and loaded the 'bods'. Staff Sergeants Baker and Winsper were the reserves and were not coming, much to their chagrin.*

15 Bill Howard's section: *Alf Porter was the Lance-Corporal, Glyn Roberts the Bren gunner, 'Buck' Read, 'Killer' Roach, Galbraith, a long-serving soldier – Indian sweat, Sandy Ferguson we left at home, came next day with the ammo cart.*

16 Rene Niepceron states that it was an unusual occurrence for the bridge to remain down overnight. However, he has no idea why the bridge was not up on the night of the *Coup de Main* operation, although it has been suggested that it could have been due to the anti-invasion exercise going on in the area. I put this question to a member of the Resistance and other French people, and no one recalls the bridge being raised at night. Certainly, until the summer of 1944, with little chance of an invasion, there would have been no reason to perform such an action. There was also the curfew in place and the guard to prevent movement across it. It could have only hindered German movement. There is no doubt that the Resistance and indeed SOE were gathering information within the area for quite some time before D-Day, and would such a vital, basic piece of information be missed? Herr Rohmer, a guard, makes no mention of the bridge being down as unusual or in fact 'unfortunate' for the defenders, considering what ensued. The Gondrees also never mentioned it at any point.

CHAPTER 6 - *THE* COUP DE MAIN *OPERATION*

1 The cabourg flak gap was around 3 miles east of the mouth of the Orne.

2 (a) Later, the nosewheel was apparently found firmly embedded in the backside of a cow. Being from a nation of animal lovers, the troops, after having found out what had happened, reportedly said, *What must have gone through the mind of that poor cow? Probably, what so and so has let the bull into the field at this time of night!* (b) The order of the glider landings has been described in this manner because of Roy Howard's statement that his glider came to rest at nine minutes past midnight, a very precise time indeed. I therefore decided to go with his statement rather than begin with Jim Wallwork's glider, the first at the canal bridge, which landed at 0018. Nothing has been found to confirm or disprove Howard's recollection, but at the very least, describing an Orne bridge glider first will hopefully raise the 'profile' of the events at that bridge.

3 The Debriefing Report states that they went into cloud for two minutes fifteen seconds, but Peter Boyle believes this should have read, ' . . . just into cloud for fifteen seconds.'

4　There is an apparent quotation of Jim Wallwork's that states that he did indeed 'fly by the seat of his pants' i.e. did not follow the designated procedure. This was checked with Jim and he stated that it was untrue. The course was adhered to religiously.

5　Glider 91 photos prove that the left-hand undercarriage survived.

6　John Howard stated to Stephen Ambrose that the landing caused his watch to stop at 0016 as did another man's in his glider. The glider report states 0018.

7　Wally Parr always describes his 'accomplice' in this action as Gus Gardner, but as Bill Bailey explains, it was he who inserted the other grenade – Gardner was the Bren gunner.

8　There were two sentries actually on the bridge when No 1 Glider landed. These were Helmut Rohmer and Erwin Sauer. Rohmer stated: *Suddenly we heard a swishing noise and saw a large, silent aircraft flying low towards the canal bridge. It crashed in a small field next to the bridge, only about 50 metres away. At first we thought it was a crippled bomber. We wondered whether to take a look at it or wake our sergeant. We were moving forward cautiously when we heard what seemed to be the sound of running feet. Before we knew it, we were confronted by a bunch of about 10 wild-looking men who were charging towards us. They were armed, but didn't shoot. We were two boys alone – and we ran. We could see that we were outnumbered by these menacing, war-like looking men. But I still managed to fire off a signal flare to try to warn the rest of our garrison of about 20 men who were sleeping nearby. About 100 metres off, we plunged into some thick bushes by the track running alongside the canal. There were two more crashes. We knew that the British were landing in force. Firing had started all around the bridge and we could see tracer bullets whizzing in all directions. At first it was non-stop, then it died down to occasional bursts. We remained hidden throughout the night, scared to move in case we would be seen and shot. Sometime after noon next day, we heard and saw some more troops with a piper at their head moving from the direction of the beaches to cross the bridge. We stayed under cover for the rest of the day and the next night. Then, hungry and thirsty, we decided to surrender. We plucked up our courage, put our hands in the air and walked out of the bushes. The British didn't fire at us. I'll always be grateful to them for that. We knew it was the end of the war for us and we were bloody glad of it.*

　　Rohmer told Frank Bourlet on the 40th Anniversary: *'One of our comrades had had a birthday party the same night. They'd been drinking in the café until 10pm. So they were all well asleep!'*

　　Concerning German reaction at the bridge. Major Howard: *We knew that it was mostly the NCOs who stopped and fought us. I can't remember seeing any officers there at the time, they were mostly German NCOs and these troops, some of which were not necessarily German. They were a mixture of Russians and Poles and God knows what. They certainly weren't the tip-top troops, not that we had been led to believe in our intelligence that they would be tip-top troops. The German NCOs stopped and fought quite a bit, to the bitter end, and the skirmishing went on all the way round the bridges, not only in the trenches but also the other side as well.*

9　(a) Some of this fire came from a small group of Germans led by a Sergeant Hickmann. After the war, Bill Gray became a member of his local Parachute Regiment Association Branch: *I was up there one day and they were asking about Pegasus Bridge. So I said, 'I'll show you a photo of it.' So I took that up and he said, 'I know that bridge.' He said, 'I was on there.' I said, 'You bleedin' weren't!' He said, 'Yes I was, I was just bringing some new recruits up to . . . 'somewhere they were going, and was just passing the bridge when it all happened!' And he started firing at us. He said, 'I saw you all coming across the bridge.' It must have been true because he knew exactly what went on. He was a POW, a German Para. He got caught at Falaise, got wounded there and made POW. Came back here. His wife was in the occupied part of Germany, so after the war he was given the opportunity of either staying in England or going back to Germany. He decided to stay here . . . smuggled himself out to the Russian occupied zone, got his wife and brought here back and they lived at Daventry, just up the road. He had three sons who all joined the British Army and all finished up Warrant Officers. They were proud to be British! Heinz was his real name but we used to call him Henry.* (b) Apparently, a Corporal Weber managed to reach the office of the garrison commander in Benouville and report exactly what had occurred.

10 Oliver Boland: *Nobody got hurt as such, other than my co-pilot who got a severely pulled tendon or something in his knee, which incapacitated him, made it difficult for him to walk.* Also, concerning the landing, see Appendix B.

11 This may well have been Auguste Delaunay.

12 A report on the glider action states that Barkway's glider arrived some five minutes after Wallwork's.

13 It was discovered later, almost certainly the next morning according to Dennis Edwards, that there was one fatality during the landing of the three gliders, this being Private Fred Greenhalgh. The person that Peter Boyle saw may well have been him. Also see Appendix B.

14 Harry Wheeler also states that he cut four wires in all.

15 John Vaughan was forced to amputate his arm. When interviewed, Geoff Barkway said: 'the nerve pains are still there! I can still feel my fingers!'

16 Cyril Haslett: *We found the explosives in a hut down the bank later on the next morning.* This was a hut on the north-east bank. The explosives had not been put in place beneath the bridges because this was supposed to be carried out when the invasion alarm had been issued, but no such order had been supplied to the 7th Army. Army Group B had put the 15th Army on alert for the Pas de Calais area. This clearly shows that the German High Command was expecting the invasion in that particular area.

17 David Wood: *We used to talk in the Army about a group, that was a number of rounds in a short area. When you're firing on the range, could you get a one-inch group, a two-inch group . . . Well this chap put three rounds into my left leg, so he must have been very close indeed. I know the Schmeisser machine pistol fires very quickly, but even so . . .*
    On David Wood's wounds: one bullet shattered his femur, another began to work its way to the 'surface' and was pulled out by a nurse while in hospital in England, and the final one is still in there!

18 Lance Corporal Arthur Roberts on Godbold: *He was a sergeant before we took off, he was a corporal when we landed because he'd got busted down* [for fighting]. *Wally Parr was another one. He was up and down that many times that you didn't know whether he was a corporal, lance-corporal or a private! But they were like that, our lads. The Major called us the biggest load of rogues he ever came across!*

19 John Vaughan: *He died a couple of hours later. The fact that I knew that Margaret, his wife, was expecting a baby almost any time . . . was at the top of my mind as I saw Den carried past on that stretcher, a very sad moment for myself and for everybody concerned, particularly his platoon.*

CHAPTER 7 – ARRIVAL OF 5 PARACHUTE BRIGADE

1 In an interview with Stephen Ambrose, Brigadier Poett stated categorically that he did not see John Howard's Coup de Main Force from the ground before it landed: *I really don't know whether gliders got down before the first people in the pathfinding . . . They were planned to come*

down at exactly the same time, and which came down first I really do not know, and never thought it important.

2   Poett's wireless operator was Lt Gordon Royle. Major Guy Radmore 5 Para Bde Signals was his OC: *I had told him whatever he did he was not to get involved in a fight, he was to stay with the Brigadier, and keep his communication personally going for him. And Gordon being Gordon, of course when he had a chance he took on a German machine gun and was killed. He must have been one of the very first officers killed on D-Day. We didn't find his body, I think Sergeant Moore found his body about two days later and I actually buried him in the cemetery in Ranville, which we made by the church.*

3   A stick led by Lieutenant John Vischer, which was due to drop further south on DZ 'K', landed on the south-east edge of DZ 'N' believing it to be DZ 'K'. They had duly set up a Eureka and a 'T' of five lights coding letter K. This may well be one of the reasons why later there were 8th Battalion men on DZ 'N'.

4   Lt Rogers began flashing the Aldis lamp from what was the eastern end of the DZ.

5   Ron Perry: *I understand that the stick commanders used to carry a loaded pistol inside their jumping jackets in case somebody 'jibbed'.*

6   Bill Le Chaminant's verdict on the Stirling was as follows: *Lovely plane to jump out of . . . because you've got four engines, a lot of slipstream and because you go feet first, so the slipstream catches your feet first. Then you're flat on your back in the slipstream until your 'chute opens. The only thing, you oscillate a lot when the thing opens.*

7   The 13th Bn RV was at Map Reference 120734. The rallying signals were the hunting horns of the CO, the second in command and the company commanders.

8   A Vickers MMG Platoon comprised one officer and forty men, and was broken down as follows: Platoon HQ: officer, batman, platoon sergeant, wireless operator and range taker. Two sections, each of eighteen men that included a section commander (a Sergeant) and a second in command (Lance Sergeant). Each section had two detachments that had a Number One (carrying the tripod), a Number Two (carrying the gun) and a Number Three (carrying the condenser can which turned the steam back into water, plus a liner of ammunition) and five ammunition carriers, each carrying two liners. A liner was an aluminium case which was pre-filled with 250 rounds.

9   Geoffrey Pine-Coffin: The large number of kitbags undoubtedly slowed up the exits and resulted in some sticks being unduly long.

10 The 12th Battalion RV was at Map Reference 113749.

11 Sadly the plane subsequently crashed.

CHAPTER 8 – GERMAN REACTION AT THE BRIDGES

1   Tod Sweeney: *We found them there the next morning, but unfortunately one of the people in that bunch was a parachutist. Either he'd been captured by the Germans, or somehow or other he'd been dropped out of the way and was sneaking up, but there was a dead parachutist and two or three dead Germans there. I rather think they had caught him, and they were from the bridge garrison, they were bringing him back up to the bridge.*

2   Tod Sweeney: *Because we wanted to hit the bridge quickly, we left anything heavy behind. The PIAT was not considered necessary in the first instance, so after we had a moment to spare, after the half-track had come over the bridge, I sent back and got all the other kit out of the glider, including the PIAT.*

3   Jim Wallwork: *(a) It turned out they had been part of the discarded equipment back at Tarrant – though I still have trouble so convincing him. (b) I thought all night I had only one good eye left. With a black eye-patch, would I look like Errol Flynn?*

4   Brigadier Poett: *We made mistakes in the planning of the thing. To start with we did not allow nearly enough time for the lights to be put out. If you drop absolutely perfectly on an exercise, when there was nothing going on . . . well then that's fine, you can possibly do it in half an hour. It takes a great deal longer because there were these Rommel's Asparagus, we didn't know whether they were going to have mines on them, be wired together or what was going to happen. They* [the Pathfinders] *took a great deal longer. Double the time would have been about right.*

5   When asked who was with him, Wagger Thornton stated: *It must have been one of two people: Private Peverill or Private Hubberd.* Private Eric Woods has also been mentioned by a relative, but as can be read from the account, Alf Whitbread was the actual man with Wagger. The vehicles belonged to the 1st *Panzerjäger* (Assault Gun) *Kompanie* of 716 Infantry Division, who were the first force, along with 2nd Heavy Artillery Battery, 989 Battalion, to be sent towards Benouville.

6   John Howard: *When I thought about it at the time and also afterwards it was quite clear to me that putting that tank out of action stopped any enemy counter-attack on the bridges before the Paras arrived. It was a very lucky break as far as that was concerned. I keep on referring to luck and there's no doubt about it, we did have a fair bit of luck on this mission.*

7   The Map Reference of this lane was 102747.

8   The RV for the Forward Brigade HQ was at Map Reference 112745.

9   Dr Hewlings states that he picked up Leonard Moseley en-route to the RV: *I well remember he was wearing Army issue steel rimmed spectacles, stuck on at his temples and the bridge of his nose with white sticking plaster to prevent them being blown off during the drop. He looked comical, and a little lost and bewildered.*

10   This meeting confirms which platoon of the 7th was first to leave the RV. Archdale and his group was virtually at the bridge, and the first officer he saw was his friend, Ted Pool.

11   Quite possibly the young driver that Dr Vaughan mentions.

12   This wood on the north side of the road junction was at Map Reference 097748.

13   Lieutenant Temple and a group of No 1 Platoon had been killed when their Stirling had been shot down.

14   Bowyer died about twenty minutes later.

15   One of the planes carrying the Mortar/MMG Platoon had been shot down. It crashed near Douvres la Deliverande and this is where its crew are all buried today.

CHAPTER 9 – ARRIVAL IN RANVILLE

1   This hedge stretched from Map Ref: 097729 to 101728. The location of this hedge has been described in various other publications as being in a field situated a few hundred yards further east, nearer Le Bas de Ranville. I therefore checked with both John Sim and Gordon Medd, and they confirmed that it was the hedge at the above map reference.

2   The other part of 2 Section had been dropped wide, near Grangues.

3   Five of these vehicles were subsequently made serviceable and used to collect the wounded.

4   No 32 was owned by a Monsieur Hervieu.

5   Mark VIIIZ was the special ammunition used by the Vickers. Compared to the normal small arms ammunition (Mark VII), this had a bigger charge and a more streamlined bullet.

CHAPTER 10 – COUP DE MAIN *GLIDER 94*

1   Captain Priday: *I afterwards worked it out, and can only assume that owing to a navigational error on the part of the tug aircraft we were cast off in the wrong place. The glider pilots could not have glided the distance of error in the short, free-flying time they had after cast-off. Indeed they had made a first-class job of the landing as I well appreciated now that I could see for myself how dark it really was on the ground. The glider was right alongside a river and close up to a bridge. They had seen these as they came down to land and made for them. Not until it was too late did they realize that they were not the Orne and Caen Canal bridges, our objectives.*

2   During the Sicily operation.

3   Tich Rayner states that there were two Germans escorting Hooper. Tich also likes to relate that he was 'The only soldier to be shot by a dead German!'

4   Tich Rayner: *He was the first man killed. They say Danny Brotheridge was the first man killed. Danny Brotheridge wasn't the first man killed immediately, he was probably the first man shot, but Danny died an hour after he was shot.*

5   Sergeant Lucas belonged to the 7th Parachute Battalion.

CHAPTER 11 – THE MORNING AT BENOUVILLE AND THE BRIDGES

1   The chateau was owned by the Doix family. Guy Radmore: *General Gale arrived in his jodhpurs in great form and gave me a terrific rocket because my cook, Lance Corporal Moreno, had opened up on some snipers. I had not included Moreno (an underchef from one of the big London hotels) in my original jump, but he had been so upset that I gave him some spare equipment and let him come. He was longing to kill Germans and could not resist opening fire at the first provocation.*

2   The 5 Bde War Diary states that HQ was at Map Ref 106741, which is surely incorrect as it places it behind Divisional HQ. The initial Brigade HQ was a farm in the area Map Ref 105736.

3   (a) Lieutenant Hunter: *I've had to live with that on my conscience for the last 50 years.* (b) Timing: Hunter mentioned that "Dawn's early light was on its way". It is documented in 225 Fd Amb War Diary that first light was 0430 hours. (c) McCara's death. Gurney said he got over hedge, but having seen photo of hedge (plus ditch) this would almost certainly not have been possible. He must, as Hunter stated, have gone through a gap in it. Gurney also said he was knifed to death while Hunter said he was shot. Unclear. (d) *Oberleutnant* Hans Höller belonged to 8 Company, Heavy Panzergrenadier Regt 192. From correspondence with Herr Höller, it is apparent that his Company arrived not long after this first engagement with the 7th Battalion because he carried out a reconnaissance and saw the body of a Para near the Chateau entrance. This could have been McCara or Whittingham. Therefore, the initial attack may have been another attempt by 1st *Panzerjäger* Company 716.

4   John Butler: *Mortimore gave his life to warn those men. That is what the Victoria Cross is all about, but Mortimer received no decoration or recognition. There was no officer there to make a recommendation.*

5   There is a slight discrepancy between Thomas' and Georges Gondree's account regarding whether the door was knocked on or not. The remainder of the accounts are almost identical. Georges Gondree: *Came a knock at the door. Opening it I was confronted by a soldier with a blackened face who said 'Avez vous Allemands ici?' I replied 'Non, Pas d'Allemands. Entrez, Monsieur'. He came in and was joined by another soldier.*

6   There is always debate about such incidents and whether they involved tanks, SP guns or both, but it would appear that both were present in the fighting for Benouville.

7   Major Taylor: *Earlier on, before things had really hotted up, the windows of that house upstairs had opened and a whole lot of women, young women, were looking out and making sort of fairly inviting gestures to us. And I had my suspicions that it was perhaps the local German Army brothel. We didn't see them for the rest of the day, we did not have the opportunity to find out whether our surmise was right.*

8   This account of events has been based on lecture note headings made by Jim Webber, with of course analysis of everything else which is known and the personal accounts.

9   Captain Wagstaff believes the French people informed the Germans that they had withdrawn.

10 As at Note 7, this account has been collated using much of an interview with Dennis Fox, plus accounts of others. Information about the half-track has been put together from the aerial photo evidence plus the account of Madame Deschamps. This is the only known instance that the Germans attacked using an armoured car, and Madame Deschamps describes one being hit and all the Germans jumping out on fire. She was taking cover in that area at the time. Having enlarged and analyzed the aerial photo on p. 194 it almost certainly depicts a vehicle on a P107 chassis. The profile is distinct and the 8 Company, Heavy *Panzergrenadier* Regt 192 possessed some of these vehicles. Nigel Taylor confirms that the tank was not knocked out and came back along the main road, where it was subsequently destroyed.

11 John Butler: *My feelings in the matter didn't change for many years. I still castigated myself for cowardice and it was only many years later and after reading many books on the war that I realized my fear was the sort of thing that many other far better and braver soldiers than I had experienced.*

12 Dennis Fox managed to escape while being held in the area and was hidden by some French people for a couple of days before contacting the Commandos.

13 Guy Radmore: *Years later I met the German adjutant commanding the German battalion on the bridge and we went through it all and he said how he telephoned through to headquarters and couldn't get it and he couldn't understand why the line wasn't working, so I told him.*

14 Poett states that they left at about 9.30am.

15 Richard Todd on Colonel MacEwan: *He was absolutely covered with medals, so he was called 'Technicolour!' He had a DSO, he had a DFC as well, wings . . . He had been in the original Flying Corps in the First World War and he was a gunner, Royal Artillery. Then he qualified as a doctor and came to 6th Airborne Div. He had the choice of being CRA or an ADMS, Commander Royal Artillery or Assistant Director Medical Services. He chose the latter, to be our top doctor, because it was a full Colonel and to his fury, just after he made his choice, CRA was promoted from Lieutenant-Colonel to Brigadier!*

16 Brigadier Kindersley had arrived early so that he knew exactly what the picture was in the area before his Brigade arrived in the evening.

17 Pine-Coffin recalled the boat which was hit by the PIAT subsequently opening fire on their HQ. However, this does not appear to be correct as none of the Oxf and Bucks have mentioned this, and they would surely have opened fire again if the boat continued to fire after being hit by the PIAT. Therefore it must have been the other boat which opened up.

18 Michael Pine-Coffin has attempted to look into the casualties for this event and they do not appear to be as heavy as first thought.

19 225 Fd (Para) Amb War Diary states: '0920 – An RAP under Capt Urquhart was established in *estaminet* 098748 to collect casualties from 7 Para.' However, when John Butler entered the café, sometime after midday, the medical set-up was still minimal at that stage.

20 These sections were in the area just behind the *Café Picot*.

21 The Schirès family, which included seven children, lived in one of the houses that backed onto this wall. Due to the fighting the family had taken shelter in a trench in the back garden. One of them was Nicole Schirès: *The Germans entered the house and began firing at us in the trench, thinking we were British. As we looked up we could see the bullets passing over our heads. A young child started to cry and so the Germans stopped shooting. We were moved out of the garden and they occupied the trench. The British were on the other side of the wall.*

22 David Hunter: *I sometimes wondered if the poor chap hesitated to kill a soldier who was attending to the wounds of a comrade. It all of course happened in a flash and my man just reacted quicker. In the chaos of the day, I never found out who had saved my life. I am sorry to say that he possibly lost his own life.*

23 Jim Webber: *They missed the entry hole later on amid all the grenade fragments and the bullet is still in there!*

24 Tommy Killeen: *For the life of me I've often thought 'Didn't we do our job properly?', but there was nobody in there when we went in there first of all.* The chapel part of the church was and remains, a historic building.

25 This event is depicted in Peter Archer's evocative painting, *Go To It!* Guy Radmore: *I put him in for a DCM, he got an MM. It was a very fine, marvellous piece of initiative.*

26 It is debatable whether there were actually Germans firing from the Chateau itself. Madame Vion apparently managed to persuade the Germans not to employ it as a defensive position because of the fire it would attract. However, they certainly used it to observe the situation. Sadly, one of the French Resistance men who was being sheltered went to the window, against everybody's advice, and was killed. Madame Vion's influence certainly worked to a degree during the afternoon when Hans Höller went into the building and used it to see what the position was. He stated that he did not deploy men within it because of it being a Maternity Home.

27 Almost forty years later, Bill Bailey persuaded Joe Caine to go back to the bridge. It was the first time he had returned: *Do you know what he wanted to see more than anything else? He went back to see if they'd ever emptied the bloody bucket!*

28 Dennis Edwards found a notebook in one of the houses and used it to record his experiences. The contents were subsequently published as *The Devils Own Luck*.

CHAPTER 12 - THE MORNING IN THE RANVILLE AREA

1 List of names gathered of party (4 Platoon): Captain John Sim, Sim's batman, Sergeant Frank Milburn, Sergeant Jones, Frank Gleeson, Andrew Gradwell, L/Cpl Hateley, L/Cpl Skellett (Sniper), Pte Rudolph, Ed Ruff, Two bodies were later found with 6 Pdr, FOO & radio operator. The ship was HMS Mauritius. The anti-tank gun belonged to the 4th Airlanding Anti-tank Battery.

   Private Leonard Cole went with Gordon Medd's party: *Found two German dead and about five of ours including, Sgt Jones, Sgt Milburn, Ptes Skellett, Hateley and Dobson. 6-pounder also knocked out – Worrel wounded – Sgt Commons injured hand.*

2 Sadly Major Rogers was killed six days later during the battle of Breville.

3   Lt Dean on Frank Maclean and the balloon jump: *It was our second jump and he, as first man out, was given the order 'Action Stations Number One', but said, 'I can't jump Number One, Sergeant.' Without a second's hesitation came the order 'Action Stations Number Two', and I swung my legs into the hole. 'Go', and I pushed off with my hands and out I went. Fusilier McLean did not jump that morning and had been whisked away before we returned to camp at Ringway, but what a brave man he turned out to be.*

4   Confusion of battle is surely involved here. Staff Sergeant RC Downing: *Our 6-pounder scored a hit on one of the tanks with the first round, from about 600 yards and the second blew up. The infantry were repulsed mainly by the 13th, but I reckon I nailed one Jerry and possibly two.*

     This gun, I think, must have been the one commanded by Sergeant Bert Clements and was sited close to the farm, right rear of Lieutenant Gordon O'Brien-Hitching's Platoon of 'A' Company. Right and 200 yards forward of this gun, another was sited behind a low stone wall. Staff Sergeant R. White and Sergeant F. Eason had landed this gun in Chalk 115.

5   During this period a small reinforcement had arrived in Ranville. The glider flown by Major John Royle, 2i/c No 1 Wing, Glider Pilot Regiment, had had its towrope broken by flak and his party had subsequently landed about four miles east of DZ 'N'. They had reached their RV at around 0930 hours to find approximately fifty-three pilots had gathered. Royle formed these men into 'Force John' to fight as infantry until they were no longer required and could be sent back to England for further glider tasks. At 0945 hours, this force made contact with the 13th Battalion who requested that they defend the area to the west and south-west of the main crossroads in Ranville.

     At 1040 hours Major Royle led a patrol of five men to search houses for snipers in the area south-east of the Ranville Church, but no one was found, although they did receive an 'embarrassing but hearty reception from French females!'

     The 12th Battalion was then contacted, and were somewhat relieved to find out about the force's presence as they were expecting a counter-attack. Major Royle checked the area and ordered Major Griffith to establish standing patrols, each of ten men, at dangerous unwatched locations that were possible lines of infiltration, particularly by night. These were at a small bridge in a wood 150 yards south-east of the Ranville crossroads, the road junction 150 yards south of the crossroads. Map References: 111732 and 112733.

6   Frank Gleeson: *Long after the war I reckoned that he thought I had blasted several rounds of .45 bullets into the face of his sergeant whom we had blasted at a distance of four feet.*

7   The two self-propelled guns belonged to the 200th Assault Gun Battalion.

CHAPTER 13 - SEABORNE ARRIVALS AT THE BRIDGES

1   (a) The only group that matches the timing, requirements and type of vehicle appears to be 1626 Floating Boat Equipment (FBE) Platoon of 106 (Bridging) Company, part of the 17 Field Company Engineer Group. They had begun landing on SWORD Beach at 0920 hours. Fighting was still going with various machine gunners and snipers that remained in houses on the front, but by 1100 hours seven of the platoon's eight vehicles had managed to get off the beach and head for Benouville. (b) There is the possibility that Richard Todd took the road to St Aubin d'Arquenay.

2   The arrival of these Engineers was witnessed by a number of people before they saw any Commandos.

3   (a) Wally Parr: *On a personal note, since the original bombing of various places in England in*

1940, and seeing London and Bristol and other places bombed to smithereens, it gave me the greatest personal delight on D-Day to sit behind a German captured gun firing German ammunition up German arseholes. I thoroughly enjoyed every minute of it. (b) This boat fired upon the Chateau because it saw movement on the staircase. This was actually Hans Höller and a couple of colleagues who had entered the building to get a better view of what was happening.

4   This contingent belonged to 71 Field Company, and was either the party led by Major Upton or 1 Platoon of Lieutenant 'Jock' Whyte. Whyte was due to meet up with the evacuated Lieutenant Clarke.

5   Scotson described this field: *'which is now like a caravan camp, at that time it was a field in a wooded area.'* This location is confirmed by the map reference [101754] quoted by the Troop report in the War Diary.

6   21-year-old Alan Pyman was killed a few hours later in the grounds of what is now the Breville *Mairie*. His famous statement is regularly, and incorrectly, attributed to Lovat.

7   Gordon Fleming stated that he thought he recalled seeing cyclists start to cross the bridge just before 3 Troop, 6 Cdo. This may well have been 1 Troop, 6 Cdo, or even 3 Troop, 3 Commando. The text has explained the arrival of 3 Troop, 6 Commando before that of a Cycle Troop, because there is no doubt that the first incident of the Airborne and the Commandos meeting is that of Alan Pyman's. 1 Troop may well have been the cause of the fighting which 3 Troop heard in Le Port. See Appendix D for discussion of Commando/Seaborne engineer arrival.

8   Peter Masters' real name was Peter Arany. Of the Irishman who said sorry: *When on the next day, on a machine gun charge and was himself cut down and killed, nobody apologized to him.* Nick van der Bijl's *Commandos in Exile* states that the Bren gunner was George Thompson of the Grenadier Guards.

9   Howard's and other accounts place this earlier. Bill Bailey recalled it when Commandos were coming through: *So not only did I not end up with my champagne, I never had any tea either!* They had many cups of tea together after the war!

10   Georges Gondree had gone into his garden and with the help of a couple of soldiers, began digging up the hoard of wine and champagne that he had buried. Some have said that this was fiction. However, too many veterans have mentioned this for it to be so. John Butler's account backs this up and probably puts a perspective on it as being a more gradual process of distributing the drink! Major Howard: *There was a hell of a lot of cork-popping went on which was heard the other side of the Canal, and by the time I'd got back there, I was told that everybody wanted to report sick! Well we stopped that lark of course, but I didn't go back until I had had a sip of course. It was wonderful champagne and it was something to really celebrate.*

11   This was almost certainly Nigel Poett, who had moved back towards Le Bas de Ranville. The only other possibility of course is Hugh Kindersley. The Commando orders stated that 'Each troop will report to Bridge control point 106744 set up by 5 Para Brigade on crossing the bridges.'

12   This could really only have been the Mercedes staff car.

13   Gordon Medd: *I didn't give him much of a chance, but the stretcher bearers got him back later that day and two weeks later, I found myself in the next bed to him in Alder Hey Hospital, Liverpool. He was very ill, but he did recover.*

14   Gordon Medd: *I am sad to say I still don't know to this day who it was. Later that day I had my last sight of the hedgerow. We were 'resting up' in a farmyard after withdrawal when Joe Jenkins*

the Padre, who had borrowed a Jeep from somewhere, asked me to go with him to bring back some of the dead. We drove up the track and loaded only L/Cpl Skellett on the vehicle when we attracted fire. We raced back to the Company position with his body, regretfully leaving the others.

CHAPTER 14 - THE REMAINDER OF THE DAY

1   Peter Young: *By 3.30pm most of the Commando had crossed the bridge and was taking up defensive positions. When we had been in position for less than two hours, four German tanks were reported on the rising ground to our south. They were engaged by 3-inch mortars belonging to the Airborne Division and withdrew. At the same time HMS* Serapis *fired twenty rounds into some German infantry who had been seen digging in the forward edge of a wood.*

2   Stated by Hans Höller, who was in the grounds of the Chateau.

3   It was not until he reached Britain that it was realized that he also had a piece of shrapnel in his neck.

4   (a) War Diary confirms that 2123801 Dvr Dransfield belonged to 3 Platoon. Barnett is also confirmed wounded but not Kerr. Another man, Simpson, is named. George Dransfield is buried in the churchyard at Le Port. (b) This tank was knocked out by the gun served by Herr Höller: *At the end of the afternoon an old man made a great show of hobbling out of the village from the enemy lines, tottered up to the shrubbery where we were, turned about, and hobbled back. The Panzergrenadiere were not sure whether to let him go back, by which time he had gone. A few minutes later two tanks burst out onto the road and the first shell was aimed at our hedge. One of my guns, set up to cover our advanced party where the wall around the grounds starts, fired on the tank and it burst into flame; the second tank disappeared down the side road.*

Oberleutnant Braatz rushed up to me with unseemly haste and told me that the enemy had already turned west and that our unit had to be pulled back, or more exactly head off south towards Blainville. We received an order to assemble all our vehicles and artillery behind the grounds of the Chateau, to the east of the road. From this short range we planned to fire a few parting shells directly onto the bridge and the vicinity before pulling back. But suddenly we heard and saw a tank heading towards us from the west along the houses and up the road. It stopped 80 meters from us and its commander spoke to a crowd of villagers who were eagerly gathered around it. We were in thickets in the park, the ground was on a slight rise, and the stone wall which separated us from the road, was below us. We had a quite a job lowering the barrel of the gun without giving ourselves away to get it pointing directly at the tank. After what seemed an interminable period of time, we managed it. The first shell [it was a 7.5cm Sfl Feldwebel Guse] *struck the fuel tank or ammunition. The tank exploded and all around it was a scene from hell. The house nearest to it was completely destroyed. We did not fire any shells on the bridge. We withdrew very peacefully and were able to pull out without being noticed. Fire was coming from all directions from the village and the bridge, but nothing came near us.*

5   David Hunter: Relating to Hunter's statements on p. 256: *(1) It transpired later that I had made quite an impression on Nigel. I was quite unaware that blood was pouring from the wound in my ear and I was really quite a bloody sight. (2) I am not religious but I do recollect earlier praying quietly to God – if there was one – to get me out of this and I would be a good boy ever after. (3) I never dreamed I would be sent back to the UK, but that was what happened.*

6   Lt Hunter: *These men were terrific. They had been brought up in the Depression in humble homes when there was minimum welfare. They owed their country very little but they gave everything. I don't mind admitting I was terrified out of my skin, but I could not show it, not to these men.*

I remember thinking at the time, 'It's just as well I'm an Officer. If I wasn't, I would probably run like hell.'

7   Apart from the Ox and Bucks and the Royal Ulster Rifles, the majority of the units on this landing had been planned to form an Armoured Recce Group, which subsequently became known as 'Parkerforce' after its commander, Lt Col 'Reggie' Parker. It was planned for this group to form a small firm base outside the Divisional area in order to carry out deep reconnaissance and impede enemy movement from the east and south-east of Caen. However, the Division's situation at the end of D-Day prevented Parkerforce from being deployed. (For further information about this and on the 6th Airborne Armoured Reconnaissance Regiment, see *Airborne Armour*, Keith Flint, Helion & Company (2004).

8   Famously, just to the west, where a German counter-attack had reached the coast in the area of Luc sur Mer, the arrival of the gliders made a critical difference to the ambitions of this armoured group, which immediately began to pull back for fear of being encircled.

9   The OP tank was named 'LANDRECY'. It was knocked out at Map Ref: 089739. Herr Höller: *To get out of the trap the other vehicles had to follow and assure cover to right and left. Oberleutnant Braatz and a few grenadiere were used as couriers for our orders; since we had no radio, once the orders were given, I had to leap about like a football from vehicle to vehicle, and get right into the dark, oven-like insides of each to transmit the orders. During this difficult time one of the couriers ran up to me to warn us of an enemy tank approaching from the west under cover of infantry and coming across an open field. To the east of the road we were covered by hedges. I found our 7.5cm Pak gun aimer, Gefreiter Wleck, on the edge of the road, preparing himself some bread and butter when I came and ordered him to let the tank approach us as much as possible. All our Kampfgruppe was brought together and warned that they were to keep still. The silhouette of the tank and infantry appeared on the horizon across the open field and as there were only a few isolated shrubs, they were highly visible. Also, no other vehicles seemed to be following them. When the tank had almost reached the road on the other side, at about 20 metres, Wleck fired an armour-piercing shell at point-blank range, followed by explosive shells and then he used a machine gun on the infantrymen around it. The tank and the infantrymen were eliminated and we were able to continue our retreat.*

10   This was related to Jim Holder-Vale by another driver/operator, Bill Husband. Len Harvey saw the guns opening fire at the church. He is certain that it involved F4 Gun and also states that two Germans, young enough to be Hitler Youth, emerged from the front door waving white handkerchiefs.

     The snipers in the church were not all necessarily firing from the tower. Having inspected the interior of the church, it is apparent that there were various positions within the building that provided very good views of the surrounding area.

11   Jim Holder Vale was dug in at the T-junction for the subsequent week and one night he was on guard near the Town Hall: *A plane came over and it dropped a bomb and it landed right outside the house. There was a memorial outside there. Noticed how damaged it is? I saw it explode. I'd never seen a bomb explode before. It just exploded in a shower of sparks. That was a few days after D-Day.*

12   Major Maitland actually died of wounds the following day. John Vaughan had collected eighteen British and six German casualties.

13   (a) John Hoare: *It was I think charged with picric acid because it was yellow, rather like the old-fashioned lemonade powder, and we threw a lot of water on the bridge to get the flames on the explosives. As a result of this it quickly dissolved and made a sort of very yellow looking slush.*

Working on it, we got our boots soaked in it. The effect on the boots was that the boots shrunk down and we had to get replacement boots issued as quickly as possible! (b) This obviously signalled a drastic change in policy (and attitude?) of the German Command. This attack is perhaps backed up by Major Howard stating that the bridge was also attacked by Frogmen but were thwarted in their attempts to get near the bridge.

14 This retreat may well not have gone on without interference. During their 'advance' some of the Germans passed members of the Commando Troop in the area. When they started to fall back, the Commandos opened up on them.

15 Padre Bill Briscoe was one of these.

Captain Wagstaff: *We continued to treat and evacuate patients, until we cleared all the casualties, at 0100 hours on D+1. The 7th Battalion, having been relieved by the Warwicks, had gone over to the east side of the River Orne. The section therefore followed and reported to the MDS at Le Bas de Ranville about 0215 hours.*

16 At around 0230 hours the two groups of Oxf and Bucks who had been on Glider 94, arrived in Ranville and reported to Major Howard. After being split up when the firing started at the River Dives bridge, the groups, led by Captain Priday and Sergeant Barwick had met up again in Robehomme, before moving down into Ranville.

Sources & Bibliography

6th Airborne Division:

6th Airborne Division War Diary: WO171/425.
6th Airborne Div. Report on Operations in Normandy: PRO: CAB106/970.
6th Airborne Div. Signals: WO171/429.
6th Airborne Div. ADMS: WO177/360.
CRE; Lt Col Frank Lowman: Account: The 6th Airborne Divisional Engineers on D-Day 1944 – War Diary.
Capt Anthony Windrum (Signals) Account – War Diary.

5th Parachute Brigade:

5th Parachute Brigade War Diary – WO171/595 - PRO.
Brigadier Nigel Poett's account – *Pure Poett, The Autobiography of General Sir Nigel Poett*, Leo Cooper, 1991.
Interview with Stephen Ambrose, IWM.
Interview with General Julian Thompson, IWM Tape.
Major Guy Radmore – IWM Taped Interview, plus account in The D-Day Landings, Phillip Warner.
George Brownlee, 4th Airlanding Anti-tank Battery: Interviews with author, May and June 2008.
Fraser Edwards, 317 Airborne Security Section: Tape supplied to author by Mr Edwards and Telecon Edwards/Barber July 2004.
Dr N. Hewlings – 225 Field Ambulance – *The D-Day Landings*, Phillip Warner.
Harry Leach, Brigade HQ – Meeting in Normandy June 2008, Interview with author July 2008.
Captain David Tibbs, 225 Field Ambulance – Interview with author, April 2008.
Capt. John Wagstaff, 225 Field Ambulance – Interview with author, September 2005.

6th Airlanding Brigade:

6th Airlanding Brigade War Diary: WO171/591 & WO171/4320.

2nd Ox and Bucks:

2nd Ox and Bucks War Diary – PRO.
War Chronicles of the 52nd Light Infantry, 1952. HMSO.
John Vaughan - *All Spirits*, Merlin Books, 1988.
Capt Brian Priday – Ox & Bucks LI War Chronicle, Lt Gen Sir JEH Neville.
Lt 'Tod' Sweeney – *Men of the Red Beret*, Max Arthur, Hutchinson, 1990.
The Pegasus Diaries – Major John Howard and Penny Bates, Pen & Sword, 2006.

Audio accounts:

Major John Howard: IWM Taped Interview.
IWM Taped Interview – 1989 - 11061/2.
IWM Tape (Interview with Stephen Ambrose).
Lt Dennis Fox: IWM Tape (Interview with Stephen Ambrose).
Lt Richard 'Sandy' Smith: IWM Taped interview.
Lt 'Tod' Sweeney: IWM Tape (Interview with Stephen Ambrose).
L/Cpl Ted Tappenden: IWM Tape (Interview with Stephen Ambrose).
Lt David Wood: IWM Tape (Interview with Stephen Ambrose).
Interview with author, March 2004, plus documents lent to author.
Doug Allen: Interview with author, March 2004.
Jack 'Bill' Bailey: IWM Tape (Interview with Stephen Ambrose).
Frank Bourlet: Interview with author, September 2003.
Peter 'Rocky' Bright: Interview with author, July 2005.
Leslie Chamberlain: IWM Taped Interview.
Harry 'Nobby' Clark: Interview with author, December 2003.
Dennis Edwards Interview with author 2006, Account supplied to author and *The Devil's Own Luck*, Pen and Sword Books.
Stan Evans: Interview with author, March 2004.
Bill Gray: Interview with author, March 2004.
Bill Howard: Interviews with author, June 2004.
Paddy O'Donnell: IWM Tape (Interview with Stephen Ambrose).
Tom Packwood: Interview with author, November 2003.
Wally Parr: IWM Taped interview.
'Wagger' Thornton: IWM Tape (Interview with Stephen Ambrose), Account written in *Voices from D-Day.*
Lce Sgt 'Tich' Rayner: Interview with author, July 2004.
Arthur Roberts: Interview with author, January 2004.
Fred Weaver: Interview with author, March 2004.

Glider Pilots:

Freddie Baacke: *Soldier Magazine*, D-Day Supplement, 1984.
Geoff Barkway: Interview with author, April 2004 and *One Night in June*, Kevin Shannon & Stephen Wright, Airlife, 1994.
Oliver Boland: IWM Tape (Interview with Stephen Ambrose).
Peter Boyle: Account from David Brook of the GPRA – Featured in The Eagle.
Roy Howard: *Men of the Red Beret*, Max Arthur, Hutchinson, 1990.
Account from David Brook of the GPRA – Featured in *The Eagle*.
Stan Pearson: Account from David Brook of the GPRA – Featured in The Eagle.
Jim Wallwork: Article supplied to author by Jim Wallwork, December 2003.
Further correspondence with author, 2006–07.

249 Field Company RE:

War Diary: WO171/1605.
Cyril Haslett: Interview with author.
Cyril Larkin: IWM Taped Interview and *Remembering D-Day*, Michael J. Bowman, Harper Collins 2004.

7th Parachute Battalion:

7th Battalion War Diary: WO171/1239.
7th Battalion Responsibilities: Report by Lt-Col Pine Coffin, 7th Bn War Diary WO171/1239, PRO.
Lt Col Geoffrey Pine-Coffin: IWM Tape 1647, Source BBC 20899, recorded 18th August 1944.
Major Steele-Baume: *The Covenanter*, 1945 (Quoted from *Nothing Less Than Victory*, Russell Miller, Penguin 1994).
Major Taylor: *Ready for Anything*, Julian Thompson, Weidenfeld and Nicolson; Interview with Stephen Ambrose, IWM.
The Tale of Two Bridges, Barbara Maddox & Peter Pine-Coffin, Peter Pine-Coffin, 2003.
Capt Jim Webber: Interview with author 7-9-04; *Ready for Anything* and Newspaper interview for D-Day 50th Anniversary and *The Pegasus Trail*.
Lt Nick Archdale: Interview with author, August 2006. *Men of the Red Beret*, Max Arthur, Hutchinson, 1990; Written account via Michael Pine-Coffin. Account in Battalion War Diary.
Lieutenant Tommy Farr: Battalion War Diary.
Lt Ted Pool: Interview with author, 6-10-06; Notes from Chester Wilmot Diary, Liddell Hart Archive; *The Tale of Two Bridges*, Barbara Maddox and Peter Pine-Coffin, Peter Pine-Coffin, 2003.
Lt Dan Thomas: *Pegasus* magazine via Michael Pine-Coffin.

Lt Richard Todd: Interview with author, 23-9-04.

John Butler: Correspondence with author and Michael Pine-Coffin.

Phillip Crofts: IWM Taped Interview.

Dennis Fox: Interviews with author.

Sgt William French: IWM Taped Interview.

Freddie Fricker: *The Tale of Two Bridges*, Barbara Maddox and Peter Pine-Coffin, Peter Pine-Coffin, 2003.

Eddie Gurney: *Remembering D-Day*, Martin W Bowman, Harper Collins 2004.

Tommy Killeen: Notes from Chester Wilmot Diary, Liddell Hart Archive.

Bill Law: Interview with author, June 2008.

William Le Chaminant: IWM Taped Interview.

Sgt McCambridge: DCM Citation.

Michael McGee: Notes from Chester Wilmot Diary, Liddell Hart Archive.

Jim Moran: Correspondence with author.

Ron Perry: Interview with author, 17-8-04.

G. Skelly: MM Citation.

Bob Tanner: *D-Day 1944, Voices from Normandy*, Robin Neillands and Roderick de Normann, Orion, 1993.

Edward Traynor: MM Citation.

Eric Truman: *The Tale of Two Bridges*, Barbara Maddox and Peter Pine-Coffin, Peter Pine-Coffin, 2003.

Letters: Lt David Hunter, Vic Bettle, Eddie Gurney, RJ Davey, Bill French, Ted Lough.

8th Parachute Battalion:

War Diary, PRO, Kew.

12th Parachute Battalion:

Major G. Ritchie MC: *Para Memories*, Parapress, Eric Barley and Yves Fohlen, 1996.

Captain Phillip Burkinshaw: Interview with author, March 2008. Also, *Alarms and Excursions*, Davis Brothers, 1991.

Lt Gordon Medd: *Para Memories*, Parapress, Eric Barley and Yves Fohlen; Telecon April 08.

Captain John Sim: Notes from Chester Wilmot Diary, Liddell Hart Archive.

Account in 12th Battalion War Diary.

Interview with author, 10-7-08.

Men of the Red Beret, Max Arthur, Hutchinson, 1990.

Eric Barley: Interview with author, Feb 08; *Para Memories*, Parapress, Eric Barley and Yves Fohlen.

Frank Gleeson: *Red Devils in Normandy*, Georges Bernage, Heimdal Editions, 2002. And *Para Memories* as below.

13th Parachute Battalion:

War Diary, PRO, Kew.

Captain Nobby Clark: *The D-Day Landings*, Phillip Warner, William Kimber 1980. (Accounts now held in IWM).

Lt 'Dixie' Dean Interview with author, March 2008, plus unpublished account supplied to the author, 12-07.

Lt Jack Watson: Interview with author, October 2008.

Don Jones: Telephone interview with author, 7-8-08.

Ken Lang: Interview with author, March 2008.

Commandos:

3, 4, 6 Commando & 45 RM Commando War Diaries: PRO, Kew.

Lord Lovat: *March Past*, Weidenfeld and Nicolson, 1978.

Lt Colonel Derek Mills-Roberts: Clash by Night, William Kimber, 1956, Draft and Original held in Liddell Hart Archive.

Lt Keith Ponsford: Correspondence with author.

Capt G.B. Wilson: 'Chronicles of D-Day', Rupert Curtis, document held in IWM.

Cliff Morris: 3 Troop, 6 Commando's Exploits, personal account supplied to author, 1995.

Original Account sent to Derek Mills-Roberts, Liddell Hart Archive.

JV 'Jock' Byrne: *The General Salutes a Soldier*, Robert Hale Ltd, 1986.

Sid Dann: *True Stories of the Commandos*, Robin Hunter, Virgin Books.

George Jowett: 3 Troop, 6 Commando's Exploits, personal account supplied to author, 2004.

Murdoch McDougall: *Swiftly They Struck, The Story of No 4 Commando*, Arms and Armour Press, 1954.

Peter Masters: *Ten Commando 1942–1945*, Ian Dear, Leo Cooper, 1987.

Phillip Pritchard: Correspondence with author, 2007.

Soldiering in the British Forces in World War II, Private Publication, Phillip Pritchard.

'Chronicles of D-Day', Rupert Curtis, document held in IWM.

Geoffrey Scotson: IWM Taped Interview. (Also interviewed his wife 2006).

Stan Scott: Interviews with author, 2003–2006.

Eddie Simms: Interviews with author, April 2004, August 2005.

L/Sgt Jimmy Synott: Interviews with author.

Seaborne Engineers:

The Route Forward, History of 3rd (British) Divisional Royal Engineers.

17th Field Company Royal Engineers, 3rd Infantry Division, *A Brief History from 6th June 1944–8th May 1945*, Denis Stephenson.

War Diary 71 Field Company RE, WO171/1528.

71st Field Company RE, Orne to the Elbe, June 1944 – May 1945.
246th Field Company RE History.
246th Field Company RE War Diary, WO171/1604.
106 Bridging Company, War Diary, WO171/2383.
90 Company RASC, War Diary, WO171/2377.
RASC History.
Major David Willison (17 Fd Coy): Interview with author, January 2006.
Captain John Hoare (71 Fd Coy): Interview with author, 2005.
Bob Heath (71 Fd Coy): Interviews with author, 2005, 2006.
SR Sharman (71 Fd Coy): Interview with author 2006. Plus *D-Day Landings*, Phillip
    Warner, William Kimber 1980.

Others:

1st Battalion the Suffolk Regiment and D-Day, Eric Lummis, Les Amis du Suffolk
    Regiment, 1989.
2nd Royal Warwicks, War Diary.
7th Field Regt RA, War Diary.
13th/18th Hussars War Diary, PRO, Kew.
Lt Col NPH Tapp DSO RA commanding 7 Field Regt (SP) RA, 3rd British
    Division, Account in Firepower Museum/IWM.
Major JF Lister, 7 Field Regt RA, IWM account.
Captain H. Illing, 2nd Royal Warwicks: *No Better Soldier*, H. Illing – Private
    Publication, Royal Regiment of Fusiliers Museum.
Bob Randall: Interview with author, August 2003.
Chester Wilmot: His diary, Liddell Hart Archive.
Jim Holder-Vale, 92nd LAA, Interview with author, January 2007.

FOB Party:

Captain Francis Vere Hodge RA, Interview with author, October 2005. Written
    account supplied by Vere Hodge.
Alex Boomer RN Interview with author, March 2006.
Wilf Fortune RN Written account supplied by Alex Boomer.

French Civilians

Madame Deschamps, Newspaper article.
Monsieur Gilles Deschamps, June 2007.
Madame Arlette Gondree, Interview with author, May 2005.
Andre and Christiane Grand, Letter to author December 06 on actions of Eugene
    Meslin.

Monsieur Andre Heintz, Letter to author February 2008, interview with author, June 2008.
Madame Louise Moulin, June 2006.
Monsieur Niepceron, Interview with author, May 2005.
Madame Suzy Scheppers, June 2005, 2006.

Bibliography:

The Red Beret, Hilary St George, Michael Joseph, 1950.
Airborne Forces, Lt. Col TBH Otway DSO,.War Office 1951.
With the 6th Airborne Division in Normandy, Lt. Gen. Richard Gale, Sampson Low, Marston & Co, 1948.
Pegasus Bridge, Stephen Ambrose, George Allen & Unwin, 1984.
The Orne Bridgehead, Lloyd Clark, Sutton Publishing, 2004.
What D'Ya Do In the War, Dad, The Story of Wally Parr, Barry Parr, Trafford Publishing.
The Pegasus Trail, Audio accounts of the Operations of the 6th Airborne Division in Normandy, Brittany Ferries, 1994.
21st Panzer Division, Jean-Claude Perrigault, Heimdal, 2002.
Invasion – They're Coming!, Paul Carell, George G. Harrap & Co, 1962.
The 12th SS Hitler Jugend Division, Hubert Meyer.
One Night in June, Kevin Shannon & Stephen Wright.
Bridging – Normandy to Berlin, 1945.
Gliderborne, The Story of the 2nd Battalion The Oxfordshire & Buckinghamshire Light Infantry (The 52nd) in World War II, Michael Massey-Beresford, Private Publication.
Worst Fears Confirmed (the History of Intelligence Corps Airborne Units & the Intelligence Gathering & Security Measures Employed For British Airborne Operations), Graeme Deeley, Barny Books.
Voices from D-Day, Jonathan Bastable, David & Charles 2004.
Ten Thousand Eyes, Richard Collier, Collins, 1958.
Histoire du Maquis de Saint-Clair, Henri Lamperiere.
The Rifles Are There – 1st & 2nd Battalions The Royal Ulster Rifles in the Second World War, David Orr & David Truesdale, Pen & Sword, 2005.
The Pegasus Diaries – The Private Papers of Major John Howard DSO, John Howard and Penny Bates, Pen & Sword, 2006.

Photographic Credits

Every effort has been made to locate the copyright owners of the photographs employed within this book. However, if anyone has been omitted, please contact the publisher and it will be corrected in subsequent editions.

James Hill: 3, Penny Bates: 7, Fred Weaver: 10, Bob Randall: 11, Stan Evans: 13, Mark Hickman: 15, Michael Pine-Coffin: 16, 19, 53, 103, 114, 139, 142, 146-148, 163, 175, 177, 183 (bottom), 184, 186, 188, 192, 198 (bottom), 200, 234 (bottom), 252, Phoebe Grant: 27, Adam Howard: 29, David Brook: 31, Andre Grand: 34, Memorial Pegasus: 35, Crown Copyright: 37, 38, 166, 183 (Top), 194, 214, 219, Gilles Deschamps: 38, Gaby: 39, IWM: 40, 94, 111, 195, 236, 237, 267, 271, Carl Rymen: 45, 49, 127, 218, Museum of Army Flying (Elizabeth Frank): 47, David Tibbs: 50, Jim Wallwork: 53, Mrs Ted Eley: 56, Jim Moran: 57, Fraser Edwards: 69, Rene Niepceron: 71, 248, Major M Massy-Beresford: 73, Michael W Bowman: 75, Peter Boyle: 79, Bill Gray: 84, Electric Photo: 85, Arthur Roberts: 87, Voisin: 88, Arlette Gondree: 90, Harry Wheeler: 92, Geoff Barkway: 95, Stan Watson: 96, David Wood: 101, G Maes: 104, 258, Richard Todd: 109, Harry Leach: 116, Eric Barley: 118, Bill Law: 121, Barry & Michael Tappenden: 123, Phillip Burkinshaw: 126, John Goddard: 130, Alf Whitbread: 133, Bill Howard: 136, Jack Watson: 138, 151, 152, 156, Ted Pool: 154, Lacour: 160, 187, 223, John Wagstaff: 161, Ted Barwick: 168, Veuve Tranchard: 172, N. Barber: 174, 222, John Butler: 189 (top), Dennis Fox: 189 (bottom), Nick Archdale: 191, Nobby Clark: 198 (top), Sylvia Atkinson/Royal Signals Museum: 203, Dennis Edwards: 207, Ken Lang: 210, Don Jones: 212, Dixie Dean: 216, J. Bechet: 221, Barry Parr: 227, Peter Bowe: 230 (top), Mrs Geoffrey Scotson: 230 (bottom), Phillip Pritchard: 231, Stan Scott: 234 (top), 240 (top), Elde: 235, Harry Bell: 239, Roy Westley: 240 (bottom), Jimmy Synnott: 241, Gordon Medd: 244, John Hoare: 247, Sir David Willison: 249, Bob Heath: 251, John Webber: 253, Donald Gilchrist (Oliver & Boyd): 254, Murdoch McDougall (Special Forces Library): 256, Stan Young: 257, Len Harvey/Tom McCarthy: 264, Jim Holder-Vale: 266.

Index

320